ECONOMICS
for
CONSUMERS
THIRD EDITION

JOHN S. MORTON • RONALD R. REZNY
HOMEWOOD - FLOSSMOOR HIGH SCHOOL

GLENCOE
Macmillan/McGraw-Hill

New York, New York   Columbus, Ohio   Mission Hills, California   Peoria, Illinois

John S. Morton

John S. Morton teaches economics at Homewood-Flossmoor High School in Illinois. In addition, he is Director of the Office of Economic Education and Community Professor of Economics at Governors State University, University Park, Illinois. He has authored several publications, including the Economics Advanced Placement Instructional Package, and serves on the Publications Committee of the Joint Council on Economic Education. Mr. Morton is a recipient of the Award for Excellence in Private Enterprise Education from Freedoms Foundation at Valley Forge. He also received an award from the Joint Council on Economic Education for innovative ideas about teaching the economic reasoning process.

Ronald R. Rezny

Ronald R. Rezny teaches economics at Homewood-Flossmoor High School. In addition to teaching at the high school and college levels, he has published a number of articles. He also serves as a consultant to school districts and government agencies in Illinois and frequently conducts workshops on consumer and economic education. Together with John S. Morton, he has received a national first-place Award for Outstanding Teaching of Economics, sponsored by the Joint Council on Economic Education, and a first-place award in the Illinois Personal Economic Competence Awards Program.

ISBN: 0-395-44300-8

4 5 6 7 8 9 10 11 12 13 14 15   RRW   00 99 98 97 96 95 94 93 92

TABLE OF CONTENTS

Preface   **vii**

UNIT 1
YOUR ECONOMIC CHOICES

UNIT 2
PERSONAL FINANCIAL MANAGEMENT

UNIT 3
THE CONSUMER AND THE MARKET ECONOMY

UNIT 4

THE CONSUMER IN THE MARKETPLACE

UNIT 5

BUYING GOODS AND SERVICES

UNIT 6

THE CONSUMER AND CREDIT

UNIT 7

BUYING A CAR

UNIT 8

THE CONSUMER AND HOUSING

UNIT 9

YOUR FINANCIAL SECURITY

UNIT 10

THE CONSUMER AND THE UNITED STATES ECONOMY

Preface

Today's marketplace is becoming more and more complex. More variety of choices, intensified competition, new manufacturing and market techniques, and more government regulation combine to make the consumer's task more challenging than ever before. Consumers are bombarded with a constant stream of advertising, making the job of selecting goods and services ever more difficult. Behind all this activity, economic forces are at work that affect every citizen's ability to earn and spend money.

This book is designed to help students better understand basic economic concepts so they can make informed consumer decisions and better manage their money. It also shows how each person, by being a more effective decision maker, can influence our private enterprise system as a consumer, producer, and citizen.

Knowing and understanding basic economic concepts helps us all understand our nation and our world. In this new edition, even more emphasis has been placed on economic understandings. Units 3 and 10 now focus almost exclusively on economic concepts. To reflect the inseparable relationship between economic understanding and wise consumer choices, a new name—ECONOMICS FOR CONSUMERS—has been given to this third edition.

Objectives

This book has been written and designed with students in mind. It is written so that it is easy and interesting to read, with case studies, interviews, and special features. After reading ECONOMICS FOR CONSUMERS and completing the Student Activities workbook, students will:

1. Develop practical consumer skills such as comparison shopping, fact-finding, and negotiating.
2. Develop thinking skills such as planning, comparing, analyzing, questioning, inferring, and evaluating.
3. Develop money management skills such as financial planning, budgeting, borrowing, saving, investing, and insuring.
4. Develop mathematical skills useful in budgeting, investing, borrowing, insuring, and comparison shopping.

5. Develop interpretation skills by studying charts, graphs, tables, and cartoons.
6. Develop the knowledge and skills to make effective consumer and citizen decisions.
7. Apply economic reasoning to decision making.
8. Explain how our economic system affects consumers and citizens, as well as how consumers and citizens affect our economic system.

Organization of the Textbook

This book covers the topics experts consider most important in the consumer economics curriculum.

Unit 1 develops a framework for effective decision making. Unit 2 applies these decision-making concepts to personal financial management.

Unit 3, "The Consumer and the Market Economy," provides insight into our private enterprise market system. Combined with Unit 10, "The Consumer and the United States Economy," this coverage should ensure that students receive a basic understanding of economics.

Units 4 and 8 are designed to improve skills in shopping for goods and services. The units cover the goods and services that are most important in a budget. Chapters include information on shopping for food, clothing, medicine and cosmetics, professional services, credit, cars, housing, and insurance.

The theme of Unit 9 is financial security. Topics such as saving; investing; and insuring life, health, and income are discussed.

Since the overall objective of this book is to teach economics from the consumer's perspective, every effort has been made to provide examples of problems and choices that confront consumers every day.

Special Features

ECONOMICS FOR CONSUMERS is not intended to be an encyclopedia of consumer information. Its goal is simply to help students understand their economic environment and to become more effective consumers.

Special features make the book easy to read and understand. Each chapter has case studies that help improve thinking and decision-making skills. Self-check questions appear within the chapters for frequent reinforcement of learning. End-of-chapter materials include vocabulary building, review questions, math skill-building activities, and thought and skill development questions. "Getting Involved in Your Community" activities encourage students to go beyond the classroom walls to interview people, examine products, and get professional advice. What better way to become more competent consumers than to go out into the marketplace to practice and improve consumer skills?

Supporting Materials

In addition to the textbook, the ECONOMICS FOR CONSUMERS package contains a student activity workbook, a teacher's edition of the workbook, achievement tests, a teacher's manual, and a test generator.

The student activity workbook contains a wide variety of activities for each chapter. The teacher's edition of the workbook provides answers for all workbook exercises. The test generator package includes a printed database and software for use in preparing tests at the computer.

The teacher's manual is designed to provide help for busy teachers. There are objectives for each chapter and the answers for all questions and activities. In addition to teaching tips and suggestions, there are selected, single-concept transparency masters and solutions to the achievement tests.

Acknowledgments

Many people helped us prepare this book. Our teaching colleagues and students gave us frank opinions of the text and activities. By using the manuscript in our classes, we were able to make worthwhile revisions. In addition, many users of the preceding edition provided valuable suggestions to help us make the textbook a more effective learning tool.

Special thanks go to Kathy Morton, who helped prepare, type, and critique John Morton's manuscript and to Karen Rezny, who entertained a toddler so Ron Rezny could complete his manuscript. Finally, thanks to our families, friends, and business associates whose personal and financial sacrifices helped make this edition possible.

John S. Morton
Ronald R. Rezny

YOUR ECONOMIC CHOICES

1

DECISION MAKING

You make decisions about many things. Whether it's which record to buy or which career to pursue, you must make choices every day. What goes into a decision? How do you decide what you really want?

◆ Why do you have to make decisions?

◆ What are opportunity costs, and why does every decision involve them?

◆ How do your values influence your decisions?

◆ What are the steps to follow in making a decision?

All your life you have been making decisions. You make decisions as a **consumer**, a person who buys goods and services. You make decisions as a **producer**, a person who makes goods and services. And you make decisions as a **citizen**, a person who lives in a community, state, or country.

You are already active as a consumer. Teen-agers spend over $65 billion each year. They buy most of the records and tapes sold in the United States. They buy about half the movie tickets and cameras. Teen-age boys buy about 40 percent of all men's sportswear, and teen-age girls buy nearly 25 percent of all women's clothing and cosmetics. Overall, teen-agers spend $80 a month on things for themselves and $100 of their families' money on household items.

Even if you don't fit this pattern, you probably make some decisions every day. As time goes on, you will face bigger and more important decisions. You will have to make decisions about where to live; how to spend your money; and how to save, invest, or borrow money. You will have to decide on a career and on whom to vote for in elections.

UNLIMITED WANTS, LIMITED RESOURCES

Where to go on vacation may be a complex decision for some, as it is for this family.

We must make decisions because our wants are unlimited but our personal resources are scarce. Our **wants** are those things that we need or wish we could have. No matter what we already have, most of us wish we could have other things as well. Our wants are limited only by our imagination.

Personal Resources

Our **personal resources** are things like time, money, or skills that we use to satisfy our wants. We do this by using these resources to get goods and services. You probably can think of many examples of goods. **Goods** are things we can touch, such as cars, houses, compact discs, and clothing. **Services** are activities such as health care, bus rides, legal help, movies, rock concerts, and haircuts. We cannot have all of the goods and services we want because, unlike wants, resources are not created just by imagining them.

In the following case study, two personal resources that Charlie Lyons needs are limited. Which resources are they? Why can't he have as much of each as he wants?

CASE STUDY

Charlie had a problem. He liked Sharon and wanted to ask her out. But he didn't have enough money. He needed money to take her to a concert and have something to eat afterward.

He told his friend Leon about his problem. "What you need, Charlie, is a job," said Leon. "Why don't you come down to Disc City, the record store where I work, and sign up? They're always looking for help."

Leon was right. Disc City hired Charlie right away to work every Saturday. It was hard work, being on his feet all day, but it was fun too. And Charlie began to have some money in his pocket.

After a few weeks, Tony Cruz, Disc City's manager, asked Charlie if he could work after school during the week. "Sure," said Charlie. "The more I work, the more I make."

Soon Charlie was working every day after school and on Saturdays too. By the time Sunday came around, he was too tired even to think about Sharon.

One day, about a month later, he met Sharon in the hall in school. "I haven't seen you around much, Charlie," she said. "A bunch of us are going hiking on Saturday. Do you want to come?"

Charlie couldn't believe it—Sharon actually asked *him* out. And he even had money now to get himself some good hiking boots. Charlie started to say "Sure!" But then he remembered. He had to work. What good was having the money if he didn't have the time to spend with Sharon?

Charlie still had a problem. No matter how he looked at the situation, he couldn't seem to have it all. Either he had the time or he had the money, but he could not have both together. He had to make a decision.

1. **What is Charlie's problem?**
2. **What decision does Charlie need to make?**

The Cost of Using Resources

Like Charlie's, everyone's personal resources are limited. And, like Charlie, most people want more than they can get with the resources they have. Because our wants are greater than the personal resources available, we have to make decisions. We have to choose which wants we will satisfy with our limited resources. So we have to decide which goods or services we want the most: we have to put them in order of priority. And by deciding which wants to satisfy with our limited personal resources, we also decide which goods and services we are willing to do without.

What you pay to get something is the *cost*. There are two kinds of costs. One is the amount of personal resources—money, time, effort—you pay to get something. The cost of a pair of jeans may be, for instance, $30. The other kind of cost is the **opportunity cost**: what you give up to be able to buy something. Suppose you want some new jeans and have just enough money to buy one pair. But you'd also like to have a few new compact discs. The opportunity cost of buying the jeans is the compact discs. That is, if you spend your money on the jeans, you give up the opportunity to buy the compact discs. If you buy the compact discs instead, the opportunity cost is the jeans. The opportunity cost of any choice is the next best alternative that you give up—your second choice.

An opportunity cost does not have to involve money. Suppose your parents take you to the movies. The cost to you is a couple of hours of your time. The opportunity cost is the next best thing you could have done with that time—go out with your friends, for example, or read a book. Each alternative has its costs and benefits. We decide which goods and services to purchase by weighing these costs and benefits and then by choosing the best alternative.

Working while in school uses up one personal resource—time. But it produces another—money.

What do high school students value? In six states, 600 students were asked what they most wanted to be remembered for. They could reply "brilliant student," "athletic star," or "most popular." The largest group (43 percent) cared more about academic achievement than about popularity or athletic glory.

✓ check your understanding ✓ ✓ ✓ ✓ ✓ ✓

1. **Why do we have to make decisions?**
2. **What are wants?**
3. **What are personal resources? Name three types of personal resources.**
4. **What is an opportunity cost?**

VALUES, GOALS, AND DECISIONS

Faced with the same alternatives, different people will make different choices. This is because people base their choices on their values and goals, which are different for each person. A **value** is a person's inner feelings about what is good, desirable, and important. For example, many people may value happiness, love,

What are the goals of the people running this race? Some may want to win. Others may want to run faster than they have before. Others may want to finish what they've begun.

You may find it difficult to decide how you feel about values and goals because your feelings keep changing. Scientists have found that teen-agers can go through the whole range of emotions, from feelings of deep sadness to extreme happiness, in as little as 45 minutes. Adults take several hours to go through that many emotions.

good health, and family. Others may value popularity, money, independence, or free time.

Values help shape a person's **goals**, the things a person tries to reach or obtain in life. Many people who value education, for example, have the goal of going to college. Many people who value success in a career also have the goal of going to college. One of your goals may be to save enough money for new clothes or a car. Perhaps you want to pass a tough course or get a good job. Maybe all you want to do right now is to lose two pounds. Any time you try to get a certain thing, you have set a goal for yourself.

Getting a good grade in your biology course is a short-term goal. A *short-term goal* is one that can be met soon, maybe next week or within a year. Other goals are *long-term goals*. They may take a year, or many years, to reach. Often, short-term goals are steppingstones to long-term goals. For example, by doing well in your biology course this year, you have a better chance of reaching your long-term goal of becoming a veterinarian.

When people make decisions, they try to choose the alternative that will best satisfy their values and goals. Let's see how Charlie Lyons' values and goals affect his decisions.

Charlie had to make a decision. How much time was he going to spend working? How much money did he really need before he asked Sharon out?

Charlie knew his hours at Disc City were not working out. He asked Tony, the manager, if he could work just after school— not on Saturdays. But Tony said Saturdays were the busiest days. Tony really didn't need Charlie unless he could work Saturdays.

Charlie figured he could find a new job. But then during lunch he mentioned his problem to his friends. "Forget it," said Leon. "No one wants to hire you if you can't work Saturdays. Many places don't even let their full-time employees take Saturdays off."

"So much for that idea," Charlie thought. Maybe he should just drop out of school. Charlie was bored with reading history, and he was bored with trying to understand algebra. He didn't know what else he was going to learn from school anyway.

But there was no sense in quitting school unless he had a real job. He talked to the manager at Disc City, but Tony didn't have any full-time openings. Luckily, a job opportunity came up. A gas station attendant at Ben's Super Service quit, and Ben offered Charlie the job. At $5.50 an hour, Charlie could make about $220 a week pumping gas full-time.

When Charlie told his parents he wanted to drop out of school, they hit the roof. His mother thought he was making a mistake, even though his grades were not that great. His father suggested that Charlie stay in school and get a summer job. Both his parents suggested he talk to Jim Terry, the manager of Alfredo's Restaurant. Jim was a friend of the family and one of the reasons that they often went to Alfredo's when they ate out.

"Here's the problem," Charlie told Jim. "I've got a good job lined up and plenty of things to do with the cash. School's not doing me any good anyway."

"Have you thought about your life ten years from now?" Jim asked. "School might help you get a better job than pumping gas."

Charlie shrugged. "Most jobs are the same. Besides, if I stay there long enough, I can work on cars and maybe become a mechanic. Even if I get a better job after going to school longer, I'll still come out behind. Look at all the money I'd lose by not making my two-twenty a week right now."

"You know, I never told you," said Jim, "but I dropped out of school. At the time, my mother was a widow, and my wages helped the family. Still, we would have managed if I'd stayed in school. If I had to do it over, I'd make a different decision today.

"As a matter of fact, I was just reading this magazine article about current unemployment rates, especially for teen-agers," Jim added. "The unemployment rate for teen-agers is almost three times the national average. The article says that dropouts like me are twice as likely as high school graduates not to get a job. You may have a job for now. But as you get older, you're less likely to get or keep a job if you don't have a diploma.

"And listen to these facts," Jim said, reading from the magazine. "'High school dropouts have a median income of $14,937, whereas high school graduates earn a median income of $26,528. If you graduate from high school, you may choose to go on to college. College graduates earn a median income of $43,169.' The article also says things will get worse for people who don't finish high school. Many jobs that unskilled people now hold are going to be done by machines in the future. Most of the newly created jobs will require more education."

"Maybe I'll go back to school later," Charlie answered. "But I need money now, and I'm tired of school. Even if all gas stations become self-service, someone will still have to collect the money."

"Of course you know what you want to do now, but what about later?" asked Jim. "All jobs don't look the same after you've been working a few years, I can tell you. What if it turns out that you don't like collecting money in a gas station, or being a mechanic, after you've been at it day after day, year in and year out? If you drop out of school, what else will you be able to do? Having a high school diploma will give you more choices all through the rest of your life."

"But not everyone who drops out is a failure," said Charlie. "Look at you!" Then Charlie told Jim about an article he had read. It discussed some dropouts who had become millionaires. "I'm going to get an early start at learning the gas station business. Who knows, I might even own a string of them."

Charlie and Jim talked some more, and Charlie thanked Jim for his advice. Charlie promised to think about it. Staying in school had its advantages and disadvantages. So did dropping out. It wasn't an easy decision. How would Charlie decide?

1. **What reasons are there for Charlie to stay in school? to get a job?**
2. **What short-term goals does Charlie have? What long-term goals does he talk about?**

STEPS IN DECISION MAKING

Goals are often hard to reach. In fact, *goal* first meant "barrier." Its meaning changed to "boundary" or "end point" as it became a sports term.

When faced with a tough decision like Charlie's, it's best to think it through calmly and thoroughly. Even when the choice seems obvious, careful thought can be important. Generally speaking, there are six steps to follow in decision making.

1. **Face the problem.** The first step is recognizing the need for a decision. A person must be able to describe clearly what

problem needs to be solved. Charlie's problem was that he didn't think he had enough free time. Between working and going to school, he didn't have time to go out with his friends.

2. **Get information about the problem.** To solve a problem intelligently, a person needs facts. Charlie talked with the Disc City manager about changing his hours. He also looked into full-time job possibilities. Charlie talked with his parents and listened to their ideas about a summer job. He talked with Jim Terry and learned some facts about poor job prospects for dropouts. He also read a magazine article that gave some other facts—about dropouts who beat the odds.

3. **List the alternative ways of dealing with the problem.** Charlie had four alternatives. He could stay in school and quit his part-time job. He could stay in school and find a new part-time job with better hours. He could stay in school, quit his part-time job, and find a summer job. Or he could drop out of school and get a full-time job.

4. **Evaluate the alternatives.** What will be the results of each possible decision? What will be gained and what will be lost? Charlie knows most businesses that might hire him would require him to work Saturdays. He doesn't want to work Saturdays. So he eliminates this alternative from consideration. If Charlie stays in school and quits his part-time job, he improves his long-term job chances. But for the time being, he can't earn money. Even if he gets a summer job, he won't have any extra money until then. If he takes the full-time job now, he hurts his chances of getting a better job in the future. Each alternative has benefits, but also opportunity costs. What he decides to give up, school or work, is the opportunity cost of his decision.

5. **Reach a decision.** To reach a decision, Charlie must determine which of the alternatives will best meet his values and goals. Charlie has many values, some of which conflict with each other. For example, he loves his family and wants to make them happy by finishing high school. But he also wants to be able to date and to buy nice things with the money he earns from working. Charlie has goals to think about too. His short-term goals are to earn money and to spend time with his friends. But what about his long-term goals? Charlie thinks he wants to become a mechanic or to own a string of gas stations. But he is not too sure about either of these goals. Since Charlie doesn't know what his long-term goals are, it would probably be a good idea for him to have as many choices as possible. As Jim Terry showed Charlie, high school graduates have more choices when it comes to careers. They make more money, too, in the long term. So, staying in school would lead

Bette Davis found out what can happen if you make a decision without having all the facts. She turned down the leading role in *Gone with the Wind* because she thought the leading man was going to be Errol Flynn. The leading man turned out to be Clark Gable. And *Gone with the Wind* became the most successful movie ever made.

Charlie to his long-term goals and please his family, which is also important to him.

6. **Act on the decision.** Charlie's task is not only to reach a decision but also to act on it. What if he decides to stay in school and quit his job? He'll have to give notice at Disc City and study hard so he can graduate. He'll also have to adjust his spending to his lower income.

✓ **check your understanding** ✓ ✓ ✓ ✓ ✓ ✓

1. **List the six steps of the decision-making process.**
2. **Why is getting information so important in making a decision?**
3. **Why are values important in decision making?**
4. **What are goals? Why are they important in decision making?**

A DECISION-MAKING GRID

When making simple decisions—like choosing which clothes to wear to school—you probably don't even think about the steps in the decision-making process. For difficult decisions, though, you may find it helpful to put your alternatives, and your goals and values, on paper. A decision-making grid can help you see problems more clearly and so can help you make better decisions. In the grid on page 10, Charlie's goals and values are listed along the top, and his alternatives are listed down the left side. In this grid, a plus sign (+) shows that an alternative helps meet a goal or satisfy a value. A minus sign (–) shows that an alternative does not meet a goal or value.

Whatever decision Charlie makes, it will involve a trade-off. A **trade-off** is getting more of one thing by choosing less of something else. Charlie cannot get everything he wants at the same time. He gives up choices of future careers if he drops out of school now. He gives up having money right now if he stays in school. But if he makes his parents happy by staying in school and getting a summer job, Charlie does not have to give up many of his goals completely. He can have *some* of each of the things he wants. As he can see by looking at the decision-making grid, he can reach part of each goal and satisfy all of his values if he stays in school and gets a summer job.

Unfortunately, the answer is not so simple. For example, Charlie may feel that some goals and values are more important than others. Some alternatives may contribute more to one goal than to others. And, even if it is the best choice, a summer job may be difficult to get. Still, if Charlie knows that getting a summer job will help him reach more of his goals, he may try harder to get

Some decisions can turn out to be very expensive. Mark Twain had a choice between investing $5,000 in the Paige typesetting machine or in Alexander Graham Bell's new telephone company. He thought the typesetter would be more successful. His mistake was one reason he had to file for bankruptcy in 1894.

That decisions always involve trade-offs is clear from the word's original meaning. The word *decide* literally means "to cut off" or "to cut the knot." In other words, choosing one thing always involves cutting yourself off from something else.

Charlie Lyons' Decision-Making Grid

Alternatives	Values		Goals			
	Respect of Parents	Ability to Date and to Buy Nice Things	Time With Friends	Money Now	Money in Future	Job Choices
Drop out of School and Work Full-Time	–	+	+	+	–	–
Stay in School and Don't Work	+	–	+	–	+	+
Stay in School and Get a Summer Job	+	+	+	–	+	+

one. At least, he will know why he should try hard to get one. An orderly and reasoned approach to decision making can help you organize your thinking about problems and can lead to better decisions.

MAKING CONSUMER DECISIONS

You have seen how to use the decision-making process to make very important decisions. You can use the same steps to make smaller decisions, such as those you often make as a consumer. In this case study, follow Gail Thomas' decision-making process as she decides how to spend $300.

CASE STUDY

Gail Thomas had barely gotten over her excitement. She had just received a $300 prize for her safety suggestion at the bakery where she worked. Until now, Gail had just been meeting her regular monthly expenses with very little left over. Now she had a decision to make—what to do with the money.

Gail thought about her alternatives. She could save the money or she could spend it. She thought about two things she had wanted for a long time: a microwave oven and a video cassette recorder (VCR). She could afford either one now, but not both. She and her two daughters, Barbara and Michelle, would enjoy watching movies at home on a VCR. A microwave oven would help Gail prepare meals more quickly.

That night, Gail called a family meeting and explained her ideas. The girls were excited, especially about the VCR. Barbara, who was ten, said her mother should decide how to spend the money. After all, her idea won the prize. Eight-year-old Michelle agreed. It was up to Gail.

Using the Decision-Making Process

The decision was important to Gail, and she treated it that way. She sat down to go through the six decision-making steps calmly and thoroughly. As you see her make her decision, the six steps of the decision-making process are identified for you.

Step One: Face the problem Gail decided to spend, not save, the money. She also narrowed her choices to a microwave oven or a VCR. Now she had to decide which to buy. Her problem was that she wanted two things, but she had the resources to buy only one of them.

Step Two: Get information about the problem Gail read about VCRs in a consumer magazine at the library. She read about how easy it was to record programs even when she was away from home. Many of her friends already owned VCRs and were always talking about the great movies they watched at home.

Then she read an article in a consumer magazine about microwave ovens and found out how they could make food preparation much easier and quicker. Some of the other workers at the bakery had microwave ovens, and it seemed that they were able to spend a lot less time making meals. After a long day at work, that would be great.

Step Three: List alternative ways of dealing with the problem Gail had narrowed down her alternatives when she first faced the problem. Since she already knew that her alternatives were to buy either the microwave oven or the VCR, she quickly passed on to the next step.

Step Four: Evaluate the alternatives Gail tried to weigh the benefits of each choice against the opportunity cost of each. Buying the microwave oven meant giving up the VCR. The children would continue to go over to their friends' houses or to theaters to watch movies. They would miss favorite TV shows if they were out. Choosing the VCR could mean more family togetherness. But buying the microwave oven meant having the convenience of getting food from the freezer to the table in minutes. Having a microwave oven would give Gail more time to spend with her daughters. However, if her daughters were out watching movies, they might not be home to share her extra time with her.

When setting goals for yourself, remember that as you grow older you may discover talents and skills that you don't know you have now. Albert Einstein failed his entrance exam the first time he applied to college. President Woodrow Wilson did not learn to read until he was 11 years old.

The Wrong Way To Make Decisions

Have you ever made a bad decision, and later wondered why you'd made it? Many things can influence our decisions.

Sometimes, people decide to do something because all of their friends do it. Someone who does this is making a decision based on *peer pressure*. Peer pressure can affect your choices without your even knowing it. For example, Thomas enjoyed his part-time job delivering furniture. He especially liked helping customers rearrange their rooms. Thomas felt he'd love to be an interior decorator some day. But he sensed that his friends, who all wanted to be engineers, would laugh at him. Later, Thomas never understood why he got a degree in engineering. He didn't even like computers.

Often, people who are under stress make poor decisions. For instance, Marta had too many demands on her time. She spent hours studying to get good grades. When she wasn't studying, all her free time was divided between the varsity girls' basketball team and helping care for her younger brothers and sisters. Marta had the opportunity to take a test to qualify for a full scholarship. But she would have to go out of town to take the test. She refused to go. Why? Marta reacted as if the test were just one more demand on her time. She didn't stop to think that the reason she had been studying so hard was to try for a scholarship.

Some people never seem to be able to make a decision at all. Why? One reason is fear of making a bad decision. Although Julie had the money, she never bought a car. She was never sure which one was the best choice. Some people avoid decisions because they fear commitments. Fear of commitment can stand in the way of making big decisions wisely. For example, when Leon asked Maria to marry him, she said no. She loved Leon, but couldn't stand the idea of not being free to date anymore.

When you are faced with an important decision, take the time to go through the decision-making process. Don't let peer pressure, stress, or fear push you into making a decision you'll regret.

If you make no decision, you still have made a decision. Say, for example, that you can't decide if you want to go to college. Making no decision would be the same as deciding not to go.

Step Five: Reach a decision To reach her decision, Gail had to decide which alternative would best satisfy her values and goals. Getting the microwave oven would give her two things she valued: convenience and relaxation. Owning a VCR would make her daughters happy and might mean that her family would spend more time together.

Gail valued her family's happiness and the time they spent together even more than she valued convenience and relaxation. So in the end, Gail chose the VCR. This decision, like all decisions, involved a trade-off. Gail traded less time in the kitchen for more time with her family. She was able to make this trade-off wisely because her choice was based on what she valued most: her daughters.

Step Six: Act on the decision Having decided to buy a VCR, Gail must now go out and get one. She must act on her decision. That means she must follow up her main decision with some other decisions. Which VCR should she buy? Where should she buy it? How much of her $300 would she spend on it? This book will help you make decisions such as these in your own life.

When To Use the Decision-Making Process

Gail Thomas' decision-making process was long and careful. For most decisions, the process is much quicker and simpler. When you shop for a sweater, for example, you may go through all of the decision-making steps, but you go through them more quickly because the decision is a smaller one.

You also make many purchases without going through all of the decision-making steps. You may have made a decision in the past about something you buy often, and now you buy the same thing over and over again out of habit. You may buy one brand of toothpaste or order the same kind of pizza all the time. But if a store stops carrying your choice or if it raises its prices, you may need to make a new decision.

Whenever a decision is needed, it makes good sense to go through all of the decision-making steps. How much time and effort does a particular decision deserve? That depends on how important it is to you.

Because we have so many products to choose from, even simple consumer decisions, like which toy to buy, can be perplexing.

✓check your understanding ✓ ✓ ✓ ✓ ✓ ✓

1. **How did values affect the decision Gail Thomas finally made?**
2. **What was the opportunity cost of Gail's decision?**
3. **What trade-offs did Gail make?**
4. **Is the decision-making process essential for every decision you make as a consumer? Explain.**

SUMMARIZING
the chapter

Our wants, what we need or wish to have, are unlimited. But our resources, the things we use to satisfy our wants, are limited. So we must make decisions. We must decide what we will get with our resources.

The cost of getting what we want is the amount of the resource we use to get it. But there is another cost. When we decide to use a resource to satisfy one want, we cannot use it anymore to satisfy another want. The opportunity cost is the next best thing we give up when we use a resource to satisfy one want instead of another.

When making an important decision, take the time to go through the six steps in the decision-making process:

1. Face the problem.
2. Get information about the problem.
3. List alternative ways of dealing with the problem.
4. Evaluate the alternatives.
5. Reach a decision.
6. Act on the decision.

A decision-making grid can guide us through this process. The grid can help us identify the best alternative based on our values and goals. The more carefully we go through the decision-making process, the more satisfaction we will get from our choices.

C·H·A·P·T·E·R A·C·T·I·V·I·T·I·E·S

BUILDING CONSUMER VOCABULARY

Number your paper from 1 to 11. Then write the term that best matches each numbered definition.

citizen	producer
consumer	services
goals	trade-off
goods	values
opportunity cost	wants
personal resources	

1. Goods and services that consumers need or would like to have
2. Getting less of one thing because you choose more of another thing
3. Inner feelings about what is good, desirable, and important
4. A person who buys goods and services
5. A person who lives in a country, state, or community
6. The next best thing we give up when we use a resource to get something
7. Things we can touch that satisfy our wants
8. Things we can't touch that satisfy our wants
9. A person who makes goods or supplies services
10. Things, such as money, time, or skills, that we use to obtain goods and services
11. The things a person tries to get in life

1. You want to buy a new bike and a new pair of stereo speakers, but you have enough money for only one of them. What is the opportunity cost of each?
2. If you were Charlie, what would you decide to do? Why?
3. How can a decision-making grid help you make a difficult decision?
4. Given your own values, which product, the microwave or the VCR, would you choose if you were Gail? Why?
5. Name six items you purchase for which you no longer go through the entire decision-making process. Do you think you should use the decision-making process the next time you purchase any of these items?

After weeks of searching, you have been offered two after-school jobs. One—as a stockroom clerk—pays $4.55 per hour. The hours are 3:30 P.M. to 6:00 P.M. Monday, Tuesday, and Thursday, and 3:30 P.M. to 9:00 P.M. on Friday. The second job offer is an opportunity to work in a greenhouse—watering, selling, and caring for plants. This position pays only $4.10 per hour, but the hours are longer—3:30 P.M. to 6:00 P.M., Monday through Friday, and 8:00 A.M. to 5:00 P.M. on Saturday. One of your considerations in choosing between the two jobs is the total amount of money you earn. How much would each job pay you per week? What is the difference between these two amounts?

1. Make a decision-making grid for Gail Thomas. Use the same type of grid as in the illustration on page 10. Do you think the decision Gail made was the best one for her? Why or why not?
2. You will have to decide whether to go to college after you graduate from high school. Construct a decision-making grid with your values and goals along the top and the alternatives down the left side. Complete the grid. What alternative appears to be best for you? Why?

Try to determine how the following businesses, agencies, or organizations in your community might help people achieve their goals: health club, clothing store, employment agency, travel agency, church or synagogue, hair salon, bookstore, and sporting goods shop.

CHOOSING A CAREER

You will probably spend most of your life working. At least you will spend most of your time trying to earn money to pay for goods and services. How can you be sure to get the job you want? How can you prepare now for the jobs of the future?

◆ What will the job market be like in the 1990's?

◆ What kinds of training will be necessary for the jobs of the future?

◆ What kinds of skills and attitudes do good employees have?

Before you can spend money, you must earn it. Without work, most people would not have the money they need to be consumers. They could not get the goods and services money can buy.

But work is more than just earning a living. Work can let you satisfy many of your interests and use many of your abilities. Work can bring you recognition and a feeling of achievement. It can bring you new friends. It can help you obtain the lifestyle you want.

Work can do all of these things—and more. Sometimes it's satisfying, and sometimes it's not. It depends on the job, and it depends on the person. Let's look at some case studies adapted from the Bureau of Labor Statistics' publication *Exploring Careers.* You'll see that there is a great variety of occupations. In fact, there are more than 20,000 kinds of jobs.

> By the time you turn 65, you will probably have spent more than 75,000 hours at work.

CASE STUDY

Joe Jaramillo grumbled and rubbed his eyes. The clock on his nightstand read 4:08—4:08 on a Sunday morning! A phone call had awakened him moments before, and a faraway voice had told him to come down to the bank right away. "So much for catching up on my sleep," he thought.

"Almost six years," he remembered, "six years next week since I was promoted from programmer to programmer/systems analyst. What a change! Back then I handled the computer all the time. Writing programs, running them, finding the 'bugs.' All I saw was my own little slice of the bank. Now I work with people from consumer lending, internal operations—all the different bank departments. I see the whole show. I help people understand what the computer can do for them—how it can help them do their work. And I have lots of room to be creative. After I find out exactly what people need, I think things through and design a new system. Then I install and test it.

"The head of the check-processing department, Tom Arnold, wanted a new system for processing checks. With the new system that Tom and I developed, checks can be proofed, encoded, and automatically sorted into several categories. With the new proof machine, Tom can easily get the information he wants about any account whenever he wants it. The checks are microfilmed while they're sorted on a high-speed reader/sorter so we can make a record of them as the bank receives them.

"The new equipment has already been installed and tested, and we've linked it to the bank's computer. Now all we have to do is switch over to the new system. It has to be ready to process checks by tomorrow morning when the bank opens. I thought the technicians would be able to handle the job, but obviously they've run into a problem if they need me at this hour. Well, fortunately, I don't have to make many of these night calls."

1. What skills does Joe need in his job as programmer/systems analyst that he didn't need as much in his job as a programmer?
2. What do you think provides the most job satisfaction for Joe?

CASE STUDY

Holly Krantzler attended technical school for two years after high school to get a First Class Radiotelephone Operator's license. Now she wants to increase her knowledge of electronics to keep up with new developments and to remain competitive in her occupation. The community college offers a degree in electronics, and Holly hopes to get hers at the end of next term.

Control Room 3 at radio station WELL is where Holly spends most of her time. She sits at a control board directly in front of a window facing into the studio. The board has dozens of buttons, dials, meters, and slide switches. These controls allow her to set sound levels in the studio and mix sounds from different sources (such as a speaking voice and background music). From this board she can also operate the turntables, tape recorders, and compact disc players in the room. She can even control a live broadcast coming from outside the studio. Holly is particularly proud of this equipment, which she installed herself. At a larger station she might not have been given this opportunity.

She spends several days each month in "solitary confinement" at the transmitter. The transmitter, located on a hill five miles from the studio, is the source of the station's radio signal. One person stays at the transmitter the entire time the station is on the air to make sure everything runs smoothly and according to federal regulations. These tasks often require very little time, so the job can get lonely.

1. What do you think provides the most job satisfaction for Holly?
2. What disadvantages do you think Holly has in her job?

CASE STUDY

Mark Kohn works as a forester for a medium-sized forest products company. He is responsible for managing 60,000 acres of company timberland scattered over a ten-county area. Mark didn't just suddenly decide to become a forester. As a boy, he was active in scouting. Then he attended a college with a forestry program and earned a bachelor's degree in forestry. While in college, Mark took part in a work-study program six months out of each year. In this program, Mark gained practical work experience at the national parks in Montana.

On this particular day, Mark's first activity is to visit a section of land being "cruised" by forestry aides. The aides are trying to determine how much marketable wood there is in this section of forest. They mark off a sample area and carefully count and measure the trees. After recording the information, Mark will enter it into a computer and onto detailed maps he has prepared.

Mark then moves on to another section of the forest. Here he must decide which trees will be left to provide windbreaks and cover for wild game and protection from erosion. Bulldozers will then make *windrows*, or mounds of dirt, to prevent the soil from blowing or washing away.

Next, Mark visits a site where inexperienced laborers are planting 1,000 trees. When he arrives at the site, Mark is not at all happy with what he sees. The laborers have begun planting, but Mark knows many of the trees cannot possibly survive. Some seedlings have even been planted upside down! Mark doesn't lose his temper, though. He knows it would do no good. Instead, he patiently and clearly shows the workers how the job should be done. Later he has a budget meeting, finishes some paperwork at his office, and visits a nearby farmer to discuss damage to the farm possibly caused by lumbering equipment. The day ends with an evening talk to a high school science club about forestry. It's a typical full day for Mark, one with a lot of variety.

1. **Describe the training necessary for the job of forester.**
2. **What do you think provides the most job satisfaction for Mark?**

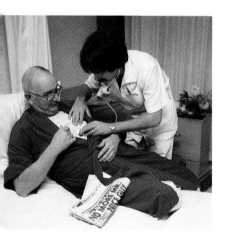

Our economy is expected to need more than 100,000 additional nurses in the 1990's.

WHICH CAREER IS RIGHT FOR YOU?

Perhaps you have been thinking about the career you would like to have. Maybe you already have a job. Your first job probably won't be your last. Why? For one reason, new graduates rarely get the most desirable jobs. Half of all 16- to 24-year-olds are low-paid service workers, clerks, or non-farm laborers. Only about 5 percent are administrators or managers. So, few people stay in their first jobs for long. Only about one worker in 100 is with the same employer ten years later. One in five workers leaves his or her job each year.

Although a first job doesn't have to lead to a career, for some people it does. For example, they might start during high school by taking a part-time job working at the counter in a restaurant. After they graduate, they find that their experience makes it easy for them to get full-time jobs in better restaurants. Five years—and three jobs—later, they are still working in the food service

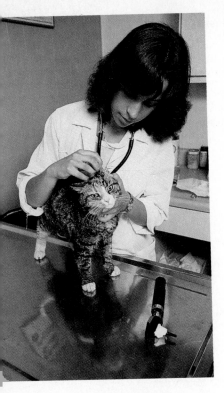

industry. If they like the work they're doing, everything is fine. But if they don't like what they're doing and want to change careers, they may find it difficult to do so.

Good planning can help you get on the right track. There are four steps to effective career planning:

1. Learn about your interests and abilities.
2. Identify careers that fit your interests.
3. Find out if job opportunities will exist in those careers in the future.
4. Find out what skills and education you must have to qualify for your favorite career, and get the necessary training.

You also need to figure out what is most important to you in a job. You may answer "money." Yet you might be unhappy if you choose a high-paying job that doesn't match your interests. When considering a job, think about how it will fit in with your interests, values, and goals. There are many reasons to work. Which of these match your own reasons for wanting to work?

- I want a job that lets me use the skills and knowledge I learned in school.
- I want a job that provides prestige—recognition from others.
- I want a job that offers a variety of activities.
- I want a job in which I can make lots of friends and can work with others.
- I want a high-paying job.
- I want a job that gives me the chance to help build a better world.
- I want a job in which I can be independent.
- I want a job that lets me be creative.
- I want a job that allows me to be in charge.
- I want a job that is difficult and challenging.

If it reflects your interests, a job you take part-time after school or one you have in the summer may become the first step on the road to building a career.

You may want many of these things, but, as with other decisions, there are trade-offs. For example, a job that meets your interests may not pay the highest salary. A job in which you can make a lot of friends may not be one that allows you to be in charge. Before you choose a career, find out who you are. Then explore career fields that spark your imagination and use your interests, education, skills, and experiences.

✓ check your understanding ✓ ✓ ✓ ✓ ✓ ✓

1. Why do few people stay in their first jobs?
2. What are the four steps in effective career planning?
3. Why should you find out what's important to you before exploring possible careers?

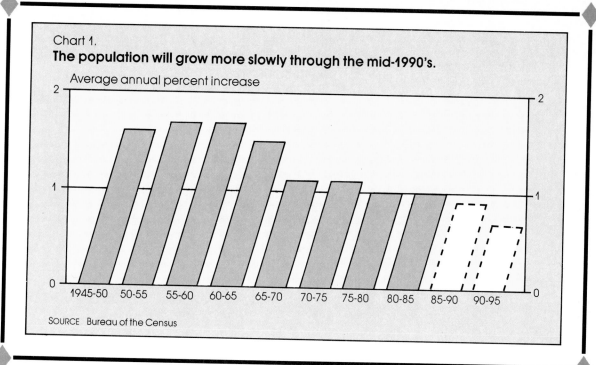

Chart 1.

The population will grow more slowly through the mid-1990's.

Average annual percent increase

SOURCE Bureau of the Census

TOMORROW'S WORKING WORLD

The economic factors that create and change jobs are themselves constantly changing. The jobs that employers offer are based on the types of goods and services consumers want to buy. Change in consumers' demands for goods and services will affect the number and types of jobs available. Economists call this relationship **derived demand**

Although new inventions and changing tastes will create jobs in the future that no one dreams of today, we can try to predict the future by looking at the past. The charts and tables on pages 21 through 26 show what has happened in the job market in the recent past and what is predicted for the future. The charts come from the United States Department of Labor's *Occupational Outlook Handbook*, an excellent source of career information. In addition to articles about where to find career information and predictions about changes in tomorrow's economy, the *Handbook* describes about 200 occupations in detail. These occupations account for three out of every five jobs in the United States.

Population Changes

Chart 1 above shows that the population will grow very slowly through the mid-1990's. The population is also aging. That is, the number of people over 65 will rise sharply while the number of 14- to 25-year-olds will decline. There should be more children

What do welders, fishing instructors, motorboat mechanics, comparison shoppers, animal trainers, air traffic controllers, ambulance drivers, fire fighters, sheep herders, and zoo keepers have in common? They are all in jobs that require a high school diploma and a number of years of on-the-job training.

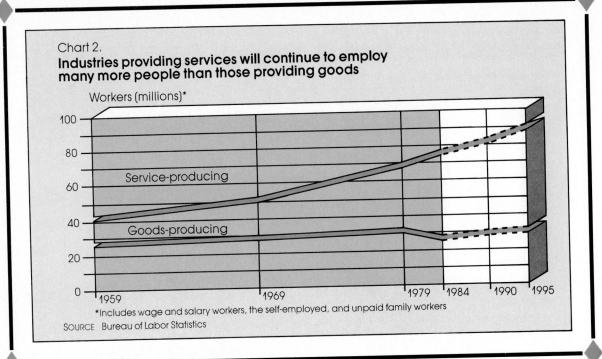

Chart 2.

Industries providing services will continue to employ many more people than those providing goods

Workers (millions)*

Service-producing

Goods-producing

1959 1969 1979 1984 1990 1995

*Includes wage and salary workers, the self-employed, and unpaid family workers

SOURCE   Bureau of Labor Statistics

under 13 as the baby boomers have children of their own. The **baby boomers** are the large number of people born after World War II (1945) and before 1960. They make up the largest segment of the population and strongly affect which goods and services are provided. For example, in 15 to 20 years, baby boomers will begin to retire. Because there are so many baby boomers, their retirement will increase the demand for health care services and leisure activities.

The Service Economy

Chart 2 above shows that the United States economy is moving from one whose industries produce goods to one whose industries produce services. As you know, goods-producing industries make products that you can touch, such as corn flakes, televisions, automobiles, and houses. Another term for products you can touch is **tangible** products. Service-producing industries sell activities you can't touch, or **intangible** products, to the consumer. Services include health care, education, recreation, restaurants, transportation, banking, and insurance. Today slightly more than seven out of every ten jobs are found in industries that produce services. Employment in service-producing industries has been growing more quickly than employment in goods-producing industries, and this trend is expected to continue. Some service-producing jobs are low-wage jobs, such as retail clerks and hospital orderlies. Other service-producing jobs in finance, insurance, and real estate are higher paying jobs.

Because their goals may change as they grow older, many people can expect to change careers at some point. A number of famous people have ended up in fields far from where they started. Paul Revere, for example, before he took his midnight ride, was a dentist. J. Edgar Hoover, the first director of the FBI, began as a librarian.

New Technology

Technology is the application of scientific knowledge in business or industry. New technology will continue to have a large impact on the workplace. Rapid technological advancement, however, doesn't mean that everyone has to become a scientist or a computer programmer. Everyone didn't have to become a mechanic when the car was invented. Yet the automobile changed the way people live just as the computer and other forms of **automation**, the use of machines to produce goods, continue to change the way people work. Just about every worker will have to learn to do new things or to do some old things in new ways. Workers unwilling to learn these new skills will have trouble finding or keeping jobs.

Using computer graphics, this man is designing equipment for an assembly line. Only a decade ago, this job would have been done with paper and pencil.

The International Economy

Future careers also will be influenced by trade with other countries. Many economists predict that more manufacturing will be done abroad. One result is that jobs will probably decline in the consumer electronics industries (industries that make electronic goods for the home, such as televisions and compact disc players). Fewer jobs are also expected in the automobile, steel, and clothing industries. On the bright side, economists believe that the United States is more competitive in service industries and in other areas of high technology, such as robotics and medical equipment. Therefore, jobs in the legal services, finance, insurance, real estate, and computer industries may increase. Almost every industry will need to compete with foreign industry. This will mean that businesses in the United States must improve quality and hire more capable workers.

Jobs of the Future

The table on page 25 shows the 40 fields that are expected to create most of the new jobs in the next few years. This information can be helpful in planning your career. Keep in mind, though, that the trends these predictions are based on could change. For example, if consumer buying patterns change, the businesses that meet these demands will also change. So don't rule out any career. Even in those industries that are expected to grow slowly, workers will retire or die. New workers will be needed to replace them.

Careers: A Place to Begin

Do you feel frustrated because you don't have any career goals? Vocational aptitude tests may be able to help. Here's how they work.

The test asks you a series of questions about what you like to do and what your interests are. Your answers are compared with answers given by people in many different occupations. Types of jobs that seem to fit your interests and personality are then suggested.

For example, the test may ask you if you would rather spend your spare time reading a book or talking to your friends. Suppose you answer that you'd rather talk to your friends. The test might conclude that you may be happier in a job working with people, such as a teacher, than in a job in which you would work alone, as writers often do.

Vocational aptitude tests won't drop a career in your lap. However, they can be used as guides to help you find out what would make you happy in a career. Ask your guidance counselor if vocational aptitude tests are available at your school.

✓ check your understanding ✓ ✓ ✓ ✓ ✓ ✓

1. **How will population changes affect the types of jobs available?**
2. **Will more jobs be created in goods-producing industries or in service-producing industries?**
3. **How will new technology affect the workplace?**
4. **How will foreign competition affect the workplace?**
5. **Why will there still be jobs in industries that are not growing or are growing very slowly?**

Forty Occupations Will Account for About Half of All New Jobs Generated between 1982 and 1995

	Employment Change (thousands)	Percentage of Change	Percentage of Total Job Growth
All occupations	**25,600**	**25**	**100.0**
Building custodians	780	28	3.0
Cashiers	740	47	2.9
Secretaries	720	30	2.8
General clerks: office	700	30	2.7
Salesclerks	690	24	2.7
Nurses: registered	640	49	2.7
Waiters and waitresses	560	34	2.2
Teachers: kindergarten & elementary	510	37	2.0
Truck drivers	430	27	1.7
Nursing aides and orderlies	420	35	1.7
Sales representatives: technical	390	29	1.5
Accountants and auditors	340	40	1.3
Automotive mechanics	320	38	1.3
Supervisors of blue-collar workers	320	27	1.2
Kitchen helpers	300	36	1.2
Guards and doorkeepers	300	47	1.2
Food preparation & service workers: fast food restaurants	300	37	1.2
Managers: store	290	30	1.1
Carpenters	250	29	1.0
Electrical and electronics technicians	220	61	0.9
Licensed practical nurses	220	37	0.9
Computer system analysts	220	85	0.8
Electrical engineers	210	65	0.8
Computer programmers	210	77	0.8
Maintenance repairers: general utility	190	28	0.8
Helpers: trades	190	31	0.7
Receptionists	190	49	0.7
Electricians	170	32	0.7
Physicians	160	34	0.7
Clerical supervisors	160	35	0.6
Computer operators	160	76	0.6
Sales representatives: nontechnical	160	27	0.6
Lawyers	160	34	0.6
Stock clerks: stockroom & warehouse	160	19	0.6
Typists	160	16	0.6
Delivery and route workers	150	19	0.6
Bookkeepers: hand	150	16	0.6
Cooks: restaurants	150	42	0.6
Bank tellers	140	30	0.6
Cooks: short order, specialty, and fast food	140	32	0.6

Source: Table compiled from George T. Silvestri *et al.* "Occupational Employment Projections Through 1995," *Monthly Labor Review,* Vol. 106, No. 11, November 1983, Table 2, p. 45.

PREPARING FOR A CAREER

Suppose you've decided on a career in a growing field that really interests you. You start getting the skills, education, or experience you need to qualify for the position you want. But other people are doing the same thing. How can you increase your chances of getting the job—and keeping it?

Getting a Good Education

Every year they work, high school dropouts fall further behind people who have high school diplomas. When both are 25, the graduate earns $1.50 for every $1.00 the dropout makes. Each year, the graduate gets a raise twice as high as the dropout's. By the time both are 65, the graduate earns $2 for every $1 the dropout makes.

Employers try to hire the best qualified workers available. As a future worker, you will compete with an increasingly educated work force. Chart 3 below shows that in 1970 only about a quarter of the work force had gone to college. But by 1984, closer to one half of the workers had some college training. Because so many people are graduating from college today, a college degree does not guarantee success in the job market. Although employment of college graduates grew 127 percent between 1970 and 1984, one out of five of those graduates took jobs that did not require a college degree.

But if the college graduates are getting the jobs that don't require a college degree, what jobs are left for the people who don't go to college? Statistics show that they are having a harder time finding a job. Therefore, the more education you obtain, the less likely you are to be unemployed. The unemployment rate among 20- to 24-year-olds who dropped out of high school is approximately 27

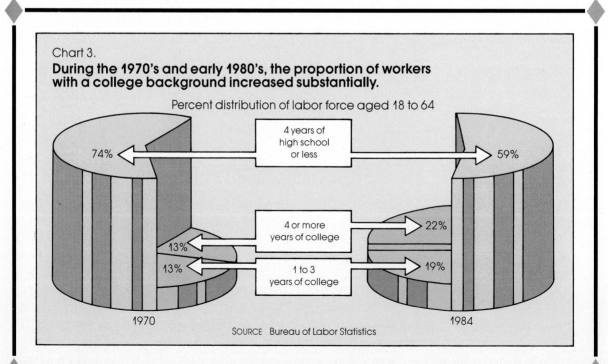

Chart 3.
During the 1970's and early 1980's, the proportion of workers with a college background increased substantially.

Percent distribution of labor force aged 18 to 64

74% ← 4 years of high school or less → 59%

13% ← 4 or more years of college → 22%

13% ← 1 to 3 years of college → 19%

1970   1984

SOURCE Bureau of Labor Statistics

percent. The **unemployment rate** is the percentage of people who are looking for work but can't find a job. High school graduates between the ages of 20 and 24 have an unemployment rate of approximately 13 percent. Those who attend college but do not graduate have an unemployment rate of about 8 percent. College graduates have the lowest unemployment rate—5 percent. Clearly, education increases your chances of getting a job.

Having the Basic Skills

Degrees are not enough, however. Your ability to use the basic skills—reading, writing, mathematics, problem solving, and science—is what will impress employers most. In addition, once hired, you will have to get along with other people on the job and contribute to the company's growth.

A panel of leading business people and educators organized by the National Academy of Sciences, the National Academy of Engineering, and the Institute of Medicine asked employers to describe the type of employee they will need in the future. All agreed that the successful employee will be one who is willing and able to learn. But only a person who has at least basic skills will be able to learn on the job. Panel members worried that young people today do not have those basic skills:

> It is precisely in the basic intellectual skills, however, that young employees show the greatest deficiencies. Many lack the ability to draw correct inferences from written, pictorial, or mathematical information; to understand oral instructions; to develop alternatives and reach conclusions; to express their ideas intelligibly and effectively; and to apply such basic concepts of economics as profit and cost. All of these skills are important, even in entry-level jobs. Advancement to more responsible posts requires skills of an even higher order, including the ability to compose tables and reports, to consult reference and source materials, to apply mathematical concepts and procedures, to control complex equipment, and to address groups.

Having a Good Attitude

Not only are employers looking for people with basic skills, they are also looking for people who can work well with others. People will depend on you to come to work on time. You will be expected to understand the standards of behavior, speech, and dress appropriate to the workplace. These standards will probably differ from those you are used to as a student. As a student, you are expected to work primarily on your own. As an employee, you must work with others, and your work must fit in with the work of others. Cooperation is expected—often demanded—on the job. Most employers insist on behavior that does not offend customers, co-workers, or the general public. In addition, private employers

It's no surprise that doctors, lawyers, and scientists need college degrees. But did you know that many nurses, TV station managers, fashion designers, veterinarians, airplane salespeople, recreation center directors, military officers, city managers, flight attendants, farmers, and optometrists need college degrees as well?

Would you like to be a park ranger, a chef, a barber, a commercial artist, a surveyor, a golf course manager, or an X-ray technician? If so, you need training at a specialized technical institute.

As is true for most jobs, this one, assembling printed-circuit boards, is a group effort.

appreciate employees who understand that a business must sell a good or service at a profit in order to survive. Public employees must realize that taxpayers expect good service for their tax dollars.

✓ check your understanding ✓ ✓ ✓ ✓ ✓ ✓

1. **What happens to your chances of keeping a job when you obtain more education?**
2. **What basic skills are most important in getting and keeping a job?**
3. **What attitudes do employers expect from their employees?**

*S*UMMARIZING
the chapter

In choosing a career, you should first determine your interests. You want a career that matches your interests, values, and goals.

Next, examine the future job market. By the year 2000, our economy will be even more service oriented than it is today. A changing population, advanced technology, and foreign competition will affect the types of jobs available and the way workers do those jobs. Remember, too, because of replacement needs, jobs will become available even in industries that are not growing or are growing very slowly.

Finally, get the proper training for work in a rapidly changing economy. No matter what job you want, you must be competent in basic skills, such as reading, writing, and arithmetic. In fact, the more education you have, the better your chances of getting and keeping a good job. But degrees do not guarantee you a job. You must also have the cooperative attitude that will make you a valuable employee to your company.

C H A P T E R  C T I V I T I E S

BUILDING CONSUMER VOCABULARY

Number your paper from 1 to 7. Then write the term that best matches each numbered definition.

automation	tangible
baby boomers	technology
derived demand	unemployment rate
intangible	

1. Something that can be touched
2. The relationship between consumer demand for goods and services and the types of jobs available
3. The application of science to industry
4. The percentage of people who want to work but cannot find a job
5. The large group of people born between 1945 and 1960
6. The use of machines to produce goods and services
7. Something that can't be touched

BUILDING CONSUMER UNDERSTANDING

1. Of the three careers described at the beginning of the chapter, which ones would be suited to a person who wants a lot of variety? Which ones would be suited to a person who likes to work alone?
2. What do you think would make one job boring and another one challenging?
3. List and explain three ways the economy is changing. How do you think these changes might affect the job market for either teachers or mechanics? (Choose one.)
4. What are three advantages of getting a college education?
5. Why is it so important for employees to get along with each other? Why is it important for employees to come to work on time?
6. What do employers mean when they say they are looking for employees with "good attitudes"?

Refer to the charts and table in this chapter, and answer the questions that follow.

1. Assume that the population of the United States was 240 million in 1976. Using Chart 1 on page 21, determine what the population was in 1977. What was the population in 1978?
2. Using Chart 2 on page 22, find out how many more workers will be employed in the service-producing industries than in the goods-producing industries in 1995.
3. According to the table on page 25, which three occupations will create the most jobs between 1982 and 1995? How many new jobs will they create together? Which three occupations will grow the fastest (as measured by percent change)? How many jobs are these three occupations expected to create?
4. There were about 125 million workers between the ages of 18 and 64 in 1984. According to Chart 3 on page 26, how many of them had four or more years of college?

In this activity, you will use the decision-making grid you learned about in Chapter 1. Construct a grid with at least five career goals you may have along the top. Rank your career goals from most important (closest to the left) to least important (furthest to the right). Write the three careers you are most interested in down the left side. In each square, put a plus sign (+) if the career helps achieve the goal or a minus sign (–) if it does not. Based on your grid, which career should you choose? Do you think a grid like this is a good way to analyze possible career choices? Why or why not?

Choose the career that most interests you, and interview a person in your community who hires people in that occupation. In the interview, be sure to get the following information:

1. Duties of the job
2. Educational requirements
3. Entry-level (beginning) salary
4. Top salary
5. Expected growth of jobs in the occupation
6. Fringe benefits offered by this company
7. Name, position, and company of the person you interview.

Summarize the information (using the categories listed) and create a classroom career file for others to review.

THINKING ABOUT:

Job Interviews

Success in a job interview depends on three things: how you look, how you act, and how you answer questions.

Experts advise all job seekers to wear conservative, well-pressed business clothes. Wearing torn or wrinkled clothing is disrespectful and implies that the wearer is careless. What judgments might you make about these job seekers? (Answer all questions on a separate sheet of paper. Use complete sentences.)

1. A man with spiked hair who wears black leather.

2. A woman wearing a tight-fitting dress and a lot of makeup.

3. A man wearing a suit and reflective-lens sunglasses.

Actions are important, too. Job seekers should appear competent and able to work with customers and other employees. A person who rocks back in a chair and asks, "So, what do you guys do here, anyway?" will seem cocky and lazy. A person with a cocky attitude can appear to be difficult to work with. What negative impressions could the following actions create?

4. A man who never looks the interviewer in the eye.

5. A man who brings a friend to the interview.

6. A woman who giggles and flirts with the interviewer.

Interviewers ask many questions. You can anticipate some of an interviewer's questions, such as "What are your career goals?" "What subjects did you study in school?" "Do you have experience?" The interviewer may ask negative questions you won't have anticipated. Negative questions "weed out" applicants. If someone asks you what your greatest weakness is, turn the question around to make your weakness a strength. One possible answer is "I get so involved in what I'm doing, I forget to stop for lunch." How could an applicant answer the following questions positively but honestly?

7. What kind of work is difficult for you?

8. What have you been criticized for by past employers?

9. What do you think you'll like least about this job?

ACTIVITY: Cut pictures from magazines of three people who are appropriately dressed and three people who are inappropriately dressed for a job interview. Explain your choices.

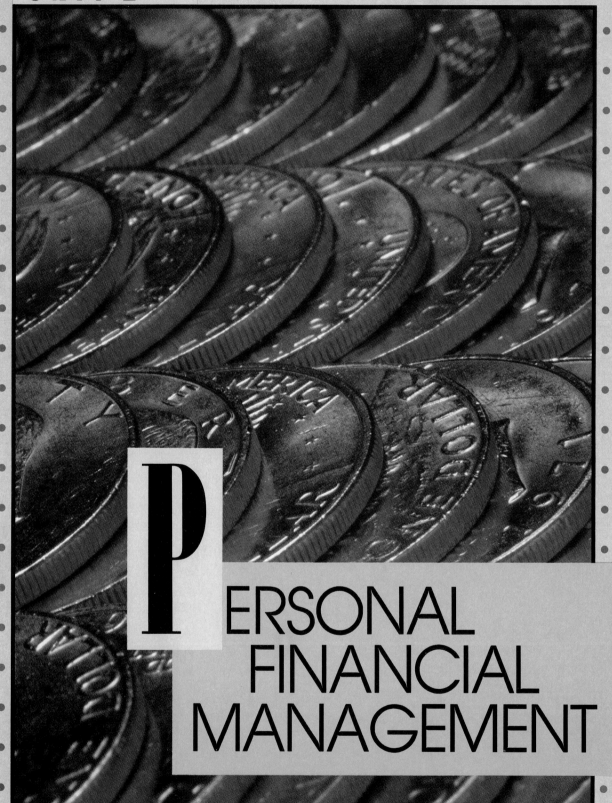

PERSONAL FINANCIAL MANAGEMENT

BUDGETING AND MONEY MANAGEMENT

③

Have you ever had that sinking feeling when you've opened your wallet to pay for something—and found nothing in it? Money may not buy happiness, but it certainly makes life a little easier if you have it. If you know how, you can plan your spending so that you have money for the things you want and need.

● How can a budget help you reach your spending goals?

● How do you determine what your financial resources are?

● What kinds of expenses might you have?

● How can you solve spending problems?

WHY YOU NEED A BUDGET

Many people need a **budget**—a plan for spending and saving money—to help them reach their goals. A budget is like a road map. It helps you reach your spending goals, just as a road map helps a driver reach a destination.

Perhaps you feel that budgets are just for your parents or for other older people. Maybe you feel that you don't need a budget because you don't have a lot of money or because you don't have many bills to pay. Maybe you don't like the idea of a budget because you think it's just one more thing limiting what you can do.

But the truth is just the opposite. Rather than limiting what you can do, budgets let you do more of the things you want to do. A budget won't make you richer than you are. It won't make you poorer, either. A budget can help you use the money you have to achieve your spending goals, both long-term and short-term.

HOW TO SET UP A BUDGET

The steps to setting up a budget are the same no matter what your income, expenses, or goals may be. The five steps are:

1. Decide on your spending goals.
2. Estimate your income.
3. Estimate your expenses.
4. Plan for your savings.
5. Evaluate and adjust your budget.

Decide on Your Spending Goals

Before you start on a trip, you need to know where you want to go. The same is true of budgets. You need to decide what your goals are and which of them can be achieved with money. Some will be long-term spending goals, like buying a car or paying for college tuition. Others will be short-term goals, such as buying running shoes or going out with your friends to the movies.

It is important that your budget be based on spending goals that reflect your values. Also, because your financial resources are limited, you may need to limit some of your spending goals. For example, if you have only $20 and no job, it may be unrealistic to expect to buy a car. If your spending goals are realistic, there's a good chance you can live within your income and reach your destination.

Estimate Your Income

How do you know if your spending goals are realistic or not? To answer that question you need to know how much money you

The word *budget* originally meant "wallet." In the 1700's when the English Chancellor of the Exchequer (finance minister) presented his plan for spending to the king, he was said to be "opening his budget," or opening the country's wallet. Eventually, the word came to mean the plan for spending money rather than the place to keep it.

What should you do with your money if you get a pay raise? You may want to revise your whole budget. Your goals may change when your resources increase. Or you may want to use the money to increase your savings. An easy way to increase savings is to keep to your original budget. Then put the whole raise into savings before you get used to spending it.

have. That sounds simple enough, but it's easy to make mistakes in figuring it out. In the following example, what mistake does Carrie North make in figuring her income?

CASE STUDY

Carrie North was lucky. After graduation, she got a job as a buyer in a large mail-order house. The job paid $18,000 a year. Now, she thought, dividing $18,000 by 12, she would have $1,500 a month to live on. That was a lot of money. It was certainly enough for a nice apartment, some furniture, some new clothes, and even a vacation. But, when she looked at her first paycheck (shown below), it was not for $1,500. It was for only $1,120.48. Where was the rest of the money?

Carrie had forgotten about **deductions**—money that is taken out of her pay before she receives her check. Her total pay, or **gross income**, was indeed $1,500. But Carrie had deductions for taxes and insurance. So, her **disposable income**, her take-home pay after deductions, was only $1,120.48. That was the amount she really had to spend each month.

Philadelphia Products, Inc.
230 Freedom Lane
Philadelphia, PA 19001

No. 5139

May 19 _____ 19 __

3-50 / 310

Pay to the Order of _Carrie North_ _____ $ 1,120 48/100

One thousand one hundred twenty and 48/100 Dollars

Fb Fidelity Bank
Philadelphia, PA 19001

David S. Freeman

⑆0310⑈0050⑆ 222167 ⑈

Employee Pay Statement

No. 5139

Detach and retain this statement.

Period Ending	Gross Pay	Federal Income Tax	State Income Tax	FICA	Life Insurance	Health Insurance	Union Dues	Savings Plan	Total Deductions	Total Pay
				Deductions						
5/13	1,500	187.00	60.47	112.65	5.22	14.18			379.52	1,120.48

Like Carrie, just about everyone who earns a paycheck has deductions. Two major deductions from your paycheck are required by federal law. One of these is federal income tax. Your employer automatically withholds a part of your gross pay for this tax. This withholding helps prepay most or all of the federal tax you owe. It guarantees that you will have the money to pay your taxes every year.

The other deduction required by the federal government is social security taxes. This deduction appears on your paycheck as FICA taxes. **FICA** stands for Federal Insurance Contributions Act. FICA tax money is used to provide income for disabled workers and dependents of deceased taxpayers. It also pays retirement benefits to workers covered by social security.

Other amounts may be deducted from your paycheck. Most states have an income tax, and some cities do as well. Union members are often required to pay dues, and that money can be deducted from each paycheck too. In addition, workers often choose to have deductions for company life and health insurance, personal savings, or contributions to charities taken out of their paychecks.

So you see, there's a big difference between your gross income and your disposable income. In planning your budget, it is important that you plan to spend only what you take home.

✓check your understanding ✓ ✓ ✓ ✓ ✓ ✓

1. **Why is it important to decide on spending goals before you set up a budget?**
2. **Give four examples of paycheck deductions.**
3. **What is Carrie North's largest deduction?**
4. **What is Carrie North's disposable income for the year? For each week?**

Estimate Your Expenses

The next step in planning your budget is to figure your expenses. There are two kinds of expenses: fixed expenses and variable expenses. **Fixed expenses**—such as insurance, mortgage, rent, or loan payments—are the same each time you pay them.

One fixed expense that many people forget about is money for emergencies. Budget experts say that, before anything else, you should set some money aside for this purpose. If you set money aside every month, you will have enough for expenses that you can't control, like large medical bills or car repairs.

Other expenses—such as those for food, clothing, and recreation—are usually different each month or each week. They are called **variable expenses.** You have more choice about how much you spend for these goods and services than you do for fixed expenses. Although you need clothes, for example, you do not have to buy a new pair of the latest designer jeans every month.

One way to save money is to pay your bills on time and avoid late charges. Federal law requires companies to send bills to you at least 14 days before you have to pay them. But to be sure your payment gets to the company on time, you should mail it at least five days *before* it's due, so that it has time to get through the mail.

What do cable TV bills, education loans, music lessons, and charges for trash collection have in common? They are all fixed expenses.

Most income is spent on housing, transportation, and food. Budget experts advise that an emergency fund also be set aside for expenses you can't control.

Housing	Clothing	Transportation	Medical	Food	Insurance/
30%	7%	20%	4%	18%	Pension
					9%

You can choose to buy a less expensive pair or decide to wait a while before you buy them.

A form you may find useful in estimating your expenses, both fixed and variable, is an *expense record*. An expense record for Scott Jameson is shown below. He's a high school senior who works 20 hours a week as an intern for his hometown newspaper. You can use a form like his to keep track of how you spend your money.

If you have a checking account, you can use it to help you keep track of your spending. Few people pay for everything with checks, but many people write checks for their fixed expenses and for many of their larger variable expenses. If you combine the record of the checks you have written with a record of the expenses you paid for with cash, you'll have a good idea of how much money you usually spend. You will know better whether your budget is realistic or not.

EXPENSE RECORD FOR Scott Jameson

Date	Explanation	Income	Payments	Savings (College)	Food	Clothing	Gifts & Contributions	Health & Personal	Household	Car	Entertainment
Mar 2	gas		8 00							8 00	
3	jacket		28 95			28 95					
5	pizza with Mary	105 60	81 50	75 00	6 50						
8	school supplies		4 98					4 98			
9	gas		10 00							10 00	
10	auto insurance		65 00							65 00	
11	movies		4 50								4 50
12		105 60	—								
15	car payment		114 67							114 67	
17	gas		9 00							9 00	
18	haircut		16 00					16 00			
19	concert with Mary	105 60	18 50								18 50
22	birthday present		15 95				15 95				
24	gas		8 00							8 00	
25	movies		4 50								4 50
26		105 60	—								
31	oil change		18 00							18 00	
	TOTALS	422 40	407 55	75 00	6 50	28 95	15 95	20 98		232 67	27 50

To save money, stick to your budget and buy only what you need.

Plan for Your Savings

When you plan your budget, you must consider your long-term spending goals. Long-term spending goals can be reached by putting money into savings.

How do you know how much to save for long-term spending goals and how much to spend each month on short-term, variable expenses? For your budget to work, your expenses cannot be larger than your income. Unless you have very few spending goals or a very high disposable income, chances are you will not be able to satisfy all of your goals. You must choose which ones to fulfill.

Spending money should bring satisfaction. You have to decide how much satisfaction each of your spending goals will bring you. You may have to choose among some spending goals. You may, for example, decide to give up some short-term spending goals—skip a movie or pass up a new album each month—to reach a long-term goal, such as buying a car.

Evaluate and Adjust Your Budget

Once you have estimated your income, expenses, and savings, it may be useful for you to put your budget decisions on paper. An example of a budget plan is shown on page 40. In this plan, developed for the Penn family, spending is divided into fixed expenses, variable expenses, and savings. You may find this plan useful, or you may want to make your own plan using different categories.

Pay yourself first. As soon as you get your paycheck, put aside not only the money you've budgeted for emergencies but also the amount you've decided to put into savings. Don't wait until the end of the month to see if you have anything left over to put into savings.

Budget experts say there is one item in a budget that people most often underestimate. What is it? Food.

The budget plan is a map to your spending goals. But a map is just a guide. For the budget plan to work, you must follow it. After you make out your budget, you should continue to keep track of your spending. The expense form can help you do this. At the end of a couple of months, compare your actual spending with your planned spending to see if you are keeping to your budget.

✓check your understanding ✓ ✓ ✓ ✓ ✓ ✓

1. **Why is it more difficult to estimate variable expenses than fixed expenses?**
2. **Look at Scott Jameson's expense form on page 38. What is his biggest expense?**
3. **Which of Scott's expenses are fixed? Which are variable?**
4. **Why would you want to put money into savings?**

HAL AND MARILYN PENN'S MONTHLY BUDGET

INCOME

Take-home Pay	$1,405	
INCOME TOTAL		$1,405

FIXED EXPENSES

Emergency Fund	$ 50	
Debt Payments	115	
Rent	425	
Car Insurance	30	
Renters' Insurance	10	
TOTAL		$630

VARIABLE EXPENSES

Food	$ 260	
Clothing	75	
Telephone, Electricity, Heat	90	
Personal Care	30	
Transportation (gas, oil)	70	
Household Operation	25	
Recreation and Entertainment	50	
Gifts and Contributions	25	
TOTAL		$ 625
SAVINGS		$ 150
EXPENSES AND SAVINGS TOTAL		$ 1,405

The Penn family budget

Hal and Marilyn Penn support themselves and their 12-year-old daughter on an income of $21,000 a year. Of that, $4,140 is withheld for taxes, union dues, and company life and health insurance. Their budget plan for each month is shown on page 40.

As you can see, the Penns have a balanced budget. Their savings plus expenses equal their income. The family has only a few spending and savings goals. They would like to buy new living room furniture and eventually send their daughter to college. For now, Hal and Marilyn just want to pay their bills, have a comfortable home, and get out once in a while for dinner or a movie. If their income goes up, they might like to buy a house. But, if it doesn't, they can live comfortably in their current apartment. Hal and Marilyn seem to have realistic spending goals for their income. And they seem to have a good chance of reaching those spending goals.

1. How much disposable income do the Penns have each month? How much do they have each year?
2. How much money do the Penns spend each month?
3. How much money are the Penns saving each year?
4. How much money do the Penns put in their emergency fund each year?

WHEN YOUR BUDGET NEEDS HELP

If you find that you are not keeping to your budget, you have two choices. You can try harder, or you can change your original budget. Roads other than the one you have mapped out may take you to your spending goals.

Every part of your budget can be changed if you find that it is not working. Although variable expenses are most easily changed, they are usually not the problem. The reason most people fail to keep to their budget is that their fixed expenses are too high. Fixed expenses can be changed, with some effort. For example, if you live on your own, you can get a roommate or try to find an apartment at a lower rent.

If you can't keep to your budget because you do not want to give up any spending goals, you can try to increase your income by working more hours or getting a different job. How much effort you make to change your budget depends on how much you want to reach your spending goals. The couple in the following case study need to make a big effort just to pay their bills.

Over their heads

Nate and Nicole Thompson live in a growing city in the South. Nate's take-home pay from his job at a dry cleaner's is about $13,800 a year, or $1,150 a month. They have a new baby—and lots of bills.

When they added up their bills, Nate and Nicole found they owed $1,600. They owed $500 to Nicole's brother for a vacation loan, $590 to a furniture store for baby furniture, $370 to other stores (mainly for baby clothes), and $140 to a garage for a new muffler and exhaust system for their car.

The Thompsons knew that things couldn't go on like this forever. They decided that what they needed was a good budget plan. But when Nate and Nicole estimated their monthly expenses, they came up with the figures shown on page 43. This budget plan used all of Nate's take-home pay and didn't even include their $1,600 worth of debts. And they hadn't set aside money for emergencies. Clearly, this budget wasn't going to work. They needed to get out of debt and control their spending. But how?

In many cities, people can get free help with financial problems from the local United Fund, the Public Assistance Office, or other family counseling agencies. Nate and Nicole found a family budget counselor in their neighborhood and used her to help them get out of debt. The counselor explains how she helped the Thompsons work out their financial problems:

In my meetings with the Thompsons, we tried to plan a so-called survival budget. That's a budget that would meet their most important needs while they paid their debts. It wasn't easy. Nicole did not want to be away from the baby, and Nate did not want to take a second job. I had to help them separate wants from needs.

Some expenses couldn't be cut. Nate and Nicole were not prepared to move, so their rent was fixed. Their auto, health, and renters' insurance were already as low as could be. Not much could be done about the electric or telephone bills either. We had to look elsewhere.

The Thompsons were going out once a week. They agreed to go out every other week instead and so cut what they spent each month on recreation by $65. They also agreed to cut in half the amount they were spending on clothes, saving another $50. Nicole thought she could buy some baby clothes second-hand. She also

NATE AND NICOLE THOMPSON'S MONTHLY BUDGET

INCOME

Take-home Pay	$1,150	
INCOME TOTAL		$1,150

FIXED EXPENSES

Emergency Fund	$ —	
Debt Payment	—	
Rent Payment	425	
Renters' Insurance	10	
Auto Insurance	31	
Health Insurance	48	
Life Insurance	28	
TOTAL		$542

VARIABLE EXPENSES

Food	$346	
Telephone, Electricity, Heat	70	
Household Operation	25	
Clothing	100	
Personal Care	30	
Car gas and oil	60	
Recreation	130	
Church	40	
Charity	30	
Gifts	25	
TOTAL		$856
SAVINGS		—
EXPENSES AND SAVINGS TOTAL		$1,398

thought she could cut her food bill by $10 a week if she made an effort to shop more carefully. That would save $43 a month. Our last battle was about the amount Nate and Nicole spent on charities and gifts, which were very important to them. They finally agreed to cut each by $10 a month.

So we found ways to cut spending by $178 a month. But we were still $70 short. And we hadn't even touched any of the back debts. The only way out then was for someone to get an extra job. They finally agreed that this was the only way to pay their bills, pay their debts, and buy the things that were important to them. We found Nate a job conducting telephone surveys two nights a week. The extra income, plus the spending cuts, would balance their budget and allow them to pay off their debts in about a year.

HARRIET WEAVER
Family Budget Counselor

Electronic Budgeting

Are you having budget problems? Perhaps a computer can help you. Many software companies have produced programs to help you computerize your budget. Programs vary widely. For example, some programs just keep track of your spending. Others help you plan your spending and investments. Not surprisingly, the more a program can do, the more it costs.

The simpler programs help you compare your spending to your budget. The program asks you to select budget categories, such as food, clothing, entertainment, and so on. As you spend money, you enter your expenses under the appropriate category. The program adds up these expenses in each category automatically, as you go along. At the end of the month, you can see how much you spent in each category. At the end of the year, you will have a summary of all expenses for tax purposes.

The more complex programs allow you to plan expenditures, chart a course for investments, and evaluate investment opportunities. Many also suggest tax strategies.

The good thing about these personal budget programs is that you don't need to be an accountant to use them. Most of them are designed with a non-professional user in mind. Some don't even have a user's manual. Everything you need to know is built right in.

The bad thing about these programs is that you still have to take the time to put in the data. And if you don't already have one, the computer itself can put a big dent in your budget.

Computers can help you keep track of your budget. It may take you some time to put the data into the computer, but you will save time later when you need to look up your records—especially for income tax purposes.

1. Which type of expense can be most easily changed?
2. Why do most people fail to spend within the limit of their budgets?
3. Name two places where people can get free financial help.
4. Explain the term *survival budget*. What types of expenses are probably included in this type of budget?

UMMARIZING
the chapter

Many people reach their financial goals by making a budget and sticking to it. There are five steps to setting up a budget:

1. Decide on your spending goals.
2. Estimate your income.
3. Estimate your expenses.
4. Plan for your savings.
5. Evaluate and adjust your budget.

Your spending goals should be realistic and not too large for your income. You should estimate your income accurately, remembering that your take-home pay is not as much as your gross income.

There are two kinds of expenses. Fixed expenses are those that stay the same, such as a car loan, a mortgage, or insurance payments. Variable expenses are usually different each time. They are such things as electric bills, food, and concert tickets. Many experts say that—before anything else—money for emergencies should be set aside each month.

Unless your income is very large and your spending goals very few, you probably will have to choose which of your spending goals you will try to meet. You will have to make trade-offs between spending money now and saving it for long-term goals.

If you find that your budget is not working, you can change any part of it. Some things, however, are much harder to change than others. Fixed expenses are usually the hardest to change. To lower the amount you pay for housing, for example, you would probably have to move or find an additional roommate. If nothing you do works, you can go to financial counseling agencies for help. A realistic budget not only helps to keep you out of debt but also helps you reach your goals.

BUILDING CONSUMER VOCABULARY

Number your paper from 1 to 7. Then write the term that best matches each numbered definition.

budget
deductions
disposable income
FICA

fixed expenses
gross income
variable expenses

1. The total amount of money one earns
2. A plan for spending and saving money
3. Bills for rent, loans, and insurance
4. Money taken out of a paycheck for such things as federal income tax, union dues, and health insurance
5. The take-home pay, or amount left over after deductions
6. Bills for food, clothing, or recreation
7. A law that requires employers to withhold money from their employees' pay to help workers if they become disabled

BUILDING CONSUMER UNDERSTANDING

1. Compare the budgets of the Penn family and the Thompson family. What are the two largest expenses in each of these budgets?
2. Which of the following expenses are fixed and which are variable: rent, movies, food, home insurance, telephone, real estate taxes, loan payments, vacation trips?
3. Using the budget counselor's figures determine how much extra income Nate Thompson needs to take home each month to be able to meet his expenses and pay off his debts in a year.
4. Create a new budget for the Thompsons based on the family budget counselor's recommendations. (Add in the extra income you calculated for question 3.)
5. Why is disposable income less than gross income? Which figure should be used when creating a budget?

BUILDING CONSUMER MATH SKILLS

Wendi Avanti's weekly paycheck has this stub attached to it:

Gross Pay	Federal Income Tax	Social Security	State Income Tax	Net Pay
$400.00	$56.00	$30.04	$16.00	$297.96

1. What is Wendi's gross income for the year?
2. What is her largest deduction?
3. What is her weekly disposable income?
4. How much does Wendi take home in a year?
5. How much does she take home in a month?
6. What percentage of her weekly gross income is her weekly take-home pay?

APPLYING CONSUMER SKILLS

Prepare a monthly budget plan for Wendi Avanti using the following information. Wendi has estimated these monthly expenses:

Rent (shared with roommate)	$266.00
Electricity and telephone	50.00
Renters' insurance	5.00
Public transportation	84.00
Loan payments	150.00
Car insurance	35.00
Car gas and oil	35.00
Food at home	126.00
Food at work	70.00

Wendi also wants to spend 5 percent of her monthly take-home pay on each of the following: clothing, personal care, recreation, and contributions to charity. She puts $100 each month into an emergency fund.

1. How much is Wendi saving each month?
2. Which of Wendi's expenses can be most easily changed? Which are hardest to change? Why?
3. Wendi's number one long-term spending goal is to save $2,000 in 12 months so that she can take a trip to Europe. How would you advise her to reach her goal? Be specific.

GETTING INVOLVED IN YOUR COMMUNITY

Obtain a copy of the budget of your town or city and bring it to class. Answer the following questions about the budget:

1. Where does the income for your community come from?
2. What is the disposable income?
3. Is money for emergencies set aside?
4. What is the largest expense? Can this expense be controlled?
5. What are some of the fixed expenses? variable expenses?
6. Is your community trying to add to its income? How?

USING CHECKING ACCOUNTS

Keeping track of your money is often a difficult process. In our economy some services help you to better manage your money. What substitutes can you use for cash? How can you become a more effective consumer by managing your money better?

- What are the advantages of using checks instead of cash to make payments?

- How do you shop for a checking account?

- How do you balance your checkbook?

- How are computers used to make payments?

Today's financial institutions offer consumers a wide variety of services. One service they offer is a checking account. Some checking accounts pay you for keeping your money in the account, and some don't. Many financial institutions charge fees for various types of services, and others don't. No matter where you choose to have one, however, a checking account can allow you to use your money safely almost anytime you want and anywhere you choose.

ADVANTAGES OF CHECKING ACCOUNTS

A **check** is a written order telling your financial institution to take money out of your checking account and give it to someone else. A checking account is one of your most important money management tools. Checks are better than cash for several reasons.

- **Safety**. If you use checks, you don't have to carry a lot of cash. Cash is easily lost and can be stolen. Money in checking accounts is safe. Most checking accounts are insured for up to $100,000 by federal or state government agencies. In addition, a check is a safe way to send money through the mail.

- **Convenience**. If you carry cash, you can spend only as much as you thought to bring with you. But if you carry a checkbook, you can write a check for any amount in your account. You don't have to guess how much money to bring with you to cover your needs.

- **Proof of Payment**. Most financial institutions return the checks you have written every month. These checks can serve as receipts and proof that you have paid your bills.

- **Recordkeeping**. When you write a check, you record the amount you spent in your checkbook. Your checkbook therefore provides an accurate record of your spending. You can see how closely you are following your budget. When you pay by cash, you don't have these records unless you remember to write down each expense or to get a receipt.

SHOPPING FOR A CHECKING ACCOUNT

To attract your business, financial institutions offer many types of checking accounts. Such variety is good for the consumer, but it also can be confusing. Each institution calls its accounts by different names, making it difficult to compare them. Basically, however, you should compare four things when deciding which checking account is best for you. Those things are interest, service charges, transaction charges, and minimum balance requirements.

The word *check* comes from the game of chess. Its original meaning is "to stop and examine closely," which is what you do if someone puts your king in check during a chess game. In banking, the term first meant to stop and examine your account closely before writing an order to take money out— something you would still be wise to do.

Do you know what a rubber check (or a bouncing check) is? It's a check written for more money than you have in your checking account. Understandably, banks do not want you to bounce checks. So they charge very high fees if you do. For each check you bounce, you could be charged as much as $25.

Interest

Some financial institutions will pay you to keep your money in an account. What they pay is called **interest**. Checking accounts that pay interest are called *interest-bearing* accounts. Those that do not pay interest are called *non-interest-bearing* accounts.

Interest is paid as a percentage of the balance in your account. The **balance** is simply the amount of money you have in your account. Suppose a bank offers to pay you 5 percent interest on your balance. If you put $1,000 in your account and keep it there for a year, the bank will pay you an extra $50 in interest (5 percent of $1,000). A bank generally pays part of your interest sooner— every three months (quarterly), for example, every month, or (what is most common) every day.

Service Charges

To pay for the cost of operating a checking account, financial institutions often charge a service fee. This *service charge* is a fixed amount of money taken directly out of your account every month. Different accounts have different service charges. They can range from less than $2 to as much as $10.

Transaction Charges

Financial institutions may also charge you a fee for each check you write. This fee is called a *transaction charge*, since financial institutions refer to each check you write as a "transaction." The amount of this fee can vary from 15 cents per check to more than $1.

Minimum Balance Requirements

Many financial institutions will reduce the monthly service charge and the transaction charge if you keep a certain amount of money in your account at all times. This amount is called a *minimum balance*. For example, a bank may reduce your monthly service charge from $10 to $5 if you keep a minimum of $250 in your checking account. Another bank may not require any service charges or transaction charges if you keep at least $500 in your account. Accounts with no charges are sometimes advertised as "free" checking accounts. But they are not really free. If you keep a lot of money in your checking account, you cannot put it somewhere else. You cannot put it someplace that would pay you more interest—in a savings account, for example. Therefore, the opportunity cost of the "free" checking account is the interest you lose by keeping the large balance in an account paying low or no interest.

Because there are so many kinds of accounts, you should compare the different features of each account carefully. The best account is one that has low service and transaction charges, low

Service charges may not seem too high if you consider that it costs your financial institution between 10 cents and 30 cents to process each of your checks.

When shopping for a bank, find out if the ones you are considering base their service charges on an *average daily balance*. In that case, your balance could slip below the minimum every once in a while. As long as your *average* balance for the month stays above the minimum, you would not have to pay the extra service charges.

minimum balance requirements, and a high interest rate. However, you may have to make some trade-offs. For example, to get a high interest rate, you may have to settle for a high minimum balance. Or, to avoid service charges, you may have to give up interest.

✓check your understanding ✓ ✓ ✓ ✓ ✓ ✓

1. **What are four advantages of using checks instead of cash when paying bills?**
2. **What four things should you compare when choosing a checking account?**
3. **Why do some financial institutions have monthly service charges and transaction fees?**

CASE STUDY

Shopping for a checking account

Ray Garcia has just graduated from college, and he is shopping for a new checking account. His first account, at his parents' bank, was a special account for college students. It had no charges and no minimum balance. But now he is starting a new job. He no longer qualifies for the student account, so he is shopping around.

His first stop was the First State Mutual Bank. He talked to the New Accounts Manager. She told him that the bank has two types of checking accounts. The Classic Checking account requires a $400 minimum balance. If his balance ever falls below $400 during the month, he will be charged a $5 service charge.

If Ray wants to earn interest on his checking account, the manager told him, the bank offers a Performance account, paying 5½ percent interest. However, if his balance falls below $1,000, he will have to pay a $7 service charge.

Next, Ray went to the Security Savings Bank. The savings counselor there told Ray about Security's Money Market account, which offers an interest rate of 7 percent. This account requires a $1,500 minimum balance and a transaction charge of 25 cents per check.

Finally, Ray checked the credit union at his new company. The credit union's checking account pays 6 percent interest. There are no transaction charges or service charges, but no interest is paid on balances of less than $500.

1. **If Ray plans to keep a lot of money in his checking account (over $1,500) and expects to write few checks, which account should he choose?**
2. **If Ray plans to keep very little money in his account (less than $200) and wishes to write a lot of checks, which account would be best?**

When shopping for food, it's easy to spend more money than you brought. Many supermarkets will cash checks for you.

USING YOUR CHECKING ACCOUNT

A checking account is the most useful tool you have for managing your money. As with any tool, you should follow some basic procedures to use it effectively.

Opening an Account

The very first thing you must do to open a checking account is to fill out a *signature card*. This card is a permanent record of your signature. The institution uses it to make sure that all checks written on your account carry your actual, not a forged, signature. The signature card also requires your address, telephone number, and social security number, as well as the name of your employer (if you have a job).

You may want another person to be able to sign checks and to use your account. In this case, the account is called a *joint checking account*. The other person must sign the signature card as well.

When you open your account, order checks. Most banks offer checks printed with your name and account number. You can include your address and telephone number, as well, if you wish. You will also receive a supply of *deposit tickets* printed with your name and account number. You will need these to put money into your account.

When filling out a signature card, many financial institutions ask you for a piece of personal information, such as your mother's maiden name. If you want to get information about your account by phone, bank employees will ask you to repeat this personal information to make sure they are talking to the right person.

Writing a Check

You can use a check to pay a bill or to give someone money. When writing a check, you should use the following steps:

1. Write with a pen so that the check cannot be changed easily.
2. Write in the date.
3. Write in the correct number of the check, if it is not already printed on the check, usually in the top right-hand corner.
4. Write the name of the **payee**—the person, place, or group getting the check—to the immediate right of the words "Pay to the order of." If you are taking money out of your account for yourself, put your own name as the payee.
5. In the space with the dollar sign, write the amount of the check in *numbers*. Write the numbers as close to the dollar sign as possible so additional numbers cannot be put in.
6. On the line below the name of the payee, write the amount of the check out *in words*. If the amount is for $145.95, for example, write "One hundred forty-five and 95/100." If any space is left, fill it in with a wavy line drawn to the word *Dollars*. This will keep anyone else from filling in another amount of money after you have written out the check.
7. Finally, sign the check in the lower right-hand corner. Sign the check the same way you signed your name on your signature card. You are the **drawer**, the one who is ordering the institution to "draw" money out of your account and pay it to someone else. The banking institution is the **drawee**, the one that pays out the money.

Why do you have to write the amount of a check twice? It's easy to make a mistake when writing numbers, to write "$100" when you mean "$10," for example. It's much harder to make this kind of mistake in words. Few people would write "one hundred" when they mean "ten."

If you write two different amounts on a check, the bank will pay the amount in words.

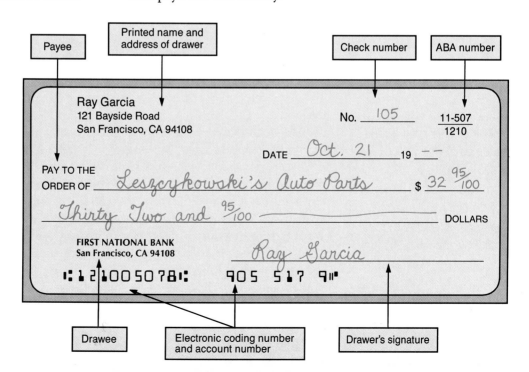

Payee

Printed name and address of drawer

Check number

ABA number

Ray Garcia
121 Bayside Road
San Francisco, CA 94108

No. 105

11-507
1210

DATE *Oct. 21* 19 --

PAY TO THE
ORDER OF *Leszcykowski's Auto Parts* $ 32 95/100

Thirty Two and 95/100 DOLLARS

FIRST NATIONAL BANK
San Francisco, CA 94108

Ray Garcia

⑆ 1 2 ⑈ 0 0 5 0 7 8 ⑆ 9 0 5 5 1 7 9 ⑉

Drawee

Electronic coding number and account number

Drawer's signature

Ray Garcia

DATE _Oct. 7_ 19 ___

FIRST NATIONAL BANK

San Francisco, CA 94108

CASH		20	00
C H E C K S	LIST SINGLY 63-420	59	60
TOTAL		79	60

DEPOSIT TICKET

⑆121005078⑆   905 517 9⑈

ITEMS CREDITED SUBJECT TO VERIFICATION AND DEPOSIT AGREEMENT OF THIS BANK

The ABA number and the amount of each check you deposit are written on a separate line of the deposit slip.

Making a Deposit

When you put money into your checking account, you make a **deposit**. You may deposit either cash or checks. You can make deposits by mail if the deposit is a check. Carefully fill out a deposit ticket by writing the date and the amount of your deposit. You should indicate how much of the deposit is in cash and how much is from checks, identifying each check by its American Bankers Association (ABA) number. The ABA number is the fraction that is printed on the top right-hand corner of the check. It aids in check processing by identifying the location of the drawee (the bank that issued the check). You need use only the top half of the fraction on the deposit slip.

Often your deposit will be a check given to you by someone else. When someone gives you a check, you must **endorse** it by signing your name on the back. Three ways to endorse a check are: a blank endorsement, a restrictive endorsement, and a special endorsement.

A _blank endorsement_ is your signature only. To make a blank endorsement, just sign your name on the back of the check. The problem with a blank endorsement is that, if you lose the endorsed check, anyone can cash it. All a person has to do is sign her or his name below yours. Therefore, blank endorsements must be used with care. You should use a blank endorsement only when you are standing in your bank, ready to cash a check.

A _restrictive endorsement_ is used when you deposit a check in your savings or checking account by mail. A common restrictive endorsement is "For deposit only." This endorsement means the check may be deposited only in your account. It can be used for no other purpose. It is important to use a restrictive endorsement if you are depositing the check by mail because the check could be lost or stolen.

Not all checks need to be endorsed. If you make a check out to "cash," anyone can cash it. People often make checks out to "cash" to take out money from their checking account. Since it is the least safe way to make out a check, however, it is wise not to use it unless you are standing in your bank.

Ray Garcia

For Deposit Only

Ray Garcia

Pay to the Order of

Ralph Garcia

Ray Garcia

If you use an ATM to withdraw cash, remember to write the amount in your check register.

A *special endorsement* is used if you want to give a check you received from one person to someone else. Let's say you received a check for $25 as a birthday gift from your Aunt Felicia. You can really use the money, but you don't have time to cash the check. So you sign the check over to your brother Ralph in exchange for cash. You write "Pay to the order of" and then put his name. Then you sign your name underneath. Ralph gives you $25 in cash, and he can take the check to his bank to cash it or put it in his account.

Using a Check Register

When you get your checks, you also get a **check register**. It is usually a separate record booklet in your checkbook. Some checkbooks have a stub attached to each check instead of a separate check register. Each time you make a deposit in your checking account, write the date and amount of the deposit in your check register. Some people also add a description of the deposit. They might write "Paycheck" or "Birthday gift from Mom," for example. Be sure to add the amount of the deposit to the money you already have in your account to determine your balance.

When you write a check, you must also record it in your check register. First, write the check number. Then fill in the date, the person or organization to which you are writing the check, and the amount. Finally, subtract the amount of the check from the amount of money in your account to find your balance.

It is very important to keep your check register up to date. Write the information in your register *before* you make the deposit or write the check. Otherwise, you may forget to record the amount. Then your register will not show the real amount of money in your account. If you forget to write down a check in your register, for example, you will have less money in your account than you think. This is the most common mistake people make with their checking accounts.

RECORD ALL CHARGES OR CREDITS THAT AFFECT YOUR ACCOUNT

Number	Date	Description of Transaction	Payment/Debit (−)		✔	Fee (If Any) (−)	Deposit/Credit (+)	BALANCE $	
								149	23
104	10-1	McNeil's Dept. Store shoes	25	65				123	58
	10-7	Deposit					79 60	203	18
105	10-21	Leszcykowski's Auto Parts	32	95				170	23
	10-22	Deposit					72 80	243	03
106	10-27	Sarah Miller repay loan	30	00				213	03
	11-1	Bank Service Charge				2.00		211	03

STATEMENT

Ray Garcia	ACCOUNT NUMBER	905-517-9
121 Bayside Road		
San Francisco, CA 94108	DATE OF STATEMENT	Nov 3, 19--

PREVIOUS BALANCE	CHECKS AND CHARGES	NO. OF DEPOSITS	NO. OF CHECKS	DEPOSITS AND CREDITS	BALANCE AT THIS DATE
149.23	60.60	2	2	152.40	241.03

CHECKS AND OTHER CHARGES		DEPOSITS AND OTHER CREDITS	DATE	BALANCE
		79.60	10-7	228.83
25.64			10-10	203.18
		72.80	10-22	275.98
32.95			10-30	243.03
2.00 S			11-1	241.03

PLEASE EXAMINE YOUR STATEMENT AT ONCE. IF NO ERROR IS REPORTED IN 10 DAYS THE ACCOUNT WILL BE CONSIDERED CORRECT. ALL ITEMS ARE CREDITED SUBJECT TO FINAL PAYMENT.

C = Certified Check   S = Service Charge   CR = Overdraft   R = Returned Check

Balancing Your Checkbook

Once a month you will receive a *statement*, like the one above, from your financial institution. It shows everything that happened in your account between the date of your last statement and the date of this statement. It shows the deposits you made, the checks the financial institution paid, all service charges, and any interest earned. The statement also shows the amount you had in your account a month ago, called the *previous balance*. And the statement shows your *current balance*—the amount in your account on the day the statement was prepared.

With most types of checking accounts, you also get your **canceled checks**. These are the checks that have cleared your account. **Clearing** is the process of transferring the money out of your account to the payee listed on your check. When you get your canceled checks back, you know that money has been taken out of your account. Any checks you write that do *not* come back with your statement have not yet cleared your account. No money has been taken out to pay those checks yet. So, you must be sure that there is money in your account to pay those checks when they do clear.

Returning canceled checks with your statement is expensive for banks. So, some have stopped doing it. Instead, they send you photocopies of the fronts of the checks. If you need the actual check, it will be provided, but you will have to pay a fee. Make sure you know whether the financial institutions you are considering return canceled checks or not.

When you receive your monthly statement, you must *reconcile your account*, or balance your checkbook. That is, you must make sure your check register agrees with the statement from the financial institution. If your check register and the statement don't agree, you must figure out why. Refer to the check register below as you read the check list for balancing your checkbook.

1. Put your canceled checks in order by check number. Check each one off in your check register in the correct box (under "√"). Be sure the amount written in your register agrees with the amount written on the canceled check.

2. Look on the statement for service charges. Write down any charges in your register that you didn't already enter. Subtract these charges from the balance in your check register.

3. If you have an interest-bearing account, add any interest that you have earned this month to the balance in your check register.

4. Copy the current balance listed on your statement on the *bank reconciliation form* included with your statement. This form can usually be found on the back of your statement.

5. Look through your check register for any deposits you made after the date the statement was issued. Add those deposits to the balance on the bank reconciliation form.

6. Look through your check register for all *outstanding checks*, the checks that have not yet cleared. These are the ones without check marks. List each check on the form, and then add the amounts to find the total of checks outstanding. Subtract this total from the balance you got in Step 5.

Suppose a check you've written gets lost, and you don't want your bank to cash it. What can you do? Ask your bank to *stop payment* by signing a stop payment form. On the form you state the date of the check, the amount, the name of the payee, the check number, and the reason for stopping payment. Banks charge anywhere from $10 to $20 for this service.

CHECKS OUTSTANDING		
NUMBER	**AMOUNT**	
106	30	00
Total of Checks Outstanding	30	00

TO BALANCE YOUR CHECKBOOK, PLEASE COMPARE YOUR CHECKBOOK RECORD WITH THE ENTRIES ON THIS STATEMENT.

1. Check off in your checkbook all the checks posted on this statement. Note that they are posted in number order so that there is no need to sort your checks.
2. List at the left any checks you wrote that are not recorded on the statement plus any checks outstanding from a prior statement period.
3. Add NOW interest, if any, to your checkbook record.
4. Subtract Service Charge, if any, from your checkbook record.
5. Enter in your checkbook any other transactions appearing on the statement that you have not yet recorded, and adjust your balance accordingly.

6. Enter statement balance (see New Balance on other side) ➤		241	03
7. Add deposits not credited on this statement. If any of these were made in a prior statement period, contact us immediately. ➤		—	
SUB-TOTAL		241	03
8. Subtract total of checks outstanding. ➤		30	00
TOTAL should agree with your checkbook balance. ➤		211	03

IF IT DOES NOT
- make sure all balances carried forward in your checkbook are correct.
- be certain you have adjusted your checkbook balance for any NOW interest, service charges, or other transactions you had not previously recorded.
- double-check all your math both in your checkbook and on the form used here.
- make certain all transaction amounts including check amounts listed on this statement are the same as those you entered in your checkbook.

If you kept careful records during the month, the balance in your check register after Step 3 will be the same as the amount you got on your bank reconciliation form after Step 6.

What should you do if these two amounts are different? First, check all addition and subtraction. Then, make sure you didn't forget to write down any deposits or checks. Finally, make sure that all information on checks and deposits is the same as that on the statement. If you still can't figure out what's wrong, contact the financial institution. If you don't call within ten days, the financial institution will assume the statement is correct.

✓ check your understanding ✓ ✓ ✓ ✓ ✓ ✓

1. **What are the differences among a blank endorsement, a restrictive endorsement, and a special endorsement? When might you use each one?**
2. **Why should you record checks in your check register before you write them?**
3. **What items are usually listed on a bank statement?**
4. **List and explain the six steps in balancing your checkbook. Which one would you skip if you didn't have an interest-bearing account?**

OTHER FORMS OF PAYMENT

Writing a check is a safe, convenient way to make a payment. There are times, though, when you need to use another method of payment. For example, you may not have a checking account, or you may find yourself doing business with a store that doesn't accept personal checks. To solve such problems, various other forms of payment have been developed. Let's find out what these other forms of payment are.

Money Orders

A **money order** is an order for the payment of a specified amount of money. It's like buying a single check from a financial institution's checking account. When you buy a money order, you pay the amount of the order plus a service fee. Different financial institutions charge different fees. There is usually a maximum dollar amount that you can buy as well. A money order is safe because it is payable only to the party named on the order. If it is lost, it can be replaced. Several different types of money orders are available.

Postal money orders can be bought at any post office. Although the maximum amount of each order is $500, more than one can be purchased if very large payments must be made.

Express money orders can be bought at travel offices, department stores, and automobile club offices (such as the American Automobile Association). American Express is the best known express money order.

Telegraphic money orders are used when money must be sent from one place to another quickly. These money orders are available from Western Union. The person sending the money pays the amount plus a service charge. Western Union then sends a telegram to another Western Union office, where the person who wants the money is waiting. The telegram tells the other office to give that money to the waiting person. Service charges are usually higher for telegraphic money orders than they are for other types of money orders. But, by using telegraphic money orders, you can send money very quickly all over the world.

Traveler's Checks

After you buy traveler's checks, make a record of the number on each check. Keep this record separate from your checks. Then, if the checks are lost or stolen, you will be able to get replacements easily.

Travelers sometimes find that their personal checks aren't accepted away from home, and carrying a lot of cash is dangerous. The answer is the **traveler's check**. You can buy traveler's checks at almost any financial institution, as well as at some travel agencies. As with a money order, you pay for the sum of the checks, which come in amounts of $10, $20, $50, $100, $500, and $1,000. Some places charge a service fee for the checks and may require that you buy a minimum amount. Others do not. When you use traveler's checks, you fill in the name of the payee only when you are ready to use each check.

Special Bank Checks

Where can you cash a check given to you by someone else? Generally, you can cash it in only two places—at the bank where you have a checking account and at the bank where the check comes from. Very few banks will cash another bank's checks.

When personal checks are not accepted, consider special bank checks. A **certified check** is a personal check that is certified, or guaranteed, by a financial institution. You can get one only from a bank in which you have an account. When you purchase a certified check, the financial institution stamps it to show that there is enough money in your account to cover the check. The financial institution then deducts the same amount from your checking account.

When might you use a certified check? Suppose you are buying a used car. The seller will probably not accept your personal check because she or he doesn't want to turn the car over to you and end up with a bad check. Using a certified check ensures that the seller will receive his or her money.

A **cashier's check** is like a certified check except the financial institution issues the check. You can buy a cashier's check at any bank. The bank writes a check on its own funds. In this way, a cashier's check is similar to a money order. However, cashier's checks can be purchased in any amount.

Electronic Funds Transfer

Electronic Funds Transfer (EFT) is a computer-run system that lets consumers, businesses, and governments transfer money from one account to another almost instantly. No cash changes hands, and no checks are written. There are three main parts to the system: automated teller machines, point-of-sale terminals, and automated clearing-houses.

Automated teller machines (ATMs) ATMs are probably the most familiar part of the EFT system. You can find them on the outside of many bank buildings and in many stores and shopping malls. As the name implies, these machines act as tellers do in a bank. They let you put money into your account, take money out, transfer money from one of your accounts to another, and find out what your balance is. To operate the machine, you need a plastic card called an *ATM card*. You usually apply for this card when you open a checking account. You also need a code number called a *personal identification number* (PIN). You choose this number when you apply for the card. To operate the ATM, you put your card in the machine, key in your PIN, and conduct your banking business. If, for example, you want to withdraw money from your checking account, the ATM sees if you have enough money in your account, automatically deducts the amount from your account, and gives you the cash. Most ATMs limit the amount of money you can withdraw at one time. Some let you take out no more than $300 a week, and others allow you to take out as much as $350 a day.

Point-of-sale (POS) terminals These terminals are computers placed in retail stores. They let you pay for goods and services by transferring funds directly from your account to the store's account. They are most often found in supermarkets, gas stations, and convenience stores—places that often do not accept checks. To use a POS terminal, you need a card called a *debit card*. You also need a PIN, generally different from the one you chose for your ATM card. Increasingly, however, financial institutions are issuing a single card that works in both the ATM and the POS terminals.

Automated clearing-houses Computer centers that allow you to deposit your paychecks and other forms of regular income without having to go to the bank are called automated clearing-houses. Such centers let you pay regular bills, such as mortgage, car payments, or insurance premiums automatically, by *direct deposit* from your account to the accounts of the various companies you do business with. In addition, requests for transfers of money can be made over the phone, by telegraph, or from a personal computer in your home.

An ATM card allows you to get cash from your account or to make a deposit if the bank is miles away and even if the bank is closed.

 check your understanding ✓ ✓ ✓ ✓ ✓ ✓

1. Why might a person or a business not accept a personal check?
2. What is the difference between a certified check and a cashier's check?
3. What advantages does the Electronic Funds Transfer system have over writing checks?

*S*UMMARIZING
the chapter

Consumers can receive help in managing their money from a wide variety of financial institutions. A checking account is one of the most important money-management tools offered by these institutions.

Compared with cash, checks are safer and more convenient. They also provide proof of payment and make recordkeeping easier. When shopping for the best checking account, compare interest rates, service charges, transaction charges, and minimum balance requirements.

A checking account must be used properly to be an effective money management tool. You must know how to make a deposit, endorse a check, write a check, use a check register, and balance your checkbook. Knowing how to do these things will help you avoid spending more than you have in your account.

Checks and cash aren't the only ways to make payments. In fact, personal checks often are not accepted by people or businesses that don't know you. However, almost everyone will accept money orders, cashier's checks, certified checks, or traveler's checks. Traveler's checks are also a good way to protect your money when you're on the road. Finally, you can use the Electronic Funds Transfer System to pay bills and transfer funds without writing checks.

·C·H·A·P·T·E·R·  ·C·T·I·V·I·T·I·E·S·

BUILDING CONSUMER VOCABULARY

Number your paper from 1 to 16. Then write the term that best matches each numbered definition.

balance	drawee
canceled checks	drawer
cashier's check	Electronic Funds Transfer
certified check	endorse
check	interest
check register	money order
clearing	payee
deposit	traveler's check

1. A written order requesting a financial institution to transfer funds out of your account to someone else
2. Money a financial institution pays you for the use of your funds in the form of a percentage of the balance in your account
3. The amount of money you have in your checking account at a particular time
4. The section of the checkbook where checks and deposits are recorded
5. A check drawn on your account that has been guaranteed by your financial institution
6. A type of check that can be bought at a post office or telegraph office
7. The process by which a financial institution transfers money out of your account to the payee listed on your checks

8. The person who orders a financial institution to draw money out of a checking account
9. The person, business, or group to whom a check is written
10. A system used to transfer funds without using checks or cash
11. Checks the financial institution paid and returned to you with your statement
12. To sign the back of a check in order to cash the check or to give it to someone else
13. To put money into an account
14. A check drawn on the funds of a financial institution that can be purchased in any amount
15. A type of check often used while traveling
16. The financial institution that pays out the money specified on a check

BUILDING CONSUMER UNDERSTANDING

1. How important would the interest rate be on your checking account if you kept a lot of money in the account? if you kept very little money in the account?
2. Which type of endorsement would you use in each of the following situations?
   a. You cash your paycheck at the bank.
   b. You deposit your paycheck by mail.
   c. You repay your Uncle Albert the money you borrowed from him by giving him your paycheck.
3. When would you make a payment with a money order? a telegraphic money order? a certified check? a traveler's check?

BUILDING CONSUMER MATH SKILLS

1. Bill and Anita just got married. They received a number of checks and some cash as wedding presents, which they are putting in their joint checking account. Below is the list of checks and cash they received.

   A check for $25 from Uncle Bob
   A $100 bill from Anita's friends at work
   $12.85 in cash from the piggy bank of Bob's niece, Amy
   A check for $50 from Bill's older brother, Scott
   In addition, Anita is putting in her paycheck for $498.72.

   a. How much money will they deposit into the bank?
   b. How much will be in cash?
   c. How much from checks?

2. Assume you are going on a trip to Japan. You have decided to take $1,000 in traveler's checks. There is a fee of $2.50 plus 1 percent of the amount of the checks. How much will you have to pay in fees for the checks?

Your bank statement came today. The balance shown is $560.20. The balance in your check register is $426.45. The following checks and deposit do not appear on your bank statement.

Check 131: Midtown Cleaners, $18.54
Check 135: Adams Department Store, $75.80
Check 137: Valley Oil Company, $89.41
Deposit: $50.00

There are no service charges. On a separate sheet of paper, balance your checkbook. Is the balance in your check register correct?

Visit or call no more than four financial institutions in your community. Ask if they have any "free" checking accounts— ones that have no transaction charges and no monthly service charges. If they do, ask what minimum balance is required for this type of account. Also ask if the account pays interest. Do any of these "free" accounts require no minimum balance? Do any pay interest? How much was the highest minimum balance required? Did that account pay interest?

As a newly married couple, Jason and Melissa make many plans for their lives together. However, when two people have different goals and values, making plans as a couple can be complicated. Here is how each of them would like to set up a budget.

JASON: I know we need to set aside money so we can buy a house, but I don't think we need to set up budget categories for all of our spending. We could just save a set amount every month and spend the rest.

We both work and can buy most of the things we want. We already have the things we need. Our folks gave us their old furniture and appliances, so we have that stuff. What I'd like to buy is a really great sound system, mag wheels for the car, and some tools. If I had my own tools, I could save money on car repairs and fix things around the house. I'd like to take Melissa on a trip to the Amazon, too. She's always reading books about it. I'd like to share the adventure with her while we're still young.

MELISSA: Our parents gave us their cast-off furniture, which is real junk. The first thing I'd like to do is replace it with new, all-white Scandinavian furniture. I also think that we should buy a personal computer. My hobby is writing, and a computer would make writing a lot easier. Jason could use the computer to keep track of bills or whatever.

After we pay for the furniture and the computer, we can save for a down payment on a house. A house is important to both of us. We'd like to have enough money saved up so that we can buy a house in three years and start a family. We both want a big family.

We could probably save money if I learned how to cook better. Right now, Jason does all the cooking. When he works late, we go out to dinner—which usually is about three nights a week.

Answer the following questions on a separate sheet of paper. Use complete sentences.

1. What are the couple's long-term goals?

2. Is replacing used furniture a want or a need? Why?

3. Do you think saving to buy a house is equally important to both Jason and Melissa? Explain.

4. Which ideas for spending seem impractical? Why?

5. Consider each person's ideas for saving and spending. What compromises could they make to attain their spending goals? savings goals?

FRESH•TULIPS
2$

THE CONSUMER AND THE MARKET ECONOMY

OUR MARKET ECONOMY

Countries, like people, have to sat-isfy wants but have limited resources. Different countries have developed different ways to solve this problem. What kinds of resources do countries have? How do countries decide which wants to satisfy?

- What are the three basic economic questions every society must answer?

- How do different societies answer these questions?

- How does the market system work?

- What is demand? What is supply? How do they determine prices?

You have been thinking about your role as a consumer of goods and services. But there is a broader picture worth looking at: the world in which you and other consumers receive those goods and services. Along with consumers, this world includes producers—the people who make goods and services available to consumers. In this world there must be a way for producers and consumers to get together. Some sort of system is needed. By understanding the system through which producers and consumers get together, you may become a better consumer. It helps to know the "rules of the game."

WHAT RESOURCES DO COUNTRIES HAVE?

Every society or nation has to make decisions about producing and providing goods and services. A society, like a person, has to make such decisions because its resources are limited, but its wants are unlimited. Resources that countries have are called **factors of production**. Economists often divide them into four categories.

What do desks, chairs, telephones, hammers, nails, thread, computers, postage stamps, paper, and robots have in common? They are all capital goods.

- **Land** is another name for natural resources. Besides land itself, natural resources include oil, water, fish, forests, and minerals like iron ore and coal. Natural resources are the starting point for production. They are used to make the goods and services we buy.

- **Capital goods** are products made from natural resources to help make other goods. They are important because they help us produce *efficiently*—that is, faster or cheaper. Machines, tools, trucks, factories, and offices are examples of capital goods.

Capital goods like boilers and turbines can be used to produce electricity. In turn, electricity is used as a capital good to produce other goods. Capital goods that can produce other capital goods are sometimes called *investment goods*. Why? Because they are an investment in production.

- **Labor** is a short name for human resources, or workers. Labor often uses capital to convert natural resources into goods and services. Labor includes both physical and mental work.

- **Entrepreneurship** is the combination of the other factors of production to form a business. An entrepreneur is someone who takes the risk of starting and managing a business. Entrepreneurs combine land, labor, and capital to make goods and services people might want. The entrepreneur takes the risk that the goods and services produced might not be the ones people want.

THE THREE BASIC ECONOMIC QUESTIONS

The amount of goods and services any country can produce depends on the land, capital, labor, and entrepreneurship available. No society has enough of these factors of production to fill all of

What do an oil rig and paper clips have in common? They are both examples of capital goods—items used to make other products.

the wants of its people. Therefore, it has to make decisions. It has to answer three basic economic questions.

■ **What goods and services should we produce?** Should we produce more cars or more buses? Should we plant more food or build more houses? Should we make more jeans or more suits? Should we provide more medical care or more legal help?

■ **How should we produce these goods and services?** What methods should we use? Should we produce them the fastest way? Should we produce them the least expensive way? How about the safest way, or the way that produces the highest quality? Should we produce them in a way that keeps the most people working?

■ **Who should get the goods and services?** Should everyone receive an equal share? Should the people who work the hardest get the most? How do we determine who gets how much?

Economists often refer to the first two of these questions as "the production problem." The last question is called "the distribution problem." Every society solves these problems in its own way. Economists, however, separate the various economic systems that countries use to answer these questions into three basic types: the traditional, command, and market economic systems.

The Traditional Economic System

The oldest approach to solving the production and distribution problems is the traditional economic system. In a **traditional economic system**, people generally repeat the decisions made in earlier times by earlier generations. Laws, religious beliefs, and customs determine what to produce, how to produce it, and for whom to produce. Although basic economic tasks get done (goods and services are produced and consumed), there is little economic change or progress. Many of the poorer developing nations in Asia, Africa, and Latin America rely heavily on traditional economic systems. Even in advanced societies, like the United States, tradition influences some economic activity. For example, some people join their parents in a family business.

> **In a traditional economy, people do things in the same way as their parents, and their parents' parents.**

The Command Economic System

In a **command economic system**, the government decides what to produce, how to produce it, and who gets the goods and services produced. The government controls the factors of production. It owns the land and capital and employs the workers. The Soviet Union and the People's Republic of China are two countries that rely mainly on the command economic system.

If the government in a command economic system decides to build cars, for example, it would build the factories, hire the workers, tell the workers how many cars to produce, decide how much the cars will cost, and determine how much the workers will be paid. Since the government makes these decisions, the personal freedom of individuals living under such a system is limited.

A command economic system requires the government to try to predict what goods and services the nation will need for many years into the future. The central government of the Soviet Union, for example, makes such plans every five years. Governments do not always predict the country's wants correctly or direct the factors of production efficiently. So, sometimes the wrong goods and services are produced. Sometimes not enough goods and services are produced.

The Market Economic System

In a **market economic system**, people, by doing what is best for themselves, decide what to produce, how to produce it, and for whom to produce. No central organization controls the factors of production. People own the land and capital and employ the labor and entrepreneurship that produce goods and services. It might seem that this approach would create confusion. But having control over the factors of production allows people to earn money if they meet the needs of consumers. So, the result is an orderly society that finds answers to both the production and distribution problems. Because the United States relies heavily on the market system, we will look at this system in more detail in the next section.

√ check your understanding √ √ √ √ √ √

1. What are the four factors of production?
2. What three basic economic questions must every society answer? Why must every society answer these questions?
3. Explain how the three basic economic questions are answered in a traditional system and in a command system.

HOW THE MARKET SYSTEM WORKS

In a market economic system, producers and consumers come together in a marketplace. A **marketplace** is not a specific place. Rather, it is the opportunity for producers to offer to sell, and consumers to offer to buy, goods and services. How are the three basic economic questions answered in the marketplace?

■ **What goods are produced in a market system?** To see how the first basic question is answered, we must look at the goals people have in a market system. Consumers have two basic goals. They wish to get the goods and services they want most. And they wish to pay the lowest price. To reach these goals, consumers make choices among the goods and services offered for sale.

Producers also have two goals. They wish to sell their goods and services. They also wish to make as much profit as they can. **Profit** is the money producers have left after selling their goods and services and paying all of their expenses.

If consumers don't buy the goods and services, producers can't make a profit. If producers don't make a profit, they can't go on producing more goods and services. So producers will soon stop offering goods and services that consumers don't want. If, however, consumers want to buy a lot of a particular good or service, producers will provide more of it in order to make a larger profit. In this way, consumers' **demand**—the amount of goods and services consumers are willing and able to buy at a certain time—affects producers' **supply**—the amount of goods or services producers are willing to sell at one time. High demand usually leads to a greater quantity supplied. Low demand usually leads to a lower quantity supplied.

Entrepreneurs must often try more than once to become successful. The owner of the Laugh-O-Gram Corporation in Kansas City, Missouri, did so poorly that he had to file for bankruptcy after two years. Not discouraged, Walt Disney left in 1923 for Hollywood with all of his belongings—one set of clothes and some drawings—to try again.

Meeting a large demand may create problems for producers. Suppose there is so much demand for a product that the producer could keep its employees working 12 hours a day, six days a week to fill the demand. A business that works its employees that hard is bound to have problems. Workers could get tired and quit, for example. Training new workers will increase costs.

- **How are goods and services produced in a market system?**
In a market system, producers determine the answer to the second question. Because producers want to make a profit, they will try to make the best, or most salable, products at the lowest cost. To meet this goal, they will try to use the most efficient combination of land, labor, capital, and entrepreneurship they can.

- **Who gets the goods and services in a market system?** Anyone who has the money and chooses to spend it can get goods and services. Those with the most money can buy the most goods and services.

OUR MIXED ECONOMY

The economy of the United States is not a pure market system. A pure market system is operated entirely by consumers and producers. The United States has a **mixed economic system**, one in which the government participates, along with consumers and producers, in the economy. In fact, consumers, producers, and government all depend upon each other to make our economy work. Economists call this interrelationship of consumers, producers, and government in the economy the **circular flow of income and expenditure**. Here's how it works.

Each of the three groups in this circle is dependent on the others because expenditures (another word for spending) by one group become income for another group. For example, consumers pay producers for goods and services. The consumers' expenditures become income for the producers. Producers, in turn, pay employees (who are consumers). These expenditures by producers become income for consumers.

Both consumers and producers pay taxes to government. These tax expenditures become income for government. In return for their tax dollars, government provides services to and employs consumers. Government also provides services to and buys goods and services from producers. These government expenditures become income for consumers and producers. This interrelationship among consumers, producers, and government in our economy can be seen in the diagram on page 74.

The welfare of each group depends on the welfare of the other two groups. If consumers spend their money, producers will make more profit. When producers make more profit, they have more money to buy the consumers' labor. Both consumers and producers will therefore have higher incomes. When consumers and producers have higher incomes, they pay more money to the government in taxes. When the government receives more money from taxes, it can provide more services, buy more goods and services from producers, and employ more labor.

The next time you see a highway, imagine the circular flow of income and expenditure. Using tax money, the government pays for workers, equipment, and materials to build the highway. In turn, the workers give part of their wages to businesses when they buy goods and services. The workers and businesses also pay part of that money in taxes, returning it back to the government.

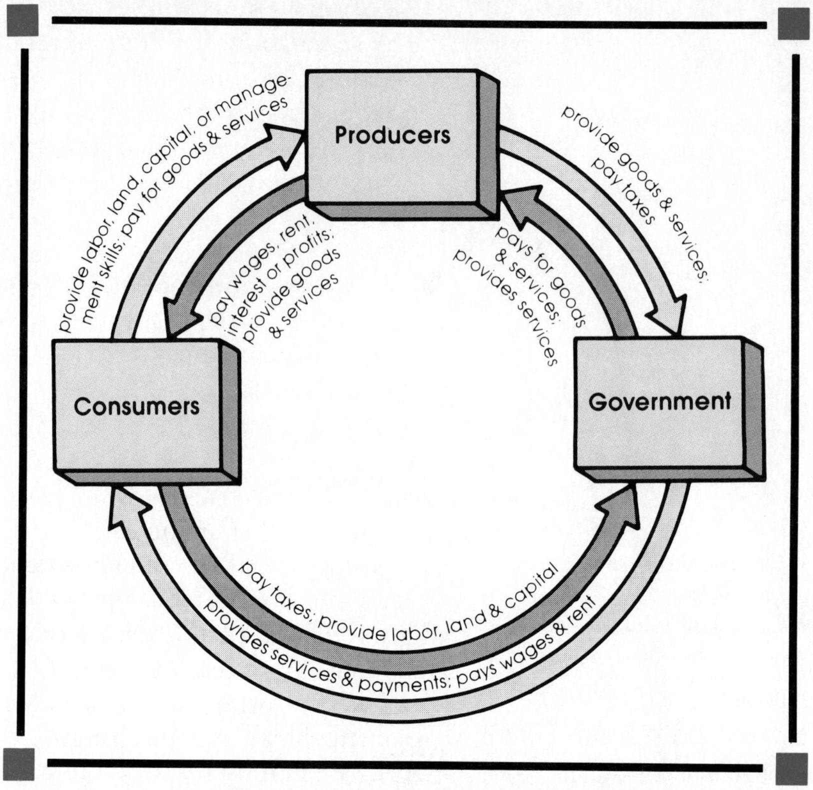
Producers
Consumers
Government
provide labor, land, capital, or management skills; pay for goods & services
pay wages, rent, interest or profits; provide goods & services
provide goods & services; pay taxes
pays for goods & services; provides services
pay taxes; provide labor, land & capital
provides services & payments; pays wages & rent

✓ check your understanding ✓ ✓ ✓ ✓ ✓ ✓

1. **How are the three basic economic questions answered in a market system?**
2. **What is the circular flow of income and expenditure? Why is it important?**
3. **What roles do consumers play in the market system? What roles do producers play? What roles does government play?**

Henry Ford was the first person to make a car cheap enough for the average person to afford. By perfecting the assembly line technology, he was able to cut the time it took to build his Model T car from more than 12 hours to less than 2 hours. He then could cut the price almost in half. Cutting the price created the first large-scale demand for automobiles.

HOW DEMAND AND SUPPLY AFFECT PRICES

In a traditional economic system, prices are set by law or custom. In a command system, a central committee or government sets prices. In a market system, prices are set through the interaction of consumers' demand and producers' supply. For a market system to answer the three basic economic questions successfully, prices must be able to move freely up or down.

We often think markets and prices are only for goods and services. However, there are markets for many things besides goods and services. There's a market for labor, and the price of labor is called a *wage*. There's a market for money, and the price of money is called *interest*. The price of using something that belongs to someone else is called *rent*. Let's see how these prices are set.

Demand and Prices

Producers can create a demand by introducing a new product. Before Sony invented the Walkman in 1979, there was no demand for personal radios. Consumers did not know they wanted them. But, once the machine was invented, demand was very high because the Walkman turned out to satisfy a want consumers did not know they had.

We already know that demand is the amount of something that consumers are willing and able to buy at a certain time. The **law of demand** says people will buy less when prices rise and more when prices fall. The higher the price, the lower the quantity demanded. The lower the price, the higher the quantity demanded.

This law should not be confused with an increase or a decrease in demand itself. Changes in demand make consumers willing to buy more or less of a product *at every price.*

What can cause a change in demand? If people want a product badly, they buy more of it. If they get tired of a product, they buy less of it. Economists call this behavior a change in consumers' tastes and habits. Also, if people have more income, they buy more. If they have less income, they buy less. In addition, we saw in Chapter 2 that an increase in the number of people of a certain age can cause an increase in the demand for products those people want.

A change in demand causes prices to change. If the demand for a product increases, its price rises. If the demand for a product decreases, its price falls. As the following case study shows, keeping up with consumers' changing tastes and habits is difficult. It's also profitable.

CASE STUDY

What is a health club?

It all started with indoor tennis. People wanted to play tennis year round. So, in response to consumer demand, indoor tennis clubs sprang up across the United States in the early 1970's. However, tennis turned out to be harder to play than many people expected. Demand dropped, and fewer tennis clubs were built. Prices for court time declined. Owners could not meet expenses, and, eventually, many clubs went out of business.

For many club owners, racquetball was the answer to their goal of staying profitable. In the early 1970's only a few college students played the game. By the late 1970's, though, it became popular as an easier substitute for tennis. Demand grew: in eight years, the number of players increased from about 75,000 to over 5½ million. Increased demand pushed prices up. Players were willing to pay as much as $8 an hour for the pleasure of knocking a little ball around a racquetball court. Club owners couldn't have been happier. They converted tennis courts to racquetball courts. Makers of racquetball equipment were also happy. In five years, sales of racquets, balls, and accessories went from practically nothing to a $100 million-a-year industry.

But smart owners of racquetball courts knew that the prosperity wouldn't last because consumers' tastes in sports tend to change rapidly. To keep up with changes in consumers' demand, many club owners added jogging tracks, gyms, saunas, and indoor swimming pools to their clubs.

Then aerobics became the "in" sport. Weightlifting machines also became popular. Club owners converted their racquetball courts into mirrored aerobics rooms and high-tech weightlifting rooms.

1. **How would a rise in consumer demand for racquetball affect the price of using a racquetball court?**
2. **Are health clubs an example of the law of demand? Why or why not?**

Supply and Prices

Supply refers to the behavior of sellers. The **law of supply** says that producers are willing to provide more of a product if the price rises and less of the product if the price falls. The higher the price, the greater the quantity supplied. The lower the price, the lower the quantity supplied.

But, as in the case of demand, this law of supply should not be confused with a change in supply. A change in supply will cause producers to want to produce more or less *at every price*. A rise in supply will cause prices to drop. A drop in supply will cause prices to rise.

What can cause supply to increase or decrease? First, it may cost more or less to make a product. New technologies often reduce the cost to make a product, for example. Such a decrease in production cost will cause supply to rise. Prices will drop.

By using technology, in this case robots, car manufacturers can keep their costs down.

What do you think will happen to the price of oranges at the supermarket in the upcoming weeks?

How low can a price go as technology cuts the cost to produce an item? The first pocket calculators cost over $400. Ten years later, similar models cost less than $5.

Suppose that the cost to produce a product goes up. If a producer raises employees' wages, for example, the cost of producing a product may rise. Supply will go down and prices will rise.

Events outside the control of producers can also cause an increase or decrease in supply. For example, good weather may increase the supply of many foods. Prices for those foods will drop. Poor weather may decrease the supply of food and raise prices.

The Market Price

Why is the cost of a pair of jeans closer to $30 than it is to $3,000 or 30 cents? We know that consumers would want to buy more jeans if they cost 30 cents. We know that producers would want to sell more jeans if they cost $3,000. How do producers and consumers settle on the price both like? Why does that price turn out to be near to $30?

To answer these questions, let's look at what would happen if the price of a pair of jeans were $3,000. Producers' profits would be very high, and so they would be willing to produce large quantities for sale at that price. But consumers would not want to buy many pairs. Producers would want to sell more than consumers would want to buy. The amount producers couldn't sell of such a product is called a **surplus**. Producers try to get rid of this surplus by lowering the price. As the price goes down, consumers want to buy more. Eventually, when the price is low enough, the surplus is eliminated. At that point (in our example, when jeans cost about $30) the quantity demanded by consumers is equal to the quantity supplied by producers. This price is called the **market price** (or *equilibrium price*).

What happens if the price starts out lower than the market price? Suppose jeans cost 30 cents. Consumers would want to buy many pairs of jeans. But producers would not want to sell many pairs at all. Consumers would therefore want to buy more than producers would be willing to sell. This situation would create a **shortage**—there would not be enough product for everyone who wants to buy it. Consumers respond to a shortage by being willing to pay higher prices. Producers raise prices and produce more. At one particular price (once again, about $30), the number of jeans that producers are willing to produce will match the number consumers are willing to buy. Once again, we are back to the market price.

✓ check your understanding ✓ ✓ ✓ ✓ ✓ ✓

1. **What is demand? What is the law of demand?**
2. **What is supply? What is the law of supply?**
3. **Name three factors that can affect demand.**
4. **What would happen if Congress passed a law setting the price of color televisions at $5?**

Graphing Supply and Demand

Graphs help us see relationships more clearly. Economists use graphs to show how supply and demand determine market prices. Let's see how this might work for jeans.

We could interview lots of people and construct a table showing the number of jeans people would be willing to buy at various prices. The table might look like this:

Price	Quantity of Jeans Demanded
$40	100
35	150
30	200
25	250
20	300
15	350

This table is called a *demand schedule*. We have plotted this demand schedule on Graph 1 below. Notice that the graph relates price on the vertical axis to quantity on the horizontal axis. The demand curve is plotted in blue. It shows that the lower the price, the more jeans people want to buy. As the price gets higher, people want to buy fewer jeans.

We could then interview companies that manufacture jeans to find out how many pairs they are willing to sell at various prices. The results of the survey might look like this:

Price	Quantity Supplied
$40	300
35	250
30	200
25	150
20	100
15	50

This table is called a *supply schedule*. We have plotted this supply schedule on the same graph as the demand schedule. The supply curve is shown in black. It shows that producers behave differently than consumers. When the price is lower, producers supply less. When the price is higher, they supply more jeans.

How will consumers and producers agree on a price? Graph 1 shows that they will eventually agree on a price of $30. This amount is the market price. Why this price? At any other price, there would be a shortage or a surplus. For example, at a price of $35, consumers would want only 150 pairs of jeans. But producers would be willing to sell 250 pairs. There would be a surplus of 100 pairs. Producers would have to lower their price to get rid of the surplus. This lower price would entice consumers to buy more until the quantity supplied equaled the quantity demanded. What would happen if jeans were priced at $25?

Graph 2 illustrates what happens if consumers' demand for jeans changed. Suppose, for example, that jeans became a fad. Everyone *had* to have them. Consumers became willing to buy 100 more pairs at every price. Curve D1 shows this increase in demand. You can see that an increase in demand will cause the market price to rise.

Suppose that everyone got tired of their jeans. Demand dropped. Curve D2 shows what happens when there is a decrease in demand at every price. The market price falls. What other factors can cause a drop in demand?

Graph 3 shows what happens if producers wish to sell more or fewer jeans at every price. Suppose a new, more efficient jeans-making machine is invented. The cost of making jeans drops. Producers want to supply 100 more jeans at every price. Curve S1 shows this increase in supply. You can see that such an increase in supply causes the market price to fall and the number of jeans exchanged to rise. But then suppose that jeans workers demand higher wages. The cost of making jeans rises. Suppliers want to decrease the supply at every price. Curve S2 shows a decrease in supply—when suppliers want to offer fewer jeans at every price. What does a decrease in supply do to the market price of jeans? What does it do to the quantity of jeans exchanged?

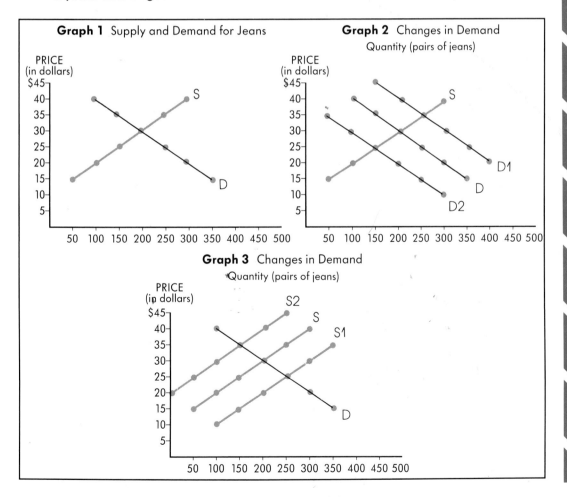

Graph 1 Supply and Demand for Jeans

Graph 2 Changes in Demand

Graph 3 Changes in Demand

Like people, countries have resources. Economists divide countries' resources into four categories: land, capital, labor, and entrepreneurship. Because these resources are limited, every society must decide what goods and services to produce, how to produce them, and who should get them. Societies use three economic systems to answer these questions: the traditional system, the command system, and the market system.

In a market economic system, consumers decide what to produce through their buying decisions. To make a profit, producers try to offer what consumers demand in the most efficient way. In a market system, anyone who has money and is willing to spend it can get goods and services.

The United States economy is not a pure market system that consists only of producers and consumers. The government plays a role as well. The roles of consumers, producers, and government in the United States economy are interrelated. This interrelationship is called the circular flow of income and expenditure. Expenditure of one group becomes income for another.

In a market system, prices are set by the interaction of supply and demand. The market price is determined when the quantity of a good or service demanded by consumers equals the quantity supplied by producers. An increase in demand or a decrease in supply will cause an increase in price. A decrease in demand or an increase in supply will cause a decrease in price.

CHAPTER ◆ ACTIVITIES

BUILDING CONSUMER VOCABULARY

Number your paper from 1 to 15. Then write the term that best matches each numbered definition.

circular flow of income and expenditure
command economic system
demand
factors of production
law of demand
law of supply
market economic system

marketplace
market price
mixed economic system
profit
shortage
supply
surplus
traditional economic system

1. Resources such as land, labor, capital goods, and entrepreneurship
2. The amount of goods and services consumers are willing and able to buy at a particular time
3. The process by which consumers, producers, and government interact in a mixed economic system
4. The amount of goods and services producers are willing to sell at a particular time
5. The money producers have left after selling their goods and services and paying their expenses
6. An economic system in which decisions are made by producers and consumers
7. An economic system in which decisions are made by the government
8. An economic system in which decisions are made based on past customs, laws, and practices
9. The price at which quantity demanded by consumers equals quantity supplied by producers
10. The result of a price higher than the market price
11. The result of a price lower than the market price
12. A rule stating that producers will provide more of a product when its price rises and less when its price falls
13. A rule stating that consumers will buy less of a product when its price rises and more when its price falls
14. The opportunity for producers to offer to sell, and consumers to offer to buy, goods and services
15. An economic system in which decisions are made by producers, consumers, and government

BUILDING CONSUMER UNDERSTANDING

1. How does consumers' demand affect what goods and services are produced? Give specific examples from the case study.
2. In the case study, when racquetball was popular, what determined who would get to play?
3. What determined which health club owners continued in business and which failed?
4. What happens to consumer demand for a good when the price of that good rises? What happens to the quantity producers are willing to supply of a good when its price rises?
5. How is the market price of a good or service affected by:
   a. An increase in demand?
   b. A decrease in demand?
   c. An increase in supply?
   d. A decrease in supply?
6. Identify which factor of production is each of the following:
   a. A tree
   b. A police officer
   c. The owner of a shoe repair shop
   d. A pencil

On a separate sheet of paper, graph the following demand and supply schedules for T-bone steaks. Label the demand curve "D" and the supply curve "S."

Price	Quantity Demanded	Quantity Supplied
$8	150	375
7	200	350
6	250	325
5	300	300
4	350	275
3	400	250
2	450	225

1. What is the market price for T-bone steaks?
2. Suppose the country has a terrible winter and many cattle die. The supply of T-bone steaks drops by 75 at every price level. Draw a new supply curve and label it "S1." What is the new market price?
3. Suppose that, after the terrible winter, the economy becomes very healthy and consumers' income increases. The quantity of T-bone steaks demanded increases by 75 at every price. Draw a new demand curve and label it "D1." What is the market price now?

Explain how the following events would affect the demand or supply and how such a change would affect prices of plane rides:

1. Consumers' income decreases.
2. The price of fuel decreases.
3. All airline pilots get big raises.
4. Many planes crash. People's fear of flying increases considerably.

Find an article in a newspaper or magazine that illustrates how a change in demand or a change in supply changed the price of a particular good or service. Explain how that price change helps determine what is produced, how it is produced, and for whom it is produced.

THE ROLE OF BUSINESS

Every time you buy a pair of jeans or go to a movie, eat a meal or visit the dentist, you are using a good or service provided by a business. If it weren't for businesses, most of our wants and needs would not be met. What would you give up if there were no businesses? How would your life be different?

◆ What types of businesses are there?

◆ How do entrepreneurs measure success?

◆ How are businesses organized?

◆ How do businesses compete?

In our market economy, businesses are responsible for supplying goods and services. In other words, they try to meet consumer demand. By so doing, they play a key part in the circular flow of income and expenditure.

You as a consumer are affected by what businesses do every day. Businesses constantly introduce new products and services that make our lives and work easier, more convenient, more enjoyable, and more interesting.

TYPES OF BUSINESSES

Entrepeneurs are not necessarily older people with plenty of money. Tina Honeycutt is a teenager whose doll-making business is so successful she was named All American Girl of the year for 1987.

Many types of businesses try to meet consumer demand. Not all businesses, however, sell directly to the consumer. Natural resources often go through a chain of businesses on their way to the consumer. There are five main types of businesses in the chain from natural resources to consumer goods and services.

First in the chain are the businesses that provide and process the natural resources. These businesses are called **raw-goods producers and processors**. Farms, mining companies, and steel companies are examples of this type of business. Raw-goods producers and processors can sell directly to consumers, as farmers sometimes do. More often, however, they sell to manufacturers.

Manufacturers take raw materials and partially finished goods and process them into finished goods. Manufacturers and raw-goods producers and processors make up the goods-producing industries discussed in Chapter 2.

Some manufacturers also sell their products directly to the consumer. But many use distributors. **Distributors** move goods from one business to another, usually from the manufacturer to the final seller. Wholesalers and transportation companies are two types of distributors.

The final sellers, the businesses that most often sell goods directly to the consumer, are called **retailers**. Retailers operate the stores and shops where you purchase food, clothes, school supplies, and other goods.

The fifth category of business is the **service firms**. These are the businesses that sell services, rather than goods, to consumers. Repair shops, hair dressers, restaurants, and employment agencies are all examples. You learned in Chapter 2 that the service firms will be producing most of the new jobs in the 1990's. So it is not surprising to find that service firms make up over 60 percent of our marketplace.

THE ROLE OF THE ENTREPRENEUR

Although businesses can grow to be so big that they employ thousands of people and earn billions of dollars, most of them start out

very small. Often, a single entrepreneur starts a business because she or he has an idea for a product or service that consumers may want. In the following case study, watch Mary Cipolla as she turns her idea into reality.

CASE STUDY

Mary's pie in the sky

The inside of Mary Cipolla's Italian restaurant is a familiar sight to the people of Rusty Springs, Montana. The restaurant is so popular that Mary believes she has made Italian dishes the favorite food in the middle of beef country. Sales top $400,000 a year.

Success didn't come easily. It took a big risk and a lot of effort before Mary's dream of owning a successful restaurant became a reality. After she graduated from college, Mary had many job interviews. The interviewers were impressed because Mary had completed her college program in food management with honors. Still, she kept losing job opportunities because she did not have much experience.

Mary believed in herself and kept trying. At last, she got a job as an assistant manager at a family pizza restaurant that was part of a large national chain. For the next two-and-a-half years she worked hard, learning all she could about the restaurant business.

After her marriage, Mary and her husband, Mike, moved west. He got a job in mining. Mary wanted to continue her career, and she thought about starting her own restaurant. She knew that raising the money could be a problem. The competition would be tough too. Rusty Springs already had two very successful steak restaurants and a few fast-food drive-ins.

One spring afternoon, Mary stopped in front of the old bank building. A sign in the window said: FOR SALE OR RENT. The bank had recently moved to a new building.

Mary liked the old building with its thick, 70-year-old beams, its large balconies, and its old-fashioned tellers' windows. She began to imagine what a family pizza restaurant could be like in the old building. Certainly, it would be different. Right then she began to make plans. There were hundreds of details to work out about furnishings, equipment, menus, employees, business hours, and so on.

Mary needed more than plans. She needed money. After several days of planning, she visited the loan officer of the bank. He said that the risk was great. More than half of all new businesses in the area failed in their first year.

Mary and Mike were willing to take the risk. They worked out plans with the loan officer to refinance their house. They put almost all of their savings into the business. In that way, they raised $60,000 to start the restaurant. Mike kept his job at the mining company but planned to help out in the restaurant at night and on weekends.

Mary rented and fixed up the old bank building. She arranged tables on the balconies and the main floor. Customers would place their orders at the tellers' windows, so Mary didn't need to hire table waiters. The bank's vault area became the kitchen, and the pizza ovens were mounted right inside the vault.

Four months later, Mary's pizza restaurant had its grand opening. The restaurant was a hit right from the start. Not only was the family atmosphere pleasant but everything moved smoothly.

Mary had developed standarized recipes for the pizza dough and sauce. Customers could always count on high-quality, good-tasting pizzas. Mary had also set up rules for cleanliness, comfort, and service with the whole family in mind. She did not want the restaurant to be a hangout, so there were no video games or vending machines.

1. **What service does Mary provide? What goods does Mary sell?**
2. **How is Mary's restaurant different from other restaurants already in the marketplace?**
3. **What type of business does Mike work for?**

Why do people like Mary want to be entrepreneurs? For Mary, owning her own restaurant gave her a chance to reach a long-term career goal. Other entrepreneurs want to be their own boss. But for all, being an entrepreneur gives them the opportunity to get financial rewards, or profits, from a business. Profits enable entrepreneurs to do many things: to buy goods and services, to save for the future, or to expand their businesses.

Figuring Profits

In Chapter 5, we learned that profit is the amount of money a business has left after selling its goods and services and paying expenses. The money a business takes in is called **income**. Let's look at income and expenses so we can better understand how difficult it is to run a business at a profit.

A recent study showed that 14½ percent of businesses fail in their first year of operation. Over 50 percent fail in the first five years. The greatest failure rates are in the areas of business services, agriculture, mining, and transportation.

Income All of the producers we discussed in Chapter 5 received income from the sale of goods and services. But there are other ways to earn income. Businesses can also earn income from investments or from the sale of capital goods (such as buildings). The amount of income taken in depends, of course, on the success of the business and the entrepreneur.

Expenses Most businesses have lots of expenses, or costs. Mary's restaurant is no exception. Mary needed pizza ovens, grills, re-

Paper is a variable cost for news publishers, depending on the number of newspapers printed.

If you doubt that entrepreneurs need to work hard to succeed, look at these figures. A survey of the fastest growing businesses in the United States revealed that less than one third of the owners took more than two weeks' vacation per year.

frigerators, dishes, and a cash register. These items, the ones she needed just to begin doing business, are called *start-up costs*. In addition to start-up costs, Mary has costs of daily operations. These include rent, employees' wages, utility bills, supplies, and interest paid on her bank loan. These costs can be divided into two major types: fixed costs and variable costs.

Businesses have to pay for some things whether they sell anything or not. These expenses are called **fixed costs**. For example, Mary must pay her rent and the interest on her bank loan even when her restaurant is closed. Fixed costs remain the same no matter how many hours a business stays open or how much it produces.

When entrepreneurs talk about fixed costs, they understand that these costs are fixed only in the short run (a year or less). In the long run (over a year), most costs will change. For example, Mary's landlord will probably raise the rent when the lease is renewed.

Variable costs are those that depend on whether the business is selling its goods and services. Mary's variable costs include the ingredients she uses to make her pizzas—the flour, tomato sauce, cheese, and so on. The more pizzas Mary sells, the more ingredients she needs. The more goods and services a business sells, the higher its variable costs.

Maximizing Profits

Most entrepreneurs try to make as much profit as possible. Economists call this *maximizing profits*. Entrepreneurs maximize profits by keeping sales high and costs low. If sales are low, and the company loses money, entrepreneurs try to keep the amount of money they lose as low as possible. Economists call this *minimizing losses*. Reducing expenses is one way to minimize losses.

When there isn't enough income to pay for all variable costs, some entrepreneurs shut down for a short time so that they have to pay only their fixed costs. For example, auto manufacturers often announce one- or two-week shutdowns until they receive enough orders to reopen.

Some businesses, like Mary's, might reduce their hours of operation in order to reduce variable costs. Let's say Mary figures that on Mondays she takes in about $350, but has fixed costs of $100 and variable costs of $300. Obviously, she's losing money on Mondays. She's losing $50 ($350 in sales −$400 in costs). Should Mary shut down on Mondays? If she does, she loses $100, her daily fixed cost. If she stays open, she loses only $50. So Mary will minimize her losses by staying open.

Measuring Success

One way to measure how well a business is doing is to compare profits with sales. This comparison is called the **return on sales**. Suppose Mary has $25,000 in profits after sales of $200,000. Mary's return on sales is 12½ percent ($25,000 ÷ $200,000 × 100).

How does Mary's business compare with other businesses in the United States? During the 1980's, the average business' return on sales was slightly less than 5 percent. In other words, the average business made about 5 cents profit for every dollar of goods or services sold. Of course, profits vary greatly from business to business.

Another way to measure success is to look at the **return on equity**. This figure compares profits with the amount the owner has invested in the business (which is called *equity*). Mary invested $60,000 in her restaurant. Therefore, with profits of $25,000, her return on equity is about 42 percent ($25,000 ÷ $60,000 × 100). Using the return-on-equity figure, Mary's restaurant is doing better than most businesses, which average about 14 percent.

A staff of six put out the first issue in 1922. Sales were expected to reach 25,000. Only 9,000 were sold, and half of the copies put on the newsstand were returned unsold. Although disappointed, its owners did not give up. They were well rewarded. Today, *Time* sells over 4 million copies a week. And the company is one of the most profitable publishers in the world.

✓check your understanding ✓ ✓ ✓ ✓ ✓ ✓

1. **What are the five main types of businesses? What is the purpose of each type of business?**
2. **Why do you think people like Mary want to be entrepreneurs?**
3. **What is the difference between a fixed cost and a variable cost?**
4. **What are the two tools entrepreneurs use to measure business success?**

HOW BUSINESSES ARE ORGANIZED

A business can have one, two, or several owners. Based on the number and type of owners they have, businesses can be organized in one of three ways: sole proprietorships, partnerships, and corporations.

Sole Proprietorships

The simplest and most numerous form of business organization is the **sole proprietorship**. It is a business owned and operated by one person. Mary's restaurant is one. Most of the small businesses around your town or neighborhood are sole proprietorships.

There are several advantages to this form of business. The owner makes all of the decisions and keeps any profits. A sole proprietorship is the easiest form of business to start. Very little paperwork is required. Of course, all businesses in the United States must obey government rules and regulations that apply to business in general. And some businesses, like restaurants or day care centers, need licenses to operate. But there are fewer government regulations controlling sole proprietorships than any other type of business in the United States. Another advantage of owning a sole proprietorship comes at tax time. A sole proprietor pays taxes only once on the profits of the business.

There are also disadvantages in owning a sole proprietorship—especially when the business loses money. The owner is personally responsible for all business debts. If the business doesn't have enough money to pay its debts, the owner's personal property can be used to pay those debts. The owner could lose a house, car, or personal savings. In legal terms, the owner has *unlimited liability* for the debts of his or her business.

In addition, some sole proprietors may have limited abilities. For example, Mary can prepare good pizza, but that's not the only skill she needs to run a restaurant. She also needs to be able to manage her finances, supervise her employees, and maintain her inventory of supplies. So, often, sole proprietors hire employees to do some of the work for them, which adds to their costs and reduces their profits.

Another disadvantage of a sole proprietorship is its *limited life*. If the owner dies or sells the business, it no longer exists legally. For someone else to continue operating the business, it must be formed again.

Success was a long time coming to Ray Kroc. He had been selling paper cups and milkshake machines to restaurants for over 17 years before he persuaded two brothers to let him franchise their hamburger stand. Ray Kroc thought he was simply working out a way to sell 80 more milkshake machines when he bought the right to franchise McDonald's.

Partnerships

A **partnership** is a business owned by two or more people. Some people may put only their money into the partnership. Others put only their talents or skills into it. In most cases, both money and talents are contributed by each owner. Partnerships can be created without putting anything down in writing, but many partners choose to sign a *partnership agreement*. This agreement lists each owner's responsibilities for running the business. It also lists their rights to profits and other benefits of ownership.

The main advantage of a partnership is that each partner can contribute his or her special skills. One person does not have to be good at every aspect of the business. Also, financial institutions are more willing to lend money to a partnership than to a sole proprietorship because the financial resources of more than one owner are backing the business.

Partnerships do have disadvantages, however. As in a sole proprietorship, the partners have unlimited liability. If one partner makes bad decisions and creates big debts, the other partners must share those debts. And, like sole proprietorships, partnerships have limited life. The death of any partner ends the partnership. For the business to continue, the surviving partners must form a new partnership.

Corporations

The largest and most complex form of business organization is the corporation. A **corporation** is a legal entity created by permission of the government. It is the form of business that produces most of the goods and services we use today.

The owners of corporations are called *stockholders*, but these owners have no role in the day-to-day operation of the business. Instead, they elect a *board of directors* that makes major policy decisions and hires managers to run the corporation.

The corporate form of business is complex because the owners of the business (the stockholders) and the business itself are legally separate. The business part is viewed as a person by law. It can do many of the things a person can do—such as own property, raise money, sue, and be sued.

This legal situation has special advantages for the owners. They are not liable, or responsible, for the corporation's actions or debts. This concept is called *limited liability*. If the corporation can't pay its debts and has to stop operating, each stockholder loses only her or his original investment. Because of this feature, corporations are able to raise large sums of money by selling stock to many owners. Investing in stocks is discussed in Chapter 27.

Another advantage of corporate organization is *unlimited life*. Because a corporation is viewed as a person, it doesn't cease to exist when a stockholder dies. In addition, ownership can be transferred from one person to another, by selling stock, without dissolving the business.

A disadvantage of the corporation is that it is harder to start than other forms of business. People who wish to start a corporation must apply to the state for a *charter*. This charter spells out what types of financing, operating procedures, and regulations the corporation must use. After receiving a charter, a corporation must prepare *bylaws*, or specific rules, spelling out the business' method of operation. More restrictions are placed on corporations by federal, state, and local governments than are placed on partnerships or sole proprietorships.

Another disadvantage of the corporation is that owners' profits are taxed twice. The corporation is taxed once when it earns a profit. Then, any of that profit distributed by the corporation to the owners is taxed again as the owners' personal income. This practice is called *double taxation*.

An individual can enjoy many of the advantages of large corporations by buying a franchise. A **franchise** is the right to use the name, employ the same business methods, and benefit from the advertising and purchasing power of another company, called the *parent company*. In return, the owner of the franchise pays a fee and gives the parent company a share in the profits. Franchises can be organized as sole proprietorships, partnerships, or corporations. Franchises are the safest way to get into businesses. Less than 5 percent of the half-million franchises operating in the United States fail each year. Many restaurants and motel chains are franchises.

> The profits of a corporation are taxed twice— once as profits for the business and once as income for its stockholders.

✓check your understanding ✓ ✓ ✓ ✓ ✓ ✓

1. What are the advantages and disadvantages of a sole proprietorship? a partnership? a corporation?
2. What two steps must a corporation take to get started?
3. What is double taxation?
4. What is a franchise? Describe two advantages of owning one.

COMPETITION AMONG BUSINESSES

Few businesses sell a good or service that no other business sells. When two or more businesses offer the same or a similar product to the consumer, they are said to be in **competition** with each other. Competition is one of the most important characteristics of a market economy because, when businesses compete, the consumer has a choice of which product to buy. When consumers have choices, they can demonstrate their demand. If, for example, you want milk but there is only one kind for sale, you must buy that kind. However, if there are two kinds of milk and one is cheaper than the other or better in another way, you can choose the one you like best. In this way you can tell producers what you want.

How Businesses Compete

Each business, of course, wants all consumers to buy its products. To get consumers' dollars, the business must give consumers a reason to buy its products instead of those offered by a competitor. Producers can convince consumers to buy their products in many ways.

Competing through price The law of demand says that consumers will buy more when the price goes down. So one way a business can compete is by offering its product at the lowest price. Then not only will consumers buy more, they will buy from one particular producer more than any other.

Competing through quality Some consumers are willing to pay more for a product if it will last longer, if it has more features, or if it is more carefully made than a less expensive product. Some companies, therefore, offer high-quality products as a way of competing against other businesses.

Competing through service Some businesses allow you to buy goods and services very quickly. Perhaps their employees seem to be extremely friendly. Maybe they will let you return an item no matter what the reason. These businesses are competing by offering good service. You may decide to buy a shirt in a store that will let you return it easily even if it costs a bit more than one from a less helpful shop.

Competing through location Many companies try to compete by being the business closest to the consumer. You may have seen places where there is a gas station on every corner. Being on a corner lets a gas station attract cars going down two roads instead of just one.

For every restaurant that succeeds in the United States, the Small Business Administration (SBA) estimates, 12 more fail. Why? The SBA says poor management is the main reason these businesses go under.

Its location near a train station makes this newsstand competitive with others.

Competing through innovation
Inventing new products or services is called **innovation**. Innovation is actually a way of eliminating competition. But a company usually can't eliminate its competition for long by inventing something new. Other companies will probably find a way to offer a similar product or service if the new one is popular. A company that wants to compete through innovation must keep inventing new products and services. Many computer companies and software firms compete in this way.

Competing through advertising
People won't buy a product or service if they don't know about it. Companies use advertising to tell consumers about their products. Many ads provide consumers with information they need to buy what they want. Other ads say little or nothing about the product. Both kinds of advertising seem to work.

When you need more horsepower, move up to BRAVO Trucks.

Does this advertisement provide enough information for you to make a decision about the product being sold?

Competing through size
Large businesses often have an advantage when competing against small businesses. Large businesses buy their raw materials in larger quantities and so can often ask their suppliers for a better price than small companies get.

Sometimes two companies try to compete by joining together to become as big or bigger than the other competing companies. If they come together to form a completely new company, with a new name, it is called a *consolidation*. If one of the companies buys the other, it is called a *merger*. In a merger, no new company is formed. The company that was purchased just stops being a separate business.

When Businesses Don't Compete

A business that sells a good or service that no other business has is called a **monopoly**. A monopoly has no competition. Some companies that provide essential services to consumers are allowed to operate as monopolies. Electric companies, water companies,

A web of wires would hide the sky, if electric companies could not operate as monopolies.

gas companies, and cable television companies are examples of this kind of monopoly. To operate, they must place pipes or wires over large areas. A tangle of pipes and wires would result if more than one company operated in each area.

These companies, however, could charge high prices for their products and services because consumers cannot go to any other company instead. To prevent such businesses from charging high prices, local, state, and federal governments limit the prices these monopolies can charge. When one of these companies wants to raise its prices, it must ask permission of the government. You will learn more about how government affects business in the next chapter.

Sometimes, one company will try to buy all of the other companies that make a particular product or provide a service and so create a monopoly. Such a company would then be able to raise its prices. Our society has decided that this kind of monopoly would not benefit the consumer. Therefore, the federal government has made the formation of a monopoly from existing companies illegal. The government will often step in to prevent the formation of a monopoly.

Sometimes, two or more companies in the same market will get together and agree on prices so that they will not have to compete with each other. This is called *price fixing*. This, too, is illegal. The federal government will step in to protect the consumer if it finds that companies have been fixing prices. In the next chapter, you will learn more about the ways in which government affects businesses.

✓ check your understanding ✓ ✓ ✓ ✓ ✓ ✓

1. **Describe three different ways that businesses can compete.**
2. **What is a monopoly? Name two ways that a monopoly could be formed.**
3. **Why is price-fixing illegal?**

SUMMARIZING
the chapter

Businesses in the United States supply consumers with a wide variety of goods and services. In return, business people hope to make a profit. Together, raw-goods producers and processors, manufacturers, distributors, retailers, and service firms take natural resources and turn them into goods and services sold to the consumer. Profit is determined in each type of business by subtracting expenses, both fixed and variable, from income. Entrepreneurs can determine how good the profit is by calculating return on sales and return on equity.

There are three major ways to organize a business: sole proprietorships, partnerships, and corporations. The main advantages of sole proprietorships and partnerships are ease of formation, control of operations and profits by owners, and single taxation of profits. The main disadvantages are limited life and unlimited liability.

The main advantages of a corporation are unlimited life and limited liability. The main disadvantages are difficulty of formation, government regulation, and double taxation. With a franchise, small-business people can enjoy many of the advantages of large corporations.

Businesses compete in a number of ways: on the basis of price, quality, service, location, innovation, advertising, and size. Monopolies have no competition. In some cases, the lack of competition lets the company raise prices. The government will step in when it feels that a company is trying to avoid competition by forming a monopoly or by fixing prices.

CHAPTER ACTIVITIES

BUILDING CONSUMER VOCABULARY

Number your paper from 1 to 17. Then write the term that best matches each numbered definition.

competition	partnership
corporation	raw-goods producers and processors
distributor	retailer
fixed costs	return on equity
franchise	return on sales
income	service firm
innovation	sole proprietorship
manufacturer	variable costs
monopoly	

1. A type of business that sells goods directly to the consumer
2. Expenses that remain the same no matter how much a business sells
3. A method of comparing business profits with the owner's investment
4. Two or more businesses selling a similar product
5. The right of one company to use the name, employ the same business methods, and benefit from the advertising and purchasing power of another company

6. The money a business takes in
7. A business organization in which the owners do not operate the business
8. Business expenses that change with the amount of goods and services a business sells
9. Businesses that provide or process natural resources
10. A method of comparing business profits with business sales
11. The invention of new products or services
12. A business owned and operated by two or more people
13. A business that moves goods and services from one company to another
14. A business that has no competition
15. A business that makes goods
16. A business owned and operated by a single person
17. A business that sells activities directly to consumers

BUILDING CONSUMER UNDERSTANDING

1. What type of business is each of the following?
   a. A salt mine
   b. A factory that makes electric guitars
   c. An airline that carries passengers
   d. An airline that flies fresh vegetables from farmers to supermarkets
   e. A sporting goods shop
   f. A doctor's office
2. Why is competition important in a market economy?
3. Corporations (and not sole proprietorships or partnerships) produce most of the goods and services supplied in our economy. Why do you think this is so?
4. What is the difference between a partnership and a corporation?
5. Identify the method of competition described in each of the following examples:
   a. "Wooly Shirts have more wool in them than any other shirt."
   b. "No matter where you are, there's a Super Saver Bank near you."
   c. "Freshstuff Supermarket will deliver any time of the day or night."
   d. "Show us the price of anyone else's bicycle and Budget Biker will beat it."

BUILDING CONSUMER MATH SKILLS

Assume that Mike Cipolla's sister goes into business designing and making work uniforms.

1. If during her first year she earns $25,000 in profits on $125,000 in sales, what is her return on sales?

2. How much are her costs?
3. Suppose she had put $50,000 into the business. What is her return on equity?

1. Did Mary use all of the factors of production to start her restaurant? Give an example from the case study of each factor of production Mary used.
2. Label each of the following expenses of Mary Cipolla's restaurant as fixed (F) or variable (V):
   a. napkins and straws
   b. interest on her bank loan
   c. fire insurance policy
   d. boxes for carryout pizza
   e. a new calculator for bookkeeping
   f. wages of employees (assume that Mary pays them by the hour)

   List three more and label them.

Interview a sole proprietor of a local business and find out the following:

1. What type of business does she or he operate (raw-goods producer or processor, manufacturer, distributor, retailer, or service firm)?
2. What are the advantages and disadvantages of being a sole proprietor in this business?
3. What are the biggest costs of the business? Are they mostly fixed or variable?
4. Has he or she considered forming a partnership or a corporation?

THE ROLE OF GOVERNMENT

Life would be simpler if we could use markets to make all of our choices. Supply and demand would set prices. Prices would determine which goods and services to produce, how to produce them, and who would get them. Unfortunately, there are situations in which markets cannot do their work alone. In these cases, government has a role to play in our economy.

7

● What is a public good?

● What services does government provide?

● How do government regulations affect us?

● What are some of the costs and benefits of government regulations?

In a pure market system, producers try to make what consumers want to buy. In this way, producers make a profit. With that money, producers can go on making what consumers want to buy. But, as the case study shows, some things that consumers want are not profitable for businesses to offer.

CASE STUDY

Who should pay for a lighthouse?

ANOTHER SHIPWRECK! Mayor Hobson frowned as she read the headline. She knew she would have to listen to the same old arguments she heard every time a ship went down in the narrow channel leading to the harbor.

Everyone agreed there should be a lighthouse. Insurance companies wanted a lighthouse so they wouldn't have to pay for so many losses due to shipwrecks. The ship owners also wanted a lighthouse. Fewer shipwrecks would lower the cost of insurance. Even more important, a lighthouse would help sailors do their jobs faster, more efficiently, and more safely. Merchants and consumers wanted a lighthouse too. They knew that the waste caused by shipwrecks made their products more expensive.

Yet no one would build the lighthouse. No business could think of a way to charge a fee to use the light. If it turned the light on for one ship, other ships could use the light without paying. No business could afford to offer the service for free.

Mayor Hobson put her paper down sadly. There was no lighthouse, and there didn't seem to be a way to build one.

WHY IS GOVERNMENT IN OUR ECONOMY?

In a pure market system, the only goods and services produced are ones that provide a profit to business. But society needs some goods and services that are not profitable. The lighthouse is an example. When our society needs a good or service that business cannot provide, we turn to government to provide it. Economists call goods and services that only government can provide **public goods**. Pure public goods have two characteristics: non-exclusion and shared consumption.

- **Non-exclusion** means that people cannot be excluded, or kept away, from the benefits of using a public good. Even if they refuse to pay for it, they can still use it. When the lighthouse turns on its light, no one can be stopped from using it. National defense is another example. Once an army is raised, or missiles

Operating a lighthouse is one of the services we expect government to provide.

are in place, all people in the country are protected whether they pay or not.

■ **Shared consumption** means that one person's using the good or service does not stop other people from using it. If one ship uses the lighthouse, others can also use it at the same time. Most private goods do not have this characteristic. After one person eats a container of yogurt, for example, other people can't eat that same portion.

Very few goods and services are pure public goods. Highways, for example, usually meet the characteristic of shared consumption. One person riding on the highway generally does not stop another person from doing so. But people can be excluded from highways by setting up toll booths.

✓check your understanding ✓ ✓ ✓ ✓ ✓ ✓

1. **Why can't businesses provide public goods?**
2. **What is non-exclusion?**
3. **Give an example of shared consumption.**

GOVERNMENT AS A PROVIDER

Obviously, if businesses don't make a profit providing these goods and services, government doesn't either. So someone must be paying for them. Who? Everyone does—businesses as well as consumers—with the money paid in taxes. Many people fail to connect the taxes they pay with the services government provides. They feel government is taking their money and giving nothing back. Or they feel that government services are free. In the following case study, Jim Wateska makes both mistakes.

CASE STUDY

Who pays for government services?

"It really makes me mad the way so much of my pay goes straight to the government," complained Jim Wateska, sitting down at the dinner table. "I wouldn't mind paying so much if I got something in return. I'm not getting anything for it!"

His son, Doug, came to dinner after watching the news on television. The news report worried him. "I'm afraid the United States might not be strong enough to keep other countries from kicking us around," he told his father. "They'll probably back us up against the wall. Pretty soon I'll be drafted into the Army instead of going to State University this fall."

Daughter Amy was still annoyed with her father for calling the police the previous night. After all, the noise in the park was just some kids having a party. They might have been wrong, she repeated once again, but not wrong enough to have a run-in with the cops.

Mrs. Wateska, however, said she was impressed that the police came so quickly. She added that the fire department was just as good. "Did you hear about the fire down the street at the Lees'? The fire department put it out even before it could spread out of the kitchen."

"How was school today?" asked Mr. Wateska.

"Okay," both children responded.

The whole family then talked about driving to the mountains during summer vacation. They were going to camp at a state park for a week. Doug wanted to take scuba diving lessons offered at the park. But Amy didn't want to miss playing in the town's summer softball league.

"Now that I'm back to work, we can afford a vacation. I'd really like to get away," said Mrs. Wateska. "Unemployment benefits helped during the three months I was out of work. But I'd like to take a real vacation now."

Grandma Wateska said she was glad she didn't have to work anymore. "I just got a raise in my social security payments, but I'm not sure I'm keeping up with rising prices," she added.

Social security taxes had just increased for both Mr. and Mrs. Wateska. "Well, I can see where my social security tax money goes," declared Mr. Wateska. "But I'm sure stumped about what the rest of my tax money is used for."

If you choose a career with the national park service, your salary will be paid by the federal government.

Some of the Services Government Provides

	Federal Level	State Level	Local Level
Aid to the poor	X	X	X
Colleges		X	
Consumer protection	X	X	X
Courts and prisons	X	X	
Fire departments			X
Foreign policy and aid	X		
Highways and other roads	X	X	X
Hospitals		X	
Housing	X	X	X
National defense	X		
Parks	X	X	X
Police protection	X	X	X
Pollution control	X	X	
Primary and secondary schools			X
Printing of money	X		
Public health programs	X	X	X
Public information programs	X	X	X
Sewage treatment		X	X
Unemployment benefits	X	X	
Water supply			X

Many services are provided for by all three levels of government.

Spending at the Federal Level

You learned in Chapter 3 that different levels of government may take money out of your paycheck for taxes. We have three main levels of government in this country: federal, state, and local. Each may take money from citizens and businesses in the form of taxes and give it back in the form of goods and services that businesses do not provide for us.

The federal government is the biggest spender of all, and the biggest part of that expense is social welfare programs. Grandma Wateska received part of that money as social security income for her retirement. Mrs. Wateska got some of it in the form of unemployment insurance benefits. The federal government provides a number of other kinds of insurance as well. In addition, the federal government pays out retirement income to government employees, including members of the military. Twenty-five years ago, such payments represented only about 25 percent of the federal budget. But the number of people retiring is increasing. And the amount of money they need to live on is also rising. Today, social welfare payments make up over 40 cents of each dollar paid out by the federal government.

The second most expensive service provided by the federal government is the national defense. Most of that money pays the salaries of people in the Army, Air Force, Navy, and Marines. It also pays for all of the airplanes, ships, and other equipment the soldiers use.

In addition, the federal government runs courts and prisons, builds highways, prints money, and runs many public information programs. It also gives money to state and local governments to help them provide goods and services—mostly for education and social programs.

Spending at the State Level

State governments spend their tax money mainly for education, social programs, health and hospitals, and construction and upkeep of highways. The states provide money to help local school districts. They also run state colleges and universities. Students at state colleges and universities pay much less than students at private universities. Tax money takes care of many costs.

Social welfare programs are run by the states, although much of the money comes from the federal government. These programs include Aid to Families with Dependent Children (AFDC), unemployment compensation, Medicaid, and other programs for the poor. The states also direct the use of funds for the maintenance and construction of highways and for public transportation. The federal government, though, contributes much of the money for these programs.

Spending at the Local Level

Local governments provide the services that most directly affect us as citizens and as consumers. They run local schools, from

Some services provided by government are not paid for by taxes. The post office, for example, gets its money mainly through the sale of its products. Tax money pays for less than 2 percent of the cost of running this service.

Tuition at state colleges and universities is less than at private schools because state schools are partially supported by tax revenues.

kindergarten through high school. They provide police and fire protection, supply water, take care of streets, and maintain local parks and playgrounds. Many local governments collect trash, provide for sewage removal, operate public libraries, and even offer emergency ambulance service.

If you go to a public high school, a lot of your costs are paid for by local tax dollars. On average, about 50 percent of the cost of education is paid for by local government, 44 percent by the states, and 6 percent by the federal government.

Many businesses that are private in this country are public in other countries. The central government owns the gas and electric companies in many Western European countries, for example. Private businesses run these companies in the United States.

✓check your understanding ✓ ✓ ✓ ✓ ✓ ✓

1. **The Wateska family mentions ten different government services for which they pay taxes. Identify them. Which are provided by the federal government? by their state government? by their local government?**
2. **List five services that local government can provide for its people.**
3. **Which levels of government pay for our public schools?**

GOVERNMENT AS A PROTECTOR

One of the major roles of government is to protect the members of society. The federal government provides national defense. State and local governments provide police and fire protection. These services protect everyone in the country.

Sometimes, however, what is good for one person or group is not good for another. Government steps in to decide how everyone's interests can best be protected. Government protects people's interests by passing laws and regulations. Some laws protect businesses. Some protect workers. Others protect our natural resources. Still others protect consumers.

Laws That Help Business

Some laws set up rules for fairness among businesses. For example, the Uniform Commercial Code is a set of business laws that is the same, or uniform, just about all over the country. It spells out what must be put in a legal contract, for example. Courts will step in to protect businesses if a contract is broken.

Patent and copyright laws prevent one company from making and selling a product that belongs to another company. Patent laws protect inventions, such as instant cameras (the ones that print their own pictures), for a limited period of time. Copyright laws protect writings, music, and software, also for a limited period of time. When the time is up, anyone can make and sell these products.

Laws That Encourage Competition

Antitrust laws set up rules for fair competition. They are the laws referred to in Chapter 6 that prevent price fixing and the formation of monopolies. Two of these laws are the Sherman Antitrust Act and the Clayton Act. These laws not only help consumers, they also help businesses. The Clayton Act, for example, prevents a large company from trying to put smaller companies out of business by selling one of its products for much less than it costs to make. And under the Federal Trade Commission Act, one company cannot try to run another out of business by spreading false rumors. This act also set up the Federal Trade Commission, which has the authority to stop unfair business practices.

Laws That Protect Natural Resources

Wise use of our natural resources benefits both businesses and citizens. Production of goods starts with natural resources. Keeping our land, water, and air clean is important to everyone's health. Adding something harmful to the land, water, or air is called **pollution**. The Air Pollution Control Act and the Water Quality Act help protect our natural resources from pollution. Also known

Citizens want the goods produced by manufacturers, but they also want protection for the environment. Is it possible to have it all?

as the Clean Air Act and the Clean Water Act, these laws stop businesses from polluting the environment with their products. For example, cars must now be made so that they do not put out as many dangerous chemicals into the air. Businesses may also have to clean up pollution already in the environment. The Environmental Protection Agency (EPA) sees to it that these laws are obeyed. It also runs Superfund. Superfund is a pool of tax money set aside to pay for cleaning up some of the most polluted places in the United States.

Laws That Promote Fair Labor Practices

Civil rights laws protect people from unfair treatment because of their race, sex, religion, or age. Businesses may not refuse to hire people just because they seem too old, for example. The Equal Employment Opportunity Commission (EEOC) can take action against businesses that do not hire or promote their workers fairly. The Occupational Safety and Health Administration (OSHA) can help if workers feel that conditions where they work are unsafe.

Laws That Protect the Consumer

Government also passes many laws especially to protect consumers. In 1962, President John F. Kennedy proclaimed that all consumers have four basic rights:

■ **The Right to Safety**. Products should not harm the user and should do what the manufacturer says they can do.
■ **The Right To Be Informed**. Manufacturers should provide complete and accurate product information.
■ **The Right to Choice**. Consumers should be able to choose from a large number of products.
■ **The Right To Be Heard**. Producers of goods and services should pay more attention to consumers' views.

In the mid-1960's, Congress passed many consumer laws. Some were intended to improve the quality and safety of products. Examples of these are The Poison Prevention Packaging Act, the Consumer Product Safety Act, and the Motor Vehicle Safety Act. Other laws were aimed at providing information about products.

Entire agencies were created, such as the Consumer Product Safety Commission and the National Highway Traffic Safety Administration. Older agencies, such as the Federal Trade Commission and the Food and Drug Administration, became more aggressive in making sure businesses obey the laws.

Today, more than 50 federal agencies and bureaus perform functions affecting consumers. More than 600 local, county, and state government agencies are involved with consumer protection. You will read more about these agencies in Chapter 10.

Government used to regulate airlines, telling them where to fly and how much to charge. Government has stopped regulating airlines. The airline industry is more competitive, and consumers save about $6 billion a year as a result. However, airlines have stopped flying to some cities because profits on those routes are too small.

1. Name three types of laws that protect the rights of business.
2. Which laws help protect the environment? How do these laws work?
3. What can the Equal Employment Opportunity Commission do?
4. Give a brief description of the basic consumer rights defined by President Kennedy.

WHO SHOULD PROTECT CONSUMERS?

Competition in the marketplace can cause consequences at the end of the line.

Some people believe there can never be too much consumer protection. After all, they argue, government exists to protect citizens. But other people believe that competition in the marketplace guards consumers better than any laws. The future direction of consumer protection may depend on your views as citizens. So let's explore the arguments for more and less legislation.

The Case for More Laws

Those who want more laws and regulations believe that consumers don't have enough information to protect themselves. After all, this is a big country. Suppose someone buys a toaster in California that is so poorly made it causes a fire. Will consumers in Rhode Island—3,000 miles away—find out about it?

Also, the argument continues, some businesses don't have enough competition, so consumers don't get all the choices they deserve. And big firms can control consumer tastes through advertising.

In the past, government regulation prevented savings banks from offering checking accounts. But in 1980, many government banking regulations were dropped. Some banks had trouble dealing with competition and went out of business. But now a wide variety of financial institutions, and even retail stores, can offer checking accounts and other services.

Court decisions have resulted in doctors and lawyers being allowed to advertise their services. Some people believe that the ads are a form of consumer education because many consumers are unaware of many medical and legal services available to them.

Firms offer what they want to produce, not what consumers really want, they say.

Another group argues for more laws for another reason. People in this group believe that consumers have too many choices, making it difficult to pick out the best goods and services. Often, consumers are forced to ask questions about a large number of similar products. How safe are they? Will they work as promised? Which one is really the best? We all aren't chemists or engineers. How can we find the answer to these questions without help from government?

The Case for Fewer Laws

Another group of people believes that government regulations harm consumers more than they help. These people point out that the market system has made this nation one of the richest in the world. Much of that wealth comes from businesses competing to satisfy the wishes of consumers.

No business can sell a product that consumers don't want, they argue. If a product causes accidents, businesses will lose customers.

And, even if standards for products are needed, this group continues, a question still remains. Who should set them? government? consumers? businesses? For example, some consumers may want to give up some safety for a lower price. Should government tell them they can't do this?

Consumer Protection Guidelines

Consumer protection is not a simple all-or-nothing affair. Some laws may benefit more people than they hurt. Others may not. Here are some guidelines you can think about when trying to judge how effective a consumer protection law will be.

■ **Are the benefits worth the cost?** A law may have many benefits, but does it have even higher costs? If we passed a law forbidding cars, we'd save thousands of lives. However, no one suggests protecting consumers in this way.

Weighing costs and benefits can be complicated. Costs are hard to determine. One study put the cost of federal regulations as high as $100 billion in a single year. But you can get other numbers, both higher and lower, depending on what you read.

Estimating benefits is even more complicated than working out costs. For example, a study found out what happened after the federal government passed regulations making cars safer by requiring seat belts and other changes. The study found an obvious benefit. Fewer drivers died in auto accidents. But more pedestrians were hit by cars. Why? No one knows. One reason may be that drivers went faster because they felt their cars were safer.

Another matter that complicates cost/benefit discussions is the fact that it is difficult to put a price tag on human life or even on human injury.

■ **Does the problem affect only the individual consumer, or does it also affect innocent bystanders?** Many people feel that government should protect citizens from each other but should not make people do things only to protect themselves. For example, a law making a motorcycle rider wear a helmet just protects the rider. These people argue that riders who do not use helmets hurt only themselves. However, poor brakes on a motorcycle can lead to injury of others. Since many other people could be affected, laws about brakes may be in the best interests of society.

■ **Can consumers use the market to obtain protection?** In many cases, the market system will automatically make sure that products and services are safe. If producers do not make safe goods, they will lose customers. But not all producers lose the same number of customers if their product is poor. Producers with little competition don't have to worry as much about quality because consumers may not be able to buy a product that is any better. Also, producers who make items meant to last a long time, such as refrigerators or new roofs, may not worry if some customers don't come back 15 or 20 years later to buy from them again. Therefore, consumer protection laws make more sense in those cases when there is little competition or business doesn't care about repeat customers.

> More than 100 chemicals in bug killers may cause cancer or brain damage to people. The Environmental Protection Agency (EPA) requires bug-killer makers to identify dangerous chemicals on the products' labels. Chemical companies object. Do these companies want to hide the dangers of their products from consumers? No. They want to hide the formulas of their products from their competitors.

√check your understanding √ √ √ √ √ √

1. Give two arguments in favor of consumer protection laws.
2. Give two arguments against consumer protection laws.
3. What are three ways to judge a consumer law?

SUMMARIZING
the chapter

When the market fails to provide essential goods and services, government may be asked to step in. Government in our economy plays the roles of provider and protector.

Government provides some goods and services because business cannot sell them at a profit. Public goods, such as national defense and lighthouses, are examples.

Businesses and citizens pay for the goods and services government provides through their taxes. Tax money collected at the federal, state, and local levels pays for such services as national defense, courts, education, parks, and roads. Some money collected at one level is used to help other levels of government provide these services.

Another major role of government is to protect members of society. Government does this by providing police and by passing laws and regulations. Government laws help business, encourage competition, protect natural resources, help workers, and protect consumers.

Some people feel that government should not protect the consumer. They feel that competition makes sure that consumers get the best products possible. Other people feel that government protection is needed if consumers don't have enough information to shop wisely or if they don't have a large choice.

Many consumer protection laws have both costs and benefits. The informed citizen must weigh the costs and benefits when judging government's role in protecting the consumer.

·C·H·A·P·T·E·R· A ·C·T·I·V·I·T·I·E·S·

BUILDING CONSUMER VOCABULARY

Number your paper from 1 to 7. Then write the term that best matches each numbered definition.

antitrust laws
civil rights laws
non-exclusion
patent and copyright laws

pollution
public goods
shared consumption

1. Adding something harmful to the land, water, or air
2. Laws that prevent a person or company from making or selling a product that belongs to another person or company
3. Goods and services that can only be provided by government
4. Laws that prevent the formation of monopolies and set up rules for fair competition
5. Laws that protect people from unfair treatment because of race, religion, sex, or age
6. A characteristic of a good or service that people can use it whether they pay for it or not
7. A characteristic of a good or service that it can be used by more than one person at the same time

1. Why do you think the federal government, and not private industry, engages in space research? Is space research a pure public good? Explain.
2. Which of the following goods and services have the characteristics of shared consumption, non-exclusion, or both?
   a. A hamburger
   b. A rock concert
   c. Street lights
   d. Traffic signs
   e. A sports stadium
   f. Police protection of a town
   g. A library
3. Where does the money come from that pays for services provided by government?
4. How do laws that encourage competition help consumers?
5. Who benefits from laws that protect the environment?
6. You are working in a factory that makes computer chips. You notice that chemicals used to make those chips are not stored safely, putting workers in danger. The company will do nothing to fix the problem. What government agency can you call for help?
7. Name three ways that government regulation helps business. Name three regulations that limit business freedom.

BUILDING
CONSUMER
MATH SKILLS

The following table is taken from information provided by the United States Census Bureau. Look at the table and then answer the questions that follow.

State and Local Government Spending in the United States

Type of Expenditure	Amount ($ billions)	Percentage of Total
Education	$ 127.7	?
Highways	31.8	?
Hospitals	16.7	?
Public Welfare	69.0	?
Natural Resources	6.5	?
Health	10.7	?
Other	34.6	?
TOTAL	$?	

1. Calculate the total amount of expenditures.
2. Calculate what percentage of the total amount is taken up by each type of expenditure.
3. What do state and local governments spend the most money on? What are three examples of state and local government spending in this area?

APPLYING CONSUMER SKILLS

Many people have been hurt riding three-wheeled motorcycles called all-terrain vehicles (ATVs). Consumer experts say the ATVs are unsafe because they tip over easily. When they tip over, they can kill the people riding them. Manufacturers say the ATVs only tip over if they are not driven properly. Manufacturers say they should not be responsible if the ATV is not used the way it is meant to be.

1. The federal government has banned these ATVs. Do you think this is a good consumer law? Why or why not?
2. Suppose government had passed a law preventing ATV manufacturers from selling ATVs to anyone under the age of 18. Do you think this would be a good consumer law? Why or why not? Whom would this law help? Whom would it hurt?
3. Suppose government had passed a law requiring manufacturers to put a label on each ATV warning that it is dangerous. Do you think this would be a good law? Why or why not?

GETTING INVOLVED IN YOUR COMMUNITY

Interview a member of your town or city government. Ask that person to identify the major goods and services provided by your local government.

1. Which goods and services have the characteristic of non-exclusion only?
2. Which ones have the characteristic of shared consumption only?
3. Which ones have both characteristics?
4. Does your town or city provide any goods and services that have neither characteristic? If so, which ones are these?

As an informed voter, Melissa wants to gather as much information as she can about issues she'll vote on. She has just read the following editorial on one such issue.

"There are many reasons to vote for—and against—raising the minimum wage. Those who say the minimum wage should be raised point out that many workers depend on minimum wage incomes to support themselves and their families. Workers who earn a minimum wage live below the poverty level. They cannot afford safe housing, or nutritious food, or sufficient clothing for themselves and their families. Social critics say these workers are being exploited by 'fat cat' business owners who are content to pay workers starvation wages.

"Those who oppose raising the minimum wage say the picture isn't so grim. They point out that 59 percent of the minimum wage work force are under age 25. A third of minimum wage workers are teenagers who live at home with parents. Statistics verify that 66 percent of the people who have a minimum wage job live with a relative who also has a job.

"Those against raising the minimum wage also argue that raising the minimum will increase unemployment. They say employers will look for ways to replace workers with machines. They also believe that an increase in wages will increase inflation. They say that if business has to pay more for production, the costs will be passed along to consumers in the form of higher prices. Opponents say these arguments are hogwash—that previous increases haven't had these effects."

Answer the following questions on a separate sheet of paper. Use complete sentences.

1. What is implied in the statement ". . . 66 percent of the people who have a minimum wage job live with a relative who also has a job"? Do you agree with what is implied? Why or why not?

2. Is the statement "59 percent of the people of the minimum wage work force are under age 25" a relevant argument? Why or why not?

3. What additional information would you want to know that you aren't given in this editorial?

4. What are some factors that would influence how different people would vote on this issue?

5. How would you vote on the issue after reading the editorial? Why?

CRITICAL THINKING

THINKING ABOUT:

Gathering the Facts

THE CONSUMER IN THE MARKETPLACE

SHOPPING WISELY

Consumers in the United States spend more than $2½ trillion on goods and services each year. With that kind of financial muscle, consumers can make businesses listen. As a consumer, you should use your buying power wisely. How can you become a wise shopper? What are the skills that turn a consumer into a smart shopper?

◆ When is comparison shopping a good idea?

◆ How can consumers compare the price and quality of goods and services?

◆ When is the best time to shop?

◆ Where is the best place to shop?

115

Do you buy the first thing you see? Or do you go from store to store looking for just the right item at just the right price? If you gather information about product prices and quality, you are **comparison shopping**. Comparison shopping takes time. Sometimes it's the best way to shop, but not always. In the following case study, Cindy and Pat Murray demonstrate the costs and benefits of comparison shopping.

CASE STUDY

When does it pay to compare?

Cindy Murray and her twin brother, Pat, each received $500 from their Uncle Fred as a birthday present. Cindy wants to buy Pat a record for his birthday. She also wants to buy a stereo for herself. By strange coincidence, Pat has the same plans.

On his way to work, Pat dropped into a convenient record store and bought Cindy's favorite album. He had seen a stereo advertised by Super Saver Sound Systems in the newspaper for $499.99. It was a brand he had heard was good, so he called the store and ordered it. His shopping took less than an hour.

Cindy shopped more carefully. She called six record shops to price Pat's favorite record. She found she could save $1.50 if she bought it at the Good Sound Record Emporium. She took the bus there and purchased the album. The bus ride cost her 80 cents each way.

She was even more thorough in her shopping for the stereo system. She went to the library and checked the quality ratings of the various stereo components—receivers, turntables, and speakers—in a consumer magazine. She found that she could save money if she bought the components separately. Twenty phone calls and two days later, she assembled the best system she could for $500. She had a better system than her brother got for the same money.

THE COSTS OF COMPARISON SHOPPING

By comparison shopping, Cindy gathered information about product prices and quality. Often such information is needed to make wise buying decisions. But there are costs involved in searching for information—time and money. These costs of obtaining knowledge about prices and quality are called **information costs**. In deciding whether to compare products, you must weigh the benefits of the information you gather against the information costs. For example, Cindy saved $1.50 on the album. Was that worth the $1.60 she spent in bus fare? What else could she have done with the time spent searching for the album?

Because time is also valuable, it is not a good idea to comparison shop for every item you buy—just the expensive ones.

Do some comparison shopping when you buy services, as well as goods. For example, one employment agency may charge you 10 percent of your first year's salary for finding you a job. Another agency may charge you a month's salary—a better deal.

Cindy spent the same amount of money on her stereo as Pat did. But her stereo is of higher quality. How should she measure this additional quality? She has to determine how much her stereo would have cost if she hadn't taken the time to buy the components separately. If, for example, the complete system would have cost $700 had she bought it at a single store, she saved $200.

In general, comparison shopping makes the most sense when you are shopping for expensive items, such as cars, large TVs, and long vacations. In these cases, there are often very large differences in price or quality from one product to another. The time spent is worthwhile because of the amount of money you can save, or the amount of extra quality you can get, if you make the best choice. Remember, though, that the full price of a product includes both the dollar cost and the information cost.

✓ check your understanding ✓ ✓ ✓ ✓ ✓ ✓

1. **What is the benefit of comparison shopping?**
2. **What is the cost of comparison shopping?**
3. **For what types of items does the benefit of comparison shopping outweigh the cost?**

PREPARING TO SHOP

To get the best value for your money, you need the right tools for shopping. These tools include doing the right research, buying at the right time, recognizing the right price, selecting the right quality, and shopping in the right place.

The Right Research

Suppose you want to gather information about a product. How do you begin? You can ask your friends and family members if they have bought the same product. But the people you know may not have bought the product you want. As you learned in Chapter 6, advertising in newspapers and magazines, on the radio, and on television can let you know about products and services. But advertisements show a product's best side. To get more information, you can do what Cindy did when she bought her stereo. You can do some research by reading consumer guides and magazines. Then you will be getting information from experts.

The best-known consumer magazine is *Consumer Reports*. It is published by Consumers Union, a non-profit organization. Each month, *Consumer Reports* publishes the results of tests done on a wide variety of products, from can openers to cars. Each year, the results are summarized in a book, called the *Buying Guide Issue*. Consumers Union accepts no advertising. Ratings are based on a product's operation, design, and construction, not on personal taste or advertisers' influence.

Other publications also provide consumer information, but they accept advertising as well. These include *Changing Times*, *Consumers' Research*, and *Money*.

When trying to gather product information, check with your local library. You can usually check out copies of magazines such as these.

The Right Time

You know that prices are set by supply and demand. If you buy when supply is high or demand is low, you can save money. For example, prices for many items are reduced after Christmas because demand is low. Many fresh fruits and vegetables are less expensive in summer because they are in greater supply. If you wait to buy camping equipment in August, you may not be able to find any to choose from. Try not to buy things you need at the last minute so that you can shop when selections are large or when goods are on sale.

The Right Price

The right price is obviously the lowest price. To many consumers, the words *sale*, *rebate*, and *coupon* automatically mean the lowest price. The wise shopper knows when to pay attention to those words and when to ignore them.

Sales "BIG SALE! 50 percent off!" Most consumers love sales. Some consumers have been known to buy things on sale they didn't need just to get a low price. And some sales do offer the consumer a good price. **Promotional sales**, for example, are sales for new items or items just coming into season. Sales of winter coats held in the fall are an example. Stores use promotional sales to compete against other shops by offering lower prices. **Clearance sales** use low prices to get rid of products that are not in great demand. A sale on winter coats held in March is an example of this type of sale. Sometimes a store will use loss leaders to help sell other products not on sale. **Loss leaders** are popular items priced so low that the seller makes little or no profit on their sale. They really are bargains. Stores offer them because once customers are in the store to buy the loss leader, they often buy other items.

Not all sales offer products at the lowest price available, however. Some retailers post a "suggested retail price" and a "sale price" or "our price," which is considerably lower. But the suggested retail price is only the price the manufacturer recommends. Few retailers may actually sell the product at that price. Also beware of tags that say "Others charge $X. We charge $Y." How do you know what "others" charge? Only by comparing prices at several stores will you know if the so-called sale price is a bargain.

In recent years, many retailers have increased their **markup**, the percentage they raise the price of an item over its wholesale price. By increasing the markup, they can then increase the percentage they take off the price during a sale and still earn a profit. The tag reads "30 percent off!" or even "50 percent off!" but the price may be the same as the regular price in another shop. Do not buy items only because they are on sale. Check the prices in other places to see if the sale price really is lower.

Rebates "Send in three labels of Grow Grain Cereal and get back 35 cents!" A **rebate** is a refund of part of a product's price. Rebates are popular on many products, ranging from food to toasters to cars.

Rebates can save you money. But many are difficult to get. Many rebates involve detailed instructions. Often, you must send in a **proof-of-purchase label**, generally some part of the box or container the item comes in. For food items, you often can't get the proof-of-purchase label until you have finished the product. By that time, you could easily forget about the rebate. Manufacturers expect that only a small number of people will take the time to follow the instructions and send in for a rebate. Don't count the rebate into the price of an item unless you understand the terms of the offer and are willing to take the time to collect on it.

Coupons A cents-off coupon states that if you buy the product you will receive some money back (the amount listed on the coupon, usually less than $1) at the cash register in the store. Coupons

Remember! When shopping for bargains, not all sales offer the lowest available prices.

Rebates are not a new idea! Henry Ford, founder of the Ford Motor Company, was the first automaker to offer a rebate on a new car. In 1915, after selling more cars than he expected to, he gave back $50 to anyone who purchased a Model T. That was a sizeable rebate considering that the car only cost about $450 at that time.

▶ ▶ ▶ ▶ ▶ ▶

▶ ▶ ▶ **Taking the time to make a shopping list and to use manufacturers' coupons for items you ordinarily buy are ways you can stretch your food dollars.**

▶ ▶ ▶ ▶ ▶ ▶

New grocery and household items sometimes have *introductory offer* printed on their labels. The idea is that the maker will sell a new item to you at a low price to introduce you to the product. By law, the introductory offer cannot last longer than six months. Then the price must go up. Otherwise, the labeling is considered to be misleading.

are often found in newspapers. Supermarkets also issue coupons. The coupons are generally good for a limited period of time, ranging from a week to as much as a year.

Why don't manufacturers just lower the regular price or put the product on sale? By issuing coupons, a manufacturer or supermarket can encourage you to buy a particular item at a particular time. In addition, coupons are a way to offer lower prices only to some people—to those who are willing to take the time to collect and use the coupons. Some people reduce their food bills by a large amount using coupons. But they have to spend the time to gather the coupons. And they have to buy the items listed on the coupons. Wise shoppers do not buy things they don't need just to get a low price. Getting 35 cents off an item you will never use is no bargain. And, even after the 35 cents is taken off the price, another product could still be cheaper.

The Right Quality

In Chapter 6, you learned that consumers are sometimes willing to pay a higher price for higher quality. How do you judge the quality of a product? One way is to read about the products in consumer magazines, such as *Consumer Reports*. Another way is to compare brands. A **brand** is the name a manufacturer gives a product or a line of products. Many manufacturers hope consumers will associate the brand name with a quality product and look for that brand again and again on other products. While some brand name products are of high quality, others are not. For example, many firms selling designer brand clothing just buy the rights to use the designer's name. In other cases, television or movie celebrities sell the right to use their names to manufacturers. Experts advise consumers to buy what they like and what looks good on them. A designer brand is not necessarily a sign of good quality.

Sometimes, you don't need to buy the highest quality product available. If you are just learning to play tennis, for example, you probably don't want to buy a $400 graphite racket. If you decide later that you really don't like the sport and don't want to play very often, you will have wasted a large amount of money. When considering quality, think about how you are going to use the product, and how often. Don't buy more quality than you will use.

Labels A wise shopper can find out about the quality of many products by reading the labels attached to the items. Furniture labels, for example, give information about construction. The label illustrated on page 122 shows you the kind of information you can find on a furniture label.

Some business organizations rate products for quality, and also for safety. The chart below shows some of the labels these organizations put on products that meet their standards.

Business Rates Its Products

The Seal	Where it is Found	What it Means
American Gas Association	On gas accessories or appliances such as stoves, heaters, clothes dryers.	Products certified by the AGA must conform to the standards of the American National Standards Institute for safety and design.
Underwriters Laboratories, Inc.	On appliances, equipment, and materials that could be hazardous and/or products used to detect or extinguish fires	Products have passed original laboratory tests and periodic factory tests and examinations, in accordance with UL Standards for Safety.
Good Housekeeping Seal	On products advertised in *Good Housekeeping Magazine*	This is a limited warranty, *not* a seal of approval. Products proven defective will be replaced or money refunded by *Good Housekeeping Magazine.*

How do these seals help you judge the safety and quality of products? What else can you do to check on a product's quality?

Information about the long-term cost of operating major appliances (like dryers, washing machines, refrigerators, water heaters, and furnaces) is displayed on yellow labels, such as the one shown below. These labels are required by federal law. They show the estimated yearly cost to operate the appliance.

The tag below tells you how much it costs to use a washing machine for one year. Are its operating costs less with a gas water heater or with an electric one?

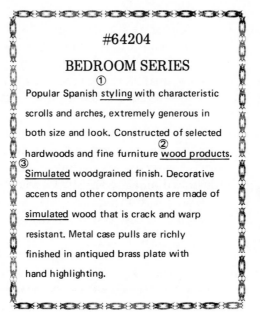

#64204

BEDROOM SERIES

①

Popular Spanish styling with characteristic scrolls and arches, extremely generous in both size and look. Constructed of selected hardwoods and fine furniture wood products. ②

③

Simulated woodgrained finish. Decorative accents and other components are made of simulated wood that is crack and warp resistant. Metal case pulls are richly finished in antiqued brass plate with hand highlighting.

Manufacturers must disclose the construction of their furniture on labels like the one on the left. The words "Spanish styling" (1) tell that this bedroom suite is not manufactured in Spain. "Wood products" (2) are not natural wood, but particleboard or fiberboard. Also, the wood has a "simulated" wood finish (3).

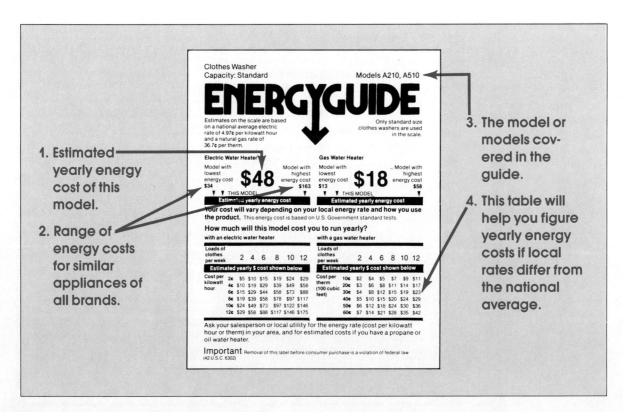

1. Estimated yearly energy cost of this model.

2. Range of energy costs for similar appliances of all brands.

3. The model or models covered in the guide.

4. This table will help you figure yearly energy costs if local rates differ from the national average.

Warranties You may want to judge the quality of a product by its warranty. A **warranty** is the manufacturer's or seller's promise that a product is of a certain quality or will perform in a certain manner. An **express warranty** is one that promises certain things to the buyer in writing. There are two types of express warranty: full or limited. The Magnuson-Moss Warranty Act requires that all written warranties be identified as one or the other. The Act also requires that the terms of both types of express warranty be fully stated on the item.

A full warranty is impressive. Although it can be limited to a certain time period, it virtually guarantees that a defective product will be repaired or replaced without charge and without unreasonable demands made on the consumer. The product must be replaced if it can't be fixed after a reasonable number of tries. Be sure, however, when looking at a full warranty that it covers the entire product and not just a part of the product.

A limited warranty is one that puts restrictions on the warranty. It generally guarantees only part of a product under certain circumstances or only part of the cost of repairing a product. Be sure to read a limited warranty carefully. While many limited warranties provide excellent guarantees, a full warranty is really your best protection.

State laws give you certain rights when you buy any product. Even if you don't get an express warranty with a product, you often have an **implied warranty**, or unwritten warranty. Most state courts have ruled that a product should do what a "reasonable person" would expect it to do. This expectation represents an implied warranty.

> Suppose you buy a compact disc player with a full warranty. You use the player to prop open your window. It rains and damages the machine. Can you claim a refund under the warranty? No. The courts say if you abuse the item or use it for a purpose other than for what it was intended, you're out of luck.

✓check your understanding ✓ ✓ ✓ ✓ ✓ ✓

1. Why is *Consumer Reports* a useful shopping tool?
2. Describe two indications that a sale may not really offer the lowest price.
3. What is a rebate? Why do you have to be careful about including the rebate when determining the price of an item?
4. Why do manufacturers offer cents-off coupons?
5. What is the difference between a limited warranty and a full warranty?

The Right Place

In our market economy, many shopping places are available to meet the changing tastes and demands of consumers. Each place provides a different mixture of product quality, prices, and convenience. We will examine the advantages and disadvantages of the most common types of stores.

Supermarkets The name suggests what they are: "super" big markets, usually offering a wide variety of food and household products. Supermarkets are able to sell food products at a lower price than other types of food stores because they buy their products in large amounts, which results in a low cost per item. Also, because they sell so much, they can keep their markups low. Although they earn a small profit on each item, they still earn enough total profit to stay in business.

Convenience stores What supermarkets often do not provide, convenience stores do. As their name implies, they can be more convenient for the consumer. Many are located in or very near residential neighborhoods. They generally stay open longer hours than supermarkets do. Some are open 24 hours a day, including holidays. However, they are more expensive than supermarkets and carry fewer products.

Full-service stores More commonly known as department stores, full-service stores carry many different types of goods, which may include clothing, furniture, automotive supplies, sports equipment, and appliances. Full-service stores often provide a great number of services, such as charge accounts, repairs, and home delivery. Many full-service stores pride themselves on standing behind the goods they sell, making it easy to return items if you are not completely satisfied.

Specialty stores A shop that sells a single type of product, such as women's clothes, children's clothes, shoes, sporting goods, or books, is called a specialty store. Specialty stores often carry only certain brands.

Specialty stores are the fastest growing segment of retailing. Many department stores now try to imitate them by having specialty departments.

A new trend in specialty stores is the category killer. A **category killer** is a store that not only offers a single category of product but offers just about every item in that category you could buy. Large toy shops, offering almost every toy on the market, are an example of a category killer. The idea is that shoppers will always find what they want in this store and won't need to go anywhere else.

Discount stores Similar to full-service stores in the variety of items they sell, discount stores offer lower prices and often fewer services. Some discount stores sell only inexpensive, lower quality goods. Most, however, carry products that display a wide range of quality. Discount stores can offer lower prices than full-service stores because they often buy in large quantities, as supermarkets do. They also generally have fewer sales clerks.

To offer the variety that full-service stores carry, they have to be pretty big. How big can they get? Macy's department store in New York City contains over 2,200,000 square feet of shopping floor space. That's as much space as 48 football fields.

There are more shopping malls in the United States than movie theaters or school districts. Americans spend more time in malls than any other place except their homes, jobs, and schools. In fact, we make about 7 billion trips to shopping malls every year.

In some areas of the country, a new type of super store is being built. It's a huge mall without walls, and it's called a hypermarket.

Although off-pricing is a hot trend, it actually started in 1909 with Filene's Basement in Boston. In 1921, Frieda Loehmann opened a high-fashion off-price store in New York. Today, both Filene's Basement and Loehmann's are chains. Other big off-price chains include Marshall's, T.J. Maxx, Syms, Burlington Coat Factory, and Clothestime.

Off-price stores A major trend in retailing is the off-price store. Off-price stores differ from discount stores in that they specialize in certain types of products, mainly clothing. They sell at lower prices than department and specialty stores because they purchase manufacturers' canceled orders, out-of-season goods, overruns (extra stock), and items with small flaws in them (called factory rejects or irregulars). They also offer few services. If you shop at an off-price store, you may not be able to buy fashions in season, and you may not be allowed to return goods.

Factory outlets Off-price stores run by manufacturers are called factory outlets. Like other off-price stores, they sell overruns and factory rejects at low prices. But they sell only the products of a single manufacturer. At first, most outlet stores were located at the manufacturer's factory. Today, factory outlets can be found in many locations far from the factory, such as shopping malls. In recent years, shopping districts have sprung up that are composed almost entirely of factory outlets.

Crooked Catalogues

Although most catalogue companies are honest, the industry has its share of crooks. Here are some ways to avoid being fooled.

- Make sure you are ordering what you think you are ordering. Read the catalogue carefully, and look for the small print. If you order from a newspaper or magazine advertisement, keep the ad so that you have evidence of any promises made in it. Items on TV can seem larger and more impressive than they really are. If you're ordering a brand name, compare the item when it comes with one in a store to see if you got what you ordered.
- Don't send cash. Pay by check, money order, or credit card so that you have proof of payment.
- Don't order from companies that have only a post office box and no street address. Many mail-order companies use post office boxes to speed up orders. But the company should also list its address. Without an address, you will find it difficult to make complaints to the company or to a consumer protection agency if you have problems. Also, a company that has only a telephone number and no address may be trying to get around federal mail fraud laws. No address may mean there is no company.
- If you pay by credit card, order by mail, not over the phone. If you give out your credit card number over the phone, you could be charged for items you did not order.
- Add in the shipping and handling charges before you order. A product that appears to be a bargain may not be such a good deal when all the charges are included. COD charges can be particularly high.
- Check the company's return policy. You should know your rights before you have a problem.
- Be suspicious of great-sounding items at very low prices. If the deal sounds too good to be true, it probably is.

Consumers buy over $40 billion a year from television home shopping networks. That amounts to more than $150 per person. Jewelry and small appliances are the most popular items sold on TV.

Mail-order companies Mail-order companies sell products through catalogues. Catalogues appeal to busy consumers who don't have the time to shop, or dislike shopping, at malls and downtown stores. The mail-order business is another fast-growing area of retailing. Many mail-order companies specialize in a single type of product, often offering high-quality items. Many times, consumers can find high-quality items at lower prices in catalogues because mail-order companies have fewer expenses than retail stores. They pay less in rent and don't employ as many salespeople. Don't assume, however, that catalogues offer the lowest prices.

The latest trend in mail-order sales is the electronic catalogue or TV shopping. Entire television stations specialize in selling items

Most state laws say you don't have to pay for items that are mailed to you if you didn't order them. If you get greeting cards or address stickers in the mail, they're yours to keep. The sender may try to pressure you into paying for them. However, by law, you owe nothing. In fact, you can charge the sender storage fees if the sender demands the goods be sent back.

shown on TV. Viewers order these goods by telephone or through the mail.

The Federal Trade Commission (FTC) has a mail-order rule that provides you with certain rights when you shop from a catalogue. The rule covers most mail-order companies. Any company that ships to more than one state is covered.

According to this rule, a mail-order company must ship your order within 30 days of receiving a complete order form or it must notify you that the order will take longer to fill. The notice must have a new shipping date and give you a chance to cancel your order. The notice must contain a postage-paid, self-addressed envelope for your reply. However, if you don't reply, the company is allowed to assume that you still want the product.

If you cancel your order, you should receive a refund within seven business days. If you paid by credit card, the refund should be deducted from your next credit card bill.

This FTC mail-order rule does not apply to credit card orders placed by phone, to companies that develop film, to companies that sell seeds and plants, to magazine subscriptions, or to COD orders (orders that you pay for when the item is delivered to you).

✓ check your understanding ✓ ✓ ✓ ✓ ✓ ✓

1. **What are two advantages of buying food at a supermarket rather than at a convenience store?**
2. **How do specialty stores differ from department stores?**
3. **What is the difference between a discount store and an off-price store? between an off-price store and a factory outlet?**
4. **Why can catalogues offer low prices?**

S UMMARIZING
the chapter

Comparison shopping pays when the benefits of comparing products outweigh the information costs. Comparison shopping is most beneficial when you are shopping for expensive items. In those cases, there are often very large differences in price or quality from one product to another.

To shop wisely, you should know where to go to get information about products. Consumer publications, such as *Consumer Reports*, are often good sources of information. You should also know when to shop. Shop at times when demand is low or supply is high. When considering sales, coupons, or rebates, compare prices from store to store. Even after the price has been reduced, an item could cost more than a similar product at another store. When searching for quality, look at a product's label and warranty. A full warranty is better than a limited warranty. Even if a product does not have an express warranty, the laws of most states grant you an implied warranty. The implied warranty holds that products should do what a reasonable person would expect them to do.

When deciding where to shop, remember that food in convenience stores costs more than food in supermarkets. Items in full-service and specialty stores generally cost more than products in discount stores, off-price stores, factory outlets, and catalogues. However, full-service and specialty stores often provide better service, and convenience stores may be open when supermarkets are not.

·C·H·A·P·T·E·R· A ·C·T·I·V·I·T·I·E·S·

BUILDING CONSUMER VOCABULARY

Number your paper from 1 to 13. Then write the term that best matches each numbered definition.

brand
category killer
clearance sale
comparison shopping
express warranty
implied warranty
information costs

loss leader
markup
promotional sale
proof-of-purchase label
rebate
warranty

1. The difference between the wholesale cost and the price of a product
2. A product sold very close to the wholesale cost to get people to come to a store
3. Gathering information about product prices and quality
4. A return to the consumer of part of the price of a product
5. A name given to a product or a line of products, which the manufacturer hopes consumers will associate with high quality
6. A specialty store that carries practically every product that exists of a certain type
7. A written warranty
8. An unwritten warranty
9. A sale to encourage consumers to buy items in low demand
10. A sale on new items or on items in season to compete with other stores on the basis of price

11. A promise made by a seller that a product is of a certain quality or will perform in a certain manner
12. Time and money spent searching for information about products
13. Something a manufacturer may require you to send in to qualify for a rebate

BUILDING CONSUMER UNDERSTANDING

1. Suppose you want to buy the following items: a new car, an apple, an air conditioner, a diamond engagement ring, a pencil. For which ones should you comparison shop?
2. How can advertising be of help in shopping?
3. Why is February 15 a good time to buy Valentine cards?
4. Why do you need to be careful when buying a brand-name product?
5. What is the difference between an implied warranty and an express warranty?
6. What is the Magnuson-Moss Warranty Act? How does it protect the consumer?
7. How do labels help you to judge a product's quality?
8. What are some of the advantages and disadvantages of shopping by mail?

BUILDING CONSUMER MATH SKILLS

1. You are going to buy a food processor. Brand A regularly costs $60, and the company is offering a $10 rebate. Brand B regularly costs $59 and the store is offering it on sale for 10 percent off the regular price. You must pay a 5 percent sales tax on either item. Which food processor is cheaper? What is the final price of each one?
2. You are at a sale where all clothing is 15 percent off the regular price. You see a pair of designer jeans regularly priced at $48. What is the sale price?

APPLYING CONSUMER SKILLS

1. Write an ad that will convince consumers to shop at the Super Suits specialty store. Write another ad convincing consumers that the off-price store Suits-for-Less is the best place to shop.
2. You ordered a sweatshirt from a mail-order company sometime ago and have not received it. What should happen if you don't receive the sweatshirt within 30 days?

GETTING INVOLVED IN YOUR COMMUNITY

Visit a shopping mall, shopping center, or group of at least five stores near you. Prepare a list of all of the stores included in the group. Categorize the stores by type—specialty store, department store, supermarket, and so on. Which type of store occurs most often? Which types of stores are not included?

ETHICS IN THE MARKETPLACE

Buying and selling involves trust. What happens if the trust breaks down, if buyer and seller try to cheat each other? Would you recognize a fraud in the marketplace? How does the consumer cheat? What can be done to help keep the marketplace free of fraud and theft?

- What are the common frauds used on consumers?

- What can consumers do to protect themselves from fraud?

- How do dishonest consumers add to the price of goods and services for everyone?

Most businesses are honest and responsible, and so are most consumers. However, businesses lose billions of dollars every year to shoplifters and other dishonest people. And consumers lose billions—sometimes without even knowing it—to crooked dealers, dishonest salespeople, and other "con artists." The marketplace is so big that consumers must be careful to protect themselves. Wise consumers know what to watch out for.

Con artists don't have to lie to mislead you. An ad promises a "complete sewing machine" for an amazingly low price. The "complete sewing machine" turns out to be a package of needles. The needles and the buyer's fingers form the sewing machine.

BUSINESS FRAUD

Getting money or other gains through some kind of deception is known as **fraud**. Taking money without delivering a promised good or service is a form of fraud. Knowingly selling a defective product is another type of fraud. Selling a product by giving false information about it is a third form of fraud.

How Frauds Work

The case studies that follow show how four types of fraud work. What are the techniques used in each case? Why are the victims so easily cheated? How can you avoid becoming a victim yourself?

CASE STUDY

In her mail, Edna McKenna received this note signed by an old friend.

> Hi Edna!
>
> In a few days, a friend of mine, Hal Smith, will call you for an appointment. He wants to tell you about a fabulous money-making plan. You can earn hundreds of dollars by working in your own home. I highly recommend this profitable idea.
>
> Sincerely,
> *Barb Williams*

When Mr. Smith phoned and said he was Barb Williams' friend, Edna set up an appointment with him. The next day, Mr. Smith arrived carrying a vacuum cleaner. He began to tell Edna about the fine points of the machine.

"But I don't need a vacuum cleaner," Edna said. "My old one works fine."

"I'm not here to sell you a vacuum cleaner," Mr. Smith said. "I just want to show you how good it is so you can sell it. You see, for every vacuum cleaner you sell, we'll pay you $75. We'll even pay you $25 for every name of a prospective customer you give us. They would be people you can't contact yourself. Now, you must buy this model cleaner to demonstrate it to your neighbors. It sells for $450. But with only six sales or 18 names, you'll have paid for it. After that, you'll be making pure profit. How can you go wrong?"

"Can't I just borrow the machine?" Edna asked.

"Well, I'd like to do that for you because I know you'll be a great salesperson. But it's against company rules. You have to invest some money to make some money. However, I can let you have it on a one-month trial. If you don't make big profits, return it for a full refund. Just sign this receipt, and you're in business."

Edna signed the paper—which was really a contract to buy the vacuum cleaner.

During the next two weeks, Edna had no luck selling the machine. She also received no money for sending the company the names of 20 prospective customers. Two neighbors pointed out to her that the same vacuum cleaner sold in a downtown store for half the price. Another neighbor had signed up for the same program and tried to sell Edna a machine.

Three weeks later, a coupon book arrived in the mail. It said that Edna must pay a finance company $63.75 a month for the next eight months. When she complained to the finance company, she was told that the problem was hers, not theirs. They just wanted their money. She called the company whose name was on the contract she had signed. No one answered the phone. Edna, who had started out to make extra money, now owed $510 for a vacuum cleaner she didn't even need.

1. **Name two mistakes Edna made.**
2. **Do you think the salesperson intended to cheat Edna? Why or why not?**
3. **What do you think the salesperson is going to do with the 20 names Edna sent in?**

CASE STUDY

For two years, Carol and Bill Upshaw had wanted to replace their living room rug. It was wearing thin, and many of the spots could not be removed. But carpet prices were just too high. Then, in Sunday's paper, they saw the answer to their problem.

Fire Sale!
Our loss is your gain!
Carpets slashed to one-fourth their original prices.
Carpet two rooms and a hall for only $329.

They drove to the store and asked a salesclerk to show them the advertised carpets. When he did, their happiness turned to gloom. The carpets on sale were badly stained. The salesclerk explained that they had suffered water damage in the fire at the warehouse.

He hated to disappoint Carol and Bill since they had driven so far. So he would give them a good deal on another carpet. This carpet usually sold for $10.99 a square yard, but could be reduced to $9.99. Of course, installation was extra. Carol and Bill found a color they liked, but the carpet would cost them $880. That was too much.

The salesclerk would give them another break. He would sell them the carpet for only $50 down and $80 a month for a year. He would even have it installed the next day. They were sold. For the time being, they wouldn't worry about where they would get the money for the monthly payments.

1. **How much will Carol and Bill pay for the carpet?**
2. **Do you think they would have gone to the store if they had known they would have to pay more than $329 for their carpet? Explain.**

CASE STUDY

Jim Garrity answered a knock at the door. The caller introduced herself as Ms. McGraw, from Education Enrichment Enterprises. She wanted to talk to Jim about his children's education.

"We know you have handsome twin boys going into first grade," she said, "and we have selected you for our new advertising program. We'll pay you well for your help—not in cash but in merchandise. We'll give you this beautiful $800 set of encyclopedias in exchange for a letter from you about the educational benefits of the encyclopedias. We might also want to use a picture of the twins holding the encyclopedias."

Jim found this hard to believe. "You mean you'll give me this set of books just for a letter?"

"I want to be absolutely clear about it. We give you the car, so to speak, but not the gas and oil. When we give you the encyclopedia set, we expect you to keep it up, so your children will always have up-to-date information. We want you to buy yearbooks for the next 12 years. A yearbook is $25. And we'd like you to buy ten research coupons each year. They're just $5 each. When your children have a question, they just write it on a card and send it to our New York office. We have experts in every field, so we can answer every question."

"But that will cost me $75 a year."

"The encyclopedias are still free, and the extras cost just about 20 cents a day. Is that too much to help your children get a good education?"

Jim decided that the books would help his boys. He signed a contract, and Ms. McGraw left.

Later, Jim read the contract he had signed. Nowhere in it was there anything about "free" encyclopedias, yearbooks, or research coupons. There was a $1,500 price in the contract that came to $2,000 with the finance charges. Ms. McGraw's words were not binding; the signed contract was.

1. **How was Jim cheated?**
2. **How could he have avoided being cheated?**

CASE STUDY

Julie Cohn was enjoying a sunny fall day on her front porch. A truck stopped, and a man walked up. He said he was a furnace inspector for the city. He checked furnaces in schools, nursing homes, and hospitals. On weekends, he moonlighted by inspecting home furnaces. His fee was only $20. Winter was just around the corner, he observed, so it was a good time to have a furnace inspected.

Why not, Julie thought. She could certainly afford $20, and the furnace hadn't been inspected in years. If it needed to be repaired, it would be better to have it done now than in the winter months. If the furnace failed then, she and her family would be without heat.

The man spent half an hour checking the furnace. Then he asked Julie to come down to the basement. He told her to look into the furnace. "You see where that pipe is burned over there? That's the flue pipe. Instead of taking all the smoke and fumes up the flue, it's letting a lot loose. See that fan in back? When it turns on, the fumes go right into the house. These fumes are worse than raw gas because you can smell raw gas. This is carbon monoxide. It's like running your car exhaust into your house. I'm not saying this to scare you but to impress you. I don't sell furnaces, you know."

"But where can I get the furnace repaired?" Julie asked.

"You can look in the phone book, or I can recommend a company. But don't mention my name. I could get in trouble if the city knew I recommended any particular company."

Julie called the company he recommended. They replaced the furnace for $3,000. Julie felt safer. She also felt poorer.

1. **Do you think Julie really needed a new furnace?**
2. **Should she have believed the furnace man? Why or why not?**

The Most Common Frauds

The Federal Trade Commission investigates frauds throughout the country. Many of the thousands of schemes it investigates are varieties of the following four kinds of fraud.

Bait-and-switch advertising If a store advertises a product that it doesn't have or is so poor in quality that no one would want it, the store is using **bait-and-switch advertising**. Bait-and-switch advertising is the most common kind of fraud.

The advertised product, the "bait," is designed only to bring you into the store. When you say you don't want the product, a salesperson tries to "switch" you to a so-called quality product—one that costs you more money and brings the store more profit.

When you find you're being switched, it's time to say no. You should not trust any merchant who uses bait-and-switch advertising. Chances are good that something could be wrong with the "quality" product you end up buying. And chances are also good that the shop will not be very helpful if you have a complaint.

Referral selling In **referral selling**, a company representative asks a customer to give the company the names of friends and neighbors who may be prospective buyers. In return, the customer will get free merchandise and maybe even earn some money. But first, the customer has to buy a sample of the product.

Consumers who let themselves get involved in referral selling usually do not get their money back. Rather, they end up buying a product they don't really want. They may also annoy their friends, who may have to resist the sales efforts of the company as well. Don't let someone fool you into buying something you don't want. If you don't want it, chances are that no one else will either.

The free gimmick We all want something for nothing. A salesperson often gets a foot in the door by offering something free, the **free gimmick**.

Why will someone offer something for nothing? The answer is no one will. In the words of one economist, "There is no such thing as a free lunch." When a person offers you something for nothing, be on guard—at least if the something-for-nothing is more than a small sample. Con artists often appeal to the greed in us. Maybe we feel we can outsmart them, but we usually end up losing money.

The fear sell Someone who scares you into buying something you don't need is using the **fear sell**. "Chimney inspectors" warn of danger from loose bricks. "Auto mechanics" warn of blowouts due to worn tires. "Tree surgeons" predict that rotten trees will fall on our houses. "Pest exterminators" find dangerous bugs in our basements. Act now or else!

Mail fraud costs consumers over $100 million a year. These frauds are often aimed at the desperate. Some common frauds include miracle diet pills, cancer cures, and baldness cures.

The first step in selling is to get customers into the store. Offering something for nothing can do the trick.

Parental fear for the health and safety of their children makes this ad for a filter to remove impurities from drinking water an effective one.

When a merchant warns you of dangerous consequences, at least check the problem out with other merchants before signing a contract. The dishonest merchant hopes you will panic and sign right away.

✓check your understanding ✓ ✓ ✓ ✓ ✓ ✓

1. Each of the case studies on the previous pages is an example of one of the four major frauds. Match each case study with the type of fraud that was used.
2. Explain how each of the four major frauds works.
3. Why did the people fall for each of the frauds?

CONSUMER FRAUD

Merchants are not the only ones who use fraud. Some consumers also practice fraud. Their activities range from staying silent when undercharged to outright theft. One of the most costly examples of theft is **shoplifting**—stealing merchandise from stores. Another example of theft is taking small items from hotels and motels.

A survey in a Midwestern city found that one out of every 15 customers has shoplifted. And the Federal Bureau of Investigation (FBI) says that one out of every three teen-agers has stolen merchandise at least once. The amount of money lost by shoplifting is huge. One researcher estimates that shoplifting costs companies over $33 billion each year. Of course, these losses result in higher prices for everyone. Each consumer's share of the bill is about $150

Shoplifted items are paid for by all of us.

Door-to-Door Sales Protection

Suppose you are sitting in your home one day, and the doorbell rings. A salesperson is at the door. Before you know it, you've signed a contract to buy a freezer and a year's supply of food for $595. The next day, you realize that you will never be able to eat all of that food. You want to change your mind. Are you stuck? No.

The Federal Trade Commission has made a rule to help protect you if you sign a contract of $25 or more in your home. You have the right to cancel that contract within three business days. Furthermore, the salesperson must give you a notice of your right to cancel the contract.

During this "three-day cooling off period," you can contact the company, cancel the agreement, and get back any money you may have already paid. It's best to send the company a registered letter with your cancellation, so the post office will have a record that the letter was sent and received. The business cannot later claim that it did not receive the cancellation request.

Many hotels try to prevent thefts by using TV cameras to monitor the activities in their corridors.

a year, or over $550 per household. And the problem seems to be getting worse. Shoplifting losses are increasing at the rate of 20 percent a year.

Hotels and motels are particularly hurt by stealing. Each year, hotel guests walk off with over $500 million worth of ashtrays, towels, sheets, bedspreads, dishes, silverware, bibles, bedside lamps—even TV sets. And that loss must be made up by increasing the room rates for all guests.

In the interview and news item that follow, two people tell about various experiences they have had with dishonest consumers.

*O*ur biggest problem, of course, is shoplifting. We've had to hire helpers in the dressing rooms to check garments in and out. We use TV cameras and plastic tags on some items. Our losses are still too high.

We have other problems. By accepting credit cards, we increase our business. But we have to guard against phony or stolen credit cards. And speaking of credit, when we make a billing mistake that charges the customer too much, we always hear about it. But I can count on the fingers of one hand the number of people who reported that we gave them credit they didn't deserve. A New York department store tried an experiment. The store overcharged 20 customers 40 cents and undercharged another 20 customers the same amount. Eighteen of the overcharged customers spoke up. Only two of the undercharged consumers said anything.

Our formal-wear department has special problems. Some women buy a dress or gown on the Friday before a big dance and return it on Monday. They say they changed their minds. But often it's obvious that the dress was bought and worn just for the dance— and they have no intention of keeping it or of paying for it. And do they get mad if the salesclerk says the dress looks worn!

We honor all returns. It's our policy. Many times a product really is defective, and we wish the customer would tell us. Some customers never say anything. They just don't come back. If we hear the complaint, maybe we can do something about it.

JEAN WATMAN
Department Store Manager

Some store security systems signal if you leave before the cashier removes this magnetically coded tag.

Michael Lasky, a reporter writing in the *New York Times*, tells of some people who steal from hotels.

> Typical of amateur pilferers . . . are Mr. and Mrs. R. of Westchester. In their comfortable home they have a whole closet full of souvenirs they have picked up from every hotel or motel they have patronized. The item they cite as "the best thing we have gotten so far" is a bedspread embroidered with a large R—taken from a Ramada Inn. "When I saw it in the motel room," says Mrs. R., "I just knew I had to have it." She adds, "There's nothing wrong with taking little things from hotels. I think they expect you to take at least a towel. Anyway, if you have something marked with their crest, it's good publicity for them. After all, I show off these things to my friends."
>
> A Long Island woman . . . boasts that she has not been to a January white sale in years because of the sheets and towels she has collected from motels. "But believe me," she asserts, "I've paid for these things. The places I've stayed haven't lost anything, because they jack up their prices so."
>
> A Miami Beach hotel executive was invited to a housewarming party given by an affluent couple who had stayed at his hotel while were looking for their "dream house." Neither the host or hostess, he relates, were the slightest bit embarrassed when he noticed that most of their flatware, plates, and tablecloths used at the party bore the name of his hotel.

> ■ Advertising puffery is not considered a fraud. It is assumed that people know the difference between fact and hype. Claims like "tastes great" or "very stylish" are matters of opinion, not fact. The difference between puffery and fraud is that puffery makes no claims that can be proved false.

✓ check your understanding ✓ ✓ ✓ ✓ ✓ ✓

1. **How serious a problem is shoplifting?**
2. **Who pays for the losses caused by shoplifting and the efforts to control it?**
3. **In addition to shoplifting, how do consumers cheat businesses?**

*S*UMMARIZING
the chapter

Most businesses and consumers are honest. But there is some fraud and dishonesty in the marketplace. The most common types of fraud are bait-and-switch advertising, referral selling, the free gimmick, and the fear sell. In bait-and-switch advertising, merchants switch consumers from the advertised products to higher priced products. In referral selling, the consumer expects to make some extra money by selling a product, but usually ends up buying it instead. Consumers should not be tempted by the free gimmick because people rarely give away something for nothing. Before buying from a fear seller, a consumer should check the problem out with another merchant.

One of the most costly kinds of dishonesty businesses face is shoplifting. Businesses lose more than $30 billion to shoplifters each year. Other dishonest activities that people practice in stores and hotels include returning used merchandise and "souvenir" shopping. Only a small number of consumers are dishonest, but all consumers wind up paying.

CHAPTER CTIVITIES

Number your paper from 1 to 6. Then write the term that best matches each numbered definition.

bait-and-switch advertising   free gimmick
fear sell   referral selling
fraud   shoplifting

1. Advertising a product at a very low price that turns out to have something wrong with it, and then pushing another, higher priced product to the consumer
2. Pressuring a consumer into buying something by warning about dangerous consequences if the consumer doesn't buy it right away
3. Getting a person to buy a product by convincing the person to try to sell it
4. Getting money or other gains through some kind of deception
5. Offering what appears to be something for nothing
6. Stealing merchandise from a store

1. Why does a consumer have to be careful when a store uses bait-and-switch sales tactics?
2. How can you avoid being cheated by a referral selling scheme?
3. Imagine that a man from the Cozy Home Roof Repair Emporium comes to your home. He tells you that he has just noticed how bad your roof is as he was driving by. He figures it won't last the winter before it leaks and ruins all of your walls. He offers to repair your roof for $2,000. What steps can you take to find out if he is honest?
4. A shop advertises "Buy two shirts, get one free." Is this an example of the free gimmick? When might the offer be a good deal? When might it be a bad deal?
5. Why should you read all papers, including receipts, before you sign them?

6. Why should you as a consumer be concerned if businesses lose money through shoplifting?

7. What reasons do people give for stealing from hotels or motels? What answer would you give to such arguments?

BUILDING CONSUMER MATH SKILLS

Assume that, like Carol and Bill Upshaw, you need a new carpet. How many square feet should you be shopping for if your living room measures 21 by 18 feet; dining room, 15 by 12 feet; and hall, 3 by 18 feet?

Suppose you find a carpet you like that costs $12 per square yard, plus $3 per square yard for padding. How much will it cost to buy enough carpet and padding for all three rooms?

APPLYING CONSUMER SKILLS

1. Develop two advertisements using two of the four different business fraud techniques described in this chapter. In each ad, how did you try to convince customers to buy your product?

2. Suppose you were the owner of a record shop. What steps could you take to prevent shoplifting in your store? What effect may these steps have on your prices? on your customers? Why?

GETTING INVOLVED IN YOUR COMMUNITY

The four most common kinds of dishonest business practices have been described. Find out what other illegal practices some businesses undertake. Contact your local Better Business Bureau, state attorney general, or Federal Trade Commission office for information. Report your findings to the class.

CONSUMER RIGHTS AND RESPONSIBILITIES

Most businesses believe that "the customer is always right."
But not every business tries to keep the customer happy.
And even those businesses that try may not always succeed.
Many organizations and agencies stand ready to help if you
have a problem. Do you know what they are? Do you
know how to contact them?

◆ How can you complain effectively if you get a bad deal?

◆ What is the Better Business Bureau, and how does it help
consumers?

◆ What are some government agencies that can help
consumers?

◆ What are the advantages and disadvantages of
small-claims courts?

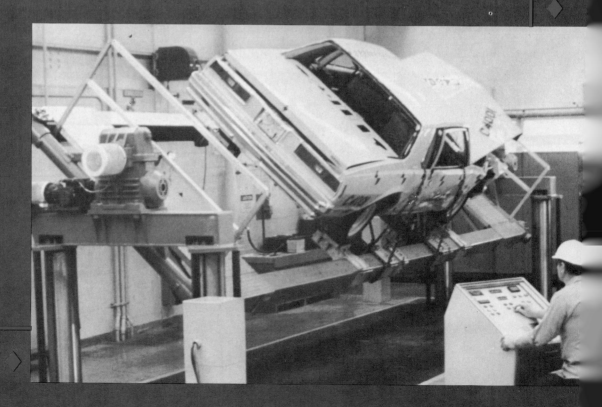

When you go into the marketplace as a consumer, you want as much know-how working for you as possible. Not only do you need to know what you are buying and with whom you are dealing, you also need to know where to go for help when necessary. An informed consumer is an effective one.

What can you do if you feel you've gotten a bad deal? Many consumers don't know. One survey revealed that over 60 percent of the consumers questioned felt they could do nothing. Many just blamed themselves. They chalked the matter up to experience or, worse, tried to forget all about it. Some felt that they were too small to fight a giant company. Others returned to the store to complain, got no help, and just gave up.

An intelligent, determined consumer does not have to give up. Honest mistakes do happen. Companies make billing mistakes. Manufacturers produce faulty goods. Clerks have bad days. The knowledgeable consumer tries to correct mistakes. The following case study shows an informed consumer in action.

CASE STUDY

Going to the source

Elaine Shultz bought a Sleepwell mattress from the DeLuxe Furniture Company. The mattress was delivered, and she took it by the handle to lift it onto her bed. The handle broke off and tore the mattress.

Elaine called the salesclerk at DeLuxe and demanded a new mattress. The clerk refused to help. He said that Elaine must have pulled too hard on the delicate fabric and caused the handle to break. Elaine was angry because she knew she was right and the mattress was probably defective. She decided to visit the store to discuss her problem in person.

When she asked for the salesclerk, she was told that he was out to lunch. She then insisted on seeing the manager. After she explained her problem to him, he asked to see her receipt. Elaine had expected that request. She had made photocopies of her receipt and the canceled check, which she showed to the manager. The manager said he would keep them and would send someone out to pick up the damaged mattress. He then apologized for the salesclerk's behavior. He said the clerk was new and was probably afraid of costing the store money.

A truck driver picked up the mattress, and a few days later the manager called Elaine. He said that the mattress had been manufactured with a defect. He offered to replace the mattress or to refund Elaine's money. Elaine could now choose the solution to her problem that would give her the most satisfaction.

If you have a complaint or wish to return an item to a store for a refund, the customer service desk is the place to begin.

HOW TO COMPLAIN EFFECTIVELY

When you have a problem with goods, services, or sellers, try to solve it at the lowest possible level. If you don't get help at that level, you can go further—all the way to the top. Here is a guide to effective consumer action when you have a complaint.

Some newspapers and television stations have consumer hotlines. These hotlines have no legal power, and they can respond to only a small number of the complaints they receive. But they can broadcast complaints to a large number of people. Sometimes they are able to embarrass a large company into settling with consumers in order to avoid bad publicity.

1. Start where you made the purchase. You may want to take the product with you. Be sure to bring copies of your sales receipt, warranty, canceled check or credit card receipt, and other important information. Be polite. People will not help you if they feel they are being attacked. If the salesclerk can't help you, don't get angry. A salesclerk may not have the authority to resolve the problem. Calmly ask to speak to someone who does have authority, such as the store manager or owner.

2. If no one at the store will help you, write to the president of the company that made the product. If the store that sold you the product is part of a chain, write to the president of the chain. Someone in the president's office will generally send the letter to the right department. A letter coming from the company president in the interoffice mail is usually given prompt attention. You can find the names and addresses of the presidents of large corporations in *Standard and Poor's Register of Corporations, Directors and Executives* or *Moody's Industrial Manual*. Many libraries carry these references.

3. A well-written letter improves your chances of getting results. A sample complaint letter is shown on page 145. Your letter should be neat and free from spelling and typographic errors. Keep the tone calm. State the facts clearly and completely, and they will speak for themselves:
   a. State the problem.
   b. Identify the product by number.

c. State the date of purchase, date of delivery to you (if it was delivered), and date you returned it (or tried to).

d. Describe what caused you to return the product (what is wrong with it).

e. Identify each person you contacted about the problem by name in the order in which you spoke to them. Describe how those people responded to your problem.

f. Enclose copies of receipts, canceled checks, and any earlier correspondence you may have (both that you wrote and that you received). Do not send original receipts.

g. Finally, tell the company what action you want it to take. Do you want your money back? Do you want the product replaced?

March 4, 1989

Ms. E. S. Cooper
President
Marigold Electronics
5000 Oxford Street
Seattle, WA 98115

Dear Ms. Cooper:

I am writing to you to ask for a replacement for my Marigold TV set. It is a portable color set, model 8974. I bought it on 2/19/89 at Video Ace Appliances, San Francisco. After my set was delivered on 2/21/89, it worked for just four hours and then went black. I called the repair department of Video Ace, and they came over the next day. They said my set had a major electrical failure, and they had to take it back to the shop. They also said the repair cost was covered in the warranty.

When they returned the set (2/26/89), the picture wasn't as good as before. They said the set needed to warm up for a few days, and they would adjust it after that.

The next day (2/27/89), while the children were watching it, the set's wiring caught fire. We had to call the fire department. I also called Video Ace again, and they came out and took the set back in (2/28/89). They said they would try to put it back in order. I said I wanted a new set. They said they couldn't give me a new set because your company's warranty does not cover full replacement.

I have been greatly inconvenienced, and my family has been endangered by this set. I'm sure that Video Ace cannot fix the set so that it will work like new.

I enclose copies of the repair orders and my sales contract. I would like a refund of my money or a replacement television.

Sincerely,

Charles W. Jefferson

Charles W. Jefferson
125 Buchanan Street
Daly City, CA 94014

1. **Where should you begin when you have a complaint about a product?**
2. **List three items you may need to bring with you when you go to a store to make a complaint.**
3. **List five pieces of information that should be included in a letter of complaint.**

FINDING ADDITIONAL HELP

Suppose you go to the salesclerk and then to the manager and finally to the president of the company that manufactured the product, and you are still not satisfied. What more can you do? You can seek help from business organizations or government agencies set up to protect consumers.

Business Groups

Businesses in many communities have formed groups to promote better business practices and to help consumers who have complaints. One such group, with chapters all over the United States, is the **Better Business Bureau**. These groups of local business people police themselves and try to keep dishonest members out of their ranks. You can write to the Better Business Bureau to complain about a local merchant. The letter will go into a permanent file. People wishing to check out the reputation of the merchant can look at that file. Understandably, merchants may not want complaints filed against them. Sometimes, if you simply show the merchant a letter you intend to send to the Better Business Bureau, you will get better cooperation.

The Better Business Bureau deals primarily with complaints involving deceptive advertising and dishonest selling techniques such as the ones described in Chapter 9. It does not judge the quality of goods and services. Neither does it give out legal advice or handle problems involving credit matters. When you complain to a Better Business Bureau, it may contact the business to try to resolve the problem. However, because the Better Business Bureau is a private organization, it can't force a settlement. The bureau may recommend other sources of help.

Local and State Agencies

Most states and big cities have laws to protect consumers against fraud, and they have regulatory agencies to uphold those laws. A **regulatory agency** is a government body that has the power to make and enforce rules.

Have you filed a consumer complaint with a regulatory agency? Get the name of the individual who takes your complaint. If you need to call the agency again, you'll know whom to ask for. You'll find that you'll get better results when you deal with the same person each time.

You know you can contact state and federal consumer agencies about consumer complaints. But did you know that your elected officials can help you too? You can contact city councilors or state and federal senators and representatives. Sometimes just one telephone call from them to a company or regulatory agency can work wonders.

The Better Business Bureau can help you settle a dispute with a local business.

At the local level, many cities and some counties have **departments of consumer affairs**. Their law enforcement divisions can take legal action against businesses that break consumer protection laws. If you have a problem with a company in your community, you can call, write, or bring your complaint personally to your city or county consumer affairs department.

In many states, the **attorney general**, the top law enforcement official in the state, enforces consumer laws for everyone in the state. Often, the attorney general has a department that deals only with consumer problems. In the following interview, the head of one of these departments explains his job.

We investigate all kinds of complaints, but most of them have to do with automobiles or with home-improvement frauds. These two take about 75 percent of our time. We watch out for false advertising, misleading prices, phony repair schemes, sales under false pretenses, and dishonest debt collection practices.

Citizens bring complaints to our attention at our neighborhood offices or by letter. All complaints have to be in writing. We investigate to find out if the complaint is legitimate. We may find that we have other complaints on file against the same firm. As we piece the information together, our office can demand to see the records of the company.

When we have a case, we ask the business to make a settlement with the citizen before we go to court. We don't seek damage money, only a full refund. If no settlement is reached, a court hearing is set. By this time, the firm knows we mean business. It may settle by a method called voluntary compliance. *That means the firm pays the citizen but does not admit guilt. We can go further if we have to and take cases to court.*

STUART BENNINGTON
Chief, Consumer Protection Division

One company's ads claimed that its mouthwash could prevent the common cold. It couldn't. The FTC forced the manufacturer to say that its product could do nothing to prevent colds in its next $10 million worth of ads.

Federal Agencies

At the federal level, the regulatory agencies listed here can help protect your rights as a consumer. These agencies rarely deal with individual cases. Instead, they watch their mail to see if patterns of complaints develop. Then they may take a company to court on behalf of a group of consumers. They also have the power to make regulations to protect all consumers better in the future. A letter to one of these agencies can help create new consumer protection laws.

The Federal Trade Commission You already are aware that the Federal Trade Commission regulates advertising and can issue rules and regulations to protect the public against deceptive selling practices. The FTC can also take legal action against businesses for false advertising, for inadequate or misleading labeling, and for unethical or dishonest sales tactics.

If a company sells a product that does not meet the standards set by the Consumer Product Safety Commission, the product can be recalled. Anyone who bought the product can then get a full refund from the manufacturer—no matter how long, or how long ago, the product was used. Product recalls are often announced in newspapers and on radio and television news programs.

The Consumer Product Safety Commission

As the name implies, the Consumer Product Safety Commission is concerned with reducing the number of injuries caused by consumer products. This agency has the power to ban unsafe products and to set standards. It has devoted much of its efforts to toy safety. You can write to the commission about any product you feel is unsafe.

The Food and Drug Administration

Problems with food, medicine, cosmetics, or medical services are handled by the Food and Drug Administration (FDA). It protects consumers from unsafe products and from deceptive labeling. In Chapters 11 and 12, you will learn more about how the FDA protects consumers from unsafe food, medicine, and cosmetics.

Department of Transportation

The Consumer Affairs Division of the Department of Transportation (DOT) will listen to your complaints about airlines. The DOT issues reports on consumer airline complaints monthly and annually. Its statistics reveal which airlines receive the most complaints.

The United States Office of Consumer Affairs

Finally, you can write to someone who works for the President of the United States. The Special Adviser to the President for Consumer Affairs heads the United States Office of Consumer Affairs. This person is the President's top assistant for consumer matters. This office is not a regulatory agency, and so cannot make or enforce rules. But it can bring complaints to the attention of federal regulatory agencies.

To receive payment for lost luggage, you must file a claim within 45 days of the loss or the airline does not have to pay.

Where to Write

Federal Trade Commission
Bureau of Consumer Protection
Pennsylvania Avenue
Washington, DC 20580

Consumer Product Safety Commission
Bureau of Complaints
Department of Health, Education, and Welfare
5401 Westbard Avenue
Bethesda, MD 20207
Toll Free: (800)-638-2772

Food and Drug Administration
Department of Health, Education, and Welfare
5600 Fishers Lane
Rockville, MD 20857

All food, drug, or cosmetics violations should be reported first to the nearest Food and Drug Administration office. You can find that address in your local telephone directory. Look under "United States Government."

Department of Transportation
Office of Consumer Affairs
400 Seventh Street, SW
Washington, DC 20590

United States Office of Consumer Affairs
1009 Premier Building
Washington, DC 20201

Small-Claims Court

Many people in our country read, write, and speak in a language other than English. To protect these people, the law says all sales contracts must be printed in the same language that the salesperson used.

Investigations by city, state, and federal agencies can take time. Often you can get faster action by going to a **small-claims court**, a court that deals with minor legal matters involving a limited amount of money. The limit varies from state to state, but ranges from $100 to $5,000. Small claims suits are often brought against store owners who sell bad merchandise; landlords who refuse to return security deposits; laundries or dry cleaners that lose or damage clothes; or people who damage homes, cars, or other property. Small-claims courts handle over 4 million cases each year.

A small-claims court provides a simple, inexpensive way to bring your complaint to a judge. The judge hears your side and

A lawyer is not necessary when you take a complaint to small claims court. The judge will not only hear the case and make a decision, but will also act as your attorney.

the other person's side, and then decides the case. In most courts, you can bring a lawyer to represent you, but few people do. A lawyer may cost more than the amount in dispute. Normally, the court fees are only a few dollars, and they are refunded to you if you win the case. The court even helps you file the necessary papers to make a complaint. In the following case study, you can see the small-claims court system in action.

CASE STUDY

The case of the damp car

Pam Ziebert bought a late-model used car from Best Buys Used Cars. It came with a 90-day warranty on all parts and labor. Pam was pleased with the car until the first time it rained. In damp weather, the car stalled at every stop. Pam told the salesperson and the manager at Best Buys about the problem. They took the car in for repair. But the next time it rained, the car stalled again. Pam returned to Best Buys and had her car fixed again. But the problem still was not corrected.

   Pam decided to take the car to another mechanic. The mechanic found the problem, but parts and labor cost Pam $210. Pam asked Best Buys to pay the bill. Best Buys refused.

Pam went to small-claims court during her lunch hour. Law students at the court helped her file the correct complaint papers. The court then agreed to hear the case about a month later.

Pam prepared for her court date. The law students told her to bring the warranty, the repair bill, and the receipts for the repair work done by Best Buys. They also recommended that she bring in the mechanic as a witness. He couldn't take time off from work, but he did give Pam a sworn statement. Pam brought a friend as a witness to testify that the car really did stall at every stop. Best Buys was notified of the court date, but no one from the company attended.

After hearing the case, the judge ordered Best Buys to pay $210 plus court costs. But Best Buys did not pay Pam any money. The law students then showed Pam how to prepare the correct forms to uphold the court's judgment. If Best Buys didn't pay, the company could face further penalties. Best Buys eventually paid Pam $210 plus $20 in court costs.

✓check your understanding ✓ ✓ ✓ ✓ ✓ ✓

1. **What is the Better Business Bureau? How can it help if you have a complaint about a business?**
2. **What types of consumer problems does the attorney general's office watch out for?**
3. **Name two ways that a federal regulatory agency helps consumers.**
4. **What is a small-claims court?**

SUMMARIZING
the chapter

When problems occur with products or businesses, informed consumers try to solve them by going first to the place of purchase. If their problems are not settled there, they can then write to the president of the store or of the company that manufactured the product.

If the company does not help, consumers can turn to private and government agencies. The Better Business Bureau will respond to complaints about its members. At the local and state levels, the attorney general's office and the department of consumer affairs protect consumers' interests. Federal agencies take companies to court on behalf of large groups of consumers and pass laws to protect consumers' rights. Small-claims courts give consumers an inexpensive and direct way to bring claims against people or businesses.

BUILDING CONSUMER VOCABULARY

Number your paper from 1 to 6. Then write the term that best matches each numbered definition.

attorney general
Better Business Bureau
department of consumer affairs

regulatory agency
small-claims court
voluntary compliance

1. A state's top law enforcement official
2. A local government agency that can take legal action against businesses as a result of consumer complaints
3. Any government body that has the power to make and enforce rules and regulations
4. A group of local businesses set up to police themselves and to record and help with consumer complaints
5. A settlement of a consumer complaint by a business without the admission of guilt
6. A court that deals with minor legal matters involving limited amounts of money

BUILDING CONSUMER UNDERSTANDING

1. Reread the Elaine Schultz case study. What wise steps did Elaine take to solve her problem? What mistakes did she make, if any?
2. Identify the following government agencies by the role each plays in consumer affairs:
   a. Enforces state laws, including complaints and problems of consumers
   b. Passes on complaints from consumers to federal regulatory agencies
   c. Protects the public from unfair business practices and regulates advertising
   d. Protects the public from unsafe cosmetics
   e. Collects complaints about airlines
   f. Regulates the safety of consumer products
3. Decide which government agency or office would handle the following consumer concerns:
   a. An unsafe child's car seat
   b. Airline flights that almost never leave on time
   c. Misleading TV advertising of a nationally known product
   d. A service station in town that charges for car repairs that were not done

4. What advantages of small-claims courts are demonstrated in The Case of the Damp Car?
5. Suppose you buy a yellow sofa on special sale at the Castle Furniture Store. The sofa is sold "as is," but there seems to be nothing wrong with it. When the sofa was delivered, you discover that the fabric under the cushions was torn. Also, the fabric on the back of the sofa is darker than in front. You call Castle and demand a refund. The salesclerk tells you that the Castle Furniture Company can do nothing to help. You want to take action. List three different things you could do.

BUILDING CONSUMER MATH SKILLS

Pam Ziebert eventually got Best Buys to pay her $230 to cover the cost of having her car repaired. But she had other expenses in connection with the car that she had to pay herself. Her car was at Best Buys for a total of six days and was with the mechanic another two days. During that time, Pam took the train to work, which cost her $3 each way. She had to take off two hours from work to go to court and lost two hours' pay. She makes $360 a week for a 40-hour week. How much money did Pam lose out of her own pocket? What percentage of her total expenses did she get back from Best Buys?

APPLYING CONSUMER SKILLS

1. You bought a new Sound Right turntable at Jack's Stereo City. After one week of normal use, you discovered that the tone arm was cracked. You called the store, and they told you there was nothing you could do. Write a letter of complaint to the Sound Right Company.
2. Suppose, after receiving no answer from your letter, you took the Sound Right Company to small-claims court. What evidence would you bring with you to support your case?

GETTING INVOLVED IN YOUR COMMUNITY

Using the telephone book, list all of the consumer protection agencies near you. Group them as private, local, state, or federal. Interview someone from one of these agencies. Ask the person to explain local consumer protection laws and the kind of help available to you under those laws.

When you read advertisements, you should be critical. Can the claims made for a product be proven? Do you need more details than you have been given to make a good decision? Where can you get consumer information to help you investigate an advertiser's claims about a product?

Jason wants to buy a birthday present for Melissa. He reads the following advertisements in the newspaper.

1. Genuine diamond necklace only $17.95! Regular price $100.00! The diamond, a full 10 points, blazes with fire and color. This beautiful stone is certified as authentic by a professional gemologist. This sensational value is available only through this limited mail-order offer.

2. Buy a BiteSize Vacuum Cleaner System at the lowest price in history, and we'll throw in a luxurious oriental carpet *and* a year's supply of bags, absolutely free. That's right, the lowest price *ever* on a Bitesize Vacuum *and* an exotic oriental carpet *and* a year's supply of bags! This offer is available only during our March Madness sale, so you must act fast! (Certain restrictions may apply.)

3. Newlywed Special!!! Silver tea service by Revere House Silversmiths. This original hand-crafted heirloom will increase in value year after year. You'll pass this treasure on to your children—and they'll pass it on to their children. Start a tradition for your family, today! Specially priced at only $499. No money down, no payment until March. Easy installments of $19.99 per month.

Answer the following questions on a separate sheet of paper. Use complete sentences.

1. Which claims in each advertisement can probably be proved? Which claims probably can't be proved?

2. For which products should Jason get more detailed information than he has been given?

3. What sources of consumer information can Jason use to help him with his purchasing decisions?

4. What are some reasons that a product might be available only by mail?

5. What are some reasons that a product might be available only for a limited time?

ACTIVITY: Choose three store ads from a newspaper. For each, list the claims that could be proved and those that could not. Based on your list, select the most reliable ad.

BUYING GOODS AND SERVICES

BUYING FOOD

Shopping for food is a familiar experience for many people. But most people probably do not realize how many decisions are involved. The average supermarket in the United States contains more than 20,000 items. Do you know which ones to choose?

- What are the four basic food groups?

- What does a food label tell you?

- What are some common food-shopping mistakes, and how can you avoid them?

- What are the differences among nationally advertised brands, house brands, and generic foods?

One of the biggest and most necessary expenses for everyone is food. It accounts for 15 to 20 percent of a typical consumer's budget. Do you know how to get the most for your money when you buy food?

What does "getting the most" mean? With food, it means getting the most pleasure and the most **nutrition**—the most use out of food for health and growth. You eat because you like to eat and because you want to stay strong and healthy. Both reasons are important. So, in shopping for food, try to meet both goals as much as you can, within the limits of your budget.

FOOD AND HEALTH

As a whole, people in the United States eat more of everything than any other people in the world. What is surprising about a country of people who eat so much is that nutrition is often a problem. In fact, over the years, the diets of our citizens have been getting worse. Furthermore, people seem to be less concerned about nutrition than they were in the past. A 1986 survey showed that the number of people concerned with the nutritional content of the foods they ate dropped significantly compared with a similar group of people questioned three years earlier.

Why should you care about the food you eat? Teen-agers need more nourishment than most people because they are growing faster than at any other time in life except infancy. Boys grow particularly fast during their teens. Some teen-agers sleep less and play harder than most people, and their bodies need good food to store up energy. Teen-age girls have a special need for good food as well. The kind of nutrition a teen-age girl gets can affect the kind of pregnancy she may have in later years.

What should you eat? Health experts say it is important to eat foods from each of the **four basic food groups**: the meat group, the milk group, the vegetable-fruit group, and the bread-cereal group. "A Daily Food Guide" on page 159 lists the foods in each of the four basic food groups and tells how much you need every day.

Many of the foods that teen-agers eat do not belong to any of the four basic food groups. These are foods high in fat and sugar—such as candy, soda, salad dressing, potato chips, and cake. Eating too much of these foods can fill you up and prevent you from eating enough healthy foods. Many teen-agers also skip meals, which is not a good nutritional practice.

Think about the food you have eaten in the last two days. Did you eat enough from each of the four basic groups? Experts say that breakfast should give you one fourth to one third of your daily nutritional needs. Did your last two breakfasts fill those needs?

If you were an "average" person in the United States, you would eat 171 pounds of meat, 33 pounds of chicken, 10 pounds of cheese, 270 eggs, and 80 pounds of sugar in a year.

American cheese was given its name after the Revolutionary War by patriotic dairy workers who wanted to distinguish their cheese from English cheddar. The modern packaging was invented in 1903. At that time, a grocery clerk from Chicago named J.H. Kraft wrapped up separate slices of cheese and sold them door to door by horse and wagon.

A Daily Food Guide

Servings recommended	What counts as a serving
Meat Group 2 or more	2 to 3 ounces of lean cooked meat, poultry, or fish. As alternates: 1 egg; ½ cup cooked dry beans, nuts, or peas; or 2 tablespoons of peanut butter may replace ½ serving of meat.

This group is a chief source of protein and supplies iron, B vitamins, and some starch.

Milk Group Child, under 9 . . . . . . 2 to 3 Child, 9 to 12 . . . . 3 or more Teen-ager . . . . . . 4 or more Adult . . . . 2 or more Pregnant woman 3 or more Nursing woman . . 4 or more	One 8-ounce cup of milk—whole, skim, buttermilk—or evaporated or dry milk, reconstituted. As alternates: 1-inch cube cheese or ¾ cup cottage cheese, ice milk, or ice cream may replace ½ cup of milk.

This group is a source of protein, vitamin A, vitamin B_2, and calcium.

Vegetable-Fruit Group 4 or more, including:	½ cup of vegetable or fruit; or a portion, for example, 1 medium apple, banana, or potato; half a medium grapefruit or cantaloupe.
1 good or 2 fair sources of Vitamin C	*Good sources:* Grapefruit or grapefruit juice, orange or orange juice, cantaloupe, papaya, raw strawberries, broccoli, brussels sprouts, green pepper, sweet red pepper. *Fair sources:* Honeydew melon, lemon, tangerine or tangerine juice, watermelon, asparagus, cabbage, cauliflower, potatoes cooked in the jacket, spinach, tomatoes or tomato juice, turnip greens.
1 good source of Vitamin A —at least every other day	*Good sources:* Dark-green and deep-yellow vegetables and a few fruits, namely: apricots, broccoli, cantaloupe, carrots, chard, cress, kale, pumpkin, spinach, sweet potatoes, turnip greens and other dark-green leaves, winter squash.

This group provides vitamins A and C, the B vitamins, calcium, iron, and fiber, which helps to regulate the intestines.

Bread-Cereal Group 4 or more	Count only if whole-grain or enriched: 1 slice of bread or similar serving of baked goods made with whole-grain or enriched flour, 1 ounce ready-to-eat cereal, ½ to ¾ cup cooked cereal, cornmeal, grits, spaghetti, macaroni, noodles, or rice.

This group is rich in vitamins and minerals, but only if the grains have not been milled or if they have been enriched.

Other Foods as Needed To round out meals and meet energy requirements	Butter, fortified margarine, other fats. Try to include some vegetable oil among the fats used.

Nutritional Labeling

How can you determine the nutritional content of the foods you buy? The Food and Drug Administration (FDA) requires **nutritional labeling**—labels that list the amount and kinds of nutrients—for many types of foods. **Nutrients** are the ingredients in a product that provide you with nutrition. There are six types of nutrients: carbohydrates, fats, proteins, vitamins, minerals, and water. The chart below shows how the body uses these nutrients and which foods provide them.

Nutrients You Need

Nutrient	What it does for your body	What to eat to get it
Vitamin A	Helps keep skin and eyes healthy	Beef liver, fish, peaches, spinach, eggs, carrots, butter, cheese
B vitamins (riboflavin, thiamine, niacin)	Release energy in food, keep digestive system working calmly, maintain healthy skin	Most meats, milk, eggs, cheese, green peas and beans
Vitamin C	Holds body cells together. It is needed for tissue strength, bone and teeth formation, and wound healing.	Orange juice, grapefruit juice, strawberries, cantaloupe, tomatoes, green leafy vegetables, sweet and white potatoes
Vitamin D	Builds strong bones and teeth	Liver, eggs, butter, fortified milk, fatty fish
Vitamin E	Is important for healthy skin	Vegetables, milk, meat, eggs, corn, soybean and peanut oils
Vitamin K	Helps blood clot	Liver, spinach, tomatoes, egg yolks, cabbage, cauliflower, soybeans, wheat
Protein	Builds muscles and fights off disease and infection. The heart, lungs, brain, muscles, and nerves are made mostly of protein.	Peanuts, meat, poultry, soybeans, cheese, eggs
Fats and carbohydrates	Provide energy and protect vital organs	Butter, margarine, cream, cheese, bacon, spaghetti, macaroni, bread, beets, pineapple, potatoes, corn, wheat
Calcium	Is needed to build bones and muscles. It helps the nervous system and heart work properly.	Milk, collards, turnip greens, cheese, salmon
Iron	Is an important part of hemoglobin, the red substance of blood, which carries oxygen from the lungs to all body tissues and assists the cells in releasing energy from food.	Liver, kidney, dry beans, raisins, enriched breads and cereals

A Nutrition Quiz

People probably have as many strong beliefs about food as about any other matter. Some are true. Some are not. See how you score on this true-false quiz by comparing your answers with those on page 165.

1. Pizza can be a nutritious main course.
2. A 1,600-calorie-a-day diet may help you lose weight, but it won't give you enough nourishment to get you through the day.
3. Fat babies are healthier than thin babies.
4. A "fast food" meal can easily provide too much fat for the average adult.
5. Some artificial ingredients in packaged foods are needed to prevent spoilage.
6. A hamburger, a frankfurter, and a bologna sandwich are just about equal in their protein value.
7. Everyone should take a vitamin pill daily.

WHOLE GRAIN
Rice

NUTRITION INFORMATION
SERVING SIZE   ⅔ cup
SERVINGS
PER PACKAGE 12
PER SERVING
CALORIES 140
PROTEIN, g. 3
CARBOHYDRATE, g. 29
FAT, g. 1
SODIUM, mg 5
**PERCENTAGE OF U.S.
RECOMMENDED DAILY
ALLOWANCES (U.S. RDA).**
PER SERVING
PROTEIN 4
VITAMIN A ....*
VITAMIN C ....*
THIAMINE 6
RIBOFLAVIN ....*
NIACIN 6
CALCIUM ....*
IRON 2
*CONTAINS LESS THAN 2
PERCENT OF THE U.S. RDA
OF THESE NUTRIENTS.
INGREDIENTS: LONG GRAIN
PARBOILED BROWN RICE.

When a company uses nutritional labeling, it must give the following facts:

- The size of a serving and the number of servings contained in the package.
- The number of calories in a serving.
- The amount (in grams) of protein, carbohydrate, and fat in a serving and the amount (in milligrams) of sodium in a serving.
- The recommended daily allowance per serving of protein, two minerals (calcium and iron), and five vitamins (A, C, and three B vitamins—thiamine, riboflavin, and niacin). This **recommended daily allowance (RDA)** is a standard set by the American Academy of Sciences for the amount of a nutrient a person needs each day to stay healthy. In fact, the RDA is generally more than enough for most people, although pregnant women and nursing mothers may need additional amounts of some nutrients. If a label says "protein, 4" it means that one serving gives you 4 percent of the RDA for protein.

Manufacturers must supply nutritional labeling when they have added nutrients that would not ordinarily be found in the food. They must also provide nutritional labeling if they make a nutrition-related claim, such as "Chunky Cheese has more calcium than an eight-ounce glass of milk." Nutritional labeling must also be placed on all low-calorie and reduced-calorie foods.

Preservatives, Additives, and Standards

Raw green peppers are a very good source of vitamin C. The green peppers you find on a pizza won't do you much good however. When you cook green peppers, the vitamins are lost.

If you see benzoic acid, sorbic acid, or sulfur dioxide on a label, what does it mean? They are preservatives used to prevent bacteria from growing in food. Glycerol and sorbitol are preservatives used to keep food from drying out. Butylated hydroxyanisol (BHA), propyl gallate, and ascorbic acid are used to prevent some foods from changing flavor when exposed to the air.

In addition to information about nutrition, labels also tell you about artificial preservatives used in food. **Preservatives** are simply things put in food to keep it from spoiling. In the past, people preserved food in a variety of ways, including cooking, freezing, drying, and smoking. They also put things in food, such as salt into meat, sugar into fruits, and vinegar into vegetables to make the food keep longer. Today, in addition to those methods, many kinds of artificial preservatives are used, which are not naturally found in any food. For example, sodium propionate is added to bread to prevent the bread from turning green and moldy. These are the kinds of preservative that must be identified on a label.

Many foods also have **additives** to improve the flavor, color, or nutritional content of the product. A label must tell you if additives have been used. A common additive in milk is vitamin D. Iron and B vitamins are often added to bread. The FDA maintains standards for and tests all artificial food preservatives and additives.

You can find a list of ingredients on many packages of food. This list is always in order, from most plentiful to least plentiful, but it does not tell you how much of each ingredient has been used. However, the Food and Drug Administration has established standard recipes for certain products, called **standards of identity**. Mayonnaise, for example, must have a certain proportion of eggs and oil. In addition, the United States Department of Agriculture has established requirements for meat and poultry products. In order for a manufacturer to label a product "Chili con carne," for example, the chili must contain at least 40 percent meat. But "Chili con carne with beans" need have only 25 percent meat. Because the ingredients are fixed, manufacturers of standard products do not have to list the ingredients on the package, although many do. All they have to list are any preservatives or additives.

✓check your understanding ✓ ✓ ✓ ✓ ✓ ✓

1. **Why is it important for teen-agers to have a healthy diet?**
2. **What are the four basic food groups?**
3. **When must a manufacturer put a nutritional label on a food item?**
4. **What is required on a nutritional label?**
5. **Do manufacturers always need to include a list of ingredients on a food label? Explain.**

THE SMART FOOD SHOPPER

What is wise grocery shopping? What mistakes should you avoid when buying food? To get an idea, try shopping with Sally Pollard.

What's in a Food Label?

Some of the terms you find on a food label are specifically defined by law. Other terms could mean just about anything. The smart shopper knows which are which.

- **"Lite" or "light."** When it comes to food and drinks, both of these terms are undefined. "Light" foods may have fewer calories or less fat, but sometimes they are light only in taste or color. Look for a specific claim such as "half the calories of our regular spaghetti sauce." This specific claim requires nutritional labeling, so you'll know for sure what's in each serving.
- **"Natural."** Most food manufacturers may call anything "natural." The use of "natural" is regulated for meats, however. "Natural meats" must be free of artificial ingredients and preservatives and only minimally processed.
- **"No preservatives added."** This phrase means what it says—no artificial preservatives. But check to be sure no artificial coloring has been added.
- **"Low-calorie."** This term is specific. It means that a product has fewer than 40 calories per serving and no more than 0.4 calories per gram. A nutritional label is required.
- **"Reduced-calorie."** Products labeled "reduced-calorie" must have one-third fewer calories than the product it replaces. Nutritional labeling is required and should compare the higher- and lower-calorie products.
- **"Sodium-free."** Another well-defined term, "sodium-free" means the product has less than 5 milligrams (mg) of sodium per serving. "Very low sodium" means 35 mg of sodium or less per serving. "Low-sodium" means 140 mg of sodium or less per serving. To compare, a teaspoon of salt has 6,000 mg of sodium. However, "low-salt" doesn't always mean "low-sodium." Sodium may be hidden in many compounds such as baking soda.
- **"Sugar-free."** Some sugar substitutes allowed by the Food and Drug Administration have as many calories as sugar has. So "sugar-free" does not always mean calorie-free. Soft drinks are an exception, however. "Sugar-free" soft drinks must use a low-calorie sweetener.

Stop after each paragraph of the following case study to see if you can figure out what she should have done differently.

CASE STUDY

Shopping with Sally

When she looked around her kitchen at about 11:00 A.M., Sally Pollard found that she was getting short of food. In fact, she didn't even have anything for the children's lunch. She remembered that the Econ-O-Mart had advertised specials on ground beef and sirloin steak. So she put her children in the car and drove off to the Econ-O-Mart.

Sally's first stop was the fruits and vegetables section. The store was giving free samples of papaya, and they tasted so good that Sally bought two at $1.69 each. Peaches were on display at the end of the aisle, and she bought a pound. Then her son Michael talked her into getting some shiny red apples.

Sally needed cereal. She saw that one brand was marked "40 cents off regular price," so she picked that one. Right next to the cereal was some chocolate candy. Sally bought a bag.

At the meat counter, Sally got some ground beef at the advertised special price. Unfortunately, the store was out of the advertised sirloin steak. Well, too bad, she thought. She bought a porterhouse steak instead. It didn't cost all that much more. Besides, she felt that porterhouse was better.

Sally still needed something for lunch. She decided on tuna salad. The cans of tuna came in several sizes: 3¼ ounces for 65 cents, 6½ ounces for 98 cents, 9¼ ounces for $1.09, and 12½ ounces for $1.59. Sally wasn't sure, but she figured that the bigger the package, the lower the price. She took the 12½ ounce size.

Next, Sally went to the canned vegetables section. She started to take the store's own brand of green beans. It was cheaper than the nationally advertised brands, but was it as good? She decided not to take a chance. Her family deserved the best.

Sally was in a rush now. She and the kids were hungry, and she still had more to buy. She hurried down the aisles, picking things that were easy to reach. She didn't have time to compare prices.

In the frozen foods section, she picked four prepared dinners to pop in the microwave and two packages of mixed vegetables that could be cooked in their own pouches.

When she returned home, Sally knew it wasn't her day. The yogurt she bought for dessert was spoiled. Well, she thought, what can you do? Maybe she'd switch her business to the Save-A-Lot store.

Planning Ahead

The largest single source of sugar in our diet is soft drinks. There are ten teaspoons of sugar in a 12-ounce soft drink. In fact, most people get ten times as much sugar from soft drinks as from candy.

How many mistakes could you find in Sally's shopping? The following are some ideas from several shopping experts. They point out mistakes that Sally made, which other consumers often make as well.

Sally made some mistakes before she even left her house. She should have read the food ads and planned her meals before deciding which store to go to. Although some stores may advertise specials that are not really reduced in price, most advertised specials do offer savings. It makes sense to be cautious, but don't ignore the ads.

Nutrition Quiz Answers

Go back to the questions on page 161 and see how well you did.

1. True. Since it has protein (cheese, meat), carbohydrate (dough), calcium (cheese), and vitamins A and D (tomato sauce), pizza is nutritious. With a salad and a glass of milk, pizza makes a nourishing meal.
2. False. A man needs about 1,600 calories a day to get the 40 essential nutrients that keep the body going. A teen-age girl needs 1,400, whereas a grown woman needs 1,200.
3. False. Fat babies face several health problems. They are more likely to get diseases, such as respiratory illnesses. When they become adults, they may remain overweight, which would make them more likely to have heart attacks and strokes.
4. True. Fast foods tend to be high in fat. Various fast food hamburgers contain 10 to 15 teaspoons of fat. With French fries added, adults can easily get more than the 15 teaspoons of fat they should limit themselves to in a day.
5. True. Calcium propionate, for instance, keeps mold from forming. It is often added to baked goods.
6. False. A three-ounce hamburger gives you 20 grams of protein (about one-third of your daily protein needs). You would have to eat three frankfurters to get 20 grams of protein. And you would need 12 or 13 slices of bologna on a sandwich to get that much protein.
7. False. A well-balanced diet and normal exposure to sunshine should give you all the vitamins you need. The average person does not need vitamin pills unless a doctor says they are necessary.

What does it mean when a product is labeled "bargain size" or "economy size"? By law, other sizes of the same product must be available, and the larger size must really be a bargain. If a larger size of a product isn't labeled as the "ecomony size," you may save money by buying the smaller size.

Next, Sally should have made a shopping list. Sally and 60 percent of today's shoppers do not. But shopping without a list leaves you wide open to all of the supermarket's attractive displays. Without a list, most shoppers end up with things they don't need, can't afford, and don't really want. Although you should be flexible about in-store specials, generally you should stick to what is on your list.

It was a mistake for Sally to do her shopping just before lunch. Everything looks good if you shop when you're hungry. You're more likely to buy foods that are not on your list. You may even buy more than you can eat within a reasonable time. Studies show that people who shop after they eat spend 9 to 17 percent less money than those who shop while hungry.

Sally should try to shop without her children. They can be distracting when you're trying to figure out the best deal and can talk you into buying things you really don't want.

Impulse Buying

Some stores encourage impulse buying by placing high-profit items where they will catch the shoppers' eye.

Stores try to take advantage of **impulse buying**—buying something without thinking first. Sally bought expensive fruits without checking for specials. The fact that peaches were in a special display at the Econ-O-Mart does not mean that they were on sale. Most fruits and vegetables are in greater supply at certain times of the year and they are likely to be priced lower then. The chart below shows the best times to buy a number of fruits and vegetables.

Giving free samples and putting things at the end of an aisle are ways of leading people to buy things they hadn't planned to buy. Another way is putting high-profit items, such as deli and bakery goods, in the outside aisles. Some in-store bakeries run their ovens all day to attract customers to buy freshly baked pies, cookies, and breads. Studies have shown that most customers shop in the outside aisles before going to the middle aisles. Customers are more open to impulse buying before the cart is full and they begin to wonder if they bought too much.

Sally also should not have bought the "40 cents off" cereal without comparing prices. One survey found that 90 percent of the "cents off" deals do offer real savings, but other brands may still be cheaper.

Best Times to Buy Fruits and Vegetables

Fruit or Vegetable	January	February	March	April	May	June	July	August	September	October	November	December
Apples	X	X	X	X	X					X	X	X
Asparagus			X	X	X							
Bananas	X	X	X	X	X	X	X	X	X	X	X	X
Broccoli	X		X	X	X	X			X	X	X	X
Brussels Sprouts	X	X								X	X	X
Carrots	X	X	X	X	X	X			X	X	X	X
Cherries						X	X					
Cucumbers					X	X	X					
Grapefruit	X	X	X	X	X						X	X
Grapes								X	X	X		
Oranges	X	X	X	X	X							X
Peaches						X	X	X	X			
Strawberries				X	X	X						
Tomatoes				X	X	X	X	X				

Source: United Fresh Fruit and Vegetable Association

Buying fruits and vegetables in season can stretch food dollars. And buying them at a farmers' market can make your money go even further.

Next to the cereal was the candy that Sally bought on impulse. Many stores put a high-profit item like candy next to high-selling products like cereal or next to this week's specials. They know that the item will sell faster there. If the candy were off on a candy shelf, Sally might not buy it.

The Econ-O-Mart was out of the special-sale sirloin, and Sally bought a steak that cost more. That wasn't impulse buying, but she could have been more careful. If a store is out of an advertised special, you can ask for a **rain check**—a written statement saying that you can buy the product at the sale price when the store gets it in again. Unless the store's ads say "limited quantities," or "no rain checks," the Federal Trade Commission requires the store to give you a rain check. But you won't get one unless you ask.

Unit Pricing

Many consumers think that a big package must be a better buy than a small package. That's not always true. When Sally bought a 12½ ounce can of tuna for $1.59, she paid almost 13 cents an ounce. The 9¼ ounce can selling at $1.09 cents was a better buy because it cost about 12 cents an ounce. But Sally is not a computer, and you can't blame her for not taking the time to figure out the price per ounce of each can of tuna.

Many stores help you by using **unit pricing**. Besides telling you the price of a product, they tell you how much the product costs per unit (per ounce or per pound, for instance). If Sally's store did that with the tuna, she would have this information in front of her:

Size of Can (ounces)	Price	Unit Price (cents per ounce)
3¼	$0.65	20.0
6½	0.98	15.1
9¼	1.09	11.8
12½	1.59	12.7

Where unit pricing is used, it makes good sense to pay attention to it. You can save money.

House Brands and Generic Foods

A store's own brand, or **house brand**, is often cheaper than a nationally advertised brand. One study found that shoppers can save an average of 21½ percent by buying house brands. Of course, to be sure of a saving, you need to compare prices.

An even less expensive type of prepared or processed food is **generic foods**—foods that have no brand name at all. Many stores have an entire section of generics. Generic products may be lower in quality than nationally advertised brands. But most experts say that nationally advertised brands, house brands, and generics are of equal nutritional value. A wise consumer should decide if the top-grade product is needed. You don't need perfect canned peaches to make fruit salad, but you might want them to serve whole.

Sally should not have thought that buying house brands was a risk. They are often just as good as other brands. In fact, many of them are packaged for the stores by the same companies that package the nationally advertised brands. A store can sell its house brand more cheaply because it does not have the same high advertising costs. Generic products can be sold at considerably lower prices because of the lack of advertising, lower labeling and packaging costs, and less expensive ingredients.

Foods in Easy Reach

By picking things that she saw first or could reach easily, Sally probably paid more than she had to. Some stores not only put higher priced items on special display, they also put them on shelves at eye level. One study found that a store could sell 63 percent more of a particular item when it was raised from waist level to eye level. Sales of another item increased 78 percent when it was moved from floor level to eye level.

Tomatoes were not very popular before the 1800's because many people thought they were poisonous. But in 1820 a courageous tomato lover named Robert Gibbon Johnson stood on the steps of the Salem County Courthouse in New Jersey and ate a whole tomato in full view of an amazed crowd. Johnson survived, and tomatoes became a staple in our diet.

Thomas Jefferson introduced pasta to the United States. In 1789, returning from a tour of duty as ambassador to France, he brought back a spaghetti-making machine, which he used to entertain friends at his home in Monticello.

People tend to buy items placed at eye level or within easy reach. Is this a good location for high priced items?

Convenience and Freshness

Frozen prepared dinners and vegetables in cooking pouches are convenience foods. **Convenience foods** are foods that are partially or completely prepared by the manufacturer to save you work and time in the kitchen. But you pay for this convenience. A study by the Department of Agriculture showed that 116 of 158 convenience foods examined cost more than the same foods prepared from scratch. Some frozen dinners cost twice as much as the same meals cooked at home. But two convenience foods were found to be cheaper: frozen orange juice and instant coffee.

Convenience foods may save time, but they certainly don't save money. Not only do they cost more, but they are often higher in salt and lower in nutrients than the same foods made from scratch.

Suppose you buy a carton
of milk, and the sell date
on it is today. Will the milk
be no good tomorrow? No.
The sell date is the last
date a product can safely
be *sold*, not the last date it
can safely be *used*. The
milk should last as long in
your refrigerator as any
other carton of milk you've
bought.

When she got home, Sally found that her yogurt had spoiled. She should have checked before she bought it to see if a date was printed on the package. Many packages show the last date on which the product should be sold. Sometimes, unfortunately, the date is in code, so that only the store workers know what it says. But **open dating**, where the date is clearly printed on the package, is also used. A customer should look for dates, especially on items that spoil quickly.

Even if Sally's yogurt does not have an open date, she should plan to return it to the store for a fresh package or a refund. Any store should take back spoiled food.

√ check your understanding √ √ √ √ √ √

1. **What is impulse buying? How does a store encourage it? How can a consumer resist it?**
2. **What is unit pricing? How can a consumer use it?**
3. **What are the differences among house brands, nationally advertised brands, and generic foods? How can a consumer decide which to buy?**
4. **Why are certain food products dated? In what ways can this dating be done by the store?**

SUMMARIZING
the chapter

People in the United States are among the best fed individuals in the world. But good nutrition is still a problem for some people. Teen-agers in particular need more nourishment than people in most other age groups because of their rapid growth and energetic lifestyle. For a healthy diet, everyone should eat foods from each of the four basic food groups: meat, milk, vegetable-fruit, and bread-cereal.

Food labels can give you a lot of information about the nutritional content of the foods you buy. Nutritional labeling tells you the percentages of the Recommended Daily Allowance of various vitamins and minerals a food item supplies. Labels also indicate whether manufacturers have used artificial preservatives or additives.

Buying nutritious foods at a price you can afford requires planning and careful shopping. You should make a shopping list and stick to it to avoid impulse buying. Use unit pricing to compare the cost when items come in many sizes. You can save by avoiding convenience foods and by buying house brands and generic products instead of nationally advertised brands. Finally, open dating on a package tells you if the product is fresh. A good consumer shops for food using more than just price as a guideline.

CHAPTER ACTIVITIES

BUILDING CONSUMER VOCABULARY

Number your paper from 1 to 15. Then write the term that best matches each numbered definition.

additives
convenience foods
four basic food groups
generic foods
house brand
impulse buying
nutrients
nutrition

nutritional labeling
open dating
preservatives
rain check
recommended daily allowance (RDA)
standards of identity
unit pricing

1. Buying something without thinking first
2. Categories of foods that are good sources of nutrients
3. Food ingredients that provide the body with nutrition
4. Food products having no brand name
5. A way to show the price of food so that consumers can compare the cost of different sizes of the same item
6. The process by which the body uses nutrients from food to maintain health and promote growth
7. Foods that are partly or completely prepared by the manufacturer
8. The amount of nutrients a person needs each day to stay healthy
9. A store's own brand
10. Extra ingredients put into food to improve flavor, color, or nutritional value
11. Information telling the consumer the last day on which a food product should be sold
12. Something put into food to slow or prevent it from spoiling
13. Labels required on some items giving information about the nutritional content of the food
14. Recipes established for certain products by the Food and Drug Administration
15. A written promise stating that if a store runs out of a sale item you can buy it later at the sale price

1. How can you know if your meals are giving you enough nutrition?
2. Name at least two items that a manufacturer must identify on a product label.
3. What should you do before you go food shopping in order to avoid mistakes at the store?
4. What can you do if a store no longer has a product it advertised at a special price?
5. What are the advantages and disadvantages of using convenience foods?
6. Using the Daily Food Guide on page 159, answer the following questions:
   a. Name three possible substitutes for meat. What quantity of each may replace ½ serving of meat?
   b. How many eight-ounce glasses of milk should a teen-ager have daily?
   c. Can you count grits or noodles as basic foods?
   d. Name three good sources and three fair sources of vitamin C.
7. Using the nutritional chart on page 160, answer the following questions:
   a. What is a good source of vitamin C? vitamin A?
   b. Why would fats and carbohydrates be good for a runner or a swimmer?
   c. If you had a skin condition such as acne, what vitamin supplement might be good for you?
   d. What nutrients are found in cheese?
   e. Why is protein essential in your diet?
8. Using the fruits and vegetables buying guide on page 166, answer the following questions:
   a. Which fruits are best to buy in the winter?
   b. Which fruits are good buys in summer?
   c. Which vegetables would probably be most expensive in the summer?

Which is the best buy:

1. A 15-ounce can of ravioli for 72 cents or a 40-ounce can for $1.69?
2. Apples at 69 cents per pound or a 3-pound bag of apples for $2?
3. Dinner rolls for 18 cents each or 6 for 89 cents?
4. A 20-ounce box of cereal for $2.59, a 15-ounce box for $1.99, or a 10-ounce box for $1.49?
5. A 32-fluid ounce carton of orange juice for 99 cents, a 96-fluid ounce carton for $2.49, or a 64-fluid ounce carton for $1.79?

1. Nutritional labels for two different brands of breakfast cereals are illustrated below.
   a. According to the labels, how big is a serving? When you eat cereal at home, how big is a serving for you?
   b. Which of the two cereals has more carbohydrates?
   c. Which cereal has more food value?

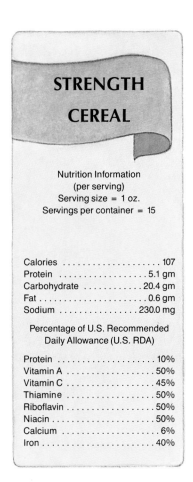

STRENGTH CEREAL

Nutrition Information
(per serving)
Serving size = 1 oz.
Servings per container = 15

Calories 107
Protein . . . . 5.1 gm
Carbohydrate . . . . 20.4 gm
Fat . . . . 0.6 gm
Sodium . . . . 230.0 mg

Percentage of U.S. Recommended
Daily Allowance (U.S. RDA)

Protein 10%
Vitamin A 50%
Vitamin C 45%
Thiamine 50%
Riboflavin 50%
Niacin 50%
Calcium 6%
Iron 40%

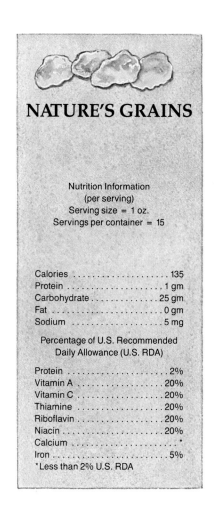

NATURE'S GRAINS

Nutrition Information
(per serving)
Serving size = 1 oz.
Servings per container = 15

Calories 135
Protein . . . . 1 gm
Carbohydrate . . . . 25 gm
Fat . . . . 0 gm
Sodium . . . . 5 mg

Percentage of U.S. Recommended
Daily Allowance (U.S. RDA)

Protein 2%
Vitamin A 20%
Vitamin C 20%
Thiamine 20%
Riboflavin 20%
Niacin 20%
Calcium . . . . *
Iron 5%
*Less than 2% U.S. RDA

2. Study your school's lunch menus for a week. Do the lunches have food from each of the four food groups? How much of your daily food needs do these lunches provide?

For ten products, compare the prices of a store's house brand with nationally advertised brands of the same size. If the store has generic products, compare the prices for the same ten products with those of the nationally advertised brands and house brands as well. How much do the ten house brand items cost all together? the nationally advertised products? the generic products?

BUYING CLOTHES

Shopping for clothes is fun for some people and boring, or even unpleasant, for others. No matter how you feel about shopping, you should use your money wisely and know what you're paying for. How can you buy the clothes you want at a price you can afford? How can you make sure your clothes will last—and keep looking good on you?

12

◆ **How does good planning help you buy clothes?**

◆ **How can you determine good quality in clothes?**

◆ **What do fabric tags and care labels on clothes mean?**

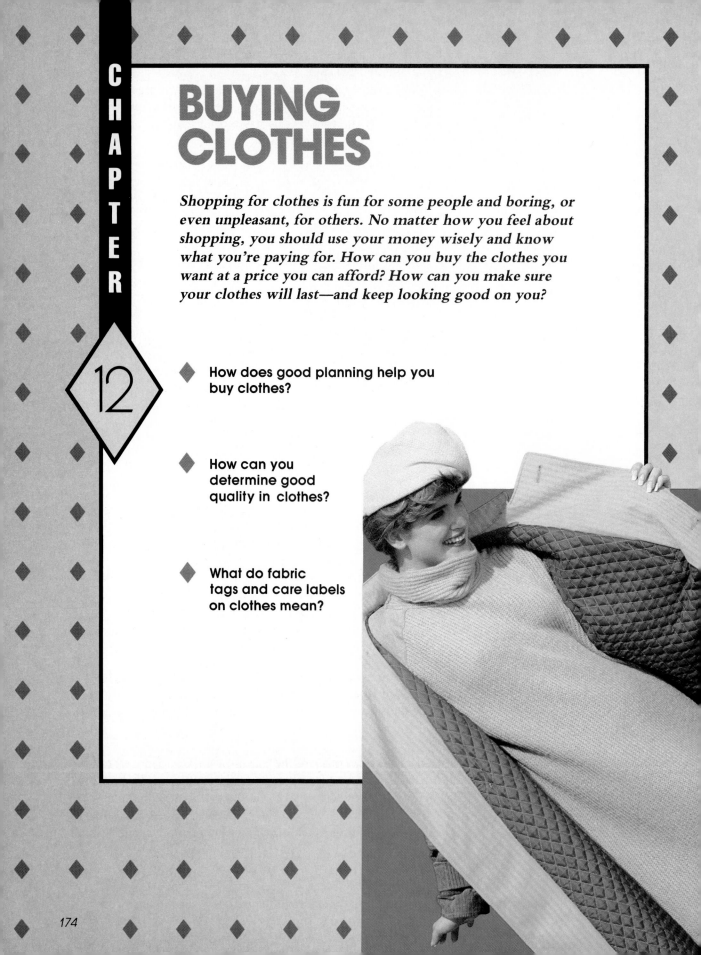

Brenda Rettig bought an expensive dress at a specialty store, figuring that anything so expensive must be well made. But, before long, the seams came apart. Brenda learned the material was expensive, but that didn't mean the dress was well made.

Ray Herrman bought a pair of jeans. When he washed them, they shrank so much he couldn't even wear them.

How can you escape such problems in buying clothes? What should you know about clothing costs, style, labeling, construction, and care? What should you think about even before you go shopping?

CLOTHES MAKE THE PERSON

You may have heard the expression "Clothes make the person." What you wear can affect people's opinions about you. Your values and lifestyle influence the type of clothing you choose and the amount of money you spend for it. Where you live, where you work, and how much money you have also influence your clothing choices. Your plans for buying should take all of those things into account. Something as important as clothing should bring forth your best consumer skills.

Planning to Save

Each year, consumers in the United States spend over $150 billion for clothes. That comes to over $600 per person each year. Since it's not a small amount, it makes sense to spend it wisely.

Your planning can start in your own closet. Take a survey of the clothing you already have. You may find, for example, that you have several sweaters but not enough shirts. Or maybe you have plenty of shirts but nothing that will go well with them.

One way to make full use of what you have is to plan around one or two colors or color combinations. Buy sweaters, shirts, or blouses that you can wear with several different slacks or skirts. That way you can stretch your clothing dollar and get the wardrobe you need for less money. The case study that follows illustrates the wisdom of planning ahead before you go shopping.

Women in pants are a common sight today in the United States. So it may surprise you to learn that women were not allowed to wear them in many restaurants and other public places just 20 years ago. Women in China, however, have been wearing pants for over 2,000 years.

Skirts have not always been worn just by women. Ancient Egyptian men wore skirts made from linen and often wore more than one at a time, one over the other.

CASE STUDY

Mike Fedder checked his closet. He found lots of jeans and T-shirts, and a couple of pairs of slacks, but not enough to fill his needs for his new job at O'Connor Hardware Store. The manager had told Mike he should wear sports shirts and casual slacks on the job. So Mike gathered up his cash, $125 in all, and headed to Savers Discount Clothes.

At the store, Mike carefully checked the prices. He found that Savers was having a big sale on one brand of sports shirts. They were very colorful, with all kinds of great designs, and were marked down to $14.95 apiece. Mike bought four of them. And he left feeling good about his budget shopping.

That night, as he hung his new shirts in the closet, Mike saw that none matched any of his slacks. Also, the shirts were short-sleeved. Mike knew that the hardware store was chilly most of the year, and he might have to be outdoors in the cold weather loading customers' cars. He needed some long-sleeved shirts. But most of all he needed some new slacks.

The next day, Mike went to Blackburn's Men's Store to get some slacks. He found that he had just enough money left to buy two pairs that would go with his shirts. He bought them and hoped that he could save some of his pay to buy more slacks and some long-sleeved shirts.

1. **What mistakes did Mike make in buying clothes?**
2. **What wise steps did Mike take in buying his clothes?**

"Clothes make the man—or woman." People's occupations can often be identified by the clothes they wear.

Thinking far ahead can save you money. Suppose you need a new winter coat. When should you buy it? Prices are not the same all year round. Many stores offer end-of-the-season sales to clear their racks and get ready for new shipments. The chart below is a general guide showing when you can expect to find some good clothing buys.

When to Buy Clothes

January
Dresses
Housecoats
Hosiery
Sportswear
Men's shirts
Boys' suits
Men's coats

February
Men's shirts
Sportswear
President's Day
   specials

March
Winter sportswear
Spring and Easter
   specials

April
Women's coats
Children's coats
Dresses
Men's and boys' suits
Infants' wear
Post-Easter clearances

May
Housecoats
Summer sportswear
Mother's Day specials

June
Dresses
Camping clothes
Men's and boys' wear
Father's Day specials

July
Housecoats
Sportswear
Children's wear
Men's shirts
Swimwear

August
Women's coats
Children's coats
Men's coats
Back-to-school specials

September
Fall fashions
Hosiery
Men's and boys' wear

October
Fall and winter
   sportswear
Women's coats
   and suits
Columbus Day
   specials

November
Women's coats
Children's coats
Men's shirts
Men's suits and coats
Women's winter clothing
Thanksgiving Day and
   Veteran's Day specials

December
Women's coats
Children's coats
Resort wear
Men's suits
Men's coats
End-of-the-year
   reductions

Sewing your own clothes can give you the style you want and the fabric and color you prefer. Plus, you can get better fit.

Another way you can save is to make some of your own clothes. One study showed that 25 percent of teen-agers own sewing machines. When you sew your own clothes, you have a wider choice of materials, colors, and styles. Not only can you save money, you can also be creative and make what's just right for you.

Being in Fashion

A few months ago, most of Ann McBain's friends started wearing cowboy boots. Ann spent a good part of her savings on a pair. This month, nobody's wearing them.

Sometimes you may buy a certain garment to be up with the latest fashion only to find that very soon nobody is wearing it. It was just a **fad**—something that is very popular for a short period of time. Of course, many clothing fashions change quickly, but not all of them do. Stop and think about what fads you've seen come and go quickly. What kinds of clothing have stayed in fashion for a long time?

✓check your understanding ✓ ✓ ✓ ✓ ✓ ✓

1. **What factors influence your choice of clothing?**
2. **What are three ways to stretch your clothing dollar?**
3. **Why do you have to be careful when buying current fashions? Describe some of today's popular styles.**

FABRICS MAKE THE CLOTHES

How long do you think this dress will stay in style?

Before you buy clothing, think about the kind of use it will get. Do you do heavy work? You may need clothing that can take stress and strain and can stand up to **abrasion**—wear caused by rubbing.

What is everybody wearing? More than three out of every four people in the world wear clothing made of cotton.

Ramie is one of the oldest known fabric fibers. It comes from a plant of the same name which first grew in Asia. The Ancient Egyptians used ramie to wrap mummies.

Do you work at a desk? You may want clothing that is comfortable and doesn't wrinkle much.

There are many kinds of clothing fabrics, or materials, made from many kinds of fibers. In general, fibers fall into two main groups. **Natural fibers**—such as cotton and wool—are made from plants or animals found in nature. **Synthetic fibers**—such as rayon and nylon—are made from chemicals. Within each of these two groups are many different fibers, each with its own characteristics.

Different fabrics are good for different uses. The table below lists the fibers most often used in clothing fabrics, along with some of the most important characteristics of each fiber. It shows, for example, that cotton is strong but wrinkles easily, whereas wool resists wrinkling but is not so strong.

A fabric may also be made from two or more fibers. Sometimes a natural fiber like wool and a synthetic one like polyester are used together to get some of the benefits of both. Although such a fabric may not "breathe" as well as one made entirely of natural fibers, it may resist wrinkling better. Sometimes a natural fiber is coated with a finish that helps it resist creases, stains, or moths. For example, clothes with permanent-press finishes do not need to be ironed.

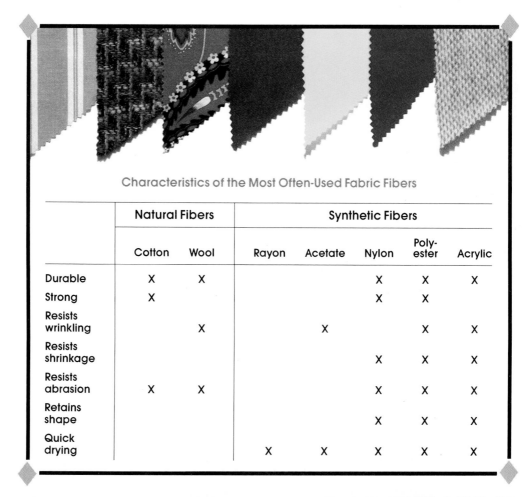

Characteristics of the Most Often-Used Fabric Fibers

| | Natural Fibers | | Synthetic Fibers | | | | |
	Cotton	Wool	Rayon	Acetate	Nylon	Poly-ester	Acrylic
Durable	X	X			X	X	X
Strong	X				X	X	
Resists wrinkling		X		X		X	X
Resists shrinkage					X	X	X
Resists abrasion	X	X			X	X	X
Retains shape					X	X	X
Quick drying			X	X	X	X	X

It looks and feels like silk, but is it? To identify today's synthetic fabrics, you often need to read the label.

The first synthetic fabric was invented in 1884 by a French chemist named Count Louis Marie Hilaire Bernigaud Chardonnet. He called it artificial silk. We know it today as rayon.

Today, linen costs a lot more than many other cloths in the United States. But it wasn't always expensive. It was the cheapest fabric for the colonists, who made it themselves from a plant called flax. Cotton became so popular, however, that today no flax is grown in North America. All of our linen is now imported.

Fabric Tags

It's difficult to tell what material a piece of clothing is made from just by looking at it. It pays to read the labels on clothing to be sure of what you're buying. Clothing may carry a tag giving the manufacturer's brand name for a particular fiber. But it must also have another tag telling you what fiber family the name belongs to. A manufacturer may call a fiber Perfecto or Supremo, but if it's really rayon, a tag must say so. Such a tag is required by the **Textile Fiber Products Identification Act**. These tags are usually found in the neck of the garment or in a side seam. If you know the strengths and weaknesses of the fibers, you will have a better idea of whether the garment will give you the kind of wear you require.

A tag must also list the manufacturer's name or **registered identification number (RN)**. If you see a tag with an RN, you can learn the manufacturer's name by writing to the Federal Trade Commission. You can find out, for instance, who made a piece of clothing sold under a house brand name by a store like Sears or J.C. Penney. This knowledge can help you in comparison shopping.

Wool Products

The **Wool Products Labeling Act** protects you when you buy clothing made of wool. It helps identify three kinds of wool used in clothing: new, reprocessed, and reused wool. A fabric may be called *new wool* or *virgin wool* only if its wool fiber has not been used before. Sometimes wool fiber has been used before to make a product that is never sold. The wool fiber is broken up, spun into yarn again, and made into another product. That fiber must be called *reprocessed wool*. If a fiber is remanufactured from wool products previously sold to consumers, it is *reused wool*. There is no difference in quality among these three types of wool. But there is a difference in price. It costs a manufacturer more to make a garment from new wool, so expect to pay less for clothing made of reprocessed or reused wool.

Moths do not eat clothes. Moths' eggs feed on the wool fibers in your clothes. Once the eggs have hatched into moths and flown out of your closet, the damage has already been done.

✓check your understanding ✓ ✓ ✓ ✓ ✓ ✓

1. **Which fabric fiber listed in the chart on page 179 has the greatest number of desirable characteristics?**
2. **What is the advantage of combining fibers?**
3. **What is the difference between reprocessed wool and reused wool?**

SMART SHOPPERS BUY QUALITY CLOTHES

Even a garment made from a strong fabric can give you problems if it isn't made well. In fact, a poorly made garment can look like a rag after you've worn it only a few times. A home economist points out some things to watch for when buying clothes.

There isn't just one standard of quality in clothing, and a high price doesn't always mean a well-made garment. You may be paying for the fabric. So you ought to check out a garment's construction carefully.

Look at the stitches on a garment to make sure they're uniform. Also the ends of the seams must be fastened so that they don't come out. Proper seams are pressed flat and are wide so that they won't fray or pull open.

Buttons, hooks, and snaps often cause complaints. They should be of good quality and reinforced from behind so they won't tear the clothing. Buttonholes should be big enough for the buttons to slide through easily. And the stitching around the buttonholes should be neat.

Make sure that the material has been cut properly so that pieces of material match. This is important in plaids, checks, and prints. Places to check are side seams in slacks and dresses, and sleeves in shirts. With permanent-press clothes, be sure to check for creases or other faults because they can't be removed. They are permanent!

Finally, be careful when buying garments with raised surfaces because they can snag. These garments shouldn't be worn for certain kinds of work.

ROBIN KENDALL
Home Economist

CARE MAKES CLOTHES LAST

Suppose you buy a wool sweater for $20. You may be getting a good price for the sweater, but are you locking yourself into heavy cleaning bills or too many evenings spent carefully washing the sweater by hand?

When you buy clothes, think about the kind of care they will need. Will it be expensive or time consuming to keep them clean and looking good? Some care in choosing clothes for ease of cleaning can pay off later in longer wear, as the following case study shows.

CASE STUDY

Len Munroe bought a pair of light-colored lightweight slacks. He wanted to look his best at a summer dance his community college was holding that night. When he got home, he tried on the slacks, checking to see how they looked with his best sports jacket. They looked good. But somehow, walking about the house, he brushed against something and got some ugly dirt marks along the side.

Luckily, there was plenty of time. Len walked down to the laundry and tossed the slacks into a machine. He sat down and talked with his neighbor Meg Roe. A half-hour later, Len took the slacks out of the machine. Not only was the dirt still there, the slacks were badly rumpled and out of shape.

Len felt awful. He couldn't understand what had happened. Meg came over and looked sympathetic. "That's like what happened to me last week," she said. "I washed some new sweats, and when I took them out, the color had run over everything. Then I found out that the label said they had to be washed separately." Len looked at the label on his slacks, which read DRY CLEAN ONLY. But it was too late for that now.

Care Labels

Dry cleaning uses little or no water to remove dirt and stains, but it is not dry. When clothes are dry cleaned, they are washed with chemicals called solvents that dissolve oils and fats not affected by soap and water.

Len and Meg did not need to have such trouble. Before washing their clothes—in fact, before buying them—they should have checked for labels telling them how to care for the clothes.

For many kinds of clothing, care labels are required by the Federal Trade Commission. Because they must be sewn on and last for the life of the clothing, these labels are called **permanent care labels**. They tell how to wash, iron, dry clean, and bleach clothing. They warn if any special care is needed. The labels discussed on page 184 are just a few of the many kinds of permanent care labels.

Following the directions on the label can make a big difference. Permanent-press clothes must be dried in a dryer and taken out of

the machine as soon as it stops or they will have to be ironed. Some other finishes are not permanent, such as water-repellent material on some raincoats. These finishes must be renewed after the clothes have been washed or cleaned a few times.

Proper care of children's pajamas or other sleepwear is very important. By law, all children's sleepwear, up to size 14, must be treated to resist fire. But you must follow the manufacturer's laundering directions to maintain the finish. The wrong kind of detergent, for example, could destroy the safety feature.

In general, following the permanent care labels will extend the life of your clothing. Knowing the particular characteristics of certain fabrics will also help. For instance, if you know that cotton has a tendency to shrink, you will be more careful of high temperatures when washing a cotton garment. A good consumer uses not only clothing labels but also common sense in making clothes last longer.

Clothing Warranties

You can avoid some problems if you can buy clothes that have warranties protecting you against faults in construction. Not many garments come with warranties, but if you buy one that does, read the warranty carefully. Many warranties hold only if you follow the manufacturer's directions on how to care for the clothing. Keep your receipts too, so you can show when you bought the clothing.

Zeroing in on Labels

In 1984, the Federal Trade Commission revised the 1972 Care Labeling Rule to standardize the terms giving information about washing and ironing. The meanings of the terms used on care labels are now clear to manufacturers. But some terms can still be confusing to consumers. Here's a list telling you what manufacturers now know.

■ MACHINE WASH SEPARATELY means wash the garment by itself. If the tag says MACHINE WASH WITH LIKE COLORS, you should wash the item only with light-colored clothes if it is light in color or only with dark-colored clothes if it is dark in color.

■ HAND WASH means just what it says. Don't assume that you can dry clean a garment carrying a hand wash tag.

■ DRY CLEAN ONLY on a tag means all methods of dry cleaning are safe. You can take the item to a professional dry cleaning shop or you can do it yourself in a coin-operated dry cleaning machine. If the tag says PROFESSIONALLY DRY CLEAN, however, the item cannot safely be cleaned in a machine.

■ DAMP WIPE ONLY means that the only way to clean the garment is by brushing it with a damp cloth or sponge.

■ IRON STEAM ONLY means that only steam, and not the iron itself, can touch the clothing.

What is not on the tags is as important as what is on them.

■ If no temperatures are mentioned on a tag, any temperature is safe to use for washing or ironing.

■ If no ironing instructions are given, the garment does not need to be ironed at all.

■ If bleach is not mentioned, any type of bleach may be used safely.

Do not buy clothes without trying them on. Different companies cut their clothes differently. The cut can vary so much that a "medium" shirt made by one company may be the same size as a "large" shirt made by another company.

If you have a complaint about clothing that has no warranty, take the garment back. Perhaps a button hole is missing, or a pocket is sewn shut. Maybe the first time you try washing your preshrunk jeans, they shrink two sizes more. A store that has sold you such a faulty garment should let you exchange it or give you your money back. If it won't, write a letter or return the garment directly to the manufacturer. The RN on the tag can help you identify the manufacturer. Remember, however, that stores do not have to take back a garment just because it doesn't fit you or because you don't like the color once you get it home. It is a good idea to check a store's return policy before you make a purchase.

✓ check your understanding ✓ ✓ ✓ ✓ ✓ ✓

1. **What are the characteristics of a well-made seam?**
2. **Why is it important to check for wrinkles in clothing made with permanent-press finishes?**
3. **What information can you find on a permanent care label?**

S UMMARIZING
the chapter

Plan ahead to get the clothes you want at a price you can afford. Take into account your lifestyle and values, the climate where you live, the type of work you do, your leisure-time activities, and the clothes you already have.

Think ahead and purchase clothes on sale. By avoiding fads, you can buy clothes that stay in fashion longer. Sewing is one other way to save money on clothes.

Knowing the characteristics of clothing fibers will give you a good idea of the kind of wear to expect and the type of care required for the garment. The fiber content of clothing can be found on fabric identification tags in the garments. But even clothes made of expensive fabrics will not last long if they are not well made. Check clothing construction for such things as smooth stitching, pressed seams, and neat buttonholes.

Once you have bought good quality clothing that is appropriate for its intended use, you should care for it correctly so that it will last. Permanent care labels tell you how to wash, iron, dry clean, and bleach the clothing.

Some clothing comes with manufacturers' warranties that protect against faulty construction. Even clothing that has no warranty may be returned to the store or manufacturer if it is not properly made.

BUILDING CONSUMER VOCABULARY

Number your paper from 1 to 8. Then write the term that best matches each numbered definition.

abrasion	registered identification number
fad	synthetic fibers
natural fibers	Textile Fiber Products Identification Act
permanent care labels	Wool Products Labeling Act

1. Fibers made from chemicals
2. A substitution for the name of the manufacturer on a clothing tag
3. Fibers made from materials found in nature, such as plants or animals
4. A law requiring that labels be sewn into clothing to identify fiber content
5. Something that is very popular for only a short period of time
6. Labels sewn into an item of clothing telling you how to clean it
7. Wear caused by rubbing
8. A law requiring types of wool used in clothing to be identified

BUILDING CONSUMER UNDERSTANDING

1. When is the best time to buy camping clothes? swimwear? back-to-school clothes?
2. What are the advantages besides saving money of sewing your own clothes?
3. Which of the natural fibers are strong? Which are quick drying? Which resist abrasion?
4. How can the information on permanent care labels help you decide what clothes to buy?
5. What can consumers do if they buy clothes that turn out to have faults in construction?
6. Suppose you bought a bathing suit and, when you got home, you decided that it made you look fat. Can you return it for that reason? Why or why not?

BUILDING CONSUMER MATH SKILLS

1. When Mike Fedder shopped for shirts and slacks for his new job, he had $125 to spend. He bought four shirts at $14.95 each at Savers Discount Clothes. If Savers also charged 7 per-

cent sales tax, how much did Mike spend there? How much money did he have left for slacks?

2. Suppose you find an end-of-season clearance sale on winter jackets. On the rack the sign reads: "30% off all jackets under $100! 40% off all jackets $100 or over!" You find two jackets that you like. Jacket A is regularly priced at $96. Jacket B normally costs $110. What is the sale price of each jacket? Which is the better deal?

APPLYING CONSUMER SKILLS

1. Answer the following questions about the tags shown below.
   a. What does the information on these tags tell you about the characteristics of each garment?
   b. Which fabrics named on the tags would be good for jeans?
   c. What does "new wool" mean in the second tag?
   d. How can you find out who made each piece of clothing? Why might you want to find out?

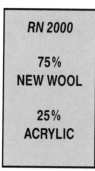

2. Examine each of the permanent care labels shown below.
   a. Suppose these labels were found on three shirts. Can all three be machine cleaned? Explain.
   b. Why is it important to follow the directions on these permanent care labels? What are some things that could go wrong otherwise?

| MACHINE WASH WARM Tumble Dry Medium Only Non-Chlorine Bleach When Needed | MACHINE WASH GENTLE Tumble Dry Low Cool Iron | DRY CLEAN ONLY |

GETTING INVOLVED IN YOUR COMMUNITY

Choose one kind of garment, such as a pair of jeans or a sweater, and shop for the best buy you can find. Visit several clothing stores in your community. Compare fabrics, construction, and the kind of care each garment needs. List the good and bad points of each. Which garment is best? Why?

CHAPTER

BUYING MEDICINES AND COSMETICS

13

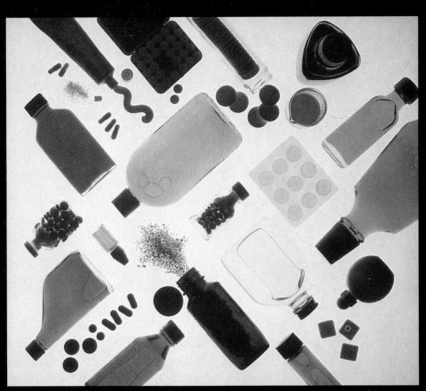

Your drugstore has thousands of medicines. For many medicines, you need a doctor's prescription. Others you can buy over the counter. How can you tell which medicines you should buy, how much you should take, how much you should pay? Can health and beauty aids make you healthy, attractive, and happy?

◆ What is the difference between prescription drugs and over-the-counter drugs?

◆ What can drugs do? What can't they do?

◆ How can you save on medicines?

◆ Who regulates and tests drugs and cosmetics?

◆ What problems can cosmetics cause?

Your medicine cabinet probably contains shampoo, medicines, brushes and combs, and maybe some cosmetics. Chances are you've bought some of the more than $7 billion worth of cosmetics sold each year. And chances are just as good that in your medicine cabinet you have at least one, and probably both, of the two categories of medicines: prescription drugs and over-the-counter drugs.

Prescription drugs, identified by the symbol "Rx," are prescribed, or ordered for you, by a doctor. In fact, you can't buy these drugs without a doctor's prescription. About 70 percent of the drugs manufactured in the United States each year are prescription drugs. All antibiotics are prescription drugs, for example. **Antibiotics**, such as penicillin, are drugs that fight diseases caused by bacteria, such as strep throat.

Over-the-counter (OTC) drugs are ones you can buy without a prescription. All of the medicines you find on drugstore shelves are OTC drugs. They include aspirin, cough medicines, and cold tablets. Prescription drugs are usually more powerful than OTC drugs. Most OTC drugs treat only the **symptoms** of a disease—the signs that something is wrong. Prescription drugs often treat the causes of a disease. Prescription drugs can also be much stronger versions of OTC drugs.

> Ibuprofen is often advertised as a substitute for aspirin. Like aspirin, it is an effective pain reliever. Also like aspirin, it can irritate the stomach. People who are allergic to aspirin are often allergic to ibuprofen as well.

THE TRUTH ABOUT MEDICINES

There are probably as many myths and misunderstandings about medicines as about any other subject. In large measure, these myths reflect the importance we all place on health. Also, special training is usually needed to know how to use medicines properly. Manufacturers make many claims for their products. The truth is often hard to find among all the claims.

The Good and Bad Sides of Aspirin

It is true that doctors recommend aspirin as one of the most effective OTC pain relievers. An American Medical Association survey found that aspirin often is "the drug of choice" when a mild (nonprescription) pain reliever is needed. Some studies have found aspirin to be as effective as some prescription pain killers, and it has fewer side effects. Still, the biggest problem with aspirin is the **side effects**—ways a drug affects the body in addition to the way it is meant to work. In addition to relieving pain, aspirin can also cause skin rashes and stomach upsets in some people. It is not recommended for children or teen-agers who have the flu or chicken pox. For these people, most doctors suggest taking another pain reliever, acetaminophen (uh SEE tuh MYN uh fuhn). It is rapidly replacing aspirin in many homes.

Many of the "extra-strength" pain relievers on the market are just combinations of aspirin, acetaminophen, and caffeine. Caffeine

> For centuries, people in various parts of the world used the bark of willow trees to stop pain and fever. Were they being foolish? No. This bark contains a chemical related to the main ingredient in aspirin.

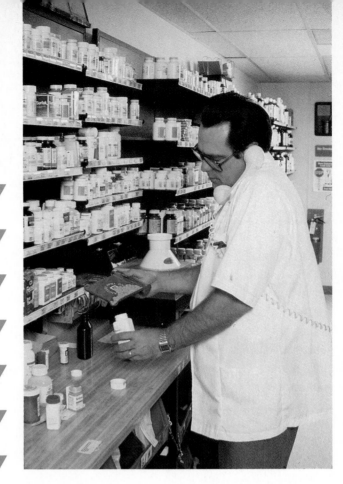

is the ingredient in coffee that keeps you awake. Most extra-strength tablets have as much caffeine as a half cup of coffee. Experts see no point in taking these extra-strength products. Plain aspirin or acetaminophen will work just as well and will probably cost less. Also, the more ingredients a product has, the greater the chance of side effects.

Cold Facts

We spend more money on cold and cough remedies than on any other over-the-counter drugs. Cold remedies can relieve some cold symptoms, such as a runny nose or stuffiness. But the American Medical Association points out that there is still no cure for the common cold.

Many manufacturers of cold products say that antihistamines relieve the symptoms of the common cold. An **antihistamine** counteracts the effects, like sneezing, of too much histamine, a substance found normally in the body. According to the American Medical Association, antihistamines are useful mainly for people with allergies. The belief that they relieve the symptoms of the common cold "is unfounded." And, like aspirin, antihistamines can have side effects. Different types of antihistamines affect people differently. Most often, however, antihistamines cause people to feel sleepy.

Every year, people in the United States buy more than 50 billion tablets containing aspirin. How much is 50 billion? If you laid 50 billion aspirin tablets side by side, they would go around the earth more than 300 times.

What Can and Cannot Be Done About Acne

Acne can be a tough matter for teen-agers. Knowing how it develops can help you decide how to treat it. Everyone has sebaceous (sih BAY shuhs) glands, which send out a white, fatty material called sebum. Growing teen-agers often have more sebum than other people. The sebaceous glands are connected to hair follicles. The follicles are lined with cells that normally die and peel off. New cells form and let the sebum come out through the skin easily. But sometimes there are too many dead cells. The cells and sebum stick together and combine with bacteria to plug the follicle. The plug grows, and so does the whole follicle. If the plug opens the pore and comes to the surface of the skin, the result is a blackhead. If, instead, the wall of the follicle breaks, the outcome is a pimple.

One way to treat acne is with drugs that cut down the amount of sebum released. This treatment must be done under a doctor's care, as the drugs used in the treatment can cause harmful side effects.

Some OTC acne products are effective, and some are not. Some simply hide the acne. Some soaps, scrubs, and lotions inflame the skin and don't reach the real problem in the follicle. Skin doctors believe that OTC products with sulfur, sulfur/resorcinol, and especially benzoyl peroxide are most effective in clearing up acne. Benzoyl peroxide gets down into the follicle, killing bacteria. It allows the dead cells to peel away, which prevents plugs from forming.

False Beliefs About Drugs and Cosmetics

One thing all medical experts seem to agree on is that mouthwashes can neither prevent colds nor help sore throats. The belief that they do either is false. Furthermore, mouthwashes don't prevent bad breath. The Food and Drug Administration (FDA) has forced mouthwash manufacturers to stop making that claim. The most manufacturers can say is that their products temporarily freshen the breath. Dentists say the best way to prevent bad breath is to brush and floss your teeth regularly.

Another false belief is that there is no difference between a deodorant and an antiperspirant. A deodorant is a cosmetic. An antiperspirant is a drug. Drugs do something to change the way the body functions. Cosmetics just cover the surface of the body. A deodorant uses perfume to cover up body odor and chemicals to slow down the growth of bacteria on the skin that cause odor. An antiperspirant helps stop the body from perspiring. Antiperspirants can irritate the skin more than deodorants can.

It is not true that dandruff is caused by germs or that a "medicated" shampoo cures dandruff by killing those germs. On the contrary, dandruff is caused by the scaling of skin, which increases when hair becomes oily. Like deodorants, dandruff shampoos are

Victorian women had beautiful complexions. Their skin was clear, pale, and unblemished. What was their secret? They wore no make-up and stayed out of the sun.

David H. McConnell started one of the first cosmetics companies in the United States after trying unsuccessfully to sell Shakespeare's plays door to door. His company became enormous, but he never forgot his roots. After 53 years in business, he changed his firm's name from the California Perfume Company to Avon, in honor of the river that flows past Shakespeare's house.

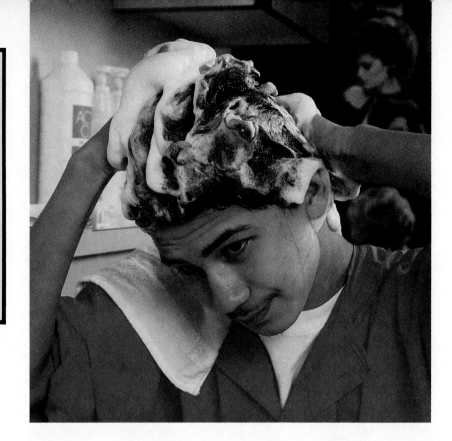

Shampoos remove the oil that attracts dirt. Without oil the outer layers of hair stand up. Conditioners put some oil back on the hair. The hair is then shinier, softer, and easier to comb.

cosmetics. At best, dandruff shampoos control flaking. They do not cure dandruff because scaling skin cannot be cured, and it happens to everyone. Consumers Union medical consultants "believe there is little evidence that scalp itching—the main symptom of dandruff—responds better to medicated shampoos than to ordinary shampoos."

✓check your understanding ✓ ✓ ✓ ✓ ✓ ✓

1. What kind of medicine is identified by the letters Rx? What kind is identified by the letters OTC?
2. What are the most recommended pain relievers?
3. What can cold remedies do? What can't they do?
4. What causes acne? What ingredients in OTC products can help people with acne?

USING MEDICINES WISELY

Buying OTC drugs without a doctor's prescription means buying them without a doctor's advice and directions. How do you know what OTC medicines will do? How do you know how much to take and how long to take it? When should you stop taking OTC drugs and call a doctor? A good source of answers is the label on a package of OTC drugs.

The Importance of OTC Drug Labels

When you take OTC drugs, the label on the bottle is your main source of information. Read the label carefully. An OTC label contains the following:

- The name of the product
- The amount of medicine contained in the bottle
- The product's active ingredients
- The name and address of the manufacturer, distributor, or packager
- Directions for safe use. These directions tell how big a dose to take, how often to take a dose, and how much you can safely take in a day or other time period.
- Warnings. People with medical conditions like high blood pressure or diabetes may be warned not to take the drug. There may be a warning to keep the drug out of reach of children. If the drug is dangerous to children, the bottle must have a safety cap as well as a warning. The FDA requires both the warning and the safety cap, because medicines are the major cause of poisoning among children under five years old.
- Drug interactions and cautions. This section warns of possible side effects. For example, some cold medicines may make you sleepy. The label will warn you about this and tell you not to drive or operate machinery.

Asking A Doctor About Prescription Drugs

You rely on your doctor to prescribe what is best for you. But it's up to you to make sure you understand what you need to know about any prescription drug you take. The FDA recommends that you find out the answers to the following questions before you leave your doctor's office with a prescription:

- What is the name of the drug? (Write it down.)
- What is the drug supposed to do for you?
- Is this the best medicine for you? (Tell the doctor about any allergies you have or any side effects you've had from drugs before. Be sure the doctor knows about any other medicines you're taking now.)
- Exactly how should you take the drug? with food? two hours after a meal?
- For how many days should you take it?
- Are there any foods you should not have while taking this drug?
- What possible side effects should you watch for? What should you do if they happen?
- Will the doctor prescribe a generic form of the drug rather than the more expensive brand-name form?

Cough No More

for Non-Narcotic
Cough Suppression

Each teaspoonful contains:
Guaifenesin, USP 100 mg and Dextro-methorphan Hydrobromide, USP 10 mg in a tasty, soothing and aromatic syrup.
INACTIVE INGREDIENTS: Citric Acid, FD&C Red 40, Flavors, Glucose, Glycerin, High Fructose Corn Syrup, Saccharin Sodium, Sodium Benzoate, Water.
DIRECTIONS FOR USE:
Adults and children 12 years of age and over: 2 teaspoonfuls every six to eight hours, not to exceed 8 teaspoonfuls in a 24-hour period; children 6 to under 12 years: 1 teaspoonful every six to eight hours, not to exceed 4 teaspoonfuls in a 24-hour period; children 2 to under 6 years: ½ teaspoonful every six to eight hours, not to exceed 2 teaspoonfuls in a 24-hour period; children under 2 years: use only as directed by physician.
Do not exceed recommended dosage.
WARNINGS: As with any drug, if you are pregnant or nursing a baby, seek the advice of a health professional before using this product.
CAUTION: Do not use if cough persists or high fever is present since these may indicate the presence of a serious condition.
FOR THE TEMPORARY RELIEF OF COUGH DUE TO THE COMMON COLD

Brand-Name and Generic Drugs

Generic drugs are similar to, but not exactly like, generic foods. A drug's generic name is given to it by the United States Adopted Names Council while it is first being tested for safety and effectiveness. If the FDA finds the drug to be safe and effective, the drug firm that developed it gives the drug a brand name. For 17 years, that drug company is the only one that can sell the drug. After that time, though, other companies can sell the drug under the generic name or under another brand name of their own.

Generic drugs are chemically the same as brand-name drugs. But many are less expensive than brand-name drugs. A recent study found that, on average, generic prescriptions cost about 50 percent less than brand-name drugs when purchased in quantities of 100 pills. The study also found that some generic drugs cost as much as 80 percent less than similar brand-name drugs. Because your doctor is the one who finally decides what drug you take, be sure to ask him or her whether a generic drug can be used.

Remember, however, that buying generic drugs does not guarantee you the best price. Drugs, like most other products, differ in price from store to store. Studies have found that some drug prices are as much as ten times higher in one store than in another. As always, it pays to shop around.

All states have some kind of a generic drug law. Even if a doctor prescribes a brand-name drug, these laws may allow pharmacists to give you the cheapest form of a drug that the drugstore carries—whether it's the brand name or the generic version.

✓check your understanding ✓ ✓ ✓ ✓ ✓ ✓

1. How can you figure out what's in an OTC drug and how much of it you should take?
2. What information should you tell your doctor before she or he prescribes any drug for you?
3. What is the difference between generic drugs and brand-name drugs?

HOW SAFE ARE YOUR MEDICINES?

The FDA is responsible for seeing that the medicines you buy are safe and effective. The agency does some testing itself, but mostly it examines and judges the testing done by drug companies.

Drug companies first test new drugs on animals. These animal tests must show that the drug is reasonably safe before it can be tested on humans. The FDA must approve all human testing. The first tests on humans help determine whether there are side effects. Only a few people are used, and the FDA believes that no one has been harmed permanently by these tests.

If your aspirin smells like vinegar, it's time to throw the bottle out. The tablets are decomposing and won't work properly.

Safety with Rx Drugs

Rx, or prescription, drugs are very powerful. When used properly, they are very effective. When not used properly, however, they can be very dangerous. You should always take the following precautions when using and storing Rx drugs.

- Take the medicine for the entire time period prescribed. Don't stop because you start to feel better.
- Don't take additional medicines without first asking your doctor since some medications interact with each other and can cause more problems than they cure.
- Never use someone else's prescription. No two people are alike. Even if you have the same problem, you may need a different drug or a different amount of the drug.
- If you lose the instructions explaining how to take the drug, don't depend on your memory. Ask your doctor or pharmacist to give them to you again.
- Keep your medicine in its original container. The container is especially made for it.
- Store all medicines out of children's reach. Containers with child-proof caps provide additional protection.
- Store all medicines away from high temperatures and humidity.

Just because you're not allergic to a drug or cosmetic today doesn't mean you won't be tomorrow. You can suddenly become sensitive to something you've been using safely for years. If a rash, headache, or dizziness occurs after using any medicine or cosmetic, stop using it immediately and call your doctor.

Next, a few patients are treated with the drug to see if it really cures or prevents the disease. If both the animal and human tests cause no unnecessary harm, the company tests the drug more widely. Thousands of patients may be involved in this part of the program.

After all this testing, the company submits a New Drug Application to the FDA's Bureau of Drugs. A team of doctors and scientists evaluates the New Drug Application. The FDA weighs benefits against risks. A drug that can cure a deadly disease may be approved even if there is a great risk of side effects. But a drug that only relaxes people may be turned down even if there is only a slight risk from side effects.

After FDA approval, the company is allowed to put the drug on the market. Then, it must keep records of the drug's safety and effectiveness and report its findings to the FDA. Reports are sent in every three months during the first year, every six months during the second year, and once a year after that. If the FDA finds any unexpected side effects, it can withdraw its approval of the drug.

HOW SAFE ARE YOUR COSMETICS?

In their never-ending search for good looks, men and women spend several billion dollars a year on cosmetics. Like anything else, consumers should shop carefully for cosmetics and use them wisely.

Large cosmetics manufacturers test new products in their own professional laboratories. Still, not all of the lotions, creams, ointments, dyes, powders, and gels are safe. The federal Food, Drug, and Cosmetics Act regulates the ingredients, cleanliness in manufacturing, and packaging of cosmetics. But the law does not require cosmetics to be tested for safety.

Care with Cosmetics

Cosmetics can bother your skin. They can cause acne. In fact, one expert says that one third of all adult women suffer from acne. Thick, greasy, oily products can increase the clogging of the hair follicles. Skin care experts advise you to use water-based or oil-free products. Wear make-up as little as possible, and wash it off as soon as you can.

Furthermore, some cosmetics can harm you if they're used improperly. For instance, eye liners, eye shadows, and mascara attract bacteria. Dirty applicators can cause eye infections. Experts advise you to note the date when you buy these products and get rid of them after four months. And never use eye make-up—or any other make-up—that belongs to someone else.

Protection in the Sun

The harmful effects of the sun are now well known. Too much sun can cause your skin to age too quickly and can also cause skin cancer. If you want to get a good tan, start out by spending just

Much of the make-up men and women used in the past was highly poisonous. For example, Englishwomen in the 1600's used to whiten their skin with something called Soliman's water. It was dangerous because it was made with mercury. It did make skin white. It also made teeth fall out.

How much sun is safe? The sun is stronger in the summer and at midday. It is more harmful the younger you are and the lighter your skin.

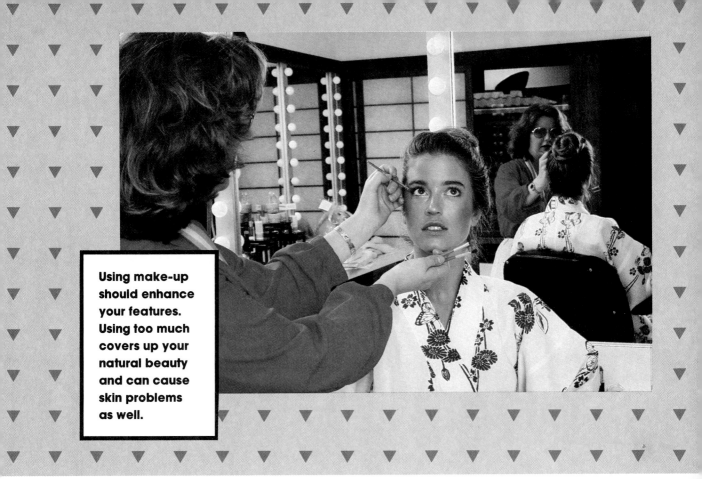

Using make-up should enhance your features. Using too much covers up your natural beauty and can cause skin problems as well.

Some foods, cosmetics, and drugs can make you more sensitive to the sun than you already are. Foods to watch out for include celery, carrots, and artificial sweeteners. Cosmetics to be concerned about include deodorant soaps and perfumes. Problem drugs include antihistamines and antibiotics.

five or ten minutes in the sun. Slowly work up to longer periods of time. Don't sunbathe during midday. And don't use suntan preparations such as mineral oil or cocoa butter. They will not protect you against the sun's harmful ultraviolet rays. Instead, use plenty of any sunscreen recommended by a consumer magazine or a pharmacist. Unlike suntan oils and butters, sunscreens block out radiation from ultraviolet rays. Sunscreens come in different strengths and are rated with a **sun protection factor (SPF)**. The higher the SPF, the better the protection. A sunscreen with an SPF of 15 or above blocks out most of the ultraviolet radiation.

Cosmetics Labels

Whatever cosmetics product you buy, read the label first. Federal law requires the following information on every package of cosmetics:

- The product's name
- The manufacturer's name and address
- The product's weight
- A list of ingredients
- A list of any artificial colorings or flavorings

Read the list of ingredients carefully to find out if the product contains anything you're allergic to. You also want to know if the product has helpful ingredients, as in the case of sunscreens. By looking at the weight, you can compare the costs of different brands and different-sized packages. Many cosmetics packages have directions for use. Follow these directions carefully.

√ check your understanding √ √ √ √ √ √

1. **Describe the procedures drug companies use to test a new drug.**
2. **Why should you throw out eye liner that is more than four months old?**
3. **What are some of the problems caused by suntanning? How can these problems be prevented?**
4. **What can you find out by reading the label on a cosmetics package?**

SUMMARIZING
the chapter

There are two types of medicines: prescription drugs and over-the-counter drugs. Prescription drugs are ordered for you by a doctor and usually treat the causes of a disease. OTC drugs are sold without a prescription, are less powerful than prescription drugs, and usually treat only the symptoms of a disease. Aspirin, the most common OTC drug, is generally considered to be one of the most effective pain killers. For those who shouldn't take aspirin, pain relievers with acetaminophen are recommended. There is no cure for the common cold, nor is there a cure for dandruff. Some OTC products may help control acne, but the ingredients should be carefully checked.

Most drugs made in the United States are prescription drugs. Be sure to learn as much as you can from your doctor about any drug prescribed for you.

Different states have different laws about selling drugs under their generic or brand names. Generic drugs often cost less than brand-name drugs. However, you should shop around because prescription drug prices vary widely from drugstore to drugstore.

The Food and Drug Administration supervises the development of new drugs and the quality of medicines already for sale. Cosmetics are not tested in the same way as drugs, so you should exercise care in using them. Always follow the directions on labels of both drugs and cosmetics.

C·H·A·P·T·E·R ◆ A ◆ C·T·I·V·I·T·I·E·S

BUILDING CONSUMER VOCABULARY

Number your paper from 1 to 7. Then write the term that best matches each numbered definition.

antibiotic
antihistamine
over-the-counter (OTC) drugs
prescription drugs

side effects
sun protection factor (SPF)
symptoms

1. Drugs that cannot be bought without a prescription
2. Signs that you may be suffering from an illness
3. A drug that relieves the symptoms, like sneezing, of allergies
4. Drugs that can be bought without a prescription
5. Ways a drug affects the body in addition to the way it is meant to work
6. A drug that is effective in fighting illnesses caused by bacteria
7. A rating system that indicates how well a product protects against the harmful rays of the sun

BUILDING CONSUMER UNDERSTANDING

1. What is the difference between prescription drugs and over-the-counter drugs?
2. What advice would you give someone buying a pain reliever? a cold remedy? an acne preparation?
3. Who should not take aspirin?
4. How does caffeine affect a person?
5. What advice would you give someone who is buying prescription drugs?
6. What is the difference between suntan oil and sunscreen?
7. What care should be taken when using cosmetics?

BUILDING CONSUMER MATH SKILLS

1. In a recent year, 1.5 billion prescriptions were written for drugs costing a total of $19.3 billion. Twenty percent of these prescriptions were for generic drugs. What was the average cost of a prescription drug in that year? How many generic prescriptions were filled?
2. The generic drug Diprydamole, a blood pressure medication, costs $9.89 for 100 tablets. The brand name drug, Persantine, costs $27.49 for the same amount. How much do you save by buying the generic drug? What is the percentage of savings?

Read the label below and answer the following questions:

This product contains safe and effective ingredients to help relieve typical cold symptoms: stuffiness, runny nose, and sneezing.

DOSAGE. Adults: 2 tablets every 4 hours as needed, not to exceed 12 tablets in 24 hours. Children 6 to 12: half the adult dosage. Under 6: consult a physician.

WARNING. Keep this medicine out of children's reach. In case of accidental overdose, consult a physician immediately. Do not use for more than 10 days unless directed by a physician. Persons with a high fever or persistent cough should not use this preparation unless directed by a physician.

DRUG INTERACTION AND CAUTIONS. Do not take without consulting a physician if under medical care. Do not drive a car or operate machinery while taking this cold remedy, as it may cause drowsiness.

ACTIVE INGREDIENTS. Each tablet contains 325 mg acetaminophen, 12 mg phenylpropanolamine HCl, 10 mg chlorpheniramine, and 18 mg dextromethorphan HBr.

1. What would you take this OTC drug for?
2. What are the active ingredients? Which are familiar to you?
3. How much should an adult take at one time? How much may an adult take in a day?
4. When should you stop taking this drug and call a doctor?
5. Can this drug cause side effects? If so, what are they?

How much do drugs cost where you live? Ask your pharmacist or your doctor to name five of the most often prescribed brand-name drugs. Then go to three drugstores in your community and price equal quantities of these drugs. Which store has the lowest prices? Which has the highest? Why do you think this is so?

BUYING PROFESSIONAL SERVICES

Some things a consumer shops for are more important than others. Two of the most important are medical and legal services. How do you find good medical and legal help? What kind do you need? How much should you pay?

◆ How should you shop for a doctor?

◆ What choices do you have in medical care?

◆ When do you need a lawyer?

◆ Where can you find legal help?

14

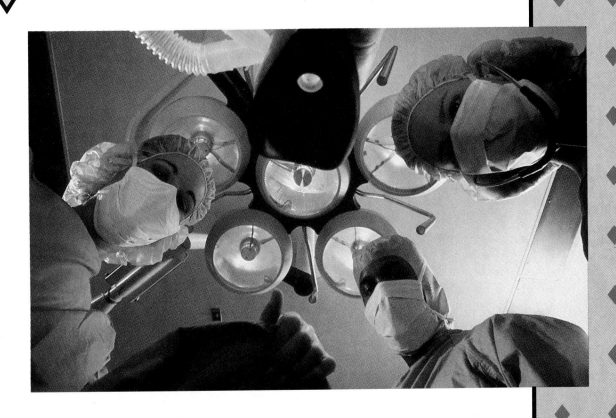

The economy of the United States depends more and more on services. Excluding farmers, nearly three out of four workers are employed by service businesses. There are educational services, financial services, health services, legal services, maintenance and repair services, and government services. Shopping for some services is so important that it requires special consumer skills.

In this chapter, we will concentrate on two of these important professional services: health care and legal help. You can apply the same shopping techniques and good consumer practices to other professional services as well.

DO YOU NEED A DOCTOR?

People often wait until they are sick to think about doctors. But the time to think about choosing a doctor is when you are healthy. In some places, people have no choice in this matter. More than 100 counties in the United States have no doctor at all. Many more have only one doctor. Doctors seem to be attracted to cities and suburbs. Fewer settle in rural areas.

Kinds of Doctors

Many people in the United States can choose from among several doctors. Faced with a choice, what kind of doctor should you look for? Most doctors agree that everyone should have a **primary-care physician**. This doctor is the one you go to on a regular basis

The best health care is the care you give yourself so that you don't get sick in the first place. To stay healthy, many experts recommend that you exercise every day, eat breakfast, and sleep no more or less than seven to eight hours a day. What shouldn't you do? Don't eat between meals, drink, or smoke.

Ophthalmologists specialize in treating eyes. After four years of college and medical school, and an internship, they must also complete a residency in their specialty.

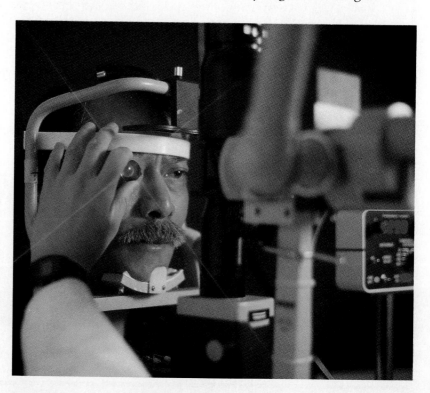

Doctors as Specialists

Many years ago, people went to "family doctors," or general practitioners, as their primary-care physicians. As more and more doctors specialize, these terms are changing. Today, your primary-care physician may be called by a different name.

- **Family practitioners** are the modern version of the old family doctors. They treat the whole body, but usually don't perform surgery. They often like to treat everyone in a family.
- **Internists** treat everything that has to do with the inside of your body. They do not perform surgery either. Many people use them as family doctors.
- **Gynecologists** treat diseases of the female reproductive organs. Many women use gynecologists as primary-care physicians.
- **Pediatricians** treat children's diseases and medical problems.

Chances are you will be referred to a specialist at some time. Here is a list of ones you may be likely to see at some point.

- **Dermatologists** specialize in diseases of the skin. Teen-agers with severe cases of acne may be referred to a dermatologist.
- **General surgeons** diagnose diseases and perform surgery on many different parts of the body.
- **Obstetricians** take care of women during pregnancy and childbirth.
- **Ophthalmologists** are eye doctors. An ophthalmologist can treat the whole range of eye problems. This doctor should not be confused with an optometrist, who is not a doctor and usually just fits you for a pair of glasses.
- **Orthopedic surgeons** treat bone and joint diseases and broken bones. If you do something to your knee playing football or break an arm, you may need to see an orthopedic surgeon.
- **Psychiatrists** diagnose and treat mental disorders.

for checkups, and the one you should see first when you have a problem. Often these doctors are certified in family practice or in internal medicine.

Once you have a primary-care physician you like, you should probably stick with that doctor. It takes time for a doctor to get to know you and your medical history.

Sometimes, your primary-care physician will suggest that you see a specialist. A **specialist** is a doctor who practices entirely in a single branch of medicine. The specialist will generally have more experience with the particular problem than your primary-care physician. The box above lists a number of primary-care doctors and specialists and describes what they do.

Choosing a Good Doctor

What should you look for in a doctor? Let's look at the views of one doctor about finding a good primary-care physician.

When choosing a primary-care physician, patients need to rate a few basic skills that physicians should have. Because we're responsible for the patient's total health—mental and physical—we must be completely familiar with the patient's medical history. We also must know all personal, family, and work circumstances. We must know when and how to use a specialist. We feel that we should stress preventive medicine and try to treat patients as individuals. We try to be friendly and answer questions honestly. In addition, I feel it's important for primary-care physicians to have the best education and training possible and to be affiliated, or connected, with a good hospital.

If patients aren't satisfied with their physician's services, they should talk to the doctor or even change physicians. Studies show that 40 percent of our patients sometime in their lives change physicians because they're dissatisfied with us.

DR. JOSIAH WOODS
Family Practitioner

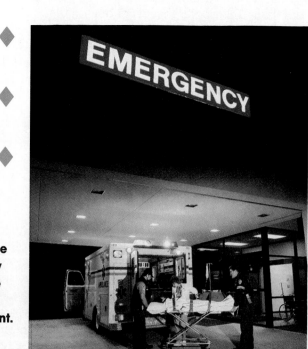

In many locations you get ambulance service by calling the police department.

How to Find a Doctor

Where should you look for a primary-care physician? As Connie Daniels finds out in the following case study, waiting until you're sick to find a doctor is a mistake.

CASE STUDY

No doctor in the house

A few months after Connie Daniels moved to a new city, she became ill. When her temperature went to 103, she knew she had to see a doctor. But whom? She didn't know any doctors, or even anyone she could ask to recommend one. She decided to try the phone book.

Connie looked in the yellow pages under "Physicians" and began calling. Dr. Anderson was completely booked but suggested that she call Dr. Polsky. Dr. Polsky said he could see her in three weeks. If that was too long, she should call Dr. Merill. Dr. Merill's answering service said he was on vacation. He wouldn't be in for another week, but Dr. Zimmerman was taking his patients. Dr. Zimmerman said she was unable to take on any new patients. She was too busy with both her own patients and Dr. Merill's.

Connie remembered seeing a 24-hour walk-in clinic as she rode the bus to work. But, instead, she decided to try the emergency room of a nearby hospital. Checking the phone book, she found a hospital not too far from her apartment. By the time she got there, she was so weak she could hardly walk. The nurse at the desk told her to fill out a form and take a seat. After two hours, a doctor was able to see her. The doctor examined her, found that she had pneumonia, and had her admitted to the hospital.

Since Connie was sick and did not have a doctor, she was wise to go to a hospital for **emergency care**—immediate medical attention for an accident or an illness. She could have gone to the walk-in clinic as well. **Walk-in clinics** are small medical offices, often found in shopping areas, set up to treat anyone who walks in. You do not need an appointment. They are staffed with doctors and other medical professionals. Many are open 24 hours a day. They have less equipment and fewer people than a hospital, but they are often less expensive and may be able to treat you more quickly.

The best thing for Connie, however, would have been to have her own primary-care physician. She should have found one before she got sick. How do you find a doctor? If, like Connie, you are moving, you can ask your old doctor to recommend someone in the new place. You can also ask a hospital, or a city or county health society, for a list of available doctors. If there is a medical school nearby, it can give you names of graduates or instructors who practice in the community. Some consumer groups publish medical directories. These directories list doctors and their fees, backgrounds, services, and methods of practice. You can check the public library to see if there is a directory for your community. Ask your friends and neighbors about their doctors too. They may give you helpful advice.

✓check your understanding ✓ ✓ ✓ ✓ ✓ ✓

1. **What are the differences between a primary-care physician and a specialist?**
2. **What should you look for in a good primary-care physician?**
3. **What sources can help you find a doctor?**

How Doctors Practice

Broadly speaking, consumers purchase health care in one of two ways: through fee-for-service arrangements and through group arrangements.

In a **fee-for-service** arrangement, consumers choose any primary-care physician and specialist they want. These doctors often are in what is called *private practice*—they operate independently from other doctors. Consumers must pay for their doctors' bills out of their savings or turn these bills over to a health insurance company to be paid.

Group arrangements are actually a form of health insurance. You will learn more about health insurance in Chapter 29. In a group arrangement, the consumer must select the primary-care physician and specialists from a particular group of doctors. The doctors are said to be in *group practice*—they are in business with other doctors. About half of all doctors practice in this way. Generally, this type of medical care is less expensive than fee-for-service arrangements.

There are three different kinds of group arrangements: health maintenance organizations, independent practitioner associations, and preferred provider organizations.

Health maintenance organizations (HMO) To join an HMO, you pay a fixed monthly fee. Then you can use the services of a group of doctors who work under one roof. Sometimes you can choose a primary-care physician from the group. In other cases, a primary-care physician is assigned to you. If you need a specialist, one from the group is chosen for you. The HMOs have their own offices, nurses, test labs, and emergency rooms. Some HMOs even have their own hospitals.

Independent practitioner associations (IPA) IPA members also get a number of medical services for a monthly fee. An IPA is an organization of doctors who work out of their own offices treating both IPA subscribers and private patients. You pick your own primary-care physician from an IPA list and are referred to specialists within the IPA by your primary-care doctor.

Preferred provider organizations (PPO) If you join a PPO, you also pay a fixed fee to use the services of a certain group of doctors and hospitals. You may also go to doctors and hospitals that are not in this group. But you will have to pay part of the bills from these outside doctors and hospitals in addition to your monthly fee.

Second Opinions

No matter how much you like your doctor, there may be times when you need a **second opinion**—another doctor's views about a medical problem. Most medical experts think you should get a second opinion if your ailment is getting worse or if your doctor tells you that you need surgery. They also suggest getting a second opinion when the treatment recommended seems very expensive, dangerous, or complex.

Some consumers are required to get second opinions by health insurance plans. Otherwise, the insurance might not pay for the treatment. Of course, consulting another doctor is wise any time you feel uncomfortable with your doctor's advice.

Health Care Costs and Malpractice

An average of about $2,000 per person is spent on health care in the United States each year. This amount includes everything from aspirin to open-heart surgery to cancer research. In the 1980's, health care costs rose much faster than most expenses in the family budget. Doctors' fees went up about twice as fast as most other expenses. Hospital charges rose almost four times as fast.

One thing that has contributed to the high cost of health care is lawsuits. A patient can sue a doctor for **malpractice**—for being careless or for making a mistake that most doctors would not make. Patients are filing, and winning, more and more malpractice suits. Doctors carry insurance against these suits, but the cost of the insurance has shot up. Some doctors pay over $50,000 a year for their malpractice insurance.

Malpractice insurance is so costly that doctors have to pass along the expense by raising charges for their services. Doctors just entering practice are steering away from high-risk specialties like surgery, where malpractice insurance is particularly costly. On the one hand, many doctors feel that there should be a limit to the

Babylonians, who lived in the Middle East around 3,000 B.C., used to put sick people in beds outside in the street. Why? In that way, passersby could offer medical advice.

The issue of whether doctors should make house calls has long been a subject of debate. In England in the late 1500's, doctors not only made house calls, they actually lived in a patient's house until the patient recovered.

amount of money received from a malpractice lawsuit. On the other hand, lawyers claim that if a patient is permanently unable to work, a million–dollar settlement is fair and reasonable.

Health care expenses have risen dramatically since 1980 because of the increase in malpractice insurance for doctors.

√check your understanding √ √ √ √ √ √

1. What are the differences among the three group arrangements for medical care?
2. How do you get a primary-care physician at an HMO? at an IPA?
3. When should you get a second opinion?
4. What is malpractice?

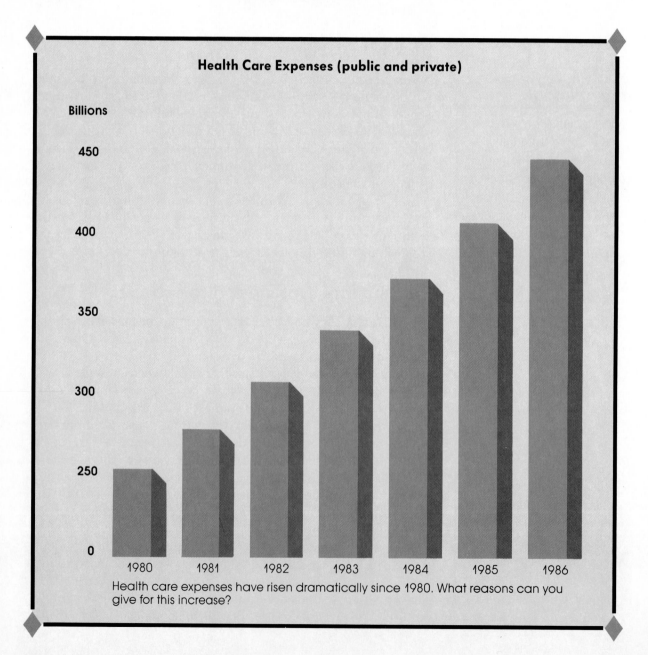

Health Care Expenses (public and private)

Billions

Health care expenses have risen dramatically since 1980. What reasons can you give for this increase?

There is more than one lawyer for every 350 people in the United States. Their help is needed with such things as contracts, lawsuits, and wills.

DO YOU NEED A LAWYER?

You may think that only people accused of crimes need lawyers, or attorneys. Most people, however, use them for civil, or non-criminal, cases. Almost everyone needs the help of a lawyer some-time. Here are some of the reasons you may need one.

■ **Contracts**. A written **contract** is any legal agreement between two or more people. The partnership agreement discussed in Chapter 6 is one example. It may be a long and complicated document or just a short letter. If the contract is important or complicated, or if it involves a lot of money, a lawyer should read it. The lawyer may suggest changes or negotiate with the other person to protect your interests.

■ **Real estate deals**. Buying or selling real estate can involve many legal problems. It is wise to have a lawyer from start to finish.

■ **Wills**. A **will** directs where your money and property will go after you die. If a person doesn't have a will, everything will be divided according to state laws. Most experts recommend that people who have property and want to divide it in a certain way have a will.

Lawyers have been involved in forming the laws of the United States from its very beginning. Of the 56 people who signed the Declaration of Independence, 25 were lawyers. And 31 of the 55 people who wrote the Constitution were lawyers as well.

- **Trusts**. A *trust* is a plan by which you turn over your property to someone else to hold and manage for your benefit or for the benefit of someone else. Often the trust is administered, or run, by an attorney.

- **Divorce**. Almost everyone needs a lawyer for a divorce, even if the divorce is *uncontested*—that is, both people already agree on the terms of the divorce. When the husband and wife disagree about the division of property or about the children, good legal help is critical.

- **Lawsuits**. If you are going to sue or if you are sued, you need a lawyer.

- **Bankruptcy**. If you can't pay your debts, you may have to declare bankruptcy. If you need to declare bankruptcy, you need a lawyer.

- **Landlord-tenant matters**. A lawyer can be useful in disputes between renters and owners. In many states, disagreements over small amounts of money, however, can be settled in small claims court without a lawyer.

How to Find a Lawyer

When trying to find a good lawyer, consumers can get some help from a **legal referral service**, a service that maintains lists of lawyers to recommend to people searching for one. This service is usually sponsored by the local **bar association**, a professional organization of lawyers. In some places, attorneys join bar associations voluntarily. In other places, they must belong to such a group in order to practice law in that state.

In addition, lawyers can advertise, and many of them include prices in the advertisements. You can find ads for lawyers in newspapers, in the yellow pages, and even on billboards. Of course, ads cannot tell you how good a lawyer is.

An attorney's first concern should be to defend the client's interests, and some lawyers can do this better than others. Judging the legal ability of attorneys is difficult. Rather than answering an ad or using a referral service, therefore, you may be wise to ask people you know for advice. Friends may be able to tell you about their experiences with lawyers. The best advice may come from someone who is an attorney but doesn't practice the kind of law involved in your case. Other good advice might come from other people experienced in your kind of case. An accountant or bank officer may know a good lawyer who specializes in wills. A real estate broker may know lawyers experienced in real estate law. A marriage counselor may know lawyers specializing in divorce.

If you want to become President, it may be a good idea to go to law school. Nearly two thirds of all Presidents of the United States have been lawyers.

To become a lawyer, most people must go through seven years of training after high school. Most lawyers have a college degree plus three years of law school. After they graduate from law school, they must pass a state bar examination in order to practice in that state.

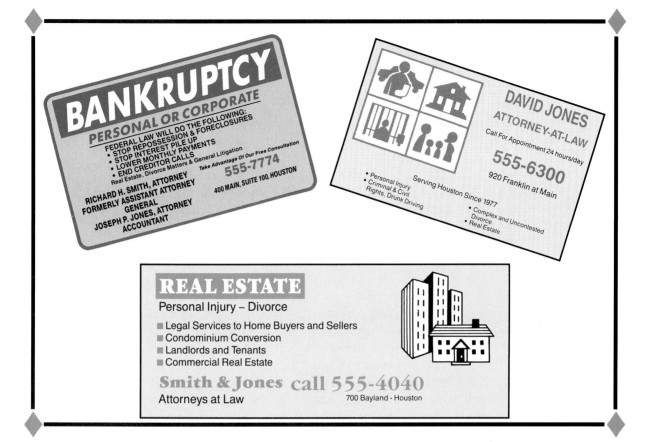

How Lawyers Practice

Like doctors, lawyers practice in a number of ways. You can go to a private lawyer who practices alone or is part of a large law firm.

Legal clinics are groups of lawyers who specialize in simple services such as wills, real estate closings, uncontested divorces, and bankruptcy. They have fixed fees for these services. Often they assign you any lawyer who is free. For complicated cases, they charge by the hour. In these cases, you should make sure the lawyer is well qualified to handle your particular problem.

Prepaid legal services are available through some professional organizations, labor unions, and credit unions. You must pay a fee to join. You can get some simple legal services at no extra charge. Members often get other services at lower fees than non-members pay. Professional organizations and unions can give a law firm a lot of business, so it may charge lower fees. However, the quality of the legal help is only as good as the lawyer or law firm that provides the service.

As with doctors, you should not wait until you need one to find a lawyer. In the following case study, Liz and Todd McKay find that so many choices make finding a lawyer difficult.

CASE STUDY

Liz and Todd McKay have decided to buy their first home. They have made a written offer to buy the house, and the owners have accepted it. The McKays know they need a lawyer to close the deal, but they don't know any. How can they get a good one?

First, they turned to the yellow pages. Hundreds of lawyers were listed. Should they just call one nearby? They couldn't decide. Then Todd found a legal referral service listed in the phone book. He called the service and got the names of two attorneys who had offices near where the McKays lived. Todd was told, however, that any lawyer can register with the service.

Liz saw several ads in the local newspaper for legal clinics. The ads gave prices for various legal services. Some of the prices for real estate closings were lower than others.

Todd had heard about prepaid legal services offered through his credit union at work. For a fixed fee, he could get a variety of legal services, including real estate closings and two free hours of a lawyer's time. However, a neighbor told Todd that she didn't like the prepaid legal service she bought. The lawyers' offices were on the other side of the city. The neighbor couldn't even make a convenient appointment with the attorney she had been assigned.

Todd and Liz need a lawyer. They still aren't sure how to choose one.

1. **Where did Todd and Liz look for a lawyer?**
2. **What problems are they encountering with these sources?**
3. **What other ways could they find a lawyer?**

How to Select the Right Lawyer for You

Whether you find lawyers through the phone book or through people's advice, you should collect the names of a number of attorneys who might help you with your problem. Then you should visit each one. Many lawyers do not charge for the first meeting. Others charge only a small fee.

When you talk to the lawyers, find out if they handle matters like yours. The more complex your problem, the more you need an experienced lawyer. Find out what percentage of the lawyers' time is spent on problems like yours. What kinds of similar cases have these lawyers handled lately? Did they win these cases or lose them?

Try to figure out which lawyer you could work with best. Do you trust the lawyer? Can you meet or speak with the lawyer at convenient times? Will the lawyer do most of the work on your problem or assign it to others?

Choose a lawyer who has experience with legal problems like yours.

Even though lawyers and doctors are experts in very complicated fields, they should be able to explain clearly to you what they are doing. Make sure you choose a doctor or lawyer who makes you feel comfortable and whose instructions and advice you understand.

The Charge for Services

Finally, you need to find out the fee. Lawyers should be clear about their charges. They should be willing to state their fees in writing. In fact, some experts advise writing a letter of agreement describing the services to be performed and the fees. Some lawyers charge a flat fee for simple legal services. High-volume legal clinics should have the lowest prices for these services.

In more complex cases, lawyers charge by the hour. Find out the hourly rate and about how much time your case will take. For lawsuits, personal injury claims, and workers' compensation claims, lawyers often charge a **contingency fee**. This fee is a percentage of the money you might win. If you lose the case, you don't have to pay the lawyer. If you win, you pay the lawyer generally about one third of any money you receive.

✓ check your understanding ✓ ✓ ✓ ✓ ✓ ✓

1. Besides criminal cases, for what other matters are lawyers used?
2. What are legal clinics? What legal services do they most often provide?
3. What are some of the advantages and disadvantages of prepaid legal services?
4. List four things you would want to know before hiring a lawyer.

SUMMARIZING
the chapter

Consumers are using more professional services every year. Health care and legal help are two of the most important professional services.

Shopping for a primary-care physician is particularly important. To evaluate a primary-care physician, consider the doctor's training, use of specialists, and hospital affiliation. To find a new doctor when you move, ask your old doctor for a recommendation. Check with a local hospital, medical society, or medical school. Look in a directory from a consumer group. Ask friends and neighbors for advice.

Doctors practice privately in fee-for-service arrangements, and they also practice in groups. Group practices, such as HMOs, are generally less expensive than fee-for-service care, but you must use the doctors in the group.

If you are not satisfied with a doctor's care, you should change doctors. If a doctor recommends expensive or dangerous treatments, you would be wise to get a second opinion. These days some insurance companies require an opinion from a second doctor before they will pay for surgical costs.

Consumers also need legal help for a variety of matters such as contracts, real estate transactions, wills, trusts, divorces, lawsuits, bankruptcy, and landlord-tenant matters. Legal clinics specialize in standardized services, including wills, real estate transactions, and simple divorces. They charge a flat fee for these services. Prepaid legal services are sometimes available through employers, professional associations, labor unions, and credit unions. Private lawyers practice separately and also in large law firms.

It is wise to interview a number of lawyers before selecting one. Make sure the lawyer you select is experienced in your type of problem, is easy to reach and to work with, and is affordable.

BUILDING CONSUMER VOCABULARY

Number your paper from 1 to 15. Then write the term that best matches each numbered definition.

bar association
contingency fee
contract
emergency care
fee-for-service
legal clinics
legal referral service
malpractice

prepaid legal services
primary-care physician
second opinion
specialist
trust
walk-in clinic
will

1. Another doctor's view about a medical problem
2. Legal services available through professional organizations, labor unions, and credit unions
3. A doctor who works entirely in a single branch of medicine
4. A description of how money and property will be divided after death
5. A percentage of the money won in a lawsuit given to the lawyer who won the case
6. A service that recommends lawyers
7. Places that specialize in simple legal services
8. The doctor you should go to for regular checkups and the one you should go to first when you have a medical problem
9. A way of receiving medical care in which you are able to select any doctor you wish
10. A professional organization of lawyers
11. Any legal agreement between two or more people
12. Carelessness or unusual mistakes made by a doctor
13. A plan by which one person holds and manages property for someone else
14. Immediate medical attention for an accident or an illness
15. A medical center that treats people without appointments

BUILDING CONSUMER UNDERSTANDING

1. If you were moving to a new town, what things should you consider in shopping for a doctor's services?
2. What are the advantages and disadvantages of choosing a fee-for-service primary-care doctor over using a group service?
3. How might the possibility of a malpractice suit affect a doctor's fees?

4. Suppose you are going to buy a new house. When is the best time to find a lawyer? Why?
5. Why is it important for a person to have a will?
6. In what ways do lawyers practice?
7. How do lawyers charge for their services? What other kind of fee do lawyers charge?

BUILDING CONSUMER MATH SKILLS

1. Together, Bill Royal and Mark Langon are buying a small apartment building to fix up and operate. Bill's lawyer charges $75 an hour for 5½ hours of related legal services. Mark has joined a prepaid legal service that charges $98 a year for membership plus $175 for real estate services. How much will Bill pay? How much will Mark pay?
2. Assume that you sue for $15,000 in a personal injury case. Your lawyer agrees to a contingency fee of one third of any money you receive. The court awards you $7,500. How much does your lawyer get paid? How much is left for you?

APPLYING CONSUMER SKILLS

1. Do you know where to go to get emergency medical treatment in your area? Make a list of all the hospital emergency rooms in your area. Then add to that a list of walk-in clinics where you can get emergency care. Describe the types of emergency treatment each provides. What is the approximate cost of each type of service?
2. Jennifer and Dan Fogarty want to make out wills. Where can they go to have wills made? How can they decide which lawyer would be best for them?

GETTING INVOLVED IN YOUR COMMUNITY

Interview three other service providers in your community. For example, you could interview a tax preparer, a dentist, an insurance agent, a carpenter, a plumber, or a repair person. What guidelines can they give about shopping for these services? Report your findings to the class.

THINKING ABOUT:

Celebrity Endorsements

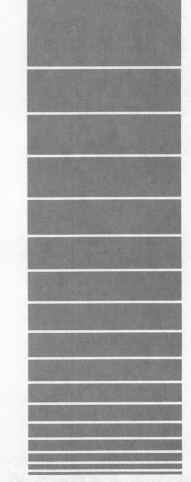

One afternoon, Jason and Melissa were watching a tennis match between two well-known players on TV. Melissa noticed that one of the players was wearing a certain brand of tennis shoes. She said, "Those must be good shoes if she wears them." Jason replied, "I don't know. She's got so many brand names on her clothes, she looks like a walking billboard."

Celebrity endorsements *are* big business. In one recent year, a 17-year-old tennis player earned $4 million—$3 million of it solely from endorsements for clothing, rackets, and tape products. Other athletes endorse not only athletic clothing and sporting goods but breakfast cereals, watches, and rental cars.

By law, athletes and celebrities are required to use the products they endorse. A tennis player who endorses a certain brand of racket must actually use that brand. A singer who promotes a certain acne cream must use that cream. Discoveries of false product testimonials have in some cases forced celebrities to give up payments from advertisers.

Advertisers think products sell better if consumers see them linked to athletes and celebrities. One year, advertisers spent $400 million for Olympic Games sponsorships. Over $1.4 billion is spent per year on other event sponsorships. Some events are created *just* so the advertiser can promote a product. Sponsorship can be an inexpensive form of advertising. When the event is televised, the advertiser's banners, billboards, and garment patches are more noticeable than commercials.

Answer the following questions on a separate sheet of paper. Use complete sentences.

1. If you like a celebrity who advertises a product, are you more inclined to buy the product? Explain.

2. Does an athlete who endorses a brand of toothpaste know any more about the product than you? Are you sure to like the product just because the athlete does?

3. Would you doubt a celebrity's sincerity if he or she is paid a huge endorsement fee? Explain. Would you be more likely to believe a celebrity who is not being paid for his or her endorsement? Explain.

4. Why do you think celebrities are required to use the products they endorse?

5. Do you think celebrity endorsements have the effect that advertisers want them to? Why or why not?

THE CONSUMER AND CREDIT

THE WHAT AND WHY OF CREDIT

Imagine a world without credit. Before you used the telephone in your home, you would have to deposit the correct change. Before you turned on a light, you would have to pay the electric company. In order to buy a car or a house, you would have to save up all of the money in advance. What are the advantages of using credit?

◆ What are the different types of credit?

◆ What is your credit rating, and why is it important?

◆ Where can you get credit?

◆ How much does credit cost?

Credit can allow you to pay for an education which will benefit you in the future.

- Sam Etheridge needs money for his college tuition.
- Jessica Chen wants a loan to purchase clothes for her dress shop.
- The citizens of Denton want to borrow money to pay for a new police station.
- The President and members of Congress want to spend $140 billion more than the government took in from taxes.

What do all of these people have in common? They all have wants, but lack the money to satisfy those wants. All of them wish to borrow the money they need to satisfy those wants. If they do borrow, they will be receiving credit. **Credit** is the opportunity to obtain money, goods, and services now in return for the promise to pay for them later. By using credit, people can add to their purchasing power, raise their standard of living, and increase their productivity.

Consumers in the United States use a tremendous amount of credit. Consumer credit—the amount of money consumers owe—grew from $60 billion in 1960 to over $600 billion 26 years later in 1986.

Businesses use even more credit. They use credit to raise funds to pay operating expenses and to pay for capital goods. In this way, businesses can increase the number of goods and services they produce and also improve the way they make or deliver those goods and services.

Studies show that people who use credit for most of their spending buy 25 to 35 percent more than people who use cash.

With credit you can also buy things that can bring pleasure to your life in the present.

Government uses credit to provide public services. Sometimes, governments wish to offer more programs and projects than can be paid for with the money collected from taxes. In order to provide these programs, governments can borrow the money.

THE CASE FOR USING CREDIT

When should you use credit? Credit allows you to have goods and services sooner than you would if you had to save up cash to pay for them. Credit lets you take advantage of sales, for example. Credit also allows you to buy things you could not have at all if you had to pay for them all at once. Very few people can save up all of the money needed to buy a house, for instance.

Buying on credit can help you in an emergency. Having a gas station credit card, for example, can come in handy if you run out of gas and cash at the same time. Or, in a more serious situation, suppose you are working your way through college and suddenly lose your job. You may be able to get a loan to tide you over until you find another job.

A disadvantage of using credit is that you often have to pay more for a purchase using credit than you would if you had paid in cash. This is because you may have to pay for borrowing money. Just as a bank may pay you interest to keep your money, you may have to

The first paper money in our country was issued by the colonists in 1690. However, the first credit union wasn't formed until 1908. And it took until 1952 before the first bank credit card was issued.

pay interest to use someone else's money. This interest you pay on a loan is called a **finance charge**. The amount of money you borrow (excluding the interest) is called the **principal**.

Often, if you don't pay a loan back quickly, interest charges mount up. Also, the ability to use credit sometimes tempts people into buying things they really don't need or can't afford.

TYPES OF CREDIT

Credit is the result of an agreement between a **creditor**, one who lends money, and a **debtor**, one who goes into debt by borrowing. Credit comes in many forms. In all, there are four main types of credit:

1. Thirty-day charge accounts
2. Revolving credit accounts
3. Retail installment credit
4. Installment cash loans

Credit cards fall under the first two categories of credit. Car loans given out by car dealers are an example of the third category. Bank loans fall under the last category. It's almost impossible to go through life without using one of these types of credit. Many people use all four kinds at the same time. In the following case study, Gina and Christopher Campbell use all four types of credit in a single month.

CASE STUDY

When Gina and Christopher Campbell opened their mail on April 20, they found four bills. One was a $65 bill from the electric company. A second was for $89.95 from their Buywise Department Store credit card. This month they had bought a toaster-oven for $39.95 with that card, and they still owed $50 from last month's bill for other purchases.

The third bill came from Wicker World furniture store and was for $90.75. It was the fourth of 12 payments for their new bedroom set. The last bill was a $195 auto loan payment due to the First National Bank.

Each bill was the result of using a different kind of credit. The electric company's bill is an example of a thirty-day charge account. With a **thirty-day charge account**, you receive a good or use a service without paying for it, and sometime later (usually within 30 days, but it varies) a bill comes. As long as you pay the bill in full, no interest is charged for this type of credit. For example, the

The telephone is one service that is available upon request and does not have to be paid for until the bill comes.

Campbells do not pay for the electricity they use when they turn on their lights. The electric company is, in effect, lending the Campbells the money, interest-free, to pay for the electricity until they pay their bill. Many retail stores, doctors, dentists, and tradespeople will give you this type of credit. Some popular credit cards, such as American Express, Diners Club, and Carte Blanche, are examples of this type of credit as well.

The bill from Buywise Department Store is an example of a **revolving charge account**. The Campbells have a Buywise store charge card. They can buy products from Buywise with the card without spending cash. And, when the bill comes, they do not have to pay all of it at once. They can choose to pay only part of the bill and pay the rest later. They must pay a finance charge, however, if they don't pay off the entire bill each month.

Buywise will allow the Campbells to charge goods only up to a certain amount on their Buywise charge card—for example, up to $1,000. This amount is called a **line of credit** (or a *credit limit*). Many department store credit cards and some national credit cards, such as MasterCard and Visa, are examples of revolving charge accounts.

The bedroom set that the Campbells bought from Wicker World cost $990. They are paying for it in 12 equal installments of $90.75 so that they can stretch the time they take to pay for it to a year. This type of credit is **retail installment credit**. The Campbells have to pay a finance charge for this kind of credit too. They are paying a finance charge of 10 percent of the cost of the furniture, or $99. At the end of the year, they will have paid $1,089: $990 in principal and $99 in interest.

The Campbells were able to borrow the entire amount of money for the bedroom set. More often, however, a seller will require a

Installment credit was first used in the 1800's by the furniture industry. Then, in 1907, a car was financed on the installment plan for the first time. Currently, about 80 percent of consumer debt is of the installment plan type. And, about half of the installment loans are for cars.

down payment. That is, the seller asks buyers to pay a certain percentage of the price of the item first. Then the seller will lend the buyer the rest of the money. Suppose Wicker World had required a 20 percent down payment. The Campbells would have paid Wicker World $198 right away (20 percent of $990). Then the Campbells would have borrowed the rest of the money.

Often, consumers borrow money from one place and buy goods and services from another place. The Campbells did this when they bought their car. They borrowed the money not from the car dealer but from a bank. The type of credit they received is a kind of installment credit, called an **installment cash loan**. It works the same way that installment credit does. The Campbells pay principal and interest in a number of equal installments. But, instead of getting a good or service from the creditor, they receive money, which they spend somewhere else.

✓check your understanding ✓ ✓ ✓ ✓ ✓ ✓

1. **What is credit?**
2. **What are the advantages of using credit? What are the disadvantages?**
3. **What are the four main types of credit?**
4. **What is a line of credit?**

YOUR CREDIT HISTORY

Not everyone is able to open a charge account or borrow money. Getting credit depends on your **credit rating**: how good or bad a risk you are thought to be. Your credit rating is based on the "three C's of credit"—your character, your capacity, and your capital.

■ **Character**. First, creditors want to know what kind of person you are. Are you honest? Are you reliable? What are your feelings about paying back the money you borrow? Creditors try to find out about your reputation in money matters by checking to see if you have paid your bills in the past.

■ **Capacity**. Second, creditors look at your capacity—your ability to earn money to pay off your debts. They want to know how much you're earning and whether you are likely to go on earning. They also look at the debts you already have.

Some bank lenders are looking beyond character, capacity, and capital when making loans. The banks are checking to see if people who want loans have a history of filing lawsuits. Why? Some borrowers have sued banks for not continuing to extend credit when the borrowers proved to be poor credit risks.

■ **Capital**. Third, creditors want to know what things of value you have. If your capacity to pay suddenly changes, what can you sell to give the creditors their money? Items of value that can be sold to repay your debt are called **collateral**. Sometimes, even if you don't sell your belongings, creditors may be able to get them by going to court.

In order to get credit, you must fill out a credit application, which may be like the one below. It asks for information that will tell the creditor about your character, capacity, and capital.

Lenders carefully screen their customers and then rate them. Some lenders use a point system. Applicants who get enough points are given a good credit rating and are able to get loans or open charge accounts.

Page 226 shows one credit rating system. Look it over. Could you qualify for credit at the Midville State Bank?

LONGWOOD DEPARTMENT STORE

APPLICATION FOR REVOLVING CHARGE ACCOUNT

NAME ☐ Mr. ☒ Ms. ☐ Mrs. ☐ Other ☐ Miss _____ (Courtesy title optional)

First Name: *MARILYN*   Initial: *M.*   Last Name: *WILLIAMS*

Family members authorized to buy on your account — Spouse: *TOM*   Others:

ADDRESS Street: *1301 FIFTH STREET*   City: *HOSKINS*   State: *NEBRASKA*   Zip Code: *68740*

Home Phone: *969-0381*   Business Phone: *969-8900*   Age: *32*   Number of Dependents: *0*   Social Security Number: *359-20-6110*

How long at present address: *1 YR.*   ☐ Own home ☐ Board   ☐ Rent — furnished ☒ Rent — unfurnished   Monthly rent or mortgage payment: *$360*

Landlord: *WAKEFIELD RENTALS*   Address: *32 MIDDLESEX ROAD, HOSKINS*

Previous address (if less than 2 years at present address): *1793 EIGHTH STREET, HOSKINS*   How Long: *6 YRS.*

EMPLOYMENT Employer: *AJAX SHIPPING + TRUCKING*   Address: *1050 MAIN STREET, HOSKINS*

How Long: *2 YRS.*   Occupation: *SALESPERSON*   Net Income: *$340*   ☒ Weekly ☐ Monthly

Former Employer (if less than 1 year with present employer):   How Long:

CREDIT Your Bank: *HOSKINS NATIONAL*   ☐ Savings ☒ Checking ☐ Loan Account   Account Number: *665-2784*

Charge Accounts or Loan References:
Name of Firm | Address | Account Number
1. *HOSKINS NATIONAL* | *501 MAIN ST.* |
2. *AJAX CREDIT UNION* | *1050 MAIN ST.* | *112*

Relative or Personal Reference: *JOSIAH STEVENS (FATHER)*   Address: *1201 LINCOLN AVE. CHICAGO, IL 60682*

MIDVILLE STATE BANK

— Credit Rating —
(450 points or more for favorable credit rating)

Income

$0-$200 per week	0 points
$200-$400 per week	200 points
Over $400 per week	300 points

Length of Employment at a Single Job

Less than 1 year	0 points
Over 1 year but less than 3 years	100 points
3-10 years	200 points
Over 10 years	300 points

Down Payment

0%-10% down	0 points
10%-30% down	100 points
Over 30% down	150 points

Past Credit Experiences

None	0 points
Favorable reference from major credit source	300 points
Favorable reference from minor credit source	100 points
Favorable reference from Midville State Bank	200 points
Bad credit report from reference	—200 points

Applicant's Credit Score

Income	_____ points
Length of employment	_____ points
Down payment	_____ points
Credit experience	_____ points
Total	_____ points

PROTECTING THE BORROWER

Creditors are expected to be careful when they lend money. They do not have to extend credit to someone who is not honest, who doesn't make enough money, or who doesn't have enough collateral. But creditors cannot refuse to lend money for other reasons. A number of laws and regulations protect borrowers. The two most important laws are the Equal Credit Opportunity Act and the Fair Credit Reporting Act.

Granting Credit Equally

The **Equal Credit Opportunity Act** bans creditors from refusing to lend money to individuals because of something besides their ability to pay. Under this law, a creditor cannot refuse to lend money to individuals just because of their race, religion, or nationality. A creditor cannot refuse to lend money to a woman just because she is a woman. A creditor cannot refuse to lend money to people just because they are married or just because they are not married. A creditor cannot refuse to lend money to people just because they are over a certain age. A creditor cannot refuse to lend money to people who receive public aid.

According to this law, a creditor must also tell applicants within a reasonable amount of time whether or not they can have credit. A creditor who turns someone down must say why, if that person asks for the reason. The creditor must also tell applicants that they have the right to ask why. People who feel that they have been denied credit illegally should contact the United States District Attorney in their area.

Granting Credit Fairly

When you apply for credit, one of the things a lender can do is ask a credit bureau to find out about you. A **credit bureau** is a company that gathers and sells information about consumers. It sells the information to employers, insurance companies, and lenders of money. If a credit bureau has a file on you, the file will probably contain information about whether you have paid your bills on time. If, for example, you did not pay your phone bill one month, the telephone company would be very likely to report that information to one or more credit bureaus in your area. If a lender makes a request, the credit bureau might go out and interview your neighbors and friends to find out about your character and your lifestyle.

People can be turned down for loans, or even jobs, because of information in their credit bureau files. But the information may be wrong or incomplete. Your file could look bad because you have the same name as someone else. Perhaps only the missed telephone bill was reported and not the many years that you paid your car loans and electric bills on time. Perhaps you've been sued, and that information is in the file. But the case was dropped, and that fact somehow did not get into the file. Maybe there are typographical errors in the file.

Because of these problems, Congress passed the **Fair Credit Reporting Act** in 1971. This act says that you have the right to know what is in your file and who has received credit reports about you in the last six months. If you do not agree with the facts in the file, you can have your version put in too. Future reports to all lenders must then include your version.

The following case study gives you an idea of how a credit bureau works and how important the Fair Credit Reporting Act is.

CASE STUDY

Matt and Amanda Kowalski were all set to buy a new car from Hub Motors—until the auto agency refused to give them an auto loan. The Kowalskis wanted to know why. Hub Motors said that they were turned down because of facts received from Lakeside Credit Bureau.

Matt and Amanda called Lakeside and asked for a meeting. They were told to come in the next afternoon and speak with Ms. LeBec. By law, there was no charge for the interview.

Ms. LeBec had the Kowalskis' file ready. She told them that Lakeside had sent out two reports on them in the past six months. One was to Manchester's Department Store and the other was to Hub Motors. She told them all about the information in the file. There was a report in it stating that they had fallen three months behind on payments for a washing machine from Norridge Appliances. Matt said that the report was wrong. The Kowalskis had never even bought anything from Norridge.

Ms. LeBec said she would call Norridge and check it out. Sure enough, it was Matt Kowalski, Jr., their oldest son, who was behind in his payments to Norridge. Ms. LeBec said that the information would be corrected and that the Kowalskis could have the corrected information sent to Hub Motors. Matt and Amanda agreed. A few days later, Hub Motors called and said that the Kowalskis' loan had been approved.

✓ check your understanding ✓ ✓ ✓ ✓ ✓ ✓

1. In determining your credit rating, what is meant by your capital? capacity? character?
2. On the Midville State Bank point system, how many points are needed for a favorable credit rating? What will make you lose points?
3. What reasons can't a lender use when refusing to give you a loan?
4. What is a credit bureau?
5. How does the Fair Credit Reporting Act protect a borrower?

WHERE TO GET CREDIT

The Campbells received credit from many different places. In general, though, there are four main places you can go to get credit or to borrow money: banks, credit unions, stores, and finance companies. In each place, your application for credit will be considered carefully. In the interviews that follow, creditors from each source discuss some of the things they consider when they give out loans.

Banks

At the bank, we lend money on a more careful basis than some other places. We screen our customers carefully and look out for bad risks. These are people who have had trouble in the past with credit.

Surprising as it may seem, however, we don't refuse many loan applications as long as we have enough money to lend. In fact, about 90 percent of our applicants get loans.

Our interest rates are about the lowest around. Sometimes credit unions beat our rates. But not everyone belongs to a credit union.

Most of our consumer loans go to people who want to buy cars or major appliances, like refrigerators or washing machines. But we also give personal cash loans, especially to our own savings account and checking account customers.

MARY DONOVAN
Bank Loan Department

Credit Unions

We lend money only to people who are members of our credit union. To become a member, you have to be an employee of our firm. You also must open a savings account with $5 or more.

We lend money at two rates. We lend money for cars at a low rate since we have the car as collateral, something of equal value to the loan that serves as protection for our money. If you don't pay the loan, we take the car. We have a higher rate for personal loans, such as those for furniture, appliances, or doctors' bills. We do have limits to how much you can borrow. It depends on how much you make and how long you've been a member of the credit union. We also find out how well you paid past loans and how much you're already in debt. All loans are approved by a committee of members.

We can lend money at low rates because we're a non-profit organization and have few costs. The officers and committee members work without pay. And we seldom lose money through bad debts since many people have their loan payments taken directly out of their paychecks. We're a good, inexpensive place to borrow money.

RICHARD SCHULTZ
Credit Union Treasurer

When many people think of credit unions, they just think of employee credit unions. However, any group of people with a common interest can form a credit union. Groups that form credit unions include labor unions, religious groups, social institutions, farm groups, and occupational groups. There are more than 19,000 credit unions in the United States.

Stores

You don't have to go outside this store to get credit for the purchases you make here. We give three kinds of credit.

First, we have installment credit. You sign a contract saying how much you will pay each month, and for how many months. Your payments include both principal and interest.

We also have a thirty-day charge account. Under this plan, we give you 30 days to pay for your purchases. We don't charge interest, but we expect you to pay your bill when it's due.

Our third plan is a revolving charge account. This is the type of account we recommend to customers who don't want to pay off their bills entirely at the end of each month. You need only pay a minimum amount each month, usually $20, but you do have to pay finance charges on the balance. If you pay the entire bill, however, there's no finance charge.

We give credit because it's a service to our customers. Of course, it helps us too. If you have an account with us, you may be more likely to buy here than somewhere else.

ANN MONTEZ
Store Credit Manager

Finance Companies

We're part of a large national company, but we're still a neighborhood operation. We give out loans to almost anyone for almost anything.

Our firm is less selective than banks and some other places in giving out loans. We do charge higher interest rates, but our rates vary. If you're a good risk, we can give you our best rates. One reason our rates are higher is that we have to go to a bank to borrow the money we lend. We also lose more than other places to bad debts. So we have to cover ourselves by charging more.

We're still a good place to borrow. We're in the neighborhood, and we're here to help you. Often, you can get a loan in a few hours on your signature only.

OSCAR ROBINSON
DFC Finance Company

√ check your understanding √ √ √ √ √ √

1. What are the four main sources of credit?
2. What is collateral?
3. If you did not want to pay finance charges, which type of account should you open at the store?
4. Why does it often cost more to borrow from a finance company than from a bank?

A lender who knowingly breaks the Truth in Lending Law can be fined up to $5,000 or be put in prison for a year, or both. Of course, a lender will be reported only by someone who knows the law and knows that it has been broken.

UNDERSTANDING INTEREST RATES

The Campbells borrowed $990 at 10 percent interest to pay for their bedroom set. How did Wicker World work out how much money the Campbells would pay in finance charges? How did the company know how much money they were giving the Campbells in principal and interest?

Lenders can calculate finance charges in any way they wish. Installment contracts often use the *simple-interest method*. Using this method, the principal (in this case, $990) is multiplied by the interest rate (10 percent or .10) and then by the number of years the money is borrowed for ($990 × .10 × 1 year = $99).

Wicker World added the $99 finance charge to the loan of $990. So the Campbells received a loan of $990 but had to pay back $1,089 ($990 + $99). This is called the *add-on method* of figuring the loan amount.

Wicker World could have deducted the finance charge in advance from the principal and given the Campbells a loan of $891 ($990 − $99). This is called the *discount method* of figuring the actual amount of a loan. Most lenders use the add-on method.

THE TRUE COST OF BORROWING

Suppose you want to borrow $100. You shop around and are given these four offers:

1. Borrow the money for six months at 20 percent add-on interest per year.
2. Keep the money for a year and pay only a dime a day interest.

3. Pay the money back in 11 monthly installments of $11 each.

4. Keep all of the money for two years and pay 2 percent per month on the unpaid balance.

Which of the four offers is the best deal? It's not easy to tell because each is stated in a different way. Yet, not so long ago, lenders could state their rates almost any way they wanted. If borrowers could not tell which rate was best, too bad for them.

Today, however, the federal **Truth in Lending Law** makes comparing credit terms easier. This law says that all lenders have to state their finance charges and interest rates in the same way. A borrower who knows what to look for in a contract can quickly decide which deal is best.

The Truth in Lending Law requires the seller to state the total finance charge—the total cost of credit. If you buy a $500 stereo on credit, for example, and have to pay $700 altogether, the finance charge is $200.

The rate that must be stated is the **annual percentage rate (APR)** of the loan. This is the rate you pay in a single year on any money you borrow. Sometimes this rate is easy to determine, but sometimes it's not. Here are some examples. In a simple case, suppose you borrow $100 and pay back $118 at the end of a year.

As the graph on the right shows, stretching loan payments out over time adds considerably to the cost of the loan.

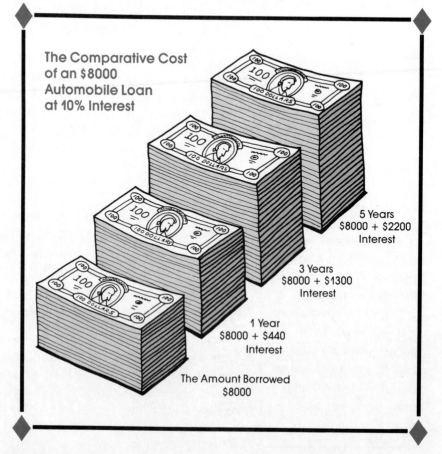

The Comparative Cost of an $8000 Automobile Loan at 10% Interest

5 Years
$8000 + $2200 Interest

3 Years
$8000 + $1300 Interest

1 Year
$8000 + $440 Interest

The Amount Borrowed
$8000

The Math of APRs

The Truth in Lending Law requires that the interest rate on all loans be stated as the annual percentage rate. The formula for figuring an annual percentage rate is:

$$APR = 2 \times M \times C \div [P \times (N + 1)] \times 100$$

M   Number of payments per year (for monthly payments this is always 12)
C   Total finance charge
P   Principal
N   Total number of payments

Let's say you borrowed $1,000 for two years at 10 percent simple interest. The finance charge is $200 ($1,000 × .10 × 2 = $200). But using the annual percentage rate formula, the APR would be: APR = 2 × 12 × $200 ÷ [$1,000 × (24 + 1)] = 4,800 ÷ 25,000 × 100 = 19.2 percent.

Your finance charge is $18, which is 18 percent of the $100 loan. Because you kept the loan for a year, that 18 percent is also the annual percentage rate.

In a slightly more complicated case, suppose you keep the $100 for two years and then pay back $118. Your finance charge is still $18, but you were only charged $9 each year, or 9 percent of $100. So your annual percentage rate in this case is 9 percent.

Some cases are so complicated that the consumer may have great difficulty figuring out the rate. Suppose you borrowed $100 for one year at a finance charge of $18. However, you pay back the loan in 12 equal monthly payments instead of all at once. Each monthly payment would be about $9.83 ($118 ÷ 12). How much is the annual percentage rate? The lender may want to say the annual percentage rate is 18 percent, since you're paying an $18 finance charge on a $100 loan in a single year. But you are not actually borrowing the entire $100 for a whole year since you are paying back one twelfth of the $100 each month. So, you are paying $18 interest to borrow less than $100 a year. The actual annual percentage rate turns out in this case to be 33.2 percent.

A consumer can't be expected to figure out the cost of a loan in such complicated cases. That's one reason why the law requires lenders to say what the rate is. When shopping for a loan, don't simply ask, "What will the loan cost?" Ask what the annual percentage rate and finance charges are. By comparing finance charges and annual percentage rates, you can shop for the lowest cost credit.

Some purchases that are minor in this country aren't in other countries. For example, in Japan, driver education classes cost $1,300. Telephone installation costs $600. Many people take out "special purpose" loans (at as much as 20 percent interest) for these purchases.

1. What process is often used to figure a loan's finance charge? How does it work?
2. How is the add-on method of figuring the amount of a loan different from the discount method?
3. What are the main requirements of the Truth in Lending Law?
4. If you get an installment loan for $750 to buy furniture, and agree to pay $825 over 12 months, what is your finance charge?

SUMMARIZING
the chapter

Credit lets people have money, goods, and services now and pay for them later. People can often buy goods and services sooner if they use credit rather than cash. Using credit also helps people in emergencies and allows them to buy very expensive items without first having to save enough money to pay for them. Unfortunately, credit can also tempt people to overspend.

The person who gives credit is called the creditor or lender. The one who borrows is the debtor or borrower.

The four main types of credit agreements are thirty-day charge accounts, revolving credit, retail installment credit, and installment loans. For all but the thirty-day charge accounts, a borrower has to pay finance charges. In some cases, the seller requires a down payment, a certain percentage of the price.

People's ability to get credit depends on their credit rating. This rating reflects a person's character, capacity to earn money, and capital worth. The Equal Credit Opportunity Act prevents lenders from refusing to lend money for other reasons. Often a lender will contact a credit bureau to find out if you are a good credit risk. The Fair Credit Reporting Act allows borrowers to know about any information a credit bureau may have about them. Consumers can get credit from banks, credit unions, stores, and finance companies.

Lenders can figure finance charges by any process. Often they use the simple interest method. They then add on this finance charge to the principal to get the amount of the loan. They can also subtract the finance charge using the discount method to get the loan's amount.

The federal Truth in Lending Law helps consumers compare the price of loans. It makes all lenders state finance charges and annual percentage rates in the same terms.

BUILDING CONSUMER VOCABULARY

Number your paper from 1 to 18. Then write the term that best matches the numbered definition.

annual percentage rate (APR)
collateral
credit
credit bureau
creditor
credit rating
debtor
down payment
Equal Credit Opportunity Act

Fair Credit Reporting Act
finance charge
installment cash loan
line of credit
principal
retail installment credit
revolving charge account
thirty-day charge account
Truth in Lending Law

1. A certain percentage of the purchase price of an item bought on credit, which the borrower pays first in cash
2. The opportunity to borrow money or to receive goods or services in return for a promise to pay later
3. A loan of money that is paid back in equal amounts each month
4. A law requiring all creditors to state finance charges and interest rates in the same way
5. Something of equal value that can be claimed if a loan isn't paid back
6. The one who borrows
7. How good or bad a credit risk you are thought to be
8. A loan that does not have to be paid back in a specified time period
9. The way lenders must state their interest rates to consumers
10. The amount borrowed
11. The one who lends money
12. The limit that can be charged on a revolving charge account
13. A company that gathers and sells credit information
14. The lender's charge for giving credit
15. A type of credit that has no limit and costs nothing in finance charges if the bill is paid in full
16. Credit given by a seller of goods and services that is paid for in equal amounts for a set period of time
17. A law granting borrowers the right to know and challenge any information credit bureaus have about them
18. A law preventing creditors from denying credit to people for a reason other than their ability to pay

1. Why do businesses use credit?
2. Is it possible to use credit without paying interest? Explain.
3. Why might using credit to pay for a vacation be a good idea? Why might it be a bad idea?
4. For what purpose might you use an installment cash loan?
5. Use the information on Marilyn Williams' application for a revolving charge account on page 225 and the Midville State Bank Credit Rating, page 226, to answer the following questions:
   a. If Marilyn Williams needed a $1,000 auto loan, could she get one from the Midville State Bank? She can pay 20 percent down. What other information might the bank want?
   b. Which questions on the application for the revolving charge account have to do with character? capacity? capital?
   c. Would Marilyn Williams have a better chance of getting a revolving credit account if she earned more money? if she had children? if she had a savings account in addition to her checking account? if she were a man?
6. Sam Clemente, a high school junior, wanted to borrow $800 to buy stereo equipment. He went to a bank and was turned down. What reasons may the bank give for its refusal? What reasons couldn't the bank give legally? Where else might Sam go?
7. How does the Truth in Lending Law make it easier for consumers to shop for credit?

1. You borrow $10,000 for two years with the finance charge figured at a simple rate of 7½ percent (or .075). What is the finance charge?
2. You borrow $2,000 and at the end of 36 months you pay back $2,440. What is the finance charge? What is the APR?
3. Compute the APR on a $500 loan for 48 months with monthly payments of $13.50.

1. Would it be possible to live without ever using coins, paper money, or checks? Explain how you might live on credit alone.
2. Explain what might happen to the economy of the United States if there were no such thing as credit. How might your lifestyle change?

List ten places in your community where people borrow money or buy things on credit. For each place, list the type of credit they offer (thirty-day charge account, revolving charge account, retail installment credit, or installment cash loans). Which places charge no interest? Which places charge interest?

16

SHOPPING FOR CREDIT

Credit usually costs money. Sometimes, it costs a lot of money. How much will it cost you to borrow? Are some lenders less expensive than others?

- What do you look for in comparison shopping for credit?

- Which type of credit card is right for you?

- How do they figure credit card finance charges?

- What should you do if your credit card bill is wrong?

- How should you shop for an installment loan?

Credit is a service consumers buy. As with other things consumers buy, it pays to shop around to get the best deal. As the Leonards learn while shopping for a television, consumers not only have to choose which item to buy, they also have to choose the best way to pay for it.

CASE STUDY

The Leonards shop for a loan

Wendy and Phil Leonard's TV was out of order again. This time, they learned, the picture tube was worn out. Rather than repair a ten-year-old set given to them by Phil's parents, they decided it made sense to buy a new one.

After checking *Consumer Reports*, they decided to buy a highly recommended set that cost $800. They had $200, which was enough for a down payment at Leo's Uptown Appliances.

Leo's Uptown Appliances

The Leonards explained to Leo what they wanted and asked if he could help them.

"Glad to," said Leo. He looked at his charts. "For an $800 set, you can pay $200 down and $56 a month. You'll be paid up in a year."

That sounded like something they could handle. But Wendy wanted all the facts. "What's the finance charge and the annual percentage rate?" she asked.

"The finance charge is $72. On a $600 loan, that's 12 percent," Leo replied.

Wendy asked, "Is that the annual percentage rate?"

"Oh, that government rate—that's about 22 percent," Leo said, "still a good deal."

The Leonards thanked Leo for the figures and said they'd be back later.

Friendly Finance Company

When they left Leo's, Phil suggested they stop at the Friendly Finance Company down the street. It was a small office, but they had heard its ads on the radio.

"Do you give TV loans?" Phil asked the manager.

"Sure," the manager replied. "I'll need to check your credit rating, but that shouldn't be a problem. How much do you need?"

"We need $600," said Wendy. "And we can pay it back in a year. What's the annual percentage rate for a $600 loan for a year?"

"It's 24 percent," he answered. "The finance charge is $78."

"Why is your loan more expensive than an installment contract?" Phil asked.

"Well, we may give you the money when they won't," the manager said. "That often happens. Besides, our costs are higher. The installment contract is sold to a bank. We often must borrow money from banks ourselves. But, remember, we're right in the neighborhood. And you might want us for future loans too."

Phil and Wendy finally told the manager that they wanted to think about it.

First City Bank

Wendy said they should try the First City Bank. Phil wasn't sure. He had heard that banks lent money only to business people, but finally he agreed to try it. Saturday morning, they went to the bank and met Mrs. Solter, a loan officer.

"We need a $600 TV loan for one year," Phil said. "How much would that cost us? How much is the annual percentage rate and the finance charge?"

"The annual percentage rate is 16.6 percent, and the finance charge is $54," Mrs. Solter answered.

"That sounds pretty good," Wendy said. "But can we qualify for a loan? We have a checking account and a small savings account here."

Mrs. Solter said that the Leonards would have to fill out a loan application. But after asking about Phil's and Wendy's jobs and salaries, Mrs. Solter said she thought they could qualify easily. She also said they might want to check another bank's rates, although she felt her bank's rate was a good one.

Appleton Company Federal Credit Union

That night, Phil and Wendy were talking about the places they might get a loan. Phil then remembered he had heard about a credit union where he worked. He had not looked into it before, but maybe he should.

On Monday, he found the credit union office in the basement of his company's building. Behind the desk was Mark Davis, a man he had talked with in the lunchroom a few times.

"Mark, can you tell me about getting loans here?"

"It's not hard, Phil. Since you work here, you can join the credit union anytime. That costs just a dollar. To borrow money, you need to have a savings account—we call it a share—of $5 or more with us. When you want a loan, you fill out this simple form. A committee will review it, and the chances are good that you'll get the loan, unless you're already too far in debt."

"What are the rates on a $600 loan for a TV set?"

"The rate is 1¼ percent a month on your unpaid balance. That's an annual percentage rate of 15 percent. The finance charge depends on how long you keep the loan. If you plan to pay back the loan and the interest in 12 equal installments, the finance charge would come to $48.75. You can also decide to pay off the loan early. The rate is the same, but the finance charge will be smaller."

Spears Department Store

When Phil got home, Wendy was waiting with a full-page ad from Sunday's newspaper. She was about to throw it out when she noticed that Spears was having a three-day clearance sale on television sets. That evening, a salesperson explained the many features on a particular set sale-priced at $200 off its regular price of $1,000.

"Can we buy it on time?" Phil asked.

"Of course—if you have our credit card and you haven't used up your line of credit yet," the salesperson replied. "Just charge it on your Spears card. Our APR is 18 percent. And you can take as long as you want to repay. Can I write it up?"

"We'll think about it tonight. The sale goes on for two more days," Phil said.

That night, Wendy did some calculations and worked out that charging the set on their Spears card would cost $78 in finance charges if they paid off the bill in 12 equal payments. But the longer they took to pay the balance, the more their finance charges would pile up.

1. **Of all the places that the Leonards shopped for a loan, which ones require a down payment? Which ones don't require a down payment?**
2. **In which places can the Leonards obtain revolving credit? Which places offer retail installment credit? Which places offer installment cash loans?**

The Leonards can choose among many ways to pay for their new television. They could take out an installment loan. They could charge it with their credit card. In either case, they need to find the best credit terms before they buy. Wise consumers know how to shop for both installment loans and for credit cards.

USING CREDIT CARDS

Will the plastic credit card someday replace the paper dollar or check as our most common form of money? Credit cards are convenient. They allow you to shop without carrying a lot of cash. Sometimes, they are necessary. Some merchants will not accept cash in certain situations.

For instance, a man wanted to rent a car in Washington, D.C. The rent-a-car clerk asked what credit card he would use. He told the clerk that he had no credit cards, but he could leave a $400 deposit. The clerk would not accept the cash and refused to rent the man a car. The man was David Bruce, a former United States ambassador to China.

Selecting the Right Card

As you learned in Chapter 15, some credit cards are examples of thirty-day charge accounts and some are revolving charge accounts. There are two types of revolving charge cards: single-purpose cards and multipurpose cards.

Like the Leonards' Spears charge card, a **single-purpose card** is one issued by a company for use in that company's stores only. Many department stores have such cards. They can be used in all of the store's branches, but not in any other store. Many oil companies have cards for use at their own service stations.

The other type of revolving charge card—the **multipurpose card**—is issued by banks, credit unions, and other financial institutions. It can be used in many different stores, at restaurants, hotels, and even with doctors and dentists. MasterCard and Visa are probably the best-known multipurpose cards. More than 200 million of them have been issued. Both multipurpose and single-purpose cards have finance charges if you do not pay off the bill each month. Both types of cards also set credit limits.

Thirty-day charge account credit cards—such as American Express, Diners Club, and Carte Blanche—are called **travel-and-entertainment cards**. Unlike multipurpose and single-purpose cards, these travel-and-entertainment cards have no finance charges and unlimited lines of credit. But you must pay the whole bill each time it comes. If you don't, you can do serious damage to your credit rating. Travel-and-entertainment cards are well known for being accepted around the world by restaurants, hotels, airlines, and other businesses that sell to travelers and tourists. A number of multipurpose cards are now accepted in many countries as well.

Shopping for a Credit Card

Lenders can make money on their cards in three ways. First, a business that accepts the cards pays the credit card companies a fee for each charge. Second, cardholders pay a yearly fee for the use of some cards. Lenders of multipurpose and travel-and-entertainment cards make money in these two ways. Third, the cardholder pays finance charges on outstanding balances. Lenders of single-purpose and multipurpose cards make money in this way.

Many different financial institutions issue MasterCard and Visa cards. Many stores issue their own cards. A number of different companies issue travel-and-entertainment cards. All of these companies try to get new customers by offering many extras with their credit cards. Most of these offers are just gimmicks. A wise consumer doesn't worry about gimmicks when shopping for a credit card. You should look for the credit card with the lowest cost and the best terms.

Roughly half of all the families in our country have at least one credit card. The average person who carries credit cards has four of them. There are about 10,000 different credit cards issued in this country.

A car rental agency is one business that does not accept cash. A major credit card is usually required before you can drive in a rental car.

When you shop for a credit card, be sure to find out about each of the following things, which vary from one card to another.

Annual fee This is the yearly charge to have a credit card account. Many single-purpose cards, and some multipurpose cards issued by credit unions, are free. Most other credit cards have annual fees that can range anywhere from $15 to more than $100. Travel-and-entertainment cards generally have the highest fees, as little money is made from finance charges.

Acceptability Where can you use it? Do many stores in your area accept the card? Is it widely accepted when you travel? Single-purpose cards, of course, are accepted only in the stores that issue them. Many shops accept one type of multipurpose card or travel-and-entertainment card and no others. Before you apply for a card, go to the stores you shop in and find out which cards they accept.

Grace period Sometimes you must pay a credit card bill as soon as it comes. Sometimes you don't have to pay the bill until a later date. The length of time between the date the bill comes and the date you must pay it to avoid finance charges is called the **grace period**. Some cards have no grace period. Some cards offer grace periods as long as 30 days. The longer the time, the better.

Interest rate Annual percentage rates for single-purpose and multipurpose cards range from about 12 to over 20 percent. This interest is charged monthly, so the APR is divided by 12 to get the rate used to figure the monthly finance charge. Often, cards issued by credit unions have the lowest rates.

Method of figuring the finance charge

The way a company determines the finance charge can make a big difference to the size of your credit card bills. The least expensive way is the **adjusted balance method**. In this case, the finance charge is applied only to the amount owed after you've paid your bill each month. For example, suppose you bought $100 worth of goods. When the bill comes, you pay $30. The next month, you charge another $200 worth of goods. If the bank uses the adjusted balance method of figuring the finance charge, it will charge interest only on the unpaid balance from the first month—on just $70 ($100 − $30 = $70).

The most expensive way to figure interest is the **previous-balance method**. It figures the finance charge on the entire amount owed from the previous month and allows no deductions for payments made. If the bank uses the previous-balance method, it will charge you interest throughout the whole month for the entire $100 of your previous balance.

Most lenders now base their charges on the **average daily balance** of your account. Using this method, the creditor works out what your balance is on each day of the billing period. The creditor then divides by the number of days in the billing period. That is the average daily balance. The creditor then applies the monthly interest rate to that amount.

However, each creditor decides what counts in the daily balance differently. Some companies will subtract payments (in this case $30), when they receive them, from the previous balance (of $100). Some count the entire $100 from the previous month into the daily balance no matter how much of that balance you pay off in the current month. Some companies add the $200 in charges from the current month to your balance. Others don't.

The law requires that you be told how the creditor will figure the finance charge. This information may be provided with the credit card application under the word *disclosure*. Sometimes it is provided when you receive the card. But before you get any credit card, ask yourself: "Do I really need it? Can I afford it? Can I afford the finance charges?"

According to Visa and MasterCard, about 30 percent of their credit card holders pay the total balance due on their bills each month. These people pay no finance charges. Statistics show that people who pay off their credit cards each month use their credit cards more often and buy more expensive items.

What do you do if a credit card is stolen? Call the issuer of the card as soon as possible. The issuer will put a "stop" on the card so no more charges can be made on your account. You must pay the first $50 of any charges you did not make. That may not sound like much money. But if you lose a wallet with ten credit cards in it, you could end up paying as much as $500.

✓check your understanding ✓ ✓ ✓ ✓ ✓ ✓

1. **What are the two types of revolving charge account credit cards? What is the difference between them?**
2. **Who offers multipurpose credit cards? How do they make money issuing these cards?**
3. **In what ways are travel-and-entertainment cards different from multipurpose credit cards?**
4. **What things should you check out when shopping for a credit card?**

Reading the Monthly Statement

The Truth in Lending Law requires creditors to send a statement to all cardholders who owe money at the end of the monthly billing period. This statement shows the current status of the account for credit card and charge account users. It must include:

- previous balance
- purchases made during the billing period with dates, prices, product descriptions (for single-purpose cards) or names of the companies from which you bought the goods or services (for multipurpose cards)
- payments made and other credits received during the billing period
- finance charges added during the billing period
- annual percentage rate and periodic (monthly, or sometimes daily) rate
- new balance

The illustration on page 245 shows how a monthly statement works. To calculate how much you owe, the creditor takes the previous balance, adds any new purchases, subtracts any payments or credits, and then adds any finance charge. On the statement, this is $74.86 + $75.36 − $50.00 + $1.62 = $101.84. The finance charge was found by taking the monthly balance (in this case the average daily balance, which was $108.30) and multiplying it by the monthly periodic rate (1½ percent or .015).

Unauthorized charges can appear on your statement even if you do not lose your card. If people get your card number, they can use it to charge items to your account over the phone. For example, concert tickets can be charged over the phone, then picked up later in person. You won't know about the charge unless you notice it on your statement.

Not only can you buy things with a credit card, but you can also get cash from an automatic teller.

READING A MONTHLY STATEMENT

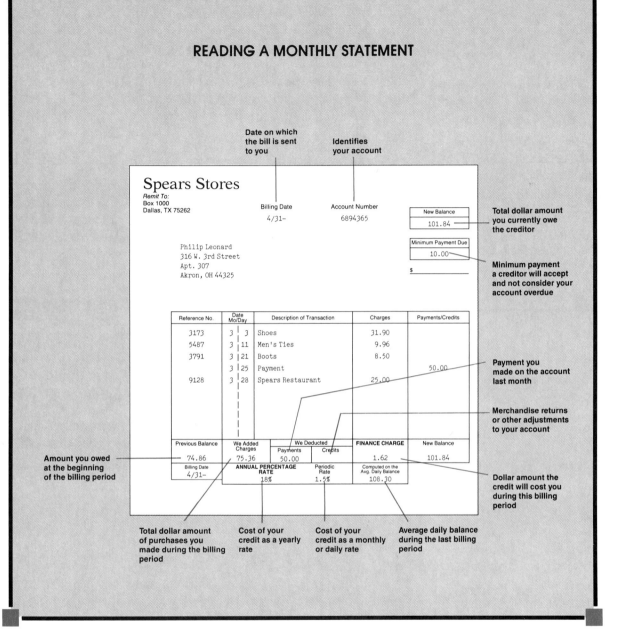

Date on which the bill is sent to you

Identifies your account

Spears Stores
Remit To:
Box 1000
Dallas, TX 75262

Billing Date
4/31-

Account Number
6894365

New Balance
101.84

Total dollar amount you currently owe the creditor

Philip Leonard
316 W. 3rd Street
Apt. 307
Akron, OH 44325

Minimum Payment Due
10.00

$

Minimum payment a creditor will accept and not consider your account overdue

Reference No.	Date Mo/Day	Description of Transaction	Charges	Payments/Credits
3173	3 3	Shoes	31.90	
5487	3 11	Men's Ties	9.96	
3791	3 21	Boots	8.50	
	3 25	Payment		50.00
9128	3 28	Spears Restaurant	25.00	

Payment you made on the account last month

Merchandise returns or other adjustments to your account

Previous Balance	We Added Charges	We Deducted Payments	We Deducted Credits	FINANCE CHARGE	New Balance
74.86	75.36	50.00		1.62	101.84

Billing Date	ANNUAL PERCENTAGE RATE	Periodic Rate	Computed on the Avg. Daily Balance
4/31-	18%	1.5%	108.30

Amount you owed at the beginning of the billing period

Dollar amount the credit will cost you during this billing period

Total dollar amount of purchases you made during the billing period

Cost of your credit as a yearly rate

Cost of your credit as a monthly or daily rate

Average daily balance during the last billing period

Handling Mistakes in Your Bill

What if you receive your monthly statement and you find something wrong? Perhaps the statement lists purchases you did not make. Maybe the amount of a purchase is wrong. Suppose you paid a bill, and the statement does not show your payment. Maybe someone used your card without your permission. Credit consumers have help. The **Fair Credit Billing Act** provides a process to allow them to correct credit card or charge account mistakes.

If you have a problem with your bill, you must write to the creditor within 90 days after the bill was mailed. In your letter, you must give your name and account number, the dollar amount of the error, and a description of the error.

The creditor has 30 days to let you know it received the letter. Then it must investigate the dispute and correct the problem within 90 days or tell you why the bill is correct.

You can refuse to pay the disputed amount until the investigation ends. If it turns out that there was a mistake in your bill, you don't have to pay any finance charge on the amount in question. But if there's no mistake, you must pay a finance charge.

The Fair Credit Billing Act also can be used to help settle disputes about the quality of merchandise. You may buy something with a credit card that turns out to be defective. Perhaps it is not what you were told it would be, or not suitable for its intended use. In these cases, you can stop payment for it. But first you must return the item and try to correct the problem with the seller. This law applies only to purchases costing more than $50 and made within 100 miles of your home.

✓ check your understanding ✓ ✓ ✓ ✓ ✓ ✓

1. **What does a monthly statement show a credit user?**
2. **How do lenders determine how much you owe on a monthly statement?**
3. **What are your rights and responsibilities under the Fair Credit Billing Act when you have a dispute with a creditor about your bill?**
4. **When can you use the Fair Credit Billing Act to stop payment for merchandise?**

USING INSTALLMENT CREDIT

Many credit cards have spending limits, and for those that don't you must pay back the amount you've spent all at once. To pay for very expensive items, such as cars, furniture, or kitchen appliances, consumers more often use installment credit.

The Leonards could decide to pay for their television with retail installment credit from Leo's or some other store. They will have to sign a contract spelling out the terms of the agreement. Taxes and delivery charges will be added. The cash down payment will be subtracted. Then the finance charge will be figured, and the total amount borrowed will be divided into monthly, or sometimes weekly, installments.

As the lender, Leo has certain rights. He will use the television as collateral, or security for the loan. If the Leonards don't make the installment payments, Leo can take the television away. This

If the borrower does not make the payments on a car loan, the car can be repossessed to satisfy the remainder of the debt.

is called **repossession**. Retail installment contracts have clauses explaining that the lender has the right to repossess the collateral.

Consumers have installment credit rights too. In addition to the finance charge and annual percentage rate required by the Truth in Lending Law, retail installment contracts must also state a third figure. This figure, called the **deferred payment price**, is the total amount of money you have to pay for your purchase. Suppose the Leonards buy the TV from Leo for $800. They pay another 5 percent in sales tax, or $40. They also pay a $25 delivery charge and a finance charge of $79.25. The deferred payment price for the $800 television is the total of all of these charges, or $944.25 ($800 + $40 + $25 + $79.25).

When shopping for retail installment credit, you should compare annual percentage rates, finance charges, and deferred payment prices. To do this correctly, you must compare loans for the same amount of money, with the same down payment, and for the same time period.

RETAIL INSTALLMENT CONTRACT

Leo's Uptown Appliances
Seller

Wendy & Philip Leonard
Buyer

Name _____

Address _1200 Main Street_

City _Akron_ State _OH_ Zip _44327_

Name _Wendy & Philip Leonard_

Address _316 W. 3rd Street - Apt 307_

City _Akron_ State _OH_ Zip _44325_

26" Staybright Color Television, Model #1200B
Description of goods and/or services to be sold

For the goods and services described above, I agree to pay $ _744.25_ in accordance with the annual terms beginning the _1st_ day of _MAY_, 19 _—_. Title to the goods included in this contract shall be retained by the seller until the balance is fully paid. I agree not to dispose of the goods or encumber them without the seller's written consent and to protect the seller against all loss or damage to the goods from the time they are delivered to me until I have fully paid for them. If more than one person signs this contract, the obligation shall be joint and several.

NOTICE: ANY HOLDER OF THIS CONSUMER CREDIT CONTRACT IS SUBJECT TO ALL CLAIMS AND DEFENSES WHICH THE DEBTOR COULD ASSERT AGAINST THE SELLER OF GOODS OR SERVICES OBTAINED PURSUANT HERETO OR WITH THE PROCEEDS HEREOF. RECOVERY HEREUNDER BY THE DEBTOR SHALL NOT EXCEED AMOUNTS PAID BY THE DEBTOR HEREUNDER.

(1) Cash Price (incl. taxes, accessories, and services) .... $ _840.00_

(2) Down Payment:
    Cash Down Payment .... $ _-200.00_

    Trade-in .... $ _____

    Total Down Payment .... $ _200.00_

(3) Unpaid Balance of Cash Price (1) – (2) .... $ _640.00_

(4) Other Charges .... _DELIVERY_ .... $ _25.00_

(5) Amount Financed (3) + (4) .... $ _665.00_

(6) FINANCE CHARGE .... $ _79.25_

(7) Total of Payments (5) + (6) .... $ _744.25_

(8) Deferred Payment Price (1) + (4) + (6) .... $ _944.25_

ANNUAL PERCENTAGE RATE .... _22%_

Monthly Payment $ _62.00_   Number of Monthly Payments _12_

Amount of Last Payment $ _62.25_

Payment to be made to the seller at the address given above.

Buyer's Signature _Philip Leonard_   Date _4/23_ 19 ___

Co-signer's Signature _Wendy Leonard_   Date _4/23_ 19 ___

Salesperson's Signature _Leo Jackson_

Reading Retail Installment Contracts

Certain information is easy to find and understand on a retail installment contract. For example, in the contract on page 248, the names and addresses of seller and buyer and the full description of the goods are easy to find. The dollar terms of the contract (Items 1–8) are clear.

Other terms are more difficult to understand. For example, why is there a last payment listed? In most situations, it's there to help adjust for division problems in getting the monthly payments to come out equally. Sometimes, however, the last payment is a lot larger than the other payments. If the last payment is more than twice as much as each of the other payments, it is called a **balloon payment**.

Balloon payments can mislead the borrower. A dishonest seller might tell you that he or she will finance a new car for only a $100 a month for four years. But when the contract is prepared, you might find that, after you've paid $100 a month for 47 months, you owe $5,000 for the last payment. If you don't make this balloon payment, the seller repossesses the car even though you haven't missed any other payments. Some states have decided that this situation is not in the interests of the public and have made balloon payment contracts illegal.

Most retail installment contracts tell you what will happen if you don't repay on time. Sometimes, the contract states that if you miss a payment, the lender can ask you to pay all of the rest of the loan back immediately. This requirement in a contract is called an **acceleration clause**. If you fail to repay the full amount, the lender may repossess the goods and can also sue for additional money in penalties.

The contract may tell you about your right to pay the full loan back before the due date. If you do, you don't need to pay any more finance charge. But the lender can use various ways to determine how much you have paid already—that is, how much of each installment payment will be counted as principal and how much will be considered interest. One method often used when someone wants to pay a loan back early is the **Rule of 78**. Using this method, the lender says the early payments of the loan are mainly just interest. In each subsequent payment, the lender will count more of it as principal and less as interest. Experts warn that if the lender uses the Rule of 78, the borrower will not save much money by paying off the loan in the early months.

Some lenders also include a charge for credit life insurance. If you have credit life insurance, your loan will be paid off by the insurance company if you die. You need this insurance only if you want to protect the people who depend on your income and you don't have enough other life insurance. It is illegal for lenders to refuse to give you a loan just because you don't buy credit life

A California man collected credit cards as a hobby. He was able to collect over 800 cards. In theory, he could have charged over $9 million in a single month. Was he a millionaire? No. He only earned about $27,000 a year.

In 1985, banks lost about $30 per card from people who paid off their bills every month. Because the cards were paid off, the banks could not collect interest. But the banks still had expenses in handling the customers' accounts. However, banks made over $47 per card on average from users who did not pay off their balances every month. That's how much those credit card holders paid in interest.

insurance. Still, a lot of it is sold. Many people probably think they must buy it. You will learn more about life insurance in Chapter 28.

Additional Lenders and Borrowers

Installment contracts can be bought and sold like any good. Your contract may be sold to another lender, such as a finance company or bank. This new owner is called a **holder in due course**. If your contract is sold, you may be required to make your payments to the new holder. The Federal Trade Commission has ruled that the new holder is as responsible as the original lender for the terms of the deal and also for the quality of the product. For example, if the product becomes defective and the original seller doesn't honor the warranty, you can turn to the holder to honor it. You also can take legal action against both parties.

The installment contract is a legal agreement between you and the lender. You must sign it.

In some cases, the lender also requires a second signature on the installment contract. Perhaps your credit rating is low. Perhaps you have not used credit much in the past. Perhaps you have used credit, but the amount of money you are looking to borrow now is much more than the amount of money you have borrowed in the past. Each circumstance increases the lender's risk.

In order to reduce the risk in such situations, the lender may require that you find someone else to agree to make the payments on the loan if you are unable to do so. The person who signs the contract and agrees to make the payments for you is called the **co-signer**. The co-signer's credit rating and experience usually have to be better than the borrower's. Who would agree to take on such a responsibility? Often the co-signer is a family member or a close friend.

Installment Cash Loans

If the Leonards go to a bank, finance company, or credit union to get the money for their television, they will get an installment cash loan. They will sign a contract very similar to the type they would sign with Leo, the seller. They will probably still need to pay Leo a down payment. Few financial institutions will give you a cash loan for the entire cost of a good.

To get an installment cash loan, the Leonards also must sign a promissory note. A **promissory note** is a written agreement stating the amount of the loan, the annual percentage rate, the terms, and the due date. They may also use the television as collateral.

Shop for an installment cash loan in the same way you would shop for credit from a seller. Make sure you read and understand every part of the contract.

Knights in medieval times used a credit card of sorts. Often a knight wore a heavy ring that was carved with his crest. To get credit, he would make an impression in wax with his ring. The impression identified him to those from whom he sought credit.

1. Why should a borrower be alert for balloon payment terms in a credit contract?
2. What actions might a lender take if you fail to repay a loan on time?
3. What happens if an installment contract is sold to another lender such as a finance company or bank?
4. When might a lender require a co-signer for a loan? What is the co-signer's obligation?

SUMMARIZING
the chapter

When you buy on credit, you should shop just as carefully for the credit as you do for the goods and services credit can buy. When shopping for single-purpose, multipurpose, and travel-and-entertainment credit cards, compare fees, acceptability, grace periods, and interest rates. Credit card companies generally use one of three ways to determine their finance charges. The adjusted balance method is the least expensive, the average-daily-balance method is more expensive, and the previous balance method is the most expensive.

Credit card and charge account users receive monthly statements showing the current status of their accounts. The Fair Credit Billing Act provides a way to help the borrower correct any errors on the statement. But the borrower needs to write promptly to the lender about any problems. The law also helps settle disputes about the quality of products.

Consumers often use installment credit for a one-time purchase of very costly items. Consumers generally make a down payment, agree to use the purchased item as collateral, and sign a contract spelling out all charges and terms of the loan. If payments aren't made on time, the creditor may require the borrower to pay the entire loan immediately. The goods may be repossessed if the borrower can't repay the whole loan. The creditor may also sue for additional money.

Read the installment contract carefully before signing to help prevent future problems. Balloon payments and Rule of 78 clauses should be avoided. Compare annual percentage rates, finance charges, and deferred payment prices. A co-signer may be required to reduce the lender's risk.

Agreements for installment cash loans are often similar to installment contracts. Financial institutions may also require a promissory note.

BUILDING CONSUMER VOCABULARY

Number your paper from 1 to 16. Then write the term that best matches each numbered definition.

acceleration clause
adjusted balance method
average-daily-balance method
balloon payment
co-signer
deferred payment price
Fair Credit Billing Act
grace period

holder in due course
multipurpose card
previous balance method
promissory note
repossession
Rule of 78
single-purpose card
travel-and-entertainment cards

1. The length of time between the date a bill comes and the date you must pay it to avoid finance charges
2. A contract term requiring you to pay back the full balance of a loan immediately if you miss a payment
3. A credit card that can be used only in one company's stores
4. A final payment of an installment loan that is more than twice as large as the other payments
5. A way to determine how much borrowers still owe when they want to pay back installment loans early
6. A way to figure credit card finance charges based on the average of the amounts you owe for each day of the month
7. A revolving credit card that can be used at many different places
8. A written agreement spelling out the terms of an installment cash loan
9. Taking the purchased item away if a loan is not repaid
10. A law requiring lenders to provide a process to help correct problems with credit card bills or with product quality
11. The new creditor when an installment contract is sold
12. A way of determining finance charges on a credit card bill using the entire amount owed from the past month and allowing no deductions for payments made
13. The total cost of a purchase made through installment credit, including down payment, principal, and finance charges
14. A way of determining credit card finance charges by basing them on the balance owed after subtracting payments made
15. Credit cards that usually don't charge interest but require you to pay off the entire balance when you get the bill
16. Someone who agrees to make the payments on a loan if the original debtor does not

1. Describe the features of a credit card plan that make it less expensive to have. Which type of card comes closest to this description?
2. Credit card A has an annual fee of $18 and an APR of 13 percent. Credit card B has a $5 annual fee, but an APR of 21.6 percent. Both have a 25-day grace period. Which card would be best for Kristen, who pays all her bills on time? Which one would be best for Jonathan, who pays only part of the balance each month?
3. What are the advantages and disadvantages of single-purpose, multipurpose, and travel-and-entertainment cards?
4. What records do you need in order to check a monthly statement for accuracy?
5. Under what circumstances should the consumer use the Fair Credit Billing Act?
6. What does credit life insurance do? When might a borrower need it? Are you required to buy it?
7. You buy a used car from Dealer A, who sells the credit contract to ABC Finance Company. Dealer A promises in the contract to install a new radio but later refuses. What actions can you take?

1. Using the information in the first case study, "The Leonards shop for a loan" on pages 238 to 240, answer the following questions on a separate sheet of paper:
   a. Make a chart showing the annual percentage rate and finance charge that Phil and Wendy Leonard would pay each of the five lenders they visited for the amount of money they asked about in each case.
   b. How much would Phil and Wendy pay for the TV set with each of the five loans? Include any down payment they plan to make.
   c. If they take one of the five loans, which one should it be? Why did you choose that one?
2. Suppose you are going to buy the following items through installment loans. In each case, the creditor requires a down payment. Figure out the down payments for the following installment purchases:

Item Purchased	Price	Percentage Required for Down Payment
Dining room table and chairs	$ 2,195	20 percent
New car	15,300	10 percent
Stereo	895	15 percent
Sofa and two chairs	1,199	10 percent
Braces and orthodontist's fee	2,350	30 percent
Clarinet	513	20 percent

1. Which of the following goods and services would you be most likely to put on a credit card? For which would you be more likely to use an installment contract?
   a. A car
   b. Airline tickets
   c. A pair of pants
   d. A bedroom set
   e. A meal in a fancy restaurant
2. Refer to the monthly statement on page 245. Assume Phil Leonard discovers that his previous balance is really $34.86. If it is, and his average daily balance declines to $74.96, what is the new finance charge? What is the new balance owed?
3. Write a letter to Spears Stores explaining the error. Be sure to include all the information required by the Fair Credit Billing Act.
4. What must Spears now do for Phil? Be specific.

Find out about the cost of credit in your own community. First, decide on an installment loan someone might want to make. For example, it might be a $10,000 loan for a new car to be repaid in installments over 36 months. Then check with a store, finance company, bank, and credit union. For each loan, find out the following information:

1. Amount of the loan
2. Repayment period
3. Annual percentage rate
4. Finance charge
5. Deferred payment price
6. Monthly payments

USING CREDIT WISELY

Consumers under 25 years old have debts that total an average of 10 percent of their household income. Consumers between the ages of 25 and 34 owe an average of 15 percent of their incomes. National credit card debt is over $160 billion. College graduates charge, on average, $400 a month. Credit use has become an important part of consumers' lifestyles. Do we use it wisely? What happens if we don't?

■ How do people get into debt?

■ What happens if you get too far into debt?

■ What are the warning signs of credit misuse?

Granting credit involves trust. In fact, the word *credit* comes from the Latin *credo* meaning "I trust." When creditors give money or goods to a person, they must trust that the person will pay them back. Most people do, but not everyone. Understandably, creditors try to be careful and lend only to people who are responsible and use credit wisely. People who do not use credit wisely find it harder and harder to get credit as time goes on.

CREDIT TROUBLE

Credit is a very useful tool for the consumer. But, like all tools, it can be misused. Tom and Jenny Gardner are among those people who let credit run away with them. Many people start the way the Gardners did. Tom and Jenny just went a little bit too far. And they didn't read the fine print on the contracts they signed. As you will see, too much borrowing can be expensive.

CASE STUDY

A diamond is forever

Tom and Jenny had been going together since their sophomore year in high school. They would graduate from college in May, and Tom had already lined up a job as a sales representative for a large manufacturing plant. They planned to be married in June.

Tom Begins To Buy

One bright April day, Tom went out to buy Jenny a diamond ring. Because he had a job lined up, he was able to find a jeweler willing to give him credit. Tom bought a $500 diamond ring on easy terms: just $50 down, $45 a month, and no payments until August. Tom felt great about using credit for the first time.

Tom and Jenny began to make plans. They planned to live in a small apartment until they had children. But they also planned to live well. Jenny had been promised a job in a real estate office. That meant they would have two incomes. With two incomes, they could get credit to buy a new car to replace Tom's old one. And they could furnish their apartment completely. They could even get a good stereo and a TV.

Tom Buys a Car

Soon after they started working, Tom and Jenny walked into the showroom of Sonny's Motors. They asked about a car they had been admiring. Sonny was glad to help them. He took Tom's old car as a down payment, which left a balance of $12,400. The payments were $435 a month for three years.

After their wedding, the Gardners moved into a three-room unfurnished apartment, with just their wedding presents and a few odds and ends of furniture that their parents and friends had given them. They started checking the furniture ads. In a few days, they found an ad for a complete living room set for just $495 at the New Age Furniture Store.

Tom and Jenny Keep on Buying

At New Age, they saw that the advertised set was not as good looking as it seemed in the ad. But the manager pointed out a better looking set for $1,295. They might as well get something they really liked. They also ordered a beautiful bedroom set for $1,199. And then they saw a fantastic home entertainment center priced at $2,000. The manager said she'd let them have it for $1,600 including tax, since they were buying so much other furniture. Why not? With this combination color TV and stereo, they might even save money by not going out to movies and concerts.

The whole package could be paid for on easy terms, about $150 a month. The good life had arrived.

Trouble at New Age

The good life lasted until the furniture was delivered. It was not the merchandise they had seen. It was junk. Tom phoned the store manager. She said it was what the Gardners had ordered. Tom said the sofa and chairs smelled of mildew. The manager said all new furniture smelled like that. Tom said the entertainment center wasn't working right. She said they'd repair it. They did repair it, but it still didn't work properly.

Tom felt New Age Furniture wasn't worth talking to. Maybe he'd sue them. He called a lawyer's office. But when the secretary said an interview would cost $50, Tom decided to forget it.

Tom and Jenny decided to stop paying for the furniture. Maybe the store would do something for them then. Or at worst, they figured, the store might take the furniture back. That would be the end of that.

Tom and Jenny Make a Big Mistake

After the Gardners stopped their payments, the store did repossess the furniture. But that wasn't the end of it. Before long, Tom and Jenny received a **deficiency judgment**, a legal notice stating that they owed the store more money in addition to the furniture that was repossessed. The notice said that the Gardners owed more than $4,000 for the remaining furniture debt, an auctioneer's charge, a storage charge, and lawyers' fees. The money was due right now. Tom decided to ignore the judgment.

About a month later, New Age wrote to Tom saying that it was turning his account over to a **collection agency**, a business that specializes in collecting bad debts. They also said that they may go to court to get part of Tom's wages to repay the debt. The collection agency called Tom at work a number of times to get him to repay. Tom's boss told him that his company didn't like these kinds of interruptions. Tom thought he'd better make his payments.

Tom went to see a finance company that advertised **debt consolidation loans**. With this loan, the Gardners could pay off all their old debts and have just one payment to make each month. The monthly payments would be quite low, but the loan would not be paid off for six years. Tom saw that the loan had a higher annual percentage rate than his auto loan and credit card accounts. But he signed up for it anyway. What else could he do?

No Way Out

A year later, Tom and Jenny had their first child. Jenny quit her job. They moved into a larger apartment. And they found there were lots of new expenses in taking care of a baby. The expenses piled up. Tom and Jenny fell behind in their loan payments. Tom didn't know what to do. He and Jenny were afraid he would lose everything, including his job. A friend told Tom about a legal aid office in town. Tom phoned and made an appointment with a lawyer.

After examining the Gardners' money problems, the lawyer could see no way out. Jenny couldn't get a job because she had to take care of the baby. The Gardners would have to declare **bankruptcy**—that is, they would have to be legally judged unable to meet their debts. Some of their possessions would be sold to help pay their creditors. They would then be out of debt—but not out of the woods.

Life would not be easy. There would be no more car loans and no more credit cards. Most lenders would not grant them credit for five to ten years.

✓ check your understanding ✓ ✓ ✓ ✓ ✓ ✓

1. **Why does credit involve trust?**
2. **What did Tom and Jenny purchase on credit?**
3. **How much money would Tom and Jenny have spent if they had paid for all of their purchases in cash?**

How Credit Mistakes Begin

What could Tom and Jenny have done to avoid their credit problems? Are there more sensible ways of using credit? Let's go back and see how the Gardners got into so much trouble.

Using easy credit The first time Tom used credit was to buy Jenny a ring. He found a jeweler happy to give him credit. That was helpful. But the trouble with easy-to-get credit is that the rates are usually high. A lender who gives credit to almost anyone will probably lose some money on unpaid accounts. To cover these losses, the lender will charge high rates.

Oddly enough, low monthly payments and other "easy terms" also mean high rates. Even though Tom was not making payments until August, his interest fees were mounting up.

NEW AGE FURNITURE CO.
FURNITURE AND RUGS

465 Middle Ave., Wilmington, MA
858-4511
monday-friday 9-9 saturday 9-5 closed mondays july and august

LOW OVERHEAD - LOW PRICE

Customer's Order No. 617-740-1710	Date 4/16 19 89

Sold to Tom & Jenny Gardner

Address 34 Garden Path

City Uptha Creek, MA 01798

Sold by Q.S.	Cash	COD	Charge NAF	Dr Acct	Mdse Ref	Paid Out	

206-C	Austin	Living Room Combo	$1,295.00
66-6-4	Pleasant Dreams Bedroom Suite (mattress not inclu.)		1,199.00
166-374	Picture Perfect Home Entertainment Center		1,600.00
			$4,094.00
		Less Deposit	-409.40
		Balance Due	$3,684.60

TERMS: 10% down - $125 monthly

Using too much credit You should use credit where you need it the most. Certainly the Gardners needed some furniture. But perhaps the new car, the stereo, or the TV could have waited. Many experts say that your installment debt should not be more than 20 percent of your net income. If you take home $10,000 a year, you should not run up debts (except for home mortgage payments) of more than $2,000 (about $167 a month). If you take home $20,000, the limit should be $4,000 (or about $330 a month). Another guideline is that a family's monthly installment debt payments should not be more than one third of their **discretionary income**—the money left over after food, clothing, housing, and utilities have been paid for.

Shopping poorly Suppose Tom truly needed a new car. Still, he should not have signed the dealer's contract without checking around for other sources of money. He may have done better if he had shopped around to find a lower interest rate and better terms. Since he had a job lined up, he may have been able to get a bank loan. Perhaps Tom's company had a credit union. Borrowers should also always check the annual percentage rate and the finance charge to see just how expensive a loan is.

At the New Age Furniture Store, Tom and Jenny really fell into a credit trap. They fell for the bait-and-switch fraud. The advertised living room set was junky, and the manager encouraged them to buy a more expensive one. Any store that uses such tactics is not likely to be reliable.

How To Get Deeper into Debt

Tom and Jenny started badly. They bought too much on credit. But they still could have solved their problems if they had acted wisely at that point. What they did—or didn't do—next made things a lot worse. Credit problems will not go away if you ignore them.

Doing nothing can cost money When they received the defective furniture, the Gardners should have done something. The lawyer may have been expensive, but Tom and Jenny were already spending over $4,000 on the furniture. The $50 cost of an interview might be money well spent. They could also check into free or inexpensive legal aid. They could contact any of the business groups and government agencies discussed in Chapter 10.

Stopping payment will not stop the problem The worst thing Tom and Jenny did was to stop paying. They thought repossession would end their debt. In most states, however, repossession does not end your obligation to pay a loan. The creditor will sell the repossessed goods. But, if the sale price does not cover the rest of your debt, the creditor can ask a court for a deficiency judgment. The creditor can ask for money to cover moving expenses, storage expenses, and legal fees, in addition to the original amount owed.

Small payments equal a long-term loan When the debt started to pile up, Tom and Jenny should have gone back to the store and explained their situation. Most lenders are willing to help. They know that they are more likely to get their money if they help you overcome your problem. They may reduce your monthly payments by giving you more time to pay back your loan. They may allow you to pay only the interest on the loan for a few months.

When businesses get into financial trouble, they can file for protection from creditors under Chapter 11 of the Federal Bankruptcy Act. The company is allowed to develop a plan to pay off its debts. If the plan is successful, the company can continue. If not, the company will go officially bankrupt. All of its funds will be divided among its creditors, and it will go out of business.

Credit and Advertising

What do the following have in common?

Easy Credit Terms

No Down Payment

Take Years to Pay

Flexible Monthly Payments

They are advertising terms for installment credit that are legal and require no further information under the Truth in Lending Law. They are so general that a credit shopper is not misled. Sure, this company probably charges high annual percentage rates and finance charges, but a wise consumer shouldn't be fooled by such advertising.

Certain advertising statements, however, if made alone, could mislead a consumer about the terms or actual costs of credit. Some examples are:

60 Months To Pay

Only 10% Down

Pay Only $10 a Month

Finance Charges under $50

If lenders make these statements, they must also give further information about the credit plan, including the annual percentage rates, as required by the Truth in Lending Law.

The Better Business Bureau suggests that anyone who wants to get a debt consolidation loan should call them first. The consolidator may have a history of complaints. Some consolidators have demanded large fees. Then, after clients paid the fees, the consolidator didn't pay the creditors.

Rather than going to their creditors, the Gardners took a consolidation loan to pay off their debts. Most credit experts do not recommend this approach. The "low monthly payments" that the loan companies advertise are low because the loan is a long-term one. Low payments every month for six years can add up to a very high finance charge.

Sometimes you can save money by grouping your smaller loan payments into one with a consolidation loan. For example, suppose you run up very high bills on your credit cards. The annual percentage rate on credit card bills can be more than 20 percent. If you could pay off these bills with a bank or credit union loan of 15 percent, you'd be saving money. But the consolidation loan the Gardners got had an interest rate that was higher than the rate on their credit card. They should have shopped around and compared loans. They should not have taken the first one that was offered.

How Creditors Can Collect Your Debt

A debt collection agency mailed out a series of five letters to debtors. The letters looked like telegrams and threatened legal action when, in fact, legal action was not even considered. Was that legal? No. The Federal Trade Commission has ruled that the telegram format and the threats are unfair and deceptive.

The finance company used a collection agency to help get payments from Tom. The collection agency must respect the debtor's rights. Therefore, the collection methods of the agency's employees, called **collection agents**, are regulated by the **Fair Debt Collection Practices Act**. Collection agents can't call you late at night. They must tell you they are collection agents when they call. They can't tell anyone else about your credit problems or threaten you in any way. And they can't contact you at work—if your boss doesn't allow it. When Tom's boss objected, Tom should have told the collection agents to stop calling him. He should have known his rights.

Taking your pay To make sure Tom paid his debt, the finance company hoped to take part of Tom's pay directly from his paycheck. This practice of "attaching" a debtor's pay is called **garnishment**. The creditor must sue in court and get a court order to garnish Tom's pay. If the creditor does so, Tom has the right to defend himself in court.

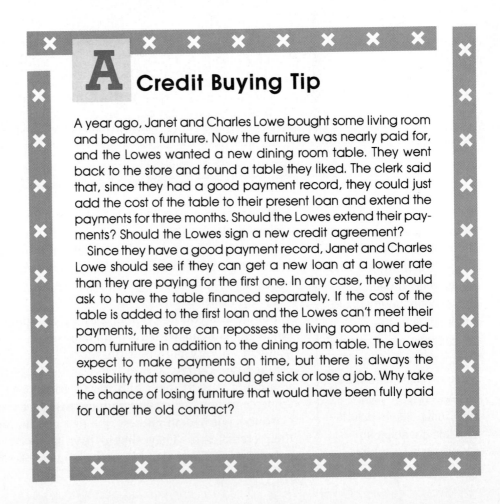

A Credit Buying Tip

A year ago, Janet and Charles Lowe bought some living room and bedroom furniture. Now the furniture was nearly paid for, and the Lowes wanted a new dining room table. They went back to the store and found a table they liked. The clerk said that, since they had a good payment record, they could just add the cost of the table to their present loan and extend the payments for three months. Should the Lowes extend their payments? Should the Lowes sign a new credit agreement?

Since they have a good payment record, Janet and Charles Lowe should see if they can get a new loan at a lower rate than they are paying for the first one. In any case, they should ask to have the table financed separately. If the cost of the table is added to the first loan and the Lowes can't meet their payments, the store can repossess the living room and bedroom furniture in addition to the dining room table. The Lowes expect to make payments on time, but there is always the possibility that someone could get sick or lose a job. Why take the chance of losing furniture that would have been fully paid for under the old contract?

In this country, the most likely people to file for personal bankruptcy are farmers.

Bankruptcy Tom Gardner did the right thing when he finally went to see a lawyer. But by that time, in the lawyer's judgment, the only way out for the Gardners was bankruptcy. By declaring bankruptcy, the Gardners did get rid of their debts, but not without a penalty.

If you are far in debt, you can go to court and ask to be found bankrupt. You file a statement listing your debts and your possessions. The cost is usually around $60 plus lawyers' fees. Your lawyer must file a petition for bankruptcy, and it may take two months for the court to act. During this time, your debts are frozen, and you are protected from your creditors.

The Gardners used Chapter 7 of the Federal Bankruptcy Act. Most debts that aren't secured by collateral are wiped out at once. With secured debts, you have to give up the collateral, unless it's special personal property, like a wedding ring. Using Chapter 7 is fairly easy and not very expensive, but it does a lot of harm to your credit rating.

When making some purchases, you could save the money spent on interest charges by living without the item until you had enough money to buy it with cash.

The Gardners should have checked on Chapter 13 of the Bankruptcy Act. Sometimes called "working bankruptcy," Chapter 13 allows you to pay off your debts under court supervision—usually in three to five years. If the Gardners succeeded with this plan, their credit rating would have been better.

When couples like Tom and Jenny declare bankruptcy, it hurts all of us. Lending places must charge high enough interest rates to cover the losses from the unpaid debts. Otherwise, they won't be lending money for long.

✓check your understanding ✓ ✓ ✓ ✓ ✓ ✓

1. What is a debt consolidation loan?
2. How does the Fair Debt Collection Practices Act help credit users?
3. What is Chapter 13 bankruptcy? What are the advantages and disadvantages of this kind of bankruptcy?

HOW MUCH CREDIT IS TOO MUCH?

The Gardners waited until their creditors decided that they were carrying too much credit. By then, they were in a lot of trouble. Credit users need to know sooner when trouble is approaching. They need to be able to turn things around and keep their good credit rating before it's too late.

Many signs can warn you that you are using too much credit. Credit counselors and other financial experts list the following warning signs most often:

- Borrowing to pay existing debts
- Spending more than 20 percent of your take-home pay on installment debt, not including rent or mortgage payments
- Being unable to pay off short-term debts, like utility bills and oil company credit cards
- Not keeping a savings account equal to at least three months' take-home pay
- Paying only some bills each month

If you see just two of these warning signs, you are heading into credit trouble. What should you do? Ask for help. It's best to seek out a non-profit financial counseling service in your community. The National Foundation for Consumer Credit can provide names of services in your area. Banks, credit unions, and employers also can help. They can analyze your situation and suggest what choices you may have to solve your problem.

Debtors in credit trouble can help themselves too. Consider cutting up all of your credit cards to avoid the temptation to spend money on things you really cannot afford and increasing your debt. Study each additional credit purchase carefully, and make sure it is really necessary. Try to pay off the debts with the highest interest rates first. See if you can sign up for a payroll deduction savings plan at work so that money is saved for you before you are tempted to spend it.

A credit counselor should not charge more than 12 percent of your debt as a fee. In fact, there are more than 200 non-profit credit counseling agencies in this country. For a list, write to the National Foundation for Consumer Credit, 8701 Georgia Avenue, Silver Springs, MD 20910.

✓ check your understanding ✓ ✓ ✓ ✓ ✓ ✓

1. **What are the five warning signs that indicate credit misuse?**
2. **What can credit users do if they believe that they are heading into credit trouble?**
3. **How much were the Gardners paying in installment bills each month before they stopped paying for the furniture? Suppose that they took home $18,000 a year. What is the maximum amount of their take-home pay per month that should go toward paying off their installment loans?**

SUMMARIZING
the chapter

Consumers should plan their use of credit wisely to avoid financial and legal problems. When consumers have difficulty in repaying a loan, the worst thing to do is nothing. If consumers just can't make the payments, they should speak to the lender. Also, non-profit financial counseling services and employers can help.

When consumers are behind in their payments, lenders may use a collection agency to get their money. The methods of collection agents are limited by the Fair Debt Collection Practices Act. Lenders also may have your wages garnisheed.

When consumers are completely unable to repay their debts, they may declare bankruptcy. They will get rid of most types of debt, but it will be hard to get credit again for many years.

Avoiding credit misuse is easier if a consumer knows some of the warning signs of credit trouble. While there are several to look for, seeing just one or two should be a signal for credit users to seek help.

CHAPTER CTIVITIES

BUILDING CONSUMER VOCABULARY

Number your paper from 1 to 8. Then write the term that best matches each numbered definition.

bankruptcy

collection agency

collection agents

debt consolidation loans

deficiency judgment

discretionary income

Fair Debt Collection Practices Act

garnishment

1. A legal notice stating more money is owed on an installment debt even though the article bought has been repossessed
2. Taking wages or salary in payment of a debt
3. A legal judgment of a person's inability to pay debts
4. Long-term loans used to pay off other loans
5. A business specializing in debt collection
6. Professional debt collectors
7. A federal law regulating the methods of collection agents
8. The money a person or family has left after paying for food, clothing, housing, and utilities

1. Why is it important to pay your bills on time?
2. What can people do if they buy defective goods with an installment loan? What can they do if they buy defective goods with a credit card?
3. Why was it a mistake for the Gardners to stop paying for their living room set?
4. Suppose you take out a loan for a new car and another one to pay for a new stereo. Then you lose your job. You find another job at a lower salary, but now you have trouble meeting your monthly installment payments. What can you do?
5. When is a debt consolidation loan a wise step? When is it a bad idea?
6. What is the difference between Chapter 7 and Chapter 13 of the Federal Bankruptcy Act?
7. Who finally pays for bankruptcy?

Assume you are comparing the costs of a $500 loan from three different lenders. Each lender offers you loans that can be paid back in monthly payments over one, two, or three years. Use the table below to answer the questions that follow.

Term of Loan	Annual Percentage Rate	Finance Charge	Monthly Payments
1 year	12%	$ 32.50	$44.38 × 12 months
	18%	48.75	45.73 × 12 months
	28%	75.84	47.99 × 12 months
2 years	12%	62.50	23.44 × 24 months
	18%	93.75	24.74 × 24 months
	28%	145.84	26.91 × 24 months
3 years	12%	92.50	16.46 × 36 months
	18%	138.75	17.74 × 36 months
	28%	215.83	19.88 × 36 months

1. How much would you save if you got a three-year loan at 12 percent rather than at 28 percent?
2. How much would you save if you got a two-year loan at 12 percent rather than at 18 percent?
3. How much would you save if you paid back an 18 percent loan in one year rather than in three years?
4. Which of the following would cost the borrower more to pay back in full: a one-year loan at 28 percent interest or a two-year loan at 12 percent interest?
5. When might you want to pay back a loan in one year rather than three? When might you want to pay it back in three years rather than in one?

1. You read the following advertisement in the paper:

> • End debt!
> • Stop lawsuits!
> • End or reduce monthly payments!
> • Prevent garnishment!
> • Get rid of the bill collector!
>
> Let us help you file for personal bankruptcy.
>
> ## Legal Eagle Law Service
> ### Phone 555-1357

    a. What are some things this ad doesn't tell you about bankruptcy?

    b. What questions should you ask if you call the service?

2. Suppose you see an ad that says: "No money down gets you a brand new Power Champ automobile. 60 months to repay. One week only! See us today."

    a. What does this ad tell you about the credit plan being offered?

    b. What other information is required by law?

Find out about credit cards in your own community. Visit two stores and two banks and find out which offer credit cards. Ask for disclosure statements. Make a chart for the cards you find showing the grace period, annual fee, annual percentage rate, monthly periodic rate, and method of figuring finance charges. For each, identify the type of credit card or charge account and give a brief summary of the requirements to get each (capacity, character, and capital).

In your own opinion, which is best and why?

As Jason and Melissa discover that credit seems to make all things possible, they also find that they must limit their use of credit. They plan to choose one or two items from the list of things they would like to buy on credit. Here are the items they are considering.

A WASHER AND DRYER

A new washer and dryer will cost $1,000. The finance charge will bring the total cost to $1,200. They currently spend $6 (and half of the day) every Saturday at a neighborhood laundry.

NEW SKI EQUIPMENT

Both of them enjoy skiing and would like to have new equipment. New equipment for both of them would cost a total of $800. A ski resort is located two hours away from their home. Lift tickets for one day and lunch usually total $60.

A VACATION

As members of a travel club, they could go on a combination cruise and overland hiking trip in Alaska. A 14-day trip for the two of them would cost $4,200, including all expenses.

A CAMERA

They want to buy 35 mm camera equipment that costs $500.

AN EDUCATION LOAN

Jason can take a two-year, part-time program at a private university in the city. If he gets a degree, he will have a much better chance of getting a promotion and a raise. He can get an education loan of $4,400—the cost of tuition and books for two years.

Answer the following questions on a separate sheet of paper. Use complete sentences.

1. Which of the potential credit purchases would eventually save money or make money?

2. What benefits, other than money, might some of the credit purchases have?

3. Do you think it's a good idea to use credit for luxuries?

4. What guidelines would you suggest to Jason and Melissa for how much they should buy on credit?

CRITICAL THINKING

THINKING ABOUT:

Credit

BUYING A CAR

BUYING A USED CAR

Next to a house, a car is probably the largest single purchase you'll ever make. If you buy a used car, it's also one of the riskiest purchases you'll ever make. How do you get a good car? How do you get a fair price?

● Where do you shop for a used car?

● How can you tell if a used car is in good shape?

● How do you know how much to pay for a used car?

● What should you know about bargaining with a dealer?

After years of waiting, you have your driver's license, your parents' permission, and some money to shop around for a used car. Where do you start?

WHERE TO BEGIN

Before looking at a single car, experts advise you to find out which cars have needed a lot of repairs in the past and which ones haven't. Ask friends and relatives about their experiences with their cars. Another place to look is the *Consumer Reports Annual Buying Guide*. In this book, you can find frequency-of-repair records from over 300,000 car owners. This information is used to find out how reliable any particular car is compared with other kinds of cars built in the same year. The guide puts this information in the form of charts listing 17 potential trouble areas (such as the fuel system, brakes, and body rust) for most models of cars and light trucks. The charts also give overall reliability ratings and cost-of-repair information for these vehicles.

Judging the Ads

Once you've narrowed down your search to a few types of cars, you need to know where to go to buy them. Many people find out by reading newspaper ads. The ads below are from a 1988 paper. To get an idea of the age of the advertised cars, imagine that you're reading the ads in 1988.

> Which costs more, a new car or the repairs on an old one? The new car, says the Department of Transportation (DOT). The most economical way to own a car, according to the DOT, is to buy one that's two to three years old and hold on to it for as long as it will keep going.

Which of the advertised cars seem like good buys? Do any of the ads make you think something is wrong? Can you tell which cars seem too high priced? Which seem too low priced? Do you know why some ads do not mention the price?

Some of the advertised cars seem inexpensive. In fact, their prices are so low they're hard to believe. Most used cars cost much more. Some of these ads may be designed just to get you to a car dealer's lot. Once you're there, you may be told that an advertised special has been sold. Or you may discover the car has been in a major accident or is full of rust. But the dealer shows you another car in fine shape for a few hundred dollars more. It's the old bait-and-switch. The best thing you can do is walk off the lot.

Another way to get you to the lot is to leave off the price. Some dealers hope that if they don't include the price in their ads, you will come in to find out for yourself. Once you are there, they hope you will stay and buy, instead of going to other dealers to compare prices.

One ad is for repossessed cars. As you learned in Chapter 16, a repossessed car is one that has been taken back from an owner who wasn't able to make the installment payments on it. Some people believe that a repossessed car must be a good deal. These cars are usually fairly new, but cost a lot less than a new car because all you have to do is take over the remaining payments. That may sound good, but these cars can turn out to be a lot of trouble. A person who couldn't make the payments probably couldn't keep the car in good condition either.

Dealers or Private Owners?

Some of the ads are from private owners, and others are from car dealers. Some people think the best buys are from private owners. Prices are often lower. But private owners provide no credit, servicing, and—most important—no warranty. Private owners sell the car "as is." If something turns out to be wrong with it after you buy it, that's your problem. Also, a private owner doesn't have to worry about maintaining a good business reputation, as an honest car dealer does.

Three types of dealers sell used cars. Higher priced used cars are usually found at new-car dealers' lots. These dealers sell the better cars that they've taken as **trade-ins**—consumers' cars taken by a dealer in place of all, or part, of the down payment for another car. Because the dealers generally sell only the trade-ins that are in good shape, they can offer good warranties and servicing.

Auto-rental agencies also sell their rentals as used cars. These cars are generally fairly new, are well equipped and maintained, and also come with good warranties. However, the cars have many miles on them and cost somewhat more than similar cars sold by private owners.

Never shop for a used car alone. Always bring a friend. Ask your friend to stand outside the car to see if all of the lights go on when you turn the switches. The friend should look for smoke coming out of the exhaust when you start the car. He or she should also watch as you drive the car to make sure that the front and rear tires line up and don't wobble.

In general, you'll get a better price if you sell your old car privately than if you let the dealer take it as a trade-in. After all, private buyers are just buying for themselves, but dealers must turn around and sell your car again at a profit.

> A used car can be a better investment than a new one since a new car depreciates as soon as it is driven off the dealer's lot.

Cars come in all shapes and sizes and so do people. Make sure you fit comfortably into any car you plan to buy. Do you have enough head room? Can you move the seat forward or back far enough to reach the pedals easily? Can you reach all of the controls when the seat belt is fastened?

Used-car dealers offer the widest range of cars and prices. You're more likely to find "beaters" for a few hundred dollars than newer, expensive cars on these lots. Like private owners, many used-car dealers sell their cars without warranties or servicing.

Both new-car and used-car dealers offer financing. Some advertise easy credit. But, as you know, easy credit often comes at high interest rates. If you buy a used car at a dealer, you don't have to finance it through the dealer. Don't, if the dealer doesn't give you the best interest rate around.

Not all dealers have to give you a warranty. Some states require dealers to give limited warranties for every car they sell. Other states have no such regulations. But in all states, if a warranty is offered, the Federal Trade Commission requires that the terms of the warranty be displayed on the car's window. Dealers must also display a check list of possible problem areas the car might have. They also have to display a reminder to get all promises in writing and a warning to have the car inspected by an independent mechanic.

✓check your understanding ✓ ✓ ✓ ✓ ✓ ✓

1. **When might you suspect that a dealer is using bait-and-switch advertising?**
2. **Why is it necessary to be careful about buying a repossessed car?**
3. **If you were looking for an inexpensive used car, where would you be most likely to find one?**

HOW TO CHECK OUT A USED CAR

No matter what the books or the ads say, the main question is, "Is the car you're looking at now a good car?" How do you find out? In the following interview, you may be surprised by what an expert tells you to look for.

My main worry is that a car may have major mechanical or body defects. We can fix the small stuff, but the big things, like pistons, valves, and the transmission, can cost a pretty penny to fix up.

If I'm checking the car on the lot, I look over the body and frame for major damage from an accident. This could cause a car to function very poorly. I always reject these accident-repair jobs.

Low mileage does not necessarily mean a good car. In fact, low mileage may mean a lot of stop-and-go city driving, which is the worst kind. A high-mileage car may have been driven mostly on the open road, which is a lot easier on the car. It might be in better shape than a low-mileage cream puff.

I can get any lemon back on the road. But give me a standard engine with a few good years left in it, and I can keep it going until they stop making parts.

LISA HORVATH
Auto Mechanic

A Used-Car Check List

Before you decide to buy any particular car, you should have a qualified mechanic look it over. But you probably can't afford to take every car that looks good to an expert to check out. How do you decide which car to take to the mechanic? You can do some checking yourself. You don't need to be an expert to follow these steps:

1. Check the outside.
2. Get in the driver's seat.
3. Start it up.
4. Check it in motion.
5. Check the engine.

Let's take a closer look at this check list so you can learn some specific warning signs to look for.

Check the outside The outside of the car should be fairly free of rust. Look at the hidden areas of the lower body, especially the rocker panels, which are the metal panels directly below the car's doors. Look behind the bumpers. Also check the paint for color mismatches. They may mean the car was damaged, repaired, and repainted.

> Cars rust from the inside out, so a car can be rusting underneath its paint. To check for unseen rust, look for bubbles, ripples, or grit in the paint surface.

Get in the driver's seat

Check out the seat belts. Are they all there, in front and back seats? Are they in good condition? Wearing them is the law in most states.

A worn gas pedal, a worn arm rest, or a badly depressed driver's seat could be signs that the car has been driven 50,000 miles or more. Of course, every car has an **odometer**, which records the number of miles the car has been driven. And the federal government and most states have laws against changing the odometers. They also require that a true statement of mileage be given to every used-car buyer. But odometer tampering does go on. The federal government says that it adds up to a multimillion-dollar fraud.

Start it up

First, turn the key, but don't start the car. All of the indicator lights on the dashboard should go on, and all the gauges should work. Check that the windshield wipers, heater, and all of the lights, inside and out, are working.

Start the car, put it in neutral, and press your foot on the gas pedal slowly. Make sure the light that says "ignition" is out at all speeds. If it is not, there may be something wrong with the electrical system. Listen for any grinding or clanging sounds. Some rattles can be fixed, but loud rattles as the car accelerates could mean problems with the valves or bearings.

Check it in motion

If the car has an automatic transmission, put it in reverse, move the car slowly backward, and then shift into drive. There should be a tight and solid catch without loud noises as the car moves forward.

If the car has a manual transmission, put in the clutch, put the car in first gear, and let the clutch out slowly. There should be no slipping or grabbing.

Accelerate the car through all of the gears up to about 45 miles per hour. If the car does not move smoothly, it may have serious

Why don't cars rust in California? Cars don't rust in places where it doesn't snow. What does snow have to do with rust? Very little. But salt is often put on roads to melt snow. And salt is a major cause of rust.

Check under the hood for such things as worn or broken wiring and leaks around hoses, gaskets, and radiator.

Shock absorbers keep a car from bouncing. Not only do they keep you from bouncing inside the car, they also keep the tires from bouncing—and skidding off the road. To check the shock absorbers, push down on each corner of the car. If the car bounces more than once, someone needs to spend anywhere from $70 to $200 to replace the shocks.

engine problems. As you drive, listen for a whining sound at the back of the car. A whine means that the rear-end gears are worn. While you drive, try a few bumpy roads. The car should not rattle and should not bounce up and down severely.

Check the brakes by making several stops from 45 miles per hour. The car should brake evenly and solidly. If the car swerves, it may need a front-end alignment. The brakes should not become soft or weak with pressure. With the car stopped, check to see that the brake pedal has three-eighths to three-fourths of an inch of play. Push down on the pedal for about a minute. The pedal should not continue to sink.

The steering wheel should not have more than two inches of free play. Try a few sharp turns at low speed to be certain that the steering wheel is sure and responsive.

Check the engine After your test drive, the engine will be warm enough for you to check it out. With the engine running, place a small piece of cardboard over the exhaust pipe. The cardboard should flap steadily. If it is sucked back against the pipe, or if it is covered with heavy blue oil smoke, the rings could be bad.

Open the hood. See if the exhaust smoke puffs out from the oil filler pipe (the place where the oil is added). This condition could also mean bad rings. Loud rattles coming from this area may mean bad valves. Look around the oil dipstick. If there is a lot of smoke, the car burns too much oil, a sign that the engine is worn out.

Now, turn off the engine. Take out the dipstick and look at the oil. Make sure the oil does not have white bubbles in it. If it does, the cooling system is leaking into the engine block.

As you inspect the engine, check for leaks under the car and around the hoses, gaskets (seals), and radiator. Also check the fluid in the radiator. It should not be brown or rusty.

The Final Check

After a car passes your own inspection, you should have it checked by an expert. Take it to a mechanic or a **diagnostic center**, a shop equipped with electronic testing equipment. Do not buy a car from anyone who will not let you have it checked out. Most used cars have very limited warranties. A careful, expert inspection can save you a lot of money in future repairs.

Plan on spending anywhere from $25 to more than $50 when you take a car to a diagnostic center or mechanic to check out. Get a written estimate of any needed repairs. You can use that estimate as a bargaining tool when deciding on the price of the car with the seller. Many sellers will pay some or all of the cost of such repairs.

✓check your understanding ✓ ✓ ✓ ✓ ✓ ✓

1. **What should you look for on the outside of the car?**
2. **Why is it important for a car to have seat belts?**
3. **What signs indicate that something is wrong with the brakes?**
4. **Why should you check the engine after you have test driven the car and not before?**

MAKING THE DEAL

After you find a car you want, you still need to make a deal, or agree on a price with the seller. Bargaining can be hard, especially if you are buying from a dealer. After all, the dealer has had plenty of experience in bargaining. Still, you can improve your bargaining position in several ways.

You can help yourself by having the car checked out by a mechanic. Then a dealer can't easily make false claims about it. You should also let the dealer know that you're shopping around. A dealer will have to offer you a price that matches the competition's. You should find out how much other cars of the same model and year cost. If you have a car to trade in, you should check the going price on that model too. Newspapers can give you some idea, but the best price information for most cars is found in the "books": the *Blue Book*, a monthly check list published by the National Automobile Dealers' Association, and the *Red Book*, published eight times a year by National Market Reports, Incorporated. These publications will give you the book value of your car. The **book value** is the price that is recognized by banks and insurance

Some cars, like this one, are so unusual that they may not be a bargain at any price.

Car **Talk**

Why should you care if a used car has a bent frame? What's it to you if the pistons are bad? Just about everything on a car can be fixed. All it takes is time and money. But some things may cost more to fix than the car is worth. Here is an explanation of some of the warning signs.

■ The *frame* is the metal skeleton that the rest of the body sits on. A bent frame is almost a sure sign of a major accident. It may cost thousands of dollars to fix, and the car may never run properly again anyway.

■ *Pistons*, *valves*, and *rings* are interrelated parts of the engine that turn the gasoline into energy. If a car needs new valves, rings, or pistons, it probably needs a new engine too.

■ The *transmission* sends the power from the engine to the wheels (to the rear wheels on a rear-wheel drive car or to the front wheels on a front-wheel drive model). A transmission can cost anywhere from $500 to $2,000 to repair. And, contrary to what many people think, a manual transmission can cost just as much to repair as an automatic.

■ *Rear-end gears* transmit the power from the transmission to the rear wheels on a rear-wheel drive car. These gears can cost more than $1,000 to fix. If you are looking at a front-wheel drive car, you will not be able to hear anything wrong with the gears, as they will be under the engine. Have the mechanic check them.

■ If a car needs a *front-end alignment*, that means the front wheels are not perfectly straight. A front-end alignment is a simple and inexpensive repair. So why is it important? If such a simple repair is needed but hasn't been done, it may be a sign that the owner did not maintain the car properly. If the owner did take the car in for an alignment and the problem did not go away, the car's frame may be bent. Other little things like broken headlights, gauges that don't work, dirty oil, or rusty radiator fluid are also signs that the car has not been properly maintained.

companies for a car of a particular model and year that's in average condition. Both books are available at banks and other financial institutions and at some libraries.

Finally, you should be on guard for tricky sales tactics. Sometimes, a dealer will offer you a high price for your trade-in. At the same time, though, the dealer will charge a high price for the car you want to buy. This tactic is called a **high ball**

Another dealer may get you excited about buying a particular car by offering a low price. But when you're ready to buy, the dealer decides that's not the price after all. Or a salesperson says the manager won't approve the price. The dealer hopes you're interested enough by now to buy the car anyway. This tactic is called a **low ball**.

Knowing the book value of the car you're trading and the car you're buying will help you spot high balls and low balls. The case study that follows shows some of these dealer tactics in operation. See how many tactics you can identify.

CASE STUDY

A used-car drama

JOAN ROBERTSON: So, I see that you like that high-performance Micro II. It's priced to move at just $6,195. I'll give you $2,715 for your old Tornado, and the difference is just $3,480. What do you say? Shall we write it up?

ED ROCKWELL: Not at that price. My Tornado is worth at least $3,000. The *Blue Book* says the average price is $2,800, and mine doesn't have a rust spot on it. It's worth far more than the average. Besides, the Micro II needs new tires. It looks like it needs new shock absorbers too.

JOAN: The Micro II's a beautiful car. Still, you've got a point there about the Tornado. But, even if it's in good shape, I can't sell it for much over the book value. I'll give you $2,800 for it.

ED: Can I have a diagnostic center check out the Micro II?

JOAN: Sure, and to show you I'm ready to deal, I'll drop the price to $6,000.

ED [*four hours later*]: Well, their mechanic says it's a pretty good car. But the muffler's worn, the front end needs alignment, and it does need new tires and shocks.

JOAN: Well, no car's perfect. It's not a new car. Shall I write it up?

ED: OK—for $6,000 minus $2,800 for my Tornado.

JOAN: Right. I'll just have to get the sales manager to approve. [*Ten minutes later.*] Sorry, the manager won't go lower than $6,075. I tried hard, but he says he can't make a buck at a lower price. I really thought he'd go for it.

✓check your understanding ✓ ✓ ✓ ✓ ✓ ✓

1. **Name three things to do before making an offer on a used car.**
2. **Where should you look to find out how much the car you want to buy is worth?**
3. **What is the difference between the low-ball and the high-ball sales tactics?**

A used car is a big purchase. It's also a risky purchase. To lower the risk, do some checking before you look at cars. Ask friends and relatives and read consumer magazines to find out which models of cars always seem to need expensive repairs and which ones don't. Read newspaper ads carefully. Don't waste your time with bait-and-switch offers that look too good to be true.

You can visit both car dealers and private owners. Cars bought from dealers usually cost more than cars bought from private owners. But private owners do not offer any credit, warranties, or servicing, as many dealers do.

Knowing how to screen out good cars from bad can save many trips to diagnostic centers or mechanics. But you'd be wise to spend the extra money to have an expert check out a car you still want to buy after it passes your inspection.

Know as much as you can about the condition of the car before you bargain with a seller over the price. Check the *Blue Book* or the *Red Book* to find out about what the price should be. If you want to trade in a car you already own as part of the deal, look up its price in the books as well.

Whether a child is riding in a new or used car, all states require that children under age 3 be protected in a safety seat.

BUILDING CONSUMER VOCABULARY

Number your paper from 1 to 6. Then write the term that best matches each numbered definition.

book value   low ball
diagnostic center   odometer
high ball   trade-in

1. Offering a high price for a trade-in and also a high price for the car a customer wants to buy
2. The price recognized by banks and insurance companies of an average car of a particular model and year
3. A shop equipped with electronic equipment to test cars
4. Offering a low price on a car and then changing to a higher price, hoping the customer is still willing to buy
5. A car taken by a dealer to cover all or part of the down payment for another car
6. An instrument on a car that measures how many miles the car has been driven

BUILDING CONSUMER UNDERSTANDING

1. If you are inspecting a used car, what can you tell about it from the following:
   a. Paint around a headlight that does not quite match the color of the rest of the car.
   b. Loud rattles from the engine as the car accelerates.
   c. An ignition light that stays on when the car is moving.
   d. Smoke visible near the oil dipstick when the engine is hot.
2. Why should you read about cars in consumer magazines before going to look at any?
3. Why might a used car be more expensive if you bought it at a new-car dealership rather than from a private owner?
4. If a used-car dealer offers easy credit, what should you watch for?
5. Why might you want to avoid buying a used car with low mileage?
6. Why is it important to have a used car checked by a diagnostic center or a mechanic before you buy it?
7. While shopping for a used car, you see a model you like priced at $4,200. Friendly Phil says his business is slow, so he'll let you have the car for the special price of $3,999. How can you find out if this is a good price?

After graduation from high school, Rich Wood plans to work full-time at Troy's Supermarket and take home about $800 a month. This won't be all his to spend, because Rich must pay his mother $150 a month for room and board, and he has to save $250 a month to be able to go to electronics school next year.

Rich also wants to buy a used high-performance ZIP Turbo II for $5,200. The bank wants 30 percent down and monthly payments of $195 for 24 months. Rich figures upkeep will cost him another $60 a month. And insurance will cost him $120 a month. Rich has the money for the down payment, but doesn't know if he can afford all of the rest of the costs.

1. How much money does Rich need for the down payment?
2. What will the total of Rich's loan payments be?
3. How much will he pay in finance charges?
4. After he pays the car payments, upkeep, and insurance each month, how much money will Rich have left over?
5. Can he afford the car?

1. Refer back to the Used-Car Drama case study on page 280 to answer the following questions:
   a. What sales technique did Joan Robertson try on Ed Rockwell?
   b. What did Ed Rockwell do correctly when bargaining with Joan Robertson?
   c. Did Ed make any mistakes? If so, what were they?
   d. What reasons can you give for Ed to take the deal? What reasons can you give for Ed to go look for another car instead?
2. Make a list of any terms you don't understand in "A Used-Car Check List." See if other members of the class can explain them. Ask them what else they would check before buying a used car.

Interview an auto mechanic and find out what major guidelines the mechanic uses to check out used cars. Using these suggestions and the Used-Car Check List in this chapter, create your own check list. Then check out your own car or a friend's car.

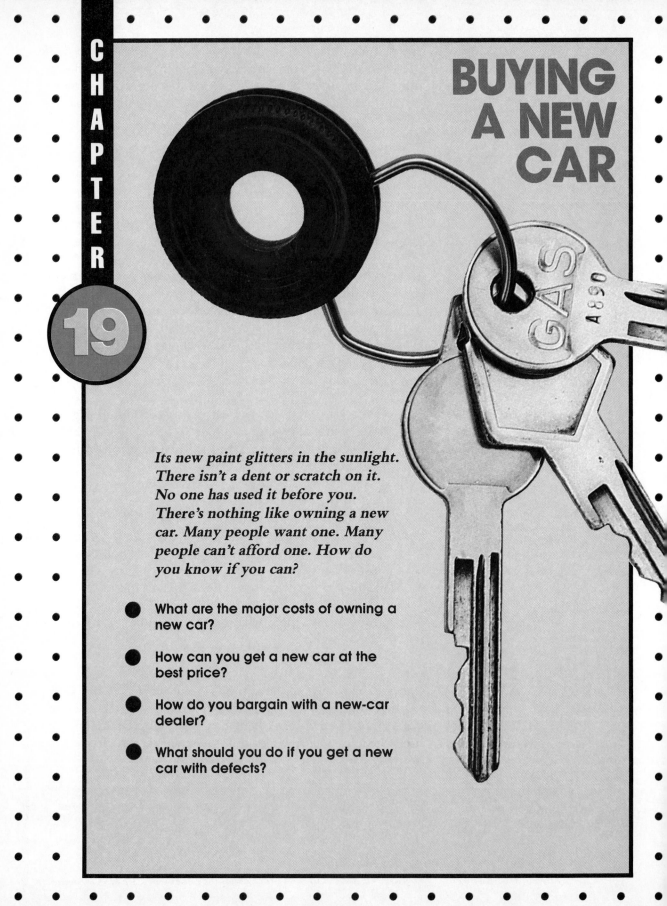

BUYING A NEW CAR

Its new paint glitters in the sunlight. There isn't a dent or scratch on it. No one has used it before you. There's nothing like owning a new car. Many people want one. Many people can't afford one. How do you know if you can?

● What are the major costs of owning a new car?

● How can you get a new car at the best price?

● How do you bargain with a new-car dealer?

● What should you do if you get a new car with defects?

A new car can have many advantages over a used car. Chances are it looks better, is safer, burns less fuel, and needs fewer repairs. But the new car has one big disadvantage—its price. How much will a new car cost you, and how much can you afford? These are the first questions you face.

THE COST

Few consumers can afford to pay cash for a new car, so they take out an installment loan. In deciding how much you can afford to pay for a new car then, one of the first things to decide is how large a monthly payment you are willing and able to make.

Many people want to pay for the car as quickly as they can. The fewer the payments, the lower the finance charge. But the longer you pay, the lower each monthly payment is. That's one reason it's common to pay for a car for 48, or even 60, months.

To find out how much you can pay for a car, estimate how much you can pay each month. Then multiply that figure by the number of months you are willing to pay. This amount will be the most you can afford to pay for a car, including the finance charge. In the case study on page 286, you can see how one couple budgeted for their new-car payments.

In addition to the cost of a new car itself, you should also consider the operating expenses for the model you choose.

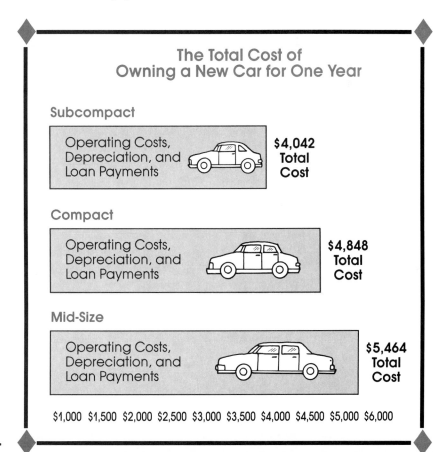

The Total Cost of
Owning a New Car for One Year

Subcompact

Operating Costs, Depreciation, and Loan Payments   **$4,042 Total Cost**

Compact

Operating Costs, Depreciation, and Loan Payments   **$4,848 Total Cost**

Mid-Size

Operating Costs, Depreciation, and Loan Payments   **$5,464 Total Cost**

$1,000 $1,500 $2,000 $2,500 $3,000 $3,500 $4,000 $4,500 $5,000 $6,000

CASE STUDY

Their old Musketeer is in bad shape, so Mike and Lisa Wayne feel they need another car. They want to get away from all the repair problems they've had with used cars, so they're looking for a new car.

Mike wants to buy a luxury Dynasty, but Lisa feels that all they can afford is a new version of their subcompact Musketeer. The Dynasty costs about $18,000 (including the finance charges), and the Musketeer is about $12,000. Mike and Lisa found some figures in a consumer magazine that told them what the operating costs (fuel, repairs, insurance, licenses) will be if they keep the car for six years. Operating costs for the Dynasty (in addition to installment payments) will be about $300 per month. The Musketeer will cost about $225 per month.

The Waynes' take-home pay is $2,500 a month. Their current budget, including the final payments on their used Musketeer, looks like this:

Rent and utilities	$850
Food and clothes	550
Car payments	250
Car operating costs	200
Other	390
Savings	260
Total	$2,500

The Waynes don't want to touch their savings account to make a down payment. But, if necessary, they'll reduce the amount they add to their savings each month. They are prepared to make payments for as long as 60 months. They think they can probably get about $1,100 when they trade in their old Musketeer.

1. **How many years would the Waynes be paying for a car if they made payments for 60 months?**
2. **What will happen to the amount they put into savings if the Waynes buy the Dynasty? Do you think they should buy the Dynasty, the Musketeer, or something else? Explain your answer.**
3. **Show what the Waynes' budget might look like if they bought the Dynasty or the Musketeer (choose one).**

How can you tell how much a car really costs you? One way is to add up your monthly payments and operating costs. That gives you the amount you need to spend each month. But you need to know one more thing. To find the total cost of your car, you need

Small cars generally get better gas mileage than large cars. But, no matter what the size, gasoline is the largest operating expense of any car.

Gas mileage varies greatly, even among cars of the same size. One compact car might get 24 miles to the gallon while another gets only 14. What difference does that make? If you drive 10,000 miles a year and gas costs you $1.25 a gallon, you'll pay almost $400 more for gas each year (or more than $7 extra every week) if you buy the less fuel-efficient car.

to figure in its depreciation. **Depreciation** is the amount the car loses in value as it gets older. If you could buy a car for $14,000 and sell it the next year for $14,000, there would be no depreciation. In the end, the car would cost you only what you put into it in operating costs. But, if your car can be sold for only $11,000 after you have owned it for a year, it has depreciated $3,000. The car has cost you operating expenses plus $3,000.

The cost of car ownership—what you pay out and don't get back—is operating costs plus depreciation (plus, if you buy on time, finance charges). Depreciation often is the greatest single cost of owning a new car. That's because depreciation is greatest in the first year of a car's life. Experts say that a new car will lose at least one quarter of its value at the end of the first year no matter how carefully it is operated or maintained. The older the car, the less it loses each year in depreciation.

Different models depreciate at different rates. For example, when fuel prices are high, fuel-efficient cars generally depreciate slower than "gas guzzlers." Cars in high demand because they are in limited supply or because they have a good reputation for reliability depreciate slowly. Cars whose design or features change a lot from year to year depreciate quickly. Smart consumers keep such facts in mind when shopping.

✓ check your understanding ✓ ✓ ✓ ✓ ✓ ✓

1. **How do you figure out how much you can afford to pay for a new car?**
2. **List all of the items that make up the total cost of owning a car. What is usually the biggest single cost?**
3. **Is it better for a car to depreciate slowly or quickly? Explain.**

THE CHOICE

You have dozens of models to choose from when you buy a new car. And each car can come with dozens of extras, such as air conditioning, a sunroof, or power steering. In some cars, these items are **standard features**—they are included in the basic price of the car. But for many other cars, these items are **options**— they cost extra. In fact, options can easily add about 20 percent to the car's price.

Because of this variety, you must make many decisions. You must decide what kind of car you want, what options you want, and how much you are willing to pay. Try to make these decisions before you visit a dealer. The chart on page 290 lists the advantages and disadvantages of some of the most common options.

Smart shoppers read reviews about new cars in newspapers and in consumer and auto magazines. Some even check *Consumer Reports'* used-car guide to determine past reliability of particular models and car companies. If you go shopping without knowing what you want, the dealer can push you toward models that are more expensive than you need. Remember, the less you want, the less you have to pay.

How to Save

When you know the general type of car you want and the options you want, shop around. Compare similar models from different manufacturers. Looks are important, but be sure to test drive the

Many cars now come with a special, smaller spare tire that is designed to save trunk space. But the tire can be used only in emergencies and then only for short distances. If you have a flat and use that tire, you must repair or replace your regular tire as soon as possible.

cars too. How comfortable are they? How do they handle in city traffic and on the highways? Test drive only the cars with features you want and need. Be sure you don't end up test driving a "look-alike" of the car you want that has a larger engine or more options than you need or can afford.

Sometimes, you can get a bargain on the type of car you want. Here are some tips for bargain shopping.

Leftovers Next year's models come on the market in the fall. Good deals can often be made on this year's leftovers in the late summer and early fall. A dealer may slash prices on these leftovers to make room for the new models. Remember, though, that the leftovers are a year old and have already depreciated. Usually, a leftover is worth buying only if you plan to keep it four or more years. Otherwise, you'll lose too much in depreciation.

Demonstrators Another possible bargain is a dealer's **demonstrator**, a car used to show to customers. Demonstrators are the cars you use to test drive, and they usually have a few thousand miles on them. They are offered at reduced prices year round. Consider a demonstrator only if the dealer will give you a complete new-car warranty with it. This will protect you against previous wear by giving you the same guarantees you would get with a brand-new car.

Group purchase Another way to save is to buy a car through a group. You may be a member of a labor union, credit union, or

An economy car may cost less to buy than a big car, but it doesn't always cost less to maintain or repair. Department of Transportation figures show that the standard maintenance needed for some subcompacts costs more than twice as much as it does for some of the largest cars.

Which Options Are for You?

Options	Price	Advantages	Disadvantages
Larger engine	$170–1,900	Quicker acceleration; usually more power for pulling trailers	Expensive; fuel economy suffers.
Turbocharged engine	$700–3,700	A way to add power to a smaller engine; saves fuel at high speeds	May not last as long as a non-turbocharged engine; may need to be serviced more often
Automatic transmission	$175–1,040	Easier to use than a manual transmission in traffic	Hurts fuel economy; can increase noise
Power steering	$215–450	Makes parking easier, which is more important the heavier the car is	Makes steering feel less responsive
Cruise control	$150–365	**Helps erratic drivers keep to the speed limit and improves fuel economy. Reduces driver fatigue on long trips**	Can make driver fail to pay attention to the road
Rear-window defogger	$35–190	Essential in rainy and cold climates for clearing fog and frost from rear window	
Rear-window wiper/washer	$110–250	Cleans off rear window in the same way that windshield wipers clear off front windows; important for hatchbacks	
Air-conditioning	$655–1,450	Reduces noise; increases comfort; keeps windows clear	Reduces fuel economy; increases maintenance costs
Tinted glass	$60–405	Reduces sun's glare and the load on the air-conditioner	Reduces nighttime vision; dark band on top may interfere with vision of tall drivers
Power windows	$145–295	More convenient	Adds weight; may increase maintenance costs. Switches can be confusing and hard to find at night.
Sun roof	$200–1,320	Can improve ventilation; may add to resale value	Reduces head room in some cars; may increase maintenance costs.
Body trim	$15–140	Vinyl moldings on the side of the car can protect it from parking-lot dents	Metal moldings are more glitter than protection
Additional rustproofing	Varies		Most new cars already have rust protection and will not benefit from additional rustproofing. If done poorly, it can actually cause your car to rust sooner

Source: Copyright © 1987 by Consumers Union of United States, Inc., Mount Vernon, NY 10553. Adapted by permission from *Consumer Reports,* April 1987. Please consult the most recent April issue of *Consumer Reports* magazine for current figures on these options.

community group. Some of these organizations can get cars for their members at special prices. But you should also shop around to make sure the group price is the best price.

How to Bargain

What sort of price can you hope to negotiate on a new car? Start with the **sticker price**. This price combines the base price of the car, as suggested by the manufacturer, and the cost of options. Dealers are required by law to display the sticker price on the car. Luckily, dealers will sell many popular new cars for less than the sticker price. How much less? They won't sell it for less than the **dealer's cost**—what the dealer had to pay the manufacturer. To find out what the dealer's cost is, write to a consumer magazine such as *Changing Times*.

Knowing the dealer's cost of the basic car and the options you want can give you an idea of where to begin when bargaining for the price of the new car. To get a detailed list of dealer's costs for a particular car, you can order a computer print-out on that car from such publications as *Consumer Reports*. Edmund's car price guides also have complete listings of dealer's costs for new cars. To the dealer's cost add the charges for taxes, freight (the cost of getting the car from the manufacturer to the dealer), and dealer's profit. Remember, a dealer needs to cover expenses and make a profit.

Dealers can make their profit in different ways. That profit can come from charging a high price for the car itself, particularly from cars in great demand but limited supply. Often, foreign cars and sports cars fall into this category. In addition, the more options you want, the more chance the dealer has to increase profit. Dealers also earn more profit from unwise shoppers who don't know what the dealer's cost is and don't drive a hard bargain.

After you negotiate the lowest price you can for the car, start all over again and bargain for a good trade-in price on your used car. Start by knowing the value of your car according to the *Blue Book* or the *Red Book*. After you negotiate the highest price for your trade-in, start bargaining for the best financing terms.

For most people, a car is too expensive an item to pay for with cash. However, a surprising number of people do manage to come up with the money. As many as 40 percent of the cars sold in the United States each year are paid for in cash.

Each new car comes with a sticker telling you what its gas mileage is according to tests made by the Environmental Protection Agency (EPA). You can use those stickers to compare one car with another. But you may not get that mileage when you drive the car. The EPA tests all cars under the same conditions. Your mileage will vary depending on how you drive.

✔ check your understanding ✔ ✔ ✔ ✔ ✔ ✔

1. **What is an option? Why is it important to decide which options you want before you go looking for a new car?**
2. **List three ways you might get the car you want at a bargain price.**
3. **How can you determine the dealer's cost for a new car?**
4. **How should you settle on the price of a new car?**

THE PURCHASE

When you're ready to buy, be sure that the dealer is not pressuring you into signing the purchase contract. If you feel pressure, get out. You have too much to lose by making mistakes. Also, don't be swayed by gifts, prizes, and other free gimmicks. Nobody gives you something for nothing.

The Contract

When the contract is drawn up, read every word. Don't be distracted. Ask questions, and if anything seems suspicious, stop the deal there. If you're not sure about any of the wording, take the contract to a lawyer for advice.

Make sure the car described in the contract is the car you saw. Also make sure that all copies of the contract say exactly the same thing.

Sign only at the bottom of each page. Make certain that there's no space above or below your name for additional words. If there is, draw several lines to the bottom of the page and cross out any blanks in the contract.

The Last Inspection

Before delivery, mechanics at the car dealership will give your car a final check.

The actual car you are buying may not be in the dealer's showroom at the time you sign your contract. It may be on order from the manufacturer and may be delivered a few weeks later. Therefore, before you accept the car and pay for it, inspect it carefully. Make sure that it has all of the equipment and options you ordered and that it has no defects.

Sometimes cars are damaged and are repaired and repainted before they're delivered to you. Check the tires for cuts and bulges. Examine the doors, trunk lid, and glove compartment door to be sure they close tightly. Test the heater, windshield wipers, lights, and turn signals. Check the steering for too much play. Finally, push on the brake pedal for about a minute. If it sinks to the floor, there's a leak in the system.

Insist on test driving the car. The dealer may hesitate because the car belongs to the dealer until you have paid the dealer for it. But the dealer should allow you the same rights you had before you signed the contract. Your test drive should be thorough, at all speeds, on a highway and also in stop-and-go traffic.

Finally, ask for a copy of the **predelivery inspection form.** Every new car dealer is required to fill out one for the manufacturer. The form is a check list of items that have been inspected by the mechanic at the car dealership. Look for missing checks and rejections. Do not accept the car you are purchasing until you are satisfied that it is in good shape.

AUTO PURCHASE FORM

Make of Car _____ Model _____

Body Style _____ Color _____ Trim Color _____

1. Price of car (sticker price):

Base price	$_____
Options	
_____	$_____
_____	$_____
_____	$_____
_____	$_____
_____	$_____
_____	$_____
_____	$_____
_____	$_____
_____	$_____
_____	$_____
_____	$_____
_____	$_____
_____	$_____
Total options	$_____
Freight charge	$_____
Total sticker price of car	$_____
Negotiated price	$_____

2. Trade-in:

Make of trade-in _____

Year _____ Model _____

Body Style _____

Trade-in allowance _____

_____

3. Calculations:

Negotiated price of car	$_____
Trade-in allowance	– $_____
Price minus trade-in	$_____
Sales tax	+ $_____
Dealer preparation charges	+ $_____
Total charges	$_____
Down payment	– $_____
Amount to be financed	$_____
_____ % annual percentage rate	
Finance charge	+ $_____
Deferred payment price	$_____
To be paid in _____ months	
Monthly payment	$_____

✓ check your understanding ✓ ✓ ✓ ✓ ✓ ✓

1. When should you refuse to sign a contract for a new car?
2. When does ownership of a new car pass from the dealer to the buyer?
3. Name three ways to check out a new car before you accept it.
4. What does a factory predelivery inspection form tell you?

THE DEALER

After you buy a new car, you still will have business with the dealer. The dealer will service the car—maintaining it, repairing it if necessary, and checking it out periodically. For many people, therefore, service is as important as price. Often, new-car buyers will buy from the dealer who gives them the best price, even if it's only a savings of $25 or $50. But such savings is not worth the sacrifice of good service.

Service and the Warranty

New cars are covered by warranties. A new-car warranty says that if a car breaks down and the problem is covered by the warranty, the dealer will fix it without charge. New-car warranties are generally limited warranties, covering only certain kinds of problems for a fixed amount of time or a fixed amount of mileage. The warranty may last for three years, for example, or until the car has been driven 36,000 miles. Only some parts of the car, such as the engine and transmission, may be covered.

The warranty will generally require you to have the car serviced and repaired by the dealer. But not all dealers give good service under the warranty. That's why it's important to buy from a dealer who will give good service and make honest agreements. Find out from your friends and neighbors what experiences they've had with dealers in your community. Consumer protection agencies can also be helpful. Some of them will tell you if they have had any complaints about a dealer.

What If It's a Lemon?

Suppose after you get your car it turns out to be a lemon. If your car has something wrong with it that is not corrected under the warranty, go to the dealer's service department right away. Ask the service manager to look into your problem personally. If that doesn't help, ask to see the person who owns the car dealership. These are the first steps to take to lodge a complaint. Sometimes they're enough.

You can also contact the car manufacturer's zone service manager. Ask the manager to meet with you and the dealer to discuss the problem. This approach may be useful if the dealer has failed to correct a problem properly. It may also be useful if the dealer says that the repairs you need are not covered by the warranty or that your complaint is not justified.

If the dealer and the manufacturer do not solve your problem, you may want to take stronger action. In the past, some people have written letters to their representatives in Congress, to federal agencies, to their state's attorney general, and to local consumer groups. Other people have hired lawyers and gone to court. Some

As you might expect, more people have driver's licenses in rural areas than in cities. For example, more than nine out of every ten people old enough to drive have licenses in Idaho. In New York, only seven out of ten people who could get a license have one.

It will come as a big surprise to people who live in cities to learn that about 45 percent of the roads in the United States are not paved. City people rarely see an unpaved road because more than 90 percent of urban roads are paved.

have even put "LEMON" signs on their cars and parked them in front of the dealer's showroom or entered them in auto shows hoping to embarrass the dealer who sold the car.

Most states have **lemon laws**. These laws give car owners a procedure to follow to settle disputes that arise with the manufacturer during the first year. Usually, the car must not have been working for 30 days or must not have been fixed in four attempts. Then the dispute is sent to a panel of individuals called an **arbitration panel**. This panel offers solutions to the manufacturer and to you. You may get a new car. You may get your money back. More often, the panel suggests a compromise. If you are unhappy with the panel's solution, you can still sue the manufacturer.

Recalled Cars

Quite often in recent years, defects have been found that affect every car made of a certain model and year. The National Highway Traffic Safety Administration (NHTSA) makes manufacturers recall those cars. In a **recall**, manufacturers ask owners to take their cars into the dealer to be fixed for free. NHTSA reports that between 1966 and 1987, 100 million cars, trucks, and motorcycles were recalled because of safety defects. If you own a car that must be recalled under NHTSA regulations, you should receive a letter informing you about the defect and telling you what to do about it. Sometimes these recalls are also announced on television and radio news programs or printed in newspapers.

✓ check your understanding ✓ ✓ ✓ ✓ ✓ ✓

1. **Why is the service a dealer gives important to you?**
2. **What kind of warranty usually comes with a new car?**
3. **What are the first steps to take if your new car has a problem that is not corrected under the warranty?**
4. **What are lemon laws? What has to go wrong with your car before you can take advantage of the lemon law?**

SUMMARIZING
the chapter

New cars are generally safer, more fuel efficient, and need fewer repairs than used cars. They also cost more. Most people cannot pay cash for a new car. Before you buy, figure out how much you can pay each month for a loan and to operate the car. Then decide what type of car and which options you want.

You may save money on a new car by buying a leftover, a demonstrator, or a group purchase deal. When bargaining with a dealer over the price of a car, it is seldom necessary to pay the sticker price. By knowing the dealer's cost and the value of your trade-in, you will put yourself in a good position to get the lowest price for a new car. Before accepting a new car, check it out thoroughly and test drive it.

The dealer should take care of any problems with a new car covered under the warranty. If your new car turns out to have many problems not covered under warranty, complain first to the service manager and then to the manufacturer's zone representative. Many states also have lemon laws that provide a way to settle these disputes. If all else fails, federal and state agencies, local consumer groups, and legal help are available. If every car of a certain model has a problem, the federal government requires car makers to recall those cars and fix the problem at no charge to you.

·C·H·A·P·T·E·R· A ·C·T·I·V·I·T·I·E·S·

BUILDING CONSUMER VOCABULARY

Number your paper from 1 to 10. Then write the term that best matches each numbered definition.

arbitration panel   options
dealer's cost   predelivery inspection form
demonstrator   recall
depreciation   standard features
lemon laws   sticker price

1. Notification to return every car of a certain model and year to the dealer to fix defects at no charge to the owners
2. The amount a car loses in value as it ages
3. Extra items, such as air conditioning or a sunroof, that add to the base price of buying a new car
4. Items that come with a new car and do not increase the base price
5. A list of the checks given to a new car by a dealer's mechanic
6. A car used by a new-car dealer to show features to potential customers
7. The base price of a new car, as suggested by its manufacturer, together with the price of any options
8. State laws designed to help consumers with new cars that have lots of problems

9. The amount a dealer pays the manufacturer for a new car
10. A group that hears and helps settle disputes between consumers and car manufacturers

BUILDING CONSUMER UNDERSTANDING

1. What are the advantages and disadvantages of buying a new car?
2. What is the advantage of taking five years to buy a new car? What is the disadvantage?
3. What is the relationship between depreciation and used-car prices?
4. When would it be a bad idea to buy a leftover? a demonstrator? a car through a group discount?
5. How does knowing the dealer's cost affect your ability to bargain for a new car?
6. What are three ways in which the dealer can make a profit?
7. Your new car stalls a lot. You've taken it to the dealer for work four times, but it still stalls out. The dealer tells you that everything will be fine. They'll work on it again next week. What should you do?

BUILDING CONSUMER MATH SKILLS

1. You want a new Cardinal, which has a sticker price of $14,750. The dealer will give you $2,250 for your old Robin and also knock $1,350 off the Cardinal. If you take the offer, how much will you pay for the Cardinal?
2. Suppose you now check a consumer publication and find the dealer's cost for the Cardinal is $12,390. How much of a profit will the dealer be making (not counting the trade-in)?
3. How much profit would the dealer make if you paid the sticker price? Approximately what percentage mark-up is this price over the dealer's cost?

APPLYING CONSUMER SKILLS

You're shopping for a brand-new Musketeer. Its total sticker price is $16,750. You go to Dealer A, where a salesperson says you can have the car for $14,400 plus your old Viking. You go to Dealer B, whose best price is $15,000 with your old Viking. When you return to Dealer A, you're told that the manager will not approve the price you were quoted. But the manager will let you have the Musketeer for $15,100 plus your old car. He'll also throw in rustproofing. What should you do? Why? Be specific.

GETTING INVOLVED IN YOUR COMMUNITY

Use an auto purchase form like that on page 293 to compare the prices of the same new car at two auto dealerships. Find out what the dealer's cost is for that car. Determine how much above the dealer's cost is the price at each dealership.

INSURING YOUR CAR

Whether your car is worth $500 or $50,000, something valuable is always at risk every time you get behind the wheel: you, your passengers, and every person you drive near. That's why most states require you to carry some kind of auto insurance. What are the different kinds of auto insurance? How can you figure out which kind you need?

◆ **Why do some drivers have to pay more than others for auto insurance?**

◆ **What should you look for when buying an auto insurance policy?**

◆ **What is the difference between liability and no-fault auto insurance?**

◆ **What are some problems with the auto insurance system?**

There are many kinds of insurance. You can insure your health, your life, and your property, for example. Insurance protects you against misfortunes such as illness, accidents, or thefts. Insurance does not help you escape these things, but it helps pay for the costs of losses that these unexpected events can cause.

HOW INSURANCE WORKS

Everyone faces risks. Risks can't be avoided, but the cost of losses can be reduced by sharing those costs with a large group of people. Insurance experts can predict pretty accurately what the expenses of a large group of people will be. How do they know? They use statistics. If you flip a coin, you can't tell whether you're going to get heads or tails. But if a million people flip a million coins, statistics show that very close to half a million people will always get heads and half a million will always get tails. No one knows what results you will get. But a large group's results can be predicted.

If you are ill, your medical bills can get very high. But the medical bills of a million people will not all be very high. If each person in the group agrees to pay one-millionth of that total, there will be enough money to pay for everyone's medical bills without everyone paying very large amounts of money. No one knows, of course, which people will have no bills and which people will have bills for thousands of dollars. But the insurance will protect all of them.

The amount each person pays for insurance is called a **premium** The money paid to insured people by insurance companies to cover the cost of losses is called a **claim**. Insurance companies set their premiums high enough to pay all expected claims over a certain period of time and also make a profit.

What causes auto accidents? Experts say there are three main causes: drivers' mistakes, poor road conditions, and something wrong with the car. In 85 percent of the cases, though, drivers cause the accidents.

Young people are involved in fatal automobile accidents almost twice as often as other drivers.

▶   ▶   ▶   ▶   ▶

THE BASICS OF AUTOMOBILE INSURANCE

The cost of your auto insurance is based on the amount of money the insurance company expects to pay out to cover the claims of the people in your group. What is "your group"? Auto insurance companies often group drivers by age. They've found that the rate of accidents and driving violations depends very much on age. The graph below shows the percentage of drivers in various age groups who had accidents in a recent year. About one out of every three drivers under the age of 25 was involved in an accident that year. Because insurance companies pay out more claims for young drivers, they charge them more.

Other factors also help determine rates. For example, teen-age boys pay more for car insurance than teen-age girls. This isn't because boys are worse drivers than girls. Both sexes have about the same number of accidents for each mile driven. But boys drive more miles and therefore have the opportunity to have more accidents.

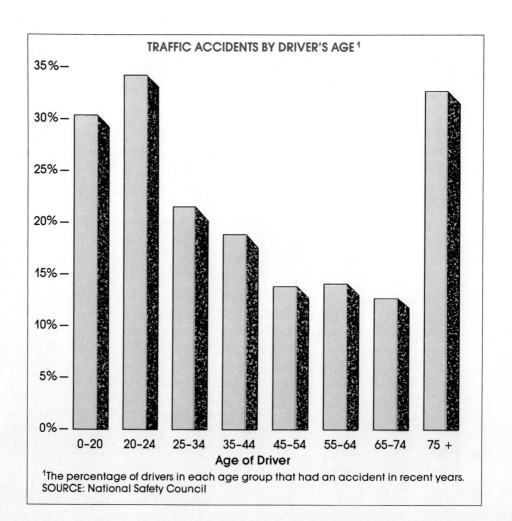

TRAFFIC ACCIDENTS BY DRIVER'S AGE [1]

[1]The percentage of drivers in each age group that had an accident in recent years.
SOURCE: National Safety Council

Drivers are grouped in other ways. People who drive in crowded city neighborhoods pay more than people who live in small towns. People who drive a long way to work pay more than those who don't. The people who pay the highest rates usually are those who have had several accidents or traffic violations.

The car itself can also make a difference. The premium depends on how easily the car is damaged, its accident record, repair costs, and theft record.

SHOPPING AROUND FOR INSURANCE

There are many places you can go to buy insurance, and they're not all alike. They don't give the same service, and they don't charge the same prices. Comparison shopping can help you find the best insurance policy at the lowest price.

One thing you want to know is how dependable the insurance company is. It does no good to save money on a policy if the company will refuse to pay your claim or will cancel your insurance after you've had one accident. A good place to find out about companies' dependability is *Consumer Reports*. Every few years, the magazine surveys its readers about auto insurance companies. It then publishes a "claims satisfaction index," which rates how satisfied the customers are who have made claims.

Another thing you want to know is the price. You can visit insurance agents in your community and compare their rates. Some companies give lower rates if you've had driver education or if you've gotten good grades in school. Some companies even offer discounts for drivers who don't smoke. When you're shopping, be sure you compare rates for identical policies.

Auto insurance can be expensive. So you should think before you buy. Buy insurance only to guard against big losses. A lawsuit for hurting another person, for example, could cost you hundreds of thousands of dollars. So protecting yourself against such a lawsuit is important. But repairing a crumpled fender might cost you only a few hundred dollars. Insurance against such a relatively small expense can cost more than it's worth.

✓check your understanding ✓ ✓ ✓ ✓ ✓ ✓

1. What is the purpose of insurance?
2. What is an auto insurance premium? Name six things insurance companies consider when determining the amount of a driver's premium.
3. How can you find out how dependable an auto insurance company is?
4. In general, what kinds of risks should you insure yourself against?

KINDS OF AUTO INSURANCE

Auto insurance is really a combination of several types of insurance. Some are more important than others. You should carefully choose the types and amount of coverage you need.

Liability Insurance

Insurance that covers the cost of bodily injury and property damage you cause to others is called **liability insurance**. If you cause an accident, your liability insurance will cover the damage you do to pedestrians, other cars, and the other people in those cars. It also helps pay the cost if someone sues you for pain and suffering caused by an accident that may be your fault. Another name for liability is *casualty*.

The insurance can be bought in different amounts. Most policies will state the amount of your coverage in a three-part number. Suppose you have a 100/300/25 policy. The "100" means that, in any accident that is your fault, the insurance company will pay personal injury expenses of anyone you have injured up to $100,000 for each person. The "300" means the company will pay a total of $300,000 in injury claims arising out of a single accident. And the

If you doubt that liability insurance is worth the money, maybe the Census Bureau can convince you. The bureau reports that more than 95 percent of the money paid to insurance companies for liability coverage is paid out in claims.

You need liability insurance to pay for the cost of damage or injury to others.

Premiums vary according to the coverage chosen.

"25" means the company will pay up to $25,000 for damage you cause to others' property (including telephone poles, fences, other people's cars, and so on). These amounts are the most the insurance company will pay. You must pay any extra expenses on your own.

Raising the limits of your liability coverage does not cost much. For example, in one state, increasing coverage from 50/100/25 to 100/300/25 costs only $21 yearly. In a time of frequent lawsuits and of rapidly rising costs for medical care and auto repairs, you should buy as much liability insurance as you can afford. Don't try to cut your auto insurance bills by trimming your liability coverage.

About half the states in the country do not have this traditional liability system. They have a **no-fault insurance** system. In these states, it doesn't matter who was at fault in an accident. Each driver's insurance company pays the personal injury expenses of its own customers. One reason no-fault insurance is used is to speed up payments to injured people. No time is wasted arguing over who caused the accident. The no-fault system is also intended to keep down auto insurance rates. Costly lawsuits can be avoided because insurance companies pay their own policy-holders' bills.

DECLARATIONS PAGE   **FAMILY COMBINATION AUTOMOBILE POLICY — PART TWO**

RENEWAL OF NUMBER
DECLARATIONS

Item 1. Named Insured and Address: (No., Street, Town, County, State)

IMPORTANT

The rates charged do not contemplate coverage for male drivers under 25.
If you have an underage driver, please call us immediately.

Item 2. Policy Period: (Mo. Day Yr.)   (Months)
From   to
      12:01 A.M., standard time at the address of the named insured as stated herein.

Occupation of the named insured is

Name and address of employer is

Item 3. The insurance afforded is only with respect to such of the following coverages as are indicated by specific premium charge or charges. The limit of the company's liability against each such coverage shall be as stated herein, subject to all the terms of this policy having reference thereto.

☐ Auto policy provisions apply unless Block contains the letter "X"

PREMIUMS		LIMITS OF LIABILITY		COVERAGES
Car 1	Car 2			
$	$	150 thousand dollars each person 300 thousand dollars each occurrence	A	Bodily Injury Liability
$	$	25 thousand dollars each occurrence	B	Property Damage Liability
$	$	$ 5,000. each person	C	Medical Payments
		(INSERT AMOUNT OR "ACTUAL CASH VALUE")	D	(1) Comprehensive—Excluding Collision
$	$	$100		(2) Personal Effects
$	$	$ 200 Actual Cash Value less deductible	E	Collision
$	$	$ Actual Cash Value less deductible	E-1	Collision (Disappearing Deductible)
$	$	$	F	Fire, Lightning and Transportation
$	$	$	G	Theft
$	$	$	H	Combined Additional Coverage
$	$	$ per disablement	I	Towing and Labor Costs
$	$	$ thousand dollars each person $ thousand dollars each accident	J	Family Protection
$	$	#154		Form numbers of endorsements attached to policy at issue:
$	$	TOTAL PREMIUM		

In a true no-fault system, victims cannot sue the person at fault in an accident for any reason. However, no-fault states do allow victims to sue for pain and suffering in some cases, although rules saying when a victim can sue differ in different states. Because no state has a real no-fault system, rates have not dropped in those states that have switched from liability to no-fault systems.

Medical Coverage

Medical coverage pays doctor and hospital expenses for injuries that happen to you, no matter who is at fault. It pays your medical bills whether you are in your car or someone else's car—even if you are hit while you are not in a car. It also pays the medical expenses of any passengers riding in your car. There is usually a limit, such as $10,000, to the amount the insurance company will pay. In no-fault states, you must buy a certain amount of medical coverage.

Collision Insurance

Collision insurance pays for the repair of your car if you are in an accident, no matter who is at fault—even when the accident is your fault. If someone else is at fault, you may collect from your own insurance company or you may choose to collect from the other person's liability insurance.

Most collision insurance policies have a **deductible clause**. That is, the insurance company deducts, or subtracts, a certain amount before paying for the damages. If, for example, you have a deductible of $250, you pay the first $250 of any repair bill yourself. The insurance company pays the rest. The higher your deductible, the lower the cost of collision insurance. But, of course, the higher your deductible, the more you will have to pay to get your car fixed if you're in an accident.

The insurance company will pay for repairs up to the book value of your damaged car as listed in the *Blue Book*. If repairs will cost $3,000 and the book value of your car is only $2,000, you will get only $2,000. If you drive an old car with a very low book value, you may want to save money by choosing not to carry collision insurance.

Comprehensive Insurance

Protection against damage to your car caused by something other than collision is called **comprehensive insurance**. It protects against damage caused by such things as vandalism, fires, windstorms, earthquakes, and falling objects. It also covers the cost of the car

if it is stolen. Like collision insurance, comprehensive insurance usually has a deductible. And, as with collision insurance, the insurance company will pay only up to the book value of the car. If your car has a very low book value, you may not want to buy comprehensive insurance either.

Uninsured Motorist Coverage

Under the liability system, if you are in an accident that is another driver's fault, that person's liability insurance should pay for your injuries and the damage to your car. But what if the other driver doesn't have liability insurance? In most states, it's required, but 10 percent of the drivers still don't have it. To protect yourself against uninsured drivers, you can buy **uninsured motorist insurance**. Usually this kind of insurance does not cost much.

In some states, drivers may also purchase **underinsured motorist insurance**. This type of insurance picks up where other people's liability insurance leaves off. For example, suppose you were in an accident caused by someone who had 15/30/10 coverage, and you had medical bills of $20,000. The other person's insurance would pay you only $15,000. Your insurance company would pay the additional $5,000.

Other Types of Insurance

In no-fault states, you must buy *wage-loss insurance*. Your insurance company will pay some of your wages lost while you're recovering from injuries suffered in an auto accident. You may buy this insurance in liability states if you wish.

If you live in some no-fault states, you must also buy *substitute service insurance*. In other no-fault states, it's not required. This insurance will pay other people to do things you normally do. For instance, it could pay someone to care for your children or shovel your driveway while you're recovering from injuries.

Emergency road service insurance covers the cost of starting or towing your car if it breaks down. If you're a member of an auto club, your club membership probably includes this coverage.

✓ check your understanding ✓ ✓ ✓ ✓ ✓ ✓

1. **If you have 100/300/25 liability insurance, what protection do you have?**
2. **Who is covered if you have medical coverage?**
3. **What is the difference between collision and comprehensive insurance?**
4. **What is the difference between uninsured motorist coverage and underinsured motorist coverage?**

PROBLEMS WITH THE SYSTEM

Many states keep tight control over insurance rates. But even in states where general rates are fixed each year, the cost of individual policies can vary from company to company. It pays to shop around no matter where you live.

Even though auto insurance is necessary, many car owners complain about it. They complain that it is difficult to get insurance and to keep it. They complain that even if they have no accidents their insurance rates keep going up. They complain that their claims aren't paid quickly or completely.

In liability states, one of the biggest causes for delay is difficulty in determining who was at fault in an accident. When a lot of money is involved, the question of who caused an accident almost always winds up in court. It can then take years to settle the matter.

The liability system is not only slow, it's unfair. Insurance companies usually settle small claims quickly and generously. When it comes to paying large amounts, some victims win big settlements, but others do not get enough to cover their losses.

In all states, a big reason for the high cost of auto insurance is lawsuits. In liability states, victims may sue for damages, medical costs, lost wages, and pain and suffering. In no-fault states, victims may sue for pain and suffering after certain conditions have been met. Large amounts of money awarded from lawsuits, along with the high cost of medical care and car repairs, are reflected in expensive premiums. The following case studies show some problems with the system.

CASE STUDY

Tyrone Neal woke up in a hospital bed, not remembering what happened to him as he was driving home from work. Later, his sister Corinne told him he was hit from the side by a driver who may have gone through a red light. Tyrone's leg was crushed.

About a week later, he had a visitor. "My name is Pat Norling," the woman said, "and I'm from Savory Insurance. We represent Janet Gustafson, the driver of the other car. I know you have many bills, and we're ready to pay you $15,000 to settle your claims."

Tyrone frowned. "My loss in pay may be more than that. Besides, the doctor said I may need some special treatment that my medical insurance won't cover. Maybe I should see a lawyer."

"Go ahead if you want," Pat said. "But a lawyer will take a third of the settlement. And we think you were probably speeding. In that case, you won't get a cent."

Tyrone called a lawyer. The lawyer explained that Tyrone could sue not only for his medical expenses but also for pain and suffering. He might get thousands of dollars, or he might get nothing. Also, it would take three years before his case would be heard in court.

CASE STUDY

Amy Sadula had just gotten into her car, the only one parked along the curb of a busy downtown street. While she was getting settled, she saw in the rearview mirror that a car was coming right at her. Sure enough, the other car hit hers, damaging the trunk and electrical system. Because Amy hadn't had time to put her seat belt on, she bumped her head and suffered a few other cuts and bruises.

Amy lived in a no-fault state, so her insurance company paid for the car repairs and the bills from her visits to the hospital emergency room and to her own doctor. Her medical bills at that point amounted to $125.

But she was angry. Dana Hearn, the driver who hit her, had been drunk when the accident occurred. Dana was arrested, tried, and convicted for drunk driving. Her license was taken away. But Amy thought Dana owed her something. She decided to sue Dana for the pain and suffering that resulted from the accident. The only problem was that, in their state, the victim had to have medical bills of over $200 before being able to sue. Amy decided her head and neck were still sore from the accident and made several more visits to her doctor. Eventually, her bills reached over $200, and she contacted her lawyer.

1. List three complaints that motorists often have about automobile insurance.
2. In what ways can the liability system be unfair?
3. Does Tyrone Neal live in a liability or a no-fault state? Why do you think so?
4. What kind of insurance coverage paid for Amy's hospital and doctor's bills?

Insurance companies offer reduced rates to drivers who have taken a driver education course.

Pinch **Hitting for an Actuary**

What are the chances of an 18-year-old girl having an accident this year? What kind of car costs the most to repair? Which cars are most likely to be stolen? Who knows the answers to these questions? An actuary knows.

An actuary decides what the premiums will be at an insurance company. To do this, the actuary uses statistics to compute insurance risks. Some of the statistics actuaries use look something like these below. They are actual figures from a major insurance company.

Category	Claims per 100 drivers	Average claim
Single males under 21	55	$645
Single females under 21	41	429
Married males under 21	38	393
Single males 21–24	37	402
Single females 21–24	32	307
Married males 21–24	29	254
Adults 25–65	20	174

The actuary does not have an easy job. She or he must make premium rates high enough to be certain that the insurance company takes in more money than it pays out in claims. The insurance company must pay its employees, meet the expenses of running its business, and make a profit. But, if the rates are too high, other companies will get all the business.

S UMMARIZING
the chapter

Insurance protects us against the costs of unexpected events. A car owner can be insured against everything from a crumpled fender to a lawsuit. Insurance is expensive, however, and should be bought only to protect against risks that would cause big losses.

The cost of your auto insurance can depend on your age, sex, neighborhood, distance you drive, driving record, and type of car. Still, different companies charge different rates, so you should shop carefully. Consider not only the rates but the reputation of the companies.

You will have to decide on the kind and amount of insurance you need. It is important to have as much liability insurance as you can afford, but if your car is old you may find that comprehensive and collision insurance are not worth the extra expense. You will need to decide how much medical coverage, uninsured motorist coverage, and other types of coverage you need and can afford as well.

About half the states have a no-fault auto insurance system. A victim's own insurance company pays for his or her medical costs no matter who was at fault. No-fault systems are meant to speed up the time it takes to settle claims by eliminating the need to determine who caused an accident. Whether a state has liability or no-fault insurance, however, many people feel the system is too slow and does not guarantee fair compensation for injuries.

CHAPTER ACTIVITIES

BUILDING CONSUMER VOCABULARY

Number your paper from 1 to 10. Then write the term that best matches each numbered definition.

claim
collision insurance
comprehensive insurance
deductible clause
liability insurance

medical coverage
no-fault insurance
premium
underinsured motorist insurance
uninsured motorist insurance

1. Pays doctors' bills and hospital expenses of you and your passengers
2. Provides protection against a driver who does not have any liability insurance
3. Requires the insured to pay a certain amount of a repair bill before the insurance company will pay the rest
4. The money paid out by insurance companies to their customers to cover losses
5. Pays for damage to your car caused by something other than a collision
6. Protects the insured person no matter who is at fault
7. Pays for damage that happens to your car if it hits another car
8. The amount of money paid by a consumer to be insured for a certain period of time

9. Pays for injuries or property damage you do to others
10. Makes up the difference if a person at fault does not have enough liability insurance to cover your losses

BUILDING
CONSUMER
UNDERSTANDING

1. How do insurance companies make a profit?
2. What is the difference between a no-fault and a liability insurance system?
3. Is it better to have a large or a small amount of liability insurance? Why?
4. Name one advantage and one disadvantage of having a large deductible?
5. If you live in a no-fault state, what types of insurance must you buy?
6. Derek Buckman has the following insurance coverage on his eight-year-old car: 30/100/20 liability, $100 deductible on collision, full comprehensive, $10,000 medical, and uninsured motorist. Derek feels he can't afford to keep paying for so much insurance. He wants to drop some of it. Which parts should he drop or reduce?
7. In a true no-fault insurance system, lawsuits for pain and suffering would not be allowed. What do you think would be the effect of the no-lawsuit rule on auto insurance premiums?

BUILDING
CONSUMER
MATH SKILLS

1. Your insurance policy will tell you how much you are paying for each type of auto insurance you select. The chart below shows what various types of insurance typically would cost for drivers of two different ages. Study the chart and then answer the questions on the next page.

Coverages	Limits of Liability	Male under 21	Driver over 25
Personal injury liability	$120,000 each person $300,000 each accident	$396.64	$144.72
Property damage	$25,000 each accident		
Medical coverage	$5,000 each person	$42.18	$15.39
Collision	Actual cash value less $200 deductible	$313.76	$114.48
Comprehensive	Actual cash value less $100 deductible	$229.40	$83.70
Uninsured motorist	$15,000 each person $30,000 each accident	$7.50	$7.50
Emergency road service	$25 per disablement	$3.30	$3.30
Total Yearly Premium		$992.78	$369.09

a. How much more does a male driver under 21 pay for liability insurance than a driver over 25?
b. How much money would a male driver under 21 save if he did not buy collision or comprehensive insurance?
c. Students with a B average save 5 percent on their insurance premium. How much would a male under 21 save if he had a B average?
d. Assume the insurance company will raise the premium of drivers over 25 by 10 percent if they have an accident. A driver over 25 has an accident with collision damage of $600. How much will the insurance company pay on the claim? How much will the premium go up?

2. Imagine that you are an actuary. Using the statistics shown in the box on page 309, answer the following questions:
a. Given only the information in the chart, whom would you charge the most for insurance? Whom would you charge the least? Why?
b. What is the average of all claims paid out by this company?
c. Assume that, to cover expenses and make a profit, the company needs to charge everyone the average claim amount plus 10 percent. If the company charged everyone the same rate, what would the premium be?
d. Who would benefit if everyone paid that rate? Who would be hurt?

APPLYING CONSUMER SKILLS

1. Insurance is meant to spread risks. Should the risks of auto accidents be spread equally among all drivers, or should they be spread just within a group, such as teen-agers or city people? What arguments can be made for each side?
2. Read the Tyrone Neal and Amy Sadula case studies on page 307 again and answer the following questions.
a. What weaknesses in the auto insurance system are shown in the Tyrone Neal case? in the Amy Sadula case?
b. What do you think Tyrone should do? Why?
c. Do you think Amy should have sued Dana? Explain.

GETTING INVOLVED IN YOUR COMMUNITY

With your class, choose a particular model and year for a car and decide the kinds and amount of auto insurance coverage that you should have if you owned that car. Then interview three auto insurance agents in your community and find out what the premiums for this coverage would be. Be sure to compare the same coverage with every agent. Do you live in a no-fault or a liability state? Do the agents offer reduced rates for people who have taken driver education? for students with good grades? for non-smokers?

Jason and Melissa's car needs major repairs. They must decide whether to buy a new car, buy a used car, or fix up the old car. Here are the issues they are considering:

BUY A NEW CAR: A new car would be covered under a warranty—giving them years of nearly trouble-free driving. The payments are much higher than for a used car, however. Insurance premiums are higher too.

BUY A USED CAR: A used car is a lot cheaper than a new one, but they could be buying someone else's headache. A used car could develop the same problems as their present car, and they could wind up with car payments *and* mechanic's bills. But they could have several years of reliable transportation that would be cheaper than buying a new car or fixing up the old car.

FIX UP THE OLD CAR: Fixing up the old car will require a bank loan, since it could cost from $500 to $1,000. The interest rate for the loan would be higher than for a new car loan. But, for what a new car will cost, they could do a lot of fixing up.

HIS IDEAS:
    "We should buy a new car—a Le Zita. It's fast and flashy, but it still gets pretty good mileage. It comes with bucket seats, a five-speed shift, and wire wheel covers. I'd also want to order a few options such as pinstriping, a tape deck, leather seats, and air conditioning. The total price would be about $25,000, but the car would hold its resale value a lot better than some little 4-cylinder brown-mouse special."

HER IDEAS:
    "We plan to start a family soon. When I'm pregnant, I wouldn't be able to drive a sports car. A sports car would also be awkward for a child's car seat or for hauling groceries. New cars depreciate so quickly, and the insurance premiums would be about twice as high as for other cars. We should just fix up the old car."

    Answer the following questions on a separate sheet of paper. Use complete sentences.

1. What features do Jason and Melissa need in a car?

2. What is the strongest argument in favor of buying a new car? Buying a used car? Fixing the old car?

3. What do you think the couple should do? Why?

CRITICAL THINKING

THINKING ABOUT:

Buying a Car

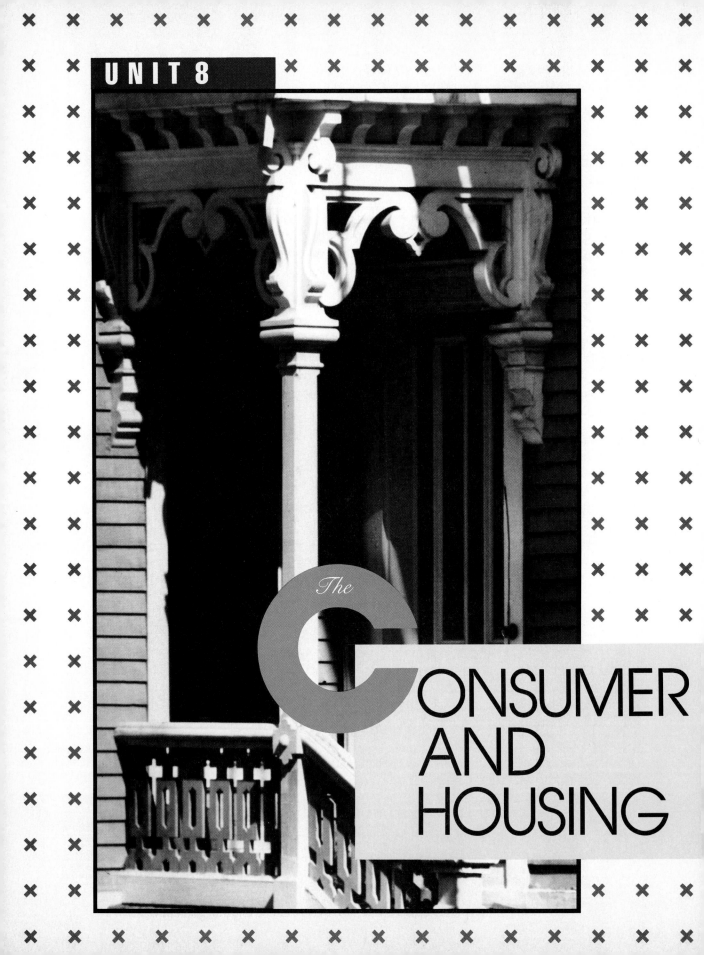

The

CONSUMER AND HOUSING

WHERE SHOULD YOU LIVE?

Deciding where to live is one of the most complicated decisions you make as a consumer. Should you move to a new community? Should you rent or buy? What information may help you make a wise choice?

- What should you think about when deciding where to live?

- What are the differences among single-family houses, mobile homes, apartments, and condominiums?

- What are the advantages and disadvantages of buying a house or condominium?

- What are the advantages and disadvantages of renting a house or apartment?

PLACES TO LIVE

Picking a place to live is not simple. You need to gather facts and make decisions. Will you live near your relatives? Will you live near your work? Will you drive to work or take public transportation? Do you want to live alone or with many people? Do you want a lot of space between your home and others? Do you like the idea of living close to other people? Do you want to live in a quiet, small community or do you prefer the faster pace of city living? Perhaps you would like to live somewhere in between a rural area and a city, in a **suburb**—an area of homes right outside a city.

City or Suburb?

Three out of every four people in the United States now live in or near a city. Some like to live right in the middle of the city. Others prefer a suburb or nearby town. The following case study shows some things to think about when deciding where to live.

Many real estate brokers say the most important feature of housing is its location. Why? Location is a major factor in a home's value. A house located in a safe, attractive neighborhood is worth more than the same house sitting next to a factory.

City living offers many advantages—but presents problems too.

"You know, Cheryl, I'm thinking about moving to the suburbs," Jackie said. "My two kids are getting to school age, and I think the schools are better out there. Besides, I'm tired of being crowded in a small place. And I could do without the parking hassles. A house with a yard and a garage is looking mighty good."

"Well, maybe I'll change my mind when Lee and I have kids," Cheryl said. "But right now I want nothing to do with the suburbs. First of all, you have the problem of getting to work. At rush hour, the expressway is a parking lot. People who ride the trains are packed in like sardines in a can. No matter how you go, getting to work costs a lot of money from out in the suburbs. Where we are now, we can go anywhere in the city by catching a bus. We can take the money we save on transportation and go to movies, ball games, and restaurants. That's more than you can say for your suburbs."

"You'll be lucky if you ever get to the movies, with all the crime in the city," Jackie replied. "It's getting worse all the time. The suburbs may not be fun city, but at least you can go out at night without being mugged."

"Suburbs have crime too," Cheryl said. "I've read a lot about house burglars and muggers in shopping centers. We've done okay in our neighborhood, haven't we? We have friends here. I'm staying put in the city."

Which is better, to have the worst house in a great neighborhood, or the best house in a bad neighborhood? The worst house in a great neighborhood is the better choice. Why? The value of the house is tied to the value of the neighborhood.

Checking Out a Neighborhood

When you move into a home, you are also moving into a neighborhood. When you choose a neighborhood, be sure you know just what you're going to get. You don't want to be surprised after you move in. The check list on page 318 can help you rate a neighborhood. Of course, different things are important to different people. So a list you make yourself will probably be a little different from this one.

✓check your understanding ✓ ✓ ✓ ✓ ✓ ✓

1. **What are some of the advantages of living in a city? What are some of the advantages of living in a suburb?**
2. **Referring to the Neighborhood Check List, describe ten things you may need to consider when checking out a neighborhood.**
3. **Will everyone's neighborhood check list be the same? Why or why not?**

A Neighborhood Check List

As you examine a neighborhood, ask yourself the following questions. You can rate the neighborhood by answering "yes" or "no" to each question.

■ **Neighborhood Appearance and Safety**
Is the neighborhood quiet enough?
Is the traffic heavy?
Are the streets well lighted?
Are the properties well maintained?
Is there a problem with pollution?

■ **Transportation**
Is there convenient public transportation?
Is there plenty of parking space?
How long will it take to get to work?
How much will it cost to get to work?

■ **Stores**
Is there an affordable food store nearby?
Is there a laundry nearby?
Are other shops easy to get to?

■ **People**
Do the neighbors seem friendly?
Are there many people about my age?
Are there people for my children to play with?

■ **Schools**
Do the schools have a good reputation?
Are the schools nearby?

■ **Important Services**
Is there a fire station nearby?
Is there a good police department?
Are the streets in good shape?
Is there a well-stocked library?
Are there parks and recreational areas?
Does the area have a good hospital?
Is garbage collected regularly?

Features people desire in their neighborhoods— like this playground—can change with their age.

Buying a house is not a one-time experience for most people. Many people stay in a house for only four or five years and then move. When you buy housing, be sure you think of it not only as something you'd like to buy but also as something you can sell to someone else.

THE COST OF HOUSING

In choosing a place to live, you must be realistic. In many places, the demand for housing is larger than the supply. You may find the perfect neighborhood, but no housing may be available.

And, although your values influence your choice of housing, in the end the decision is mainly a matter of money. Your income and savings will limit your choices. Many budget experts suggest that you pay no more than one third of your take-home pay for housing. A person who takes home $1,500 a month should spend no more than $500 a month for housing. A person making $2,000 a month could spend $666. These figures include not only rent or house payments, but also upkeep and **utilities**—heat, electricity, telephone, water, and sewerage.

You have two main choices when it comes to paying for housing. You can buy housing or you can rent housing. As you learned in Chapter 5, rent is the price of using something that belongs to someone else. People who rent are using housing that someone else owns. There can be a big difference in cost between renting and buying. Let's see what expenses are involved in each.

The most obvious cost in buying housing is the price of the home. When people buy housing, they rarely pay cash. Most people take out a form of installment loan. Installment loans for housing are called **mortgages**. They are long-term loans, usually lasting anywhere from 15 to 30 years. So, the first thing to consider in the cost of buying is the cost of the monthly mortgage payments.

Most people who buy housing also must pay **property taxes.** The more the housing is worth, the more property taxes the owners pay. These taxes are collected by local governments. Often these taxes are included in the mortgage payments.

When budget experts talk about the cost of buying a house, they also count in the cost of upkeep, utilities, and homeowners' insurance. You will learn more about homeowners' insurance in Chapter 25.

Some people feel that the biggest expense in buying a house is the down payment. This expense is not figured as part of the monthly cost of buying a home because it does not come out of monthly income. But it does have to be paid. And it's usually a large amount of money. Down payments are generally between 10 and 20 percent of the price of a home. On a $100,000 house, for example, the down payment would be between $10,000 and $20,000. Generally, the money comes out of savings. Many people simply do not have enough savings for a down payment. This is one of the main reasons why people cannot afford to buy housing.

People who rent do not have to come up with a down payment. They also do not pay property taxes, mortgage, water bills, or sewerage charges. But the owner of the property pays these bills. And the amount of the rent is usually set high enough to cover the owner's costs. Sometimes, renters pay for their own electricity

A house is probably the most expensive item anyone ever buys. It is a sign of the wealth of this country that 60 percent of the families in the United States are able to own their own homes.

Affordable housing can be a problem for many. Civic organizations, such as this, work to provide housing for the poor.

and heat. Other times, the costs of these utilities are included in the rent. When figuring out how much rent you can afford, remember to add in the cost of all utilities that are not included in the rent. And remember that renters also need insurance. Even though the owner usually carries insurance for the building, renters must insure their own possessions—their furniture and clothing.

Today housing costs are high, causing many families to spend more than a third of their take-home pay for it. How much of your income you spend for housing depends also on your own values. But remember, the more you spend on housing, the less you'll have left to spend on other things.

TYPES OF HOUSING

You have many choices when it comes to the type of housing you can live in. Basically, however, housing falls into two general categories: single-family houses and multi-family dwellings. Each type can be bought or rented. Each type has its advantages and disadvantages.

Single-Family Housing

Single-family houses are the most common type of housing in the United States. A single-family house is one that a single person or family lives in. It is not attached to any other building. Most single-family houses are owned by the people who live in them. Some are owned by one person and rented to another person or family.

Most single-family houses are *site-built*—built in the same place where they stand. But some are built in a factory and moved to another place. These are called **factory-built houses**. Factory-built houses are generally less expensive than site-built houses because they cost less to build. The first factory-built houses tended to be small and were not well made. Today, however, factory-built houses can be of very high quality and can be fairly big. It is now difficult to tell the difference between a new factory-built house and a new site-built house.

Multi-Family Housing

Buildings that contain the homes of more than one family are called **multi-family dwellings**. The smallest are two-family houses, in which two people or families live in separate parts of the house, or units. Units have their own kitchens, bathrooms, bedrooms, and so on. Buildings that contain many rental units are called apartment buildings.

More and more multi-family dwellings are condominiums. In a **condominium**, the people living in the units own their own units. As a group, they all own the common areas, such as the roof, the yard, and the hallways.

Whether you rent or own, living in a multi-family dwelling is often cheaper than living in a single-family house. But you may have less privacy and less space.

Are you living in cramped quarters? You are not alone. More than 37 percent of all homeowners say they have less living space than they need. Why? Big homes cost a lot. Families grow. And new housing does not have as much floor space as older houses do.

1. If you take home $1,100 a month, what is the most you should spend on housing?
2. What expenses do you have as a home owner that you do not have as a renter?
3. What is the difference between a single-family house and a multi-family dwelling?

The cost of housing can vary dramatically from one part of the country to another. An offer of a raise and a transfer to another city may sound great. However, if you get a $200 a month raise, but housing in the new city will cost you $500 a month more, the transfer may not seem like such a good idea.

TO RENT OR TO BUY?

Your housing needs will probably change as you grow older. Young single people and young married couples usually prefer to rent because they don't have the savings needed for a down payment or the income needed for a mortgage. Parents with growing children often prefer to buy a house. After the children have gone, the couple may sell the house and buy a smaller house or condominium, or they may rent again.

In deciding where to live, you must choose between buying or renting. The following people want you to choose from their offerings. The two interviews that follow are sales talks. The first sales talk is given by a **real estate broker**, a person who sells

Unlike renters, who depend on the landlord to do major repairs, homeowners are responsible for upkeep and maintenance of their properties.

housing. The second one is given by someone who helps people find housing to rent.

If you have the savings and income to buy a home, you should do it. You'll be ahead financially if you buy instead of rent.

Buying a house is a good way to keep up with rising prices. The price of a house rises right along with everything else. In fact, in the 1980's, many house and condominium prices went up even faster than most other prices. Although house prices sometimes level off for a while, they almost always rise again. After all, look at all of the new young families whose dream is to own a house of their own.

Owning a house also helps with your taxes. The interest you pay on your mortgage can be taken off your income tax. So can your property taxes. If you rent, your money helps pay the interest and the property taxes of the place where you live. But the owner is the one who gets to deduct those expenses from her or his income tax.

Homeowners also have more freedom of use than renters. You can remodel, or change, your house any way you want. You can paint it any color you want. You can add a room. But try making any big change in your apartment without the owner's permission!

You always come out ahead by buying a house. Your house payment is a lot like savings. The logic is simple. A renter has nothing but a pile of rent receipts to show for housing payments. The home buyer ends up owning the place.

TERRY SCARPELLI
Real Estate Broker

Many people are familiar with the 1965 Civil Rights Act. Fewer people realize that Congress passed the first Civil Rights Act as long ago as 1866. This law gave every man in this country the right to vote and to own land, regardless of his race. The worry that some day another Congress would repeal the law led to the incorporation of this act into the Fourteenth Amendment of the Constitution.

There are a lot of extra costs in owning a house. You don't have just the monthly payments. You have to keep the place up too. That means buying yard equipment, painting the house, maybe putting in a family room. And don't forget the little extras like furnace cleaning and plumbing repairs.

If you rent, you can invest the money you save on the down payment and other expenses. You can earn interest on that money. You may have quite a nest egg in a few years. You can use that money anytime you want. You don't have to sell your home if you have an emergency. Some homeowners have all their money tied up in their houses. They can't buy anything else.

Another reason for renting is that you're not tied down. If you want to move, you can. Our tenants only need to stay a year. If you own a house, you have to sell to move. That can take time.

You may have to pay a real estate broker 5 to 10 percent just to find a buyer. And your house payments! In the early years, most of your money goes for interest on the mortgage. When you sell, you'll find you don't own as much of the house as you thought.

Owning a home used to be a better deal than it is now. Most people borrowed the money they needed to buy a house at a fixed rate of interest. Time went by. Rents went up. Their mortgage payments stayed the same. But no longer. Many home mortgage interest rates can now go up or down depending on market conditions. The lenders don't want to get burned. If they raise the interest rate, your mortgage payments go up.

For many people, the best part of renting is that they don't have to worry. If something goes wrong, the owner fixes it. You don't have to mow the lawn, or shovel the snow, or paint the house. You can do the things you really want to do with your time.

SYLVIA ROSTOV
Apartment Rental Agent

"

FREEDOM OF CHOICE

What can you do if you feel that someone has denied you housing illegally? If you can't find help locally, write to the Office of Fair Housing and Equal Opportunity at the Department of Housing and Urban Development in Washington, D.C.

Everyone wants to live in a place that is friendly and makes them feel welcome. Some people try to make places friendly by keeping certain types of people out of their neighborhoods. These other people may have a different skin color. They may believe in a different religion. But singling out a group of people for unfair treatment is **discrimination**. And discrimination in housing is against the law in the United States.

The 1866 and 1968 **Civil Rights Acts** guarantee equal rights in housing. By law, no one may refuse housing to anyone because of their race, color, national origin, or sex. Many states and communities also have their own fair housing laws. Real estate brokers may not push minority groups to one area and whites to another area. A lender may not refuse housing loans to anyone with a good credit rating.

✓check your understanding ✓ ✓ ✓ ✓ ✓ ✓

1. **What are the advantages of owning a house, according to the broker?**
2. **What advantages does renting have over owning, according to the apartment rental agent?**
3. **What types of discrimination in housing are against the law?**

SUMMARIZING
the chapter

Deciding where to live is complicated. You must decide whether you want to live in a city, in the country, in a small town, or in a suburb. You must decide whether or not you want to live near work or near relatives. You must decide what type of neighborhood would best suit your values and your budget. A neighborhood check list can help you narrow down those choices.

Although values play a big role in housing decisions, cost is probably the most important factor. Budget experts say that you should pay no more than one third of your take-home pay on housing costs.

You can choose from many types of housing. You can live in single-family houses, multi-family houses, factory-built houses, condominiums, and apartments.

You have two choices when it comes to paying for housing—buying or renting. Some advantages of buying housing are that mortgage payments often stay the same over time, while rent payments usually go up. And, in the end, you own a house. Renters do not have anything to show for all of their rent payments.

Renters, however, do not have to worry about paying for repairs and maintenance. They can move more easily. And they can use the money they would have put into a house for other things.

CHAPTER ACTIVITIES

BUILDING CONSUMER VOCABULARY

Number your paper from 1 to 11. Then write the term that best matches each numbered definition.

Civil Rights Acts
condominiums
discrimination
factory-built houses
mortgage
multi-family dwelling

property taxes
real estate brokers
single-family house
suburb
utilities

1. Laws that grant equal rights in housing

2. Multi-family housing owned by all of the people who live in the units
3. A type of expense people should count in the the cost of housing that includes heat, gas, electricity, telephone service, sewerage, and water
4. An installment loan for housing
5. Taxes, collected by local government, based on the value of housing
6. A type of housing not attached to any other buildings in which a single person or family lives
7. A place to live just outside a city
8. Houses built in a factory
9. Singling out a group of people for unfair treatment
10. People who sell housing as a profession
11. A building in which more than one family lives

BUILDING CONSUMER UNDERSTANDING

1. Look at the Neighborhood Check List again on page 318 and answer the following questions.
   a. Which questions are important if you own a car?
   b. Which questions are important if you don't own a car?
   c. Which questions are particularly important if you have children?
   d. Which questions have to do with safety?
2. What is the difference between an apartment and a condominium? between a condominium and a single-family house?
3. The Andersons and the Baileys live in a two-family house. The Andersons own the unit on the first floor. The Baileys own the unit on the second floor. Together they own the roof, the basement, and the yard. What type of housing do the Andersons and the Baileys live in? If the Andersons owned the whole building, what type of housing would each family be living in? If Mr. Carrol owned the two-family house, what type of housing would the Andersons and the Baileys be living in?
4. Why do young people usually rent? Why do many parents own houses? Why do retired people often rent again?
5. Reread the interviews on pages 323–324. Are there any advantages or disadvantages of renting or buying that the two people overlooked? Explain.
6. Assume you have just graduated from college and are looking for a place to live. What type of housing would you get? Why?
7. What are some signs that a person may be a victim of discrimination in housing?

1. Your take-home pay is $15,000 a year. According to the experts, how much of this can you afford to spend each month on housing? Suppose you have a choice between two apartments that you like. Apartment A costs $350 a month plus utilities. Apartment B costs $400 a month including utilities. How much would your utility bill have to be to make Apartment B a better deal than Apartment A?

2. Lisa and Rick Shields have a monthly take-home pay of $2,100 and are thinking about moving to a larger apartment. The monthly rent at the new apartment is $550, and the owner says that the average monthly utility bill is $100. Lisa and Rick have been spending $25 monthly on upkeep. They plan to continue spending that amount. How much would they spend on housing if they moved? What percentage of their take-home pay is this? Can they afford to move? Why or why not?

1. What do you consider the biggest advantage in renting an apartment? the biggest disadvantage? Why? What do you consider the biggest advantage in buying a house? the biggest disadvantage? Why?

2. Make your own Neighborhood Check List. Be exact about what you're looking for. Use the check list in the textbook as a basis for your own. Then use your list to rate two neighborhoods in your community. Would you add anything to the Neighborhood Check List? What would you add? What is the most important category on the list as far as you're concerned?

Find out about your own housing rights. Contact local or state officials and find out whether your community or state has any fair housing laws of its own. How are those rights enforced? Where can you go for help if you feel that someone is discriminating against you in your community?

RENTING HOUSING

Your first home on your own may be a rented apartment. What should you look for in an apartment? If a landlord asks you to sign a long-term lease, what should you do? After you move in, where can you get help if things break and no one will fix them?

22

- ■ How does a smart consumer shop for an apartment?

- ■ What are some items that should be included on an apartment check list?

- ■ What are the differences between a pro-landlord lease and a pro-tenant lease?

- ■ What can tenants do if they have complaints against their landlord?

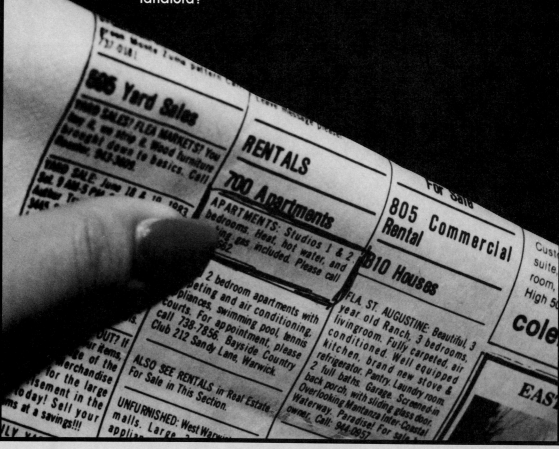

Many people can't afford to own a home. Many more don't want to. And so about two out of five families in the United States live in a house or apartment owned by someone else. The people who live there and pay the rent are called **tenants**. They pay the rent to a **landlord**, who is the owner of the building. If you're a tenant, having a good or bad landlord makes a big difference.

SHOPPING FOR AN APARTMENT

Looking for a place to rent is much like other kinds of shopping. You need to compare what's available. You should look closely at what you find to make sure you know what you're getting. The following case study tells about consumers who didn't look closely enough.

CASE STUDY

John and Kathy Novak had found jobs in the suburbs. They were looking forward to moving out of the city. Since they were both working, they could afford a place with lots of extras. They picked the Lake View Gardens Apartment Village. It had a swimming pool, tennis courts, and a wooded area around a pond in back. The rent was $675 a month. But this would be some kind of living!

The Novaks inspected the apartment they would rent. It was big, bright, and beautiful. They took it on the spot.

On the first day of the month, the Novaks put their belongings in a rented truck and drove to Lake View Gardens. After a hard day of moving, they were ready to enjoy their new home.

John went to take a hot shower—but got a cold surprise. There was no hot water. Then they decided to watch television in their air-conditioned living room. The noise of the air conditioner almost drowned out the TV. That night they had even more surprises. The ceiling creaked with every step the upstairs neighbors took. When the Novaks turned off their air conditioner, they heard not only their own TV but the TV next door.

The next day, a neighbor told them that no hot water was a familiar problem. "The building's hot-water heater isn't big enough," he said. "Besides, nothing ever gets fixed around here." John and Kathy wondered where they had gone wrong.

Before you go apartment hunting, make a check list of the things you think are important in an apartment. Take the list with you when you look at places to rent. An Apartment Check List you may use can be found on page 330.

Apartment Check List

1. What is the condition of the apartment?
   a. Is the apartment clean? Are there any bugs?
   b. Does it need to be painted? Will the landlord paint it?
   c. Are the carpets, if any, in good condition?
   d. Is the apartment free of damage? (Be sure to point out any damage to the landlord so you will not be charged for it.)
2. Does the apartment have everything I need? Does everything work?
   a. Do all of the burners on the stove work?
   b. Is there a refrigerator? Does it have a large enough freezer? Does it work?
   c. Does the apartment have air conditioning? Do I need it? Does it work? Is it too loud?
   d. Does the plumbing in all sinks, showers, and tubs work?
   e. Do doors and windows open easily? Do they lock tightly?
   f. Is there enough heat? How much does it cost?
   g. Is there enough hot water? Will I be sharing it with people in other apartments?
   h. Are there enough electrical outlets?
   i. Will a TV work in the building?
   j. Is there a place to do laundry nearby?
   k. Are there play areas for children?
   l. Is there plenty of storage space?
   m. Is there garbage collection?
   n. Are entrances and halls well lighted?
3. Is the apartment quiet enough?
4. Is there enough parking space?
   a. If there is a parking lot, are spaces assigned?
   b. If there is no lot, is there street parking? Is it easy to find a space on the street?
5. Can I afford the rent, utilities, and upkeep?
6. Do I like the neighborhood? (Use the Neighborhood Check List, Chapter 21.)

In each place you go, be sure to check the actual apartment that is for rent. Never rent an apartment you haven't seen. You should be suspicious of a landlord who finds reasons not to show you the exact apartment.

✓check your understanding ✓ ✓ ✓ ✓ ✓ ✓

1. What things should the Novaks have checked before renting their apartment?

2. **Which questions on the Apartment Check List cannot be answered just by looking at the apartment?**
3. **Why is it important to see the apartment you will be renting before you actually rent it?**

UNDERSTANDING LEASES

Before the Novaks moved into their apartment, they signed a rental agreement called a lease. A **lease** is a contract that states the rights and duties of the landlord and the tenant. The lease spells out how much rent the tenants will pay. It states in what ways the tenant can use the apartment. For example, some leases say that tenants cannot throw loud parties or have pets in the apartment.

Leases stay in effect for a certain period of time. Usually a lease lasts for a year, but tenants can sign leases for shorter or longer periods of time. If the tenants move out before the lease ends, they usually have to pay the rent until the lease is up or someone else rents the apartment. This is one reason why tenants may not want to sign a long-term lease. Usually, though, the landlord cannot raise the rent or ask the tenants to leave before the lease ends. Some tenants sign long-term leases, as long as five years, for example, to keep their rents from going up.

You do not always have to sign a lease in order to rent. In some states, renting without a lease is called **tenancy at will**. A tenant can move at any time. And the landlord can tell the tenant to move at any time. Usually both give some advance notice. In other states, tenancy without a lease is on a month-to-month basis. At the first of each month, the lease is automatically renewed for another month unless either the tenant or the landlord gives notice that the tenancy will end.

Many people find leases hard to understand and often sign a lease without reading it. This practice can be dangerous. Most leases are written by landlords or their lawyers. They strongly favor the landlords. If a problem comes up, the tenants may find they have signed away some important rights.

If you don't understand the lease you're asked to sign, get help from someone who does. Make sure you know what rights you have under the lease. If the lease contains clauses you think are unfair, try to get them taken out before you sign. Let's examine clauses that are often included in a lease.

Monthly Rent

A lease tells how much rent you will pay each month. It may say that you must pay the first month's and the last month's rent in advance, when you sign the lease. It may also have a clause like the one on the next page.

Read a lease carefully, even if you're told it's "just standard." It may not be. You may have to fix appliances that break down. Or you may be charged extra rent if a house guest stays more than three days. And, as some people have been, you may be forced to carpet your unit (at your expense) if a downstairs neighbor complains about noise.

It's usually a good idea to pay your rent with a check. Why? When you get back the canceled check, you have proof that you've paid your rent. Proof can be important if your landlord is a big corporation. Big corporations have been known to lose rent checks and then send tenants letters demanding that the rent be paid again.

The Tenant will pay the monthly rent, in the amount stated above, on the first day of each month. The payment of rent at the scheduled time is the essence of this lease.

The last sentence means that the landord can begin steps to make you leave if you don't pay the rent on time.

If you and the landlord agree that the rent should be paid on some date other than the first of the month, the date should be written into the lease. You and the landlord must put your initials by that change—and any other changes you make—in the lease.

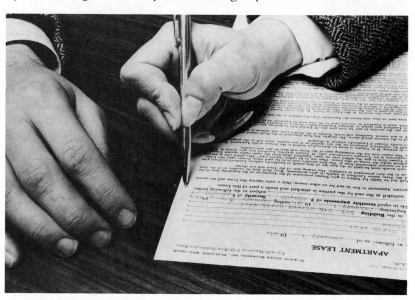

Security Deposit

A **security deposit** is money held by the landlord until the tenant moves out. It is used to cover any damage the tenant does to the apartment. A lease says whether or not you must leave a security deposit and how much it must be. Usually it is equal to one month's rent. The security deposit is in addition to the first and last months' rent you may also have to pay when you sign the lease.

The lease may also say this:

> The Tenant will deposit with the Landlord a security deposit, in the amount stated above, upon the signing of this lease. It is understood and agreed that this security deposit will be held by the Landlord as indemnity against the Tenant's neglect or failure to perform any of the covenants contained in this lease. The Landlord shall have the right to use the security deposit to pay for costs, losses, or damages caused by the Tenant's default in the performance of these covenants.

That paragraph says that the landlord holds the security deposit as insurance ("indemnity"). If you break any agreement ("covenant") in the lease, the landlord can keep the security deposit and use it to pay for any damage you caused. But what if you don't agree that you've caused any damage? In that case, you can go to court and let a judge decide who is right. Small claims courts often hear this kind of case.

Upkeep

A lease may state that the landlord is not responsible for repairs. It may have a paragraph like this:

> The Tenant has inspected the apartment and related premises and acknowledges that they are now in good order and repair. The Tenant agrees to keep and maintain the apartment as it is now, reasonable wear and tear excepted. Furthermore, the Tenant agrees that the Landlord has made no warranties or covenants concerning the order, repair, or improvement of the apartment or related premises other than those covenants contained in this lease or else in other writing signed by the Landlord.

According to that paragraph, the tenant promises not to damage the apartment ("to keep and maintain it as it is now"). The paragraph also says that the landlord has made no promises ("no warranties or covenants") about repairs except for those listed in writing. If the landlord has in fact promised to fix up the apartment, get it in writing. If you don't, the landlord doesn't have to keep the promise.

Some leases also say that even if a landlord fails to keep an apartment in good condition, you must pay your rent anyway. In some states, courts have said that leases cannot include that clause. But in many states, you must pay your rent in those cases. Otherwise, the landlord can **evict** you—force you to get out.

In some states, the landlord must put the money for the security deposit in a separate bank account. The tenant is entitled to the interest earned by that money. The landlord must give the interest to the tenant at the end of each year the tenant continues to rent.

A tenant is not responsible for normal wear and tear to an apartment. The landlord decides what is normal. If you disagree, you can take your case to small claims court.

> The landlord is responsible for major repairs and is liable if the lack of repair causes someone to be injured.

Landlord-tenant laws go back to twelfth-century England. In those days, landlords owned vast amounts of land. Tenants rented some of the land to work as farms. By the end of the 1100's, these tenants were allowed to take legal action against a landlord who wrongfully made them leave their rented farms.

Protecting Yourself with a Lease

Most leases favor the landlord. But some give about equal treatment to landlord and tenants. These **pro-tenant leases** allow the tenants more freedom and also more protection than pro-landlord leases do. A pro-tenant lease may have some or all of the following characteristics.

■ Such a lease may allow you to have pets. Usually the lease would not actually state that you can have pets. There just would be no clause saying that you could not have them.

■ Pro-tenant leases usually state that the landlord is responsible for repairs and maintenance. This is especially important if the landlord is a corporation. A pro-tenant lease may even state that, if the landlord fails to repair and maintain the apartment as promised in the lease, you do not have to pay the rent.

■ There may be a clause saying that the landlord cannot keep your security deposit unless you are given a written list of all damage for which you are being held responsible.

You sign a one-year lease. Do you have to move out at the end of the year? Perhaps, but often your landlord will give you another one-year lease (usually at a higher rent). Or the landlord may continue to rent to you on a tenancy-at-will basis.

■ A pro-tenant lease will state that you have the right to enjoy your apartment without being bothered by the landlord or other tenants. Actually, you always have that right, but it is more firmly fixed if it is written into the lease. A pro-tenant lease will say exactly when the landlord may enter your apartment. Usually the landlord has the right to come into your apartment to make repairs. He or she may also enter to show the apartment to other potential tenants if you are moving out. The landlord may also come in to see if you are breaking any of the terms of the lease. The landlord must get your permission first, however, to enter your apartment, even for these reasons.

■ Many pro-tenant leases state that the landlord can't refuse, without good reason, to let you sublease your apartment. When you **sublease**, you find someone else to live in the apartment and take over the lease if you want to move out before the lease is up. Or you may bring in someone else to share the apartment and share responsibility for the lease.

A pro-tenant lease does not let tenants do anything they want to an apartment. Remember, when you rent, you are paying for the right to use someone else's property. All leases protect landlords' rights to their own property. But a pro-tenant lease stresses the landlord's duties as much as the tenant's duties.

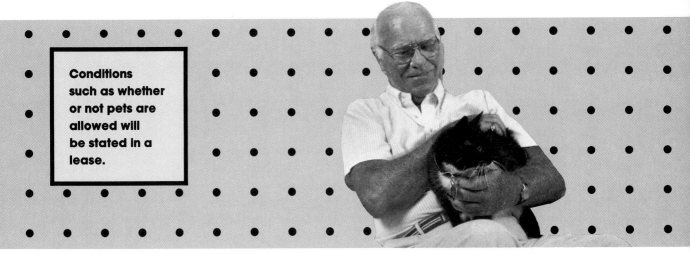

Conditions such as whether or not pets are allowed will be stated in a lease.

✓check your understanding ✓ ✓ ✓ ✓ ✓ ✓

1. What should you do if a lease contains clauses you think are unfair?
2. Suppose you rent an apartment for $350 a month. The landlord requires a security deposit equal to one month's rent. She also asks for the first and last months' rent in advance. How much money do you need to give the landlord before you can move in?

3. Can a landlord keep your security deposit if you break any rule in your lease? Explain.
4. In what ways is a pro-tenant lease different from a pro-landlord lease?

SOLVING RENTAL PROBLEMS

In a disagreement with a landlord, tenants often feel helpless. The landlord seems to have the upper hand. But many tenants have found ways to improve their living conditions. Here are some things tenants can do if they have difficulty with landlords.

■ **Tenant organizations**. Sometimes tenants get together and meet with their landlord to talk about their problems. The landlord may pay more attention to a group of tenants than to just one.

   If talking doesn't work, tenant groups may demand that the landlord answer their complaints. Some groups threaten to complain to government officials. In some places, tenant organizations have successfully put pressure on politicians to pass pro-tenant laws.

■ **Complaints to housing authorities**. If a building does not meet the local building or health codes, a tenant can complain to the housing authority. If the building is not safe, has many bugs, or has too much garbage, a tenant can complain to the local board of health. Some tenants are afraid to complain. They think the landlord might throw them out. But courts say a landlord cannot evict a tenant just for reporting building-code and health violations.

■ **Court action**. If conditions in your apartment are so bad you cannot live in it, you may go to court. Some cities have special courts just to handle disputes between tenants and landlords. Suppose, for example, the landlord won't provide heat in winter. The court could force the landlord to turn on the heat or make repairs. But going to court can be expensive and difficult. In many cities different tenant and landlord problems are handled by different courts. So tenants should check with a lawyer or a legal-aid office before taking this step.

■ **Warranty of habitability**. Some states have laws favorable to tenants. One is the **warranty of habitability doctrine**. This doctrine holds that landlords must provide a whole package of services no matter what the lease says. This package includes heat, light, plumbing, fire alarms, and locks on windows and doors. The landlord must also keep the apartment building clean and in good repair. According to this doctrine, landlords

An apartment building is heavily damaged by fire. Do the tenants still owe the landlord rent until their leases end? No. The law realizes that fires, floods, and other disasters may make a unit unfit to live in. The lease is automatically canceled in those cases. In law, this principle is called *constructive eviction*.

Your landlord says you've caused too much damage to your apartment to get your security deposit back. The damage was there before you moved in. Can you prove it? Yes, you can, if you had taken photos of the apartment before you moved in and noted the damage on the lease before you signed it. Then you'd have the evidence you need to get your deposit back.

who fail to provide all parts of this package have broken their agreement with the tenant even if these rights aren't written into the lease.

- **Rent strikes**. When tenants have a rent strike, they put their rent money in a special bank account for safekeeping until the landlord meets their demands. But a rent strike can be dangerous. In many cases, the landlord can win a court order evicting the strikers.

✓check your understanding ✓ ✓ ✓ ✓ ✓ ✓

1. **What types of problems would you report to a housing authority? to a board of health?**
2. **For what reasons might you take a landlord to court?**
3. **How does the warranty of habitability doctrine benefit renters?**
4. **Why would tenants stage a rent strike? Why might a rent strike be a bad idea?**

Because landlords will pay more attention to a group of tenants, many people have formed organizations to handle problems.

THE ECONOMICS OF RENT CONTROL

In some places, tenant organizations have asked government to help keep rents from rising. The government can help tenants fight rising rents by passing **rent control laws**. These laws tell landlords how much they can raise rent. They usually do not allow the landlords to raise the rent very much at one time.

People support rent control laws for several reasons. One reason is, of course, to keep rents low for all tenants. Another is to provide affordable housing for the elderly, whose incomes often do not rise much over time. Other people want to make sure that their city or town provides housing for people who are not well off.

In the short run, rent controls keep rents low. But laws controlling rents are the same as laws controlling other prices. You learned in Chapter 5 that if a price is set below the market price, shortages will result. Landlords are business people. They must make profits to stay in business. If their profits are cut, they will be less willing or able to provide apartments. They will also have less money for repairs. So, in the long run, rent controls lead to housing shortages and rundown buildings.

In a market economy, price and supply are controlled by demand. If there are more possible tenants than apartments, rents will rise. But higher profits will encourage people to build more housing. So, without rent control, in the long run more apartments will be built, and prices will level off.

Let's look at a case study showing how rent controls worked in one major city.

CASE STUDY

New York learns a lesson

The year was 1943. The United States was in the middle of World War II. There were shortages of everything—cars, food, housing. In that year, New York City passed its first rent control laws to deal with the housing shortage. The controls were supposed to last just a little while. When the shortage ended, the controls were supposed to come off.

But the shortage never ended. The rent control laws continued to create a shortage. Landlords did not make profits. Without profits, they could not build new apartments.

Eventually, the city decided to do something about the building shortage. Controls were lifted for new buildings. Rent ceilings were raised for other buildings. Rents became very high on the new buildings. The rich now had housing, but the poor and the middle classes were stuck in older apartments. Many of these buildings were poorly maintained and finally abandoned. The city took over the abandoned buildings and tore them down. This situation reduced both the supply of housing and the amount of money paid in property taxes. The only winners were a very small number of people who had good, cheap apartments.

✓check your understanding ✓ ✓ ✓ ✓ ✓ ✓

1. **What are rent controls?**
2. **Why do rent controls cause housing shortages?**
3. **What happened in New York City as a result of the rent controls passed in 1943?**

Looking for a place to rent, whether it is an apartment or a house, is much like shopping for any good or service. Renters can avoid problems by shopping carefully. Always use a check list, and inspect the actual unit you are planning to rent.

Most landlords require a security deposit and a lease. The security deposit is usually equal to one month's rent. If you damage the apartment, the landlord has the right to keep the security deposit. The lease is the contract signed by the tenants and the landlord. Some leases favor the landlord by spelling out mainly the tenant's duties. Pro-tenant leases also spell out the landlord's duties. Often, landlords do not have to keep promises they make to tenants unless they are made in writing.

If a landlord does not treat tenants fairly, tenants can get together to try to work things out. Tenants can also complain to local housing authorities, go to court, or withhold rent in some states. Many tenant organizations try to get the city government to pass rent control laws. Although these laws do keep rents down in the short run, they cause housing shortages in the long run.

CHAPTER ACTIVITIES

BUILDING CONSUMER VOCABULARY

Number your paper from 1 to 10. Then write the term that best matches each numbered definition.

evict	security deposit
landlord	sublease
lease	tenancy at will
pro-tenant leases	tenants
rent control laws	warranty of habitability doctrine

1. Money held by the landlord to cover any damage caused by a tenant
2. Laws telling landlords how much they can raise rents
3. The owner of a rental house or apartment
4. A law that makes landlords responsible for a package of services

5. Leases that spell out the duties of the landlord as well as those of the tenants
6. Renting without a lease
7. People who live in a house or apartment owned by someone else and pay rent to the owner
8. A rental agreement
9. To rent an apartment from a tenant
10. To force a tenant to leave an apartment

BUILDING CONSUMER UNDERSTANDING

1. Is comparison shopping important when looking for an apartment? Why or why not?
2. Why should you point out any damage an apartment may already have before you move in?
3. Why might you want to sign a long-term lease? Why might you want to rent without a lease?
4. In what ways do leases benefit or protect landlords? In what ways do they benefit or protect tenants? Why wouldn't some landlords want to have their tenants sign a lease?
5. What can you do to make sure your landlord will keep promises made about repairing your apartment?
6. What can tenant organizations do? Why might you want to join a tenant organization rather than talk to the landlord yourself?
7. Who benefits from rent control? Who does not benefit?

BUILDING CONSUMER MATH SKILLS

1. Three recent graduates of Midstate College decided to rent an apartment together and share the rent equally. The apartment they chose rents for $750 per month. How much will each person pay for rent each month?
2. Dawn Gray paid $375 a month for her apartment. She paid one month's rent as a security deposit. Dawn had a cat that scratched the kitchen cabinets badly. When she moved out, the landlord, Sean Cassidy, kept 50 percent of the security deposit to pay for repairs to the kitchen. How much of her security deposit did Dawn get back?
3. Jacob Crosser's one-year lease is about to run out. His landlord, Lynn Isaacs, says that she must raise the rent next year by 5 percent to cover increases in her maintenance costs. Jacob now pays $450 per month. What will his monthly rent be next year? How much will he pay altogether for rent in that year?

APPLYING CONSUMER SKILLS

1. Make your own Apartment Check List you could use if you were looking for an apartment.
2. Suppose you rent an apartment. The landlord has refused to fix a clogged drain, repair a broken window, or correct a short in an electric wire. There are few empty apartments

around that you can afford. What steps can you take to solve your problem?

3. Suppose your city is considering freezing rents at current levels. Apartments are in short supply, and rents have been increasing. Would you support this rent freeze? Why or why not?

GETTING INVOLVED IN YOUR COMMUNITY If your city or town has a building or housing code, get a copy of it from your city or town hall. Read over the code and find answers to these questions:

1. How and to whom do tenants report complaints?
2. How are complaints handled?
3. Are apartment inspections made?
4. How is the code enforced?
5. What are the penalties if landlords do not comply with the code?
6. May a landlord evict tenants if they complain to the authorities or take legal action against the landlord?
7. May tenants stop paying their rent in some cases?

23

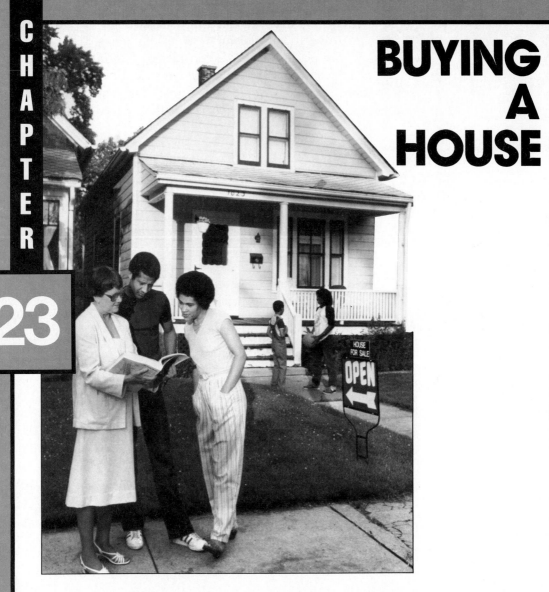

BUYING A HOUSE

Owning a house is one of many people's fondest dreams. You do not have to worry about a landlord. No one can stop you from having pets. You can fix your house up any way you like. But if you buy a house, it will probably be the most expensive purchase you ever make. What special consumer skills do you need?

▪ How do you finance a house?

▪ How do you shop for a house?

▪ Should you buy an old house or a new one?

▪ What legal problems could you run into when you buy a house?

One Sunday, Phil and Debbie Rice and their two children, Sean and Jessica, took a drive in their new car to escape the 90-degree heat in their apartment. When they came to a group of new houses, Phil asked Debbie to stop. He had read a newspaper ad saying that the builder was showing some of these new homes to the public. Three different models were open. After walking through them, the Rices stopped to talk to the salesperson in charge. When the salesperson had answered all of their questions, the Rices knew they had found their dream house. It had all of the things they wanted: a family room, a work area, and—best of all—central air-conditioning. And it would cost only $125,000.

But before they signed any contracts, the Rices decided to go back to their apartment and think things through. They asked themselves a lot of questions. Was the family outgrowing the apartment? Did they have enough money for a down payment? Could they meet the higher cost of utilities? Was everyone prepared to help out to maintain the house? First, they decided, they'd better find out if they could afford the house.

THE COST OF A HOUSE

In Chapter 21 you learned that the costs of owning a house include the down payment and the monthly costs. The monthly costs include mortgage payments, taxes, insurance, utilities, repairs, and maintenance. Budget experts recommend that you do not spend more than one third of your take-home pay on these monthly housing costs. To work out how much you can afford to pay for a house, then, you must know how much a mortgage will cost you. So, before even looking at houses, real estate experts say you should see if you can get a mortgage. Start by going to a savings and loan association, a mortgage company, a bank, or a credit union to find out how much money you are able to borrow. Phil and Debbie went to a savings and loan association first.

Shopping for a mortgage

Phil and Debbie decided to visit the Oceanview Savings and Loan Association to see about a mortgage loan. There they met Tanya Jacobs, a loan officer. "We saw a house we love for $125,000," said Phil. "Can you tell us if we can afford it?"

"Every case is different, of course," Mrs. Jacobs replied. "But we do use a general formula, which will give you some idea. First, we require 20 percent down payment. In your case, that would be $25,000," she said, working it out. "Do you have enough savings to cover that?"

"That's a lot of money," said Debbie, "but we've been saving every month for six years now, so we have enough."

Mrs. Jacobs worked out some more figures on her calculator. "You would need a $100,000 mortgage then. For a quick estimate, we say that a family should pay no more than 28 percent of their monthly gross pay for mortgage principal and interest, property taxes, and insurance."

Phil made $33,000 a year as an accountant for a company that owned a chain of florists' shops. Debbie earned $21,000 as a part-time ballet teacher. So their gross pay was $4,500 a month. "I asked the salesperson about the property taxes," said Debbie. "He said they came to $1,840 a year. And I checked into homeowners' insurance too. That would be another $500 a year."

"So that's $195 a month for taxes and insurance," said Mrs. Jacobs. "And 28 percent of your take-home pay is $1,260. So you can afford monthly mortgage payments of $1,065. Let me just get my mortgage interest table out. At our current interest rate of 11 percent for a 30-year loan, principal and interest for $100,000 comes to $952.33 a month. It seems that you can afford your house."

Debbie and Phil smiled. "But," continued Mrs. Jacobs, "I can't guarantee that we will approve your loan. Before we give you a mortgage, we look at your credit rating. And we check your other expenses, too—how much you pay for car loans and how much you owe on credit cards, for instance."

1. If the Rices get the mortgage to buy the house, how much will they be paying each month for mortgage, property taxes, and homeowners' insurance?
2. What information did the Rices need to know about the house in order to find out if they could qualify for a mortgage?

Types of Mortgages

The type of mortgage Mrs. Jacobs described for the Rices is called a **fixed-rate mortgage**. With this kind of mortgage, the interest rate and monthly payments stay the same over the life of the mortgage. The Rices, for example, will pay $952.33 every month for 30 years if they get this type of mortgage. The Rices could probably take out a fixed-rate mortgage for 20 years or 15 years. The shorter the mortgage period, the less they will pay in interest—but the higher their monthly payments will be.

Phil and Debbie could get an **adjustable-rate mortgage** (sometimes called an ARM). With this type of mortgage, the interest

Some lenders will give you a mortgage with as little as 5 percent down. But they will require that you have a higher income than you would need if you provided a higher down payment.

rate changes (is adjusted) periodically, depending on financial market conditions. If the interest rate goes up, your payments go up. If the interest rate goes down, your payments go down. Some ARMs are adjusted every six months. Others are adjusted every five years. Most often, though, they are adjusted yearly. ARMs are popular because interest rates and monthly payments usually start out lower than they would be for fixed-rate mortgages. Mrs. Jacobs explains this to the Rices.

CASE STUDY

"The interest rate on our 30-year ARM is now 9½ percent," Mrs. Jacobs told the Rices. "Your monthly payments in the first year would be only $840.86. But next year, the interest rate can rise as much as 2½ percent to 12 percent. Then your monthly payments would go up to $1,028.62. We have a 5 percent cap on our ARMs. That means the interest rate can go up or down no more than 5 percent for the life of the loan. In your case, it could go up to as high as 14½ percent or down to as low as 4½ percent. In a single year, we can only raise or lower the rate by as much as 2½ percent."

"I'm not sure whether I want to worry about interest rates every year," said Phil.

"We also offer a **balloon-note mortgage**," said Mrs. Jacobs. "This loan lasts for just three to five years. You pay off only part of the loan. At the end of the time, you must pay off the rest of the money all at once or renew the loan, usually with a new interest rate. Monthly payments are lower for this type of loan than for our other loans. The payments stay the same for the whole period. But there's no telling how much the interest rate will change when it comes time to renew. There are no caps on this type of mortgage. So, we recommend this type of loan mainly to people who are not planning to stay in their houses very long."

Phil and Debbie thanked Mrs. Jacobs. They decided to shop around some more and compare. At the Friendly Finance Corporation, they were offered a fixed-rate mortgage at 10½ percent. But it was a 15-year mortgage. The payments would be $1,105.40.

Government Guaranteed Loans

Phil and Debbie may also qualify for two kinds of loans guaranteed by the federal government. One is an **FHA loan**, a loan insured by the Federal Housing Administration. It is usually offered at an interest rate lower than commercial rates. If a borrower **defaults** on the loan (fails to make the payments), the federal government pays off the loan. The borrower pays for this insurance, which is included in the monthly payment. Usually, only people buying homes for the first time can get an FHA loan.

Home Equity Loans

Unlike most things consumers buy, houses usually increase in value over time. In some fast-growing areas, houses have been known to double in value in a single year. The amount a house is worth more than the amount owed on it is called *home equity*. House owners build home equity just by living in the house, if the market price of the house rises.

They also build home equity as they pay back the mortgage. But this equity builds very slowly because, at first, mortgage payments are almost entirely interest.

Consumers who build equity in their homes may use that equity as collateral for personal loans. These loans are called *home equity loans*. Financial institutions are often willing to give homeowners a line of credit based on a percentage of the equity they have in their house. Homeowners can borrow money as they need it, using special checks. The interest rate is lower on this type of loan than for other types of personal loans.

Home equity loans look like an easy way to get a personal loan. But experts advise you to be careful. If for any reason you fail to pay back the loan, you can lose your house. Often lenders charge points and other closing costs to establish the line of credit. And the interest rate for the loan can go up and down over time. If it rises, you may find it harder than you thought to pay off the loan.

What can you do if you buy a house when interest rates are high? Some people *refinance* their houses when interest rates drop. The process is like buying a house all over again. The owner contacts a mortgage lender for a new loan. The owner must pay closing costs again. These can amount to anywhere from $1,000 to $3,500. However, you can save well over $100 per month in mortgage payments.

If Phil or Debbie has served in the military, they might be able to get a VA loan. A **VA loan** is one guaranteed by the Veterans' Administration, another federal agency. Borrowers pay a monthly insurance fee, but, as with FHA loans, interest rates tend to be low. Also, lenders may allow longer repayment periods (which will lower the monthly payments). And lenders may accept smaller down payments. Sometimes, veterans can get VA loans that do not require any down payment at all.

✓check your understanding ✓ ✓ ✓ ✓ ✓ ✓

1. **Suppose your income is $37,000 a year. How much should your monthly payments for mortgage, property taxes, and homeowners' insurance be?**
2. **What is the difference between a fixed-rate and an adjustable-rate mortgage?**
3. **For what type of buyer is a balloon-note mortgage recommended? Why?**
4. **What advantages do FHA and VA mortgage loans have?**

CHOOSING THE RIGHT HOUSE

After deciding how much you can afford for a house, you should shop around carefully. Look at a lot of houses. Even if you find your dream house right away, you should probably take the time to see what else is available. The Rices were happy that they did.

CASE STUDY

Even though they could afford their "dream house," the Rices decided to take a look at other houses. After all, Debbie said, a little comparison shopping would probably be a good idea for something so important and so expensive. They knew they wanted to live in the northwest part of town. That section had parks, good shopping areas, and little street traffic. But they were not sure how to begin. They decided to ask Debbie's brother Mike, who had just bought a new house himself.

"You're already doing pretty well," said Mike. "You know about how much you can afford, you've saved up enough for the down payment, and you've narrowed down the neighborhoods where you want to look. I'd continue by looking through the real estate section in the newspaper for a while to get an idea of what the prices are in that neighborhood. If you see anything that sounds good, just call the number in the ad and ask to see the house."

"That sounds like it will take a lot of time," said Phil. "Isn't there a faster way?"

"You can go to a real estate broker," said Mike. "The broker will probably be able to show you a number of houses at once. The broker can also help you find the lowest cost mortgage."

"But brokers charge a fee," said Phil. "I found that they usually charge the seller between 5 and 10 percent of the selling price. On a $125,000 house that can be as much as $12,500. Some sellers add the fee onto the price of the house, so you end up paying more."

"That can happen," said Mike, "but brokers are often better at setting the price of a house than owners are. Sometimes the owner asks too much money for the house. When no one offers to buy it, the owner finally goes to a broker for help. The broker suggests that the owner lower the price.

"But remember," Mike warned. "Brokers work for the people who are selling the house, not for the people who are buying. They are supposed to tell you about the house, but they don't have to tell you about all of its bad points. Make sure you get a house inspector to check out any house before you buy."

Phil and Debbie decided to go to the Homefires Realty Office. They spoke to Jim Olmos, a real estate broker. Jim agreed that the northwest part of town was a good neighborhood. But almost all of the houses were old. "Do you want to see new houses or old ones?" Jim asked. "Each has advantages and disadvantages."

You can sometimes make purchasing a home more affordable if you are willing to buy an older house and do some work fixing it up.

Buying an Old House

Both new and old houses have bad points as well as good. Older houses usually cost less. They are often in established neighborhoods that have many services like sewerage, trash collection, nearby schools, and libraries. They may be better built than new houses, with expensive features like porches and landscaping that new houses often don't have. But older houses have disadvantages too. In the following interview, a **developer**—a builder of new housing—tells about some problems you can have with old houses.

The biggest problem with an old house is simply that it's old. Like anything old, it needs repairs. And repairs can cost you an awful lot of money.

Many older houses have termites. These insects actually eat the wood of the house away. Also, the wiring and the plumbing may be inefficient in an old house. The heating systems are often old and the roofs too. Each of these can cost thousands of dollars to replace. Old houses may have old windows and little or no insulation (padding) in the walls. That makes them expensive to keep warm in winter or cool in summer. If you find an old house without any of these problems, I'll bet it will cost a lot. Or it will have a wet basement and need to be painted.

At least look for these problems before you sign on the dotted line. If you're not an expert in all of these areas, take my advice and hire one. It'll save you plenty.

Better yet, buy a new house from us.

GORDON CASHMAN
Cashman Developers

Buying a New House

New houses do have advantages. Repair costs are usually lower. They are often less expensive to heat and cool. But a broker tells about some of the problems you can run into in a new *housing development*—a neighborhood of new homes built by a single developer.

Many buyers look at the model home in a development and fall for the glitter. Usually, the model is filled with extras you won't find in the house you buy. Or it's on a bigger piece of land than the one you'll get. You may have to pay thousands more to get carpeting, a fireplace, a finished family room, or more than one full bathroom.

Salespeople sometimes make all sorts of promises. They tell you about things planned for the community. They'll talk about future schools, parks, new streets, city water, and sewerage. You move in and there's nothing. You even wind up paying to pave the streets and hook up to the town water supply.

If you're going to move into a new development, find out about the builders. How reliable are they? Check with people living in houses they've already built. Also, insist that all promises be in writing. And don't close the deal until you've had a professional inspect the house you are planning to buy. Just because it's new, doesn't mean there's nothing wrong with it.

AMY HURLESS
Real Estate Broker

√check your understanding √ √ √ √ √ √

1. Describe two ways you could find a house to buy.
2. What construction problems should you check for before you buy an older house?
3. What can add to the cost of buying a new house?

HOW TO BUY A HOUSE

Buying a house is a complicated matter. Thousands of dollars are
at stake. Before you settle on any house, hire a lawyer. A seller or
real estate agent may suggest a lawyer to you, but you need one
who will act only for you. It's better to take the steps outlined in
Chapter 14 and get one for yourself.

Suppose you've found a house you want to buy. You'll still need
to bargain about the price. Usually the buyer and the seller settle
on a price somewhat lower than the asking price. How much lower
depends on how much you want to buy the house and how much
the seller wants to leave.

CASE STUDY

The right house for the Rices

In the end, the Rices found an older house they liked even better
than the new one. It was larger and had just about everything they
wanted. Phil would have to put in air-conditioning himself, though.
The owners, Lucy and Harry Chen, had tried to sell the house
themselves for $129,000. But three families who had liked the
house could not afford the monthly mortgage payments. The Chens
then hired Jim Olmos, the broker, who suggested they try to sell
it for $124,000.

The Rices made an offer, through Jim, of $118,000. The Chens
came down to $122,000.

Phil and Debbie then said "$120,000—and no more." The Chens accepted that offer. Phil and Debbie then had to put down a deposit, called **earnest money**. They wrote a check for $1,200 as their deposit. The Rices' lawyer prepared a contract called a **purchase-and-sale agreement**. It included a protective clause or **contingency clause**. This clause said that if the Rices couldn't get a mortgage or the house did not pass a termite inspection, they did not have to buy it. They could have their deposit money back. In addition, they would have the house inspected. If something serious was wrong, they would not have to buy the house, or they could bargain again with the sellers to lower the price. If the Rices changed their minds for other reasons, though, they would lose their deposit.

Applying for a Mortgage

The next step was to apply for the mortgage. Jim, the broker, gave the Rices a list of many of the lending institutions in the area. The list showed what kinds of mortgages and what interest rates were available that week.

The Rices expected to stay in their house for a long time. They did not want to worry about changing interest rates. So they settled on a fixed-rate mortgage. As it turned out, Oceanview's rates were the lowest around, so they went back there to apply for the mortgage. They agreed to pay a 20 percent down payment of $24,000 and to apply for a $96,000 mortgage. Oceanview charged them $200 to submit the application. It was a good thing that the Rices had shopped around for the best mortgage rates before they applied. The application fee was not refundable if they changed their minds.

A few weeks after they submitted the application, they learned that they qualified for a mortage, meaning that their credit rating was good enough for the loan. They were not sure of getting the mortgage yet, though. Oceanview still had to go through a number of other steps. Among these steps were a title search, an appraisal, and a preparation of a plot plan. These steps would take another six weeks, the Rices were told. If everything checked out, Oceanview's lawyer would contact them to set up an appointment for closing the deal.

Closing the Deal

The application fee the Rices paid to Oceanview was part of their closing costs. **Closing costs** are the costs involved in obtaining a mortgage. In addition to the application fee, the closing costs include charges for the other steps Oceanview took to approve the mortgage.

Oceanview's lawyer conducted the **title search**, which is a search through ownership records (called titles) to make sure that the Chens really owned the property and were legally allowed to sell it. Even though the Rices' lawyer did a title search, Phil and Debbie still had to pay Oceanview's lawyer to do it as well. Most mortgage lenders also require that buyers take out **title insurance**. This insurance protects the buyer and lender in case something is wrong with the title that the search did not uncover.

Oceanview also charged the Rices to have the house appraised. The appraiser checks to make sure the house is worth what the Rices are paying for it. The Rices had to pay for the time Oceanview's lawyer spent preparing documents. In addition, Oceanview sent someone to a local government office to find the official plot plan for the property. This plan shows exactly where the boundaries of the property are and where all of the buildings are on the property. The Rices had to pay for that too.

Another closing cost that lenders often require is called **points**. A point is equal to 1 percent of the amount of the loan. So one point for Phil and Debbie is $960. Usually, the lower the interest rate, the more points a lender charges. By charging points, mortgage lenders cover the costs involved in issuing a loan. Oceanview charged the Rices two points, or $1,920.

All in all, closing costs added about $3,000 to the cost of the Rices' house. In addition, of course, the Rices also had to pay for their own lawyer and for the building and termite inspectors they had hired.

Changing Ownership

Almost three months after the Rices first offered to buy the house, a date was set for the closing. A **closing** is the meeting at which the ownership of a house is transferred from the sellers to the buyers. The Rices, the Chens, the Chens' lawyer, the Rices' lawyer, and Oceanview's lawyer all attended this meeting. The Rices were told to bring a certified check for the down payment (minus the amount of their earnest money) to this meeting. They would also pay for the remaining closing costs at that time.

At the closing, Oceanview's lawyer explained all of the documents and asked the Rices to look at them and make sure they were okay. The Rices signed the mortgage agreement in which they promised to repay the mortgage loan in monthly payments. The house and land would be collateral. If the Rices default, Oceanview can foreclose. In a **foreclosure**, Oceanview would sell the house to get its money back. If Oceanview sold the house for more than the amount of the mortgage, the Rices would get the rest of the money.

After signing the rest of the documents, Oceanview turned over a check in the amount of $96,000 to the Rices. Debbie and Phil endorsed this check and the one for the down payment and gave them to the Chens' lawyer. The Rices then made out a check to Oceanview for the closing costs minus their $200 deposit. The Chens then signed the deed, transferring ownership to the Rices. Then the Chens handed the Rices the keys to the house.

That night, the whole family went out to celebrate. The very next day, they moved into their own house.

House Inspections

Buyers are always wise to have a house they want to buy inspected. But what can you expect an inspector to do? Inspectors will give you a written report. The report should answer the following questions:

- What is the condition of the heating, electrical, and plumbing systems? Are they safe? Do any of them need to be replaced? Will it cost you a lot of money to heat the house? Can the electrical system run a clothes dryer or other appliance that uses a lot of electricity?
- How sound is the structure of the house? Is it sagging anywhere? Is the foundation okay? Is there any evidence of termite damage?
- How old is the roof? Will it need to be replaced soon? Does it leak? Do the gutters drain water off the roof properly?
- Does the basement flood when it rains?
- How much insulation is in the house? Is it safe?
- Are the windows in good condition? Will they need to be replaced?

The few hundred dollars you spend on an inspection can save you thousands of dollars later on. But hiring an incompetent or dishonest inspector could also cost you money. Experts recommend comparison shopping for home inspectors. They also recommend that you stick to ones who are members of the American Society of Home Inspectors (ASHI).

Unusual houses, such as this one, may be difficult to resell. To protect your investment, make sure the house will appeal to other buyers.

1. Why are contingency clauses included in a purchase-and-sale agreement?
2. What steps do lenders take before they turn over mortgage money to a house buyer?
3. What happens at a real estate closing?

SUMMARIZING
the chapter

A house is usually a family's biggest purchase. Financial institutions use a formula to determine roughly how much money to lend to a house buyer. Under this formula, mortgage principal and interest, homeowners' insurance, and property taxes should total no more than 28 percent of the buyer's gross monthly income.

Before shopping for a house, you should understand what types of mortgages are available. You may be able to choose among fixed-rate mortgages, adjustable-rate mortgages, or balloon-note mortgages. Some people also qualify for low-cost FHA and VA loans.

Before shopping for a house, families should decide what their needs are and what neighborhoods they might like to live in. They should also consider both the advantages and the disadvantages of new and old houses.

Once you pick out a house, make sure to get a lawyer's help. The lawyer should approve the purchase-and-sale agreement and do a title search. You should also have a professional building inspector check the house, even if it is a new one.

If your mortgage application is approved, and the lender is satisfied with the results of a separate title search and appraisal, you will be able to buy the house. Ownership is transferred at the closing. After the closing, you can move in.

·C·H·A·P·T·E·R· A ·C·T·I·V·I·T·I·E·S·

Number your paper from 1 to 16. Then write the term that best matches each numbered definition.

adjustable-rate mortgage
balloon-note mortgage
closing
closing costs
contingency clause
default
developer
earnest money

FHA loan
fixed-rate mortgage
foreclosure
point
purchase-and-sale agreement
title insurance
title search
VA loan

1. A mortgage loan that is paid off monthly at a fixed rate of interest for three to five years, after which the remaining balance is due in full
2. A mortgage loan guaranteed by the Federal Housing Administration
3. The meeting at which ownership of a house is transferred from the sellers to the buyers
4. A mortgage loan in which the interest rate remains the same for the entire life of the loan
5. To fail to meet mortgage payments
6. A mortgage loan in which the interest rate changes periodically
7. A mortgage guaranteed by the Veterans' Administration that is available to people who have served in the military
8. A deposit made on a house
9. Repossession of a house by a mortgage lender because the buyer has defaulted on mortgage payments
10. A contract signed by a buyer and seller of a house setting up the terms of the sale
11. An examination of ownership records to establish the legal owners of property
12. A person or company that builds new housing
13. A charge made by a mortgage lender equal to 1 percent of the cost of a mortgage loan
14. A protective clause put in a purchase-and-sale agreement to release the buyer if specified conditions are not met
15. Charges that must be paid to a lender to obtain a mortgage
16. Insurance that protects a house buyer in case something turns out to be wrong with the title

1. Why is it important to shop for a mortgage?
2. How might the fact that the Rices just bought a new car affect their ability to get a mortgage?
3. Why is it unwise to spend all of your savings on the down payment for a house?
4. Whom does a real estate broker work for? What services can a broker perform for a buyer?
5. How can a house inspection lower the cost of buying a house?
6. At what step in the buying process should you hire a lawyer? What will the lawyer do?
7. What precautions should you take before buying a new house from a developer?
8. What can be included in closing costs?

1. Suppose Phil and Debbie Rice find an 11 percent fixed-rate mortgage from a mortgage company that charges only 1½ points. If they borrow $96,000 from this company, how much will they pay in points? How much less will they pay for points by getting this mortgage instead of the one from Oceanview Savings and Loan?
2. The house that Phil and Debbie eventually bought was less expensive than the first one they looked at. Since it was less expensive, property taxes and homeowners' insurance were lower too. The monthly mortgage payments, principal and interest, came to $914.88. The property taxes were $1,428 a year. Insurance was $360 a year.
   a. How much were the Rices' monthly payments for mortgage, property taxes, and homeowners' insurance?
   b. How much less per month are the Rices paying by buying the older house rather than the new one? How much will they save in the first year?
   c. What percentage of their monthly gross salary will the Rices be paying for mortgage, homeowners' insurance, and property taxes for their house in the first year?
3. Suppose Phil and Debbie had decided to get the 9½ percent adjustable-rate mortgage instead of the fixed-rate mortgage. In the first year, their mortgage payments would be $807.36 a month.
   a. How much money would the Rices save in the first year on mortgage payments with an adjustable-rate mortgage rather than the fixed-rate mortgage? (Do not count taxes and insurance.)
   b. If the rate went up in the second year to 12 percent, the mortgage payments would rise to $987.84. How much money would the Rices pay that year in mortgage payments? How much would the Rices pay in the second year for the fixed-rate mortgage?

After the Rices had lived in their new house a few months, they estimated their utility costs to be about $125 a month. They also put aside another $100 for maintenance and repairs.

1. What repairs might the Rices need to make on the house?
2. What sort of maintenance might they have to do that they did not have to do in their apartment?
3. Suppose that the Rices' take-home pay is $3,100 a month. What percentage of their take-home pay is spent on their total housing costs (mortgage, homeowners' insurance, taxes, utilities, maintenance, and repairs)? How does that compare with the guidelines suggested by housing experts?
4. If you were the Rices, would you have bought the house or stayed in the apartment? Why?

Read the real estate ads in your newspaper. Pick one house that interests you and determine the asking price. What are the advantages claimed for the house? How does this house compare with other houses advertised for the same price in the paper?

Visit or call three mortgage lenders in your area to find out what mortgages might be available for this house. Find out the answers to the following questions:

1. What types of mortgages are available?
2. What are the current interest rates for these types of mortgages?
3. How many points does each type of mortgage require?
4. How much will the mortgage closing costs total?
5. What size income do you need for each type of mortgage?

OTHER TYPES OF HOUSING

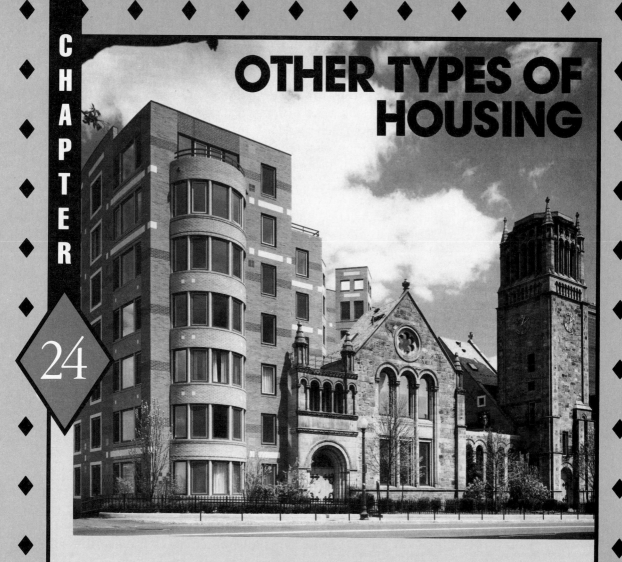

A single-family house is not the only choice home buyers have. You have alternatives. You can buy housing in multi-family dwellings. You can buy housing that is much less expensive than most single-family houses. What are the advantages to alternative housing? What are the disadvantages?

◆ What are the good points and bad points of owning a condominium?

◆ How can you avoid mistakes in buying a condominium?

◆ Why is factory-built housing becoming so popular?

◆ How should you shop for manufactured housing?

A single-family house may be beyond the reach of many families. In fact, the average sales price of a single-family house is over $125,000. Because of these high prices, many people are moving into other types of housing.

THE PROS AND CONS OF CONDOMINIUMS

The popularity of condominiums continues to grow. In the 1980's, over 10 percent of home buyers purchased condominiums. In big cities like Chicago, more than 15 percent of home buyers bought condominiums. You can probably find a condominium to buy in almost every city and suburb of the United States.

As you learned in Chapter 21, a condominium is a multi-family dwelling. Some condominiums are very small, maybe just two units in a house. Other condominium developments have many buildings and much land.

If you buy a unit in a condominium, you own your unit—that is, you own the inside walls. Together with the owners of the other units, you also own the common areas. These areas include the land, halls, grounds, elevators, heating and air-conditioning equipment, and recreational facilities (pool, exercise room), if any.

As with a house, most people buy condominiums by providing a cash down payment and obtaining a mortgage. Condominium owners pay property taxes and homeowners' insurance too. They also must pay for utilities, maintenance, and repairs to their units.

But, unlike house owners, condominium owners share the cost of insurance, utilities, maintenance, and repairs for the common areas of the condominium. These costs are paid for in a monthly **maintenance fee**. This fee is set by the **owners' association**—a group made up of everyone who owns a unit in the condominium. The owners' association decides how the common areas will be maintained. Each owner has a vote when it comes time to decide how the common areas will be maintained and how much it will cost. The vote of the majority, however, determines what all of the owners must pay. The owners as a group must cover all costs.

Many people are willing to give up the privacy of a single-family house in return for the benefits of condominiums. Often, condominiums cost less for the same living area than a single-family house would cost on the same site. Down payments are usually lower. Taxes are probably lower too. Some condominiums have pools, tennis courts, and other facilities that most owners of single-family houses could not afford to own by themselves. Owners' associations generally hire managers to maintain the buildings and grounds. These people do repairs on both the common areas and the units. They also arrange to have the snow shoveled and the grass mowed. So condominium owners spend less time repairing and maintaining their homes than house owners do.

You have bought a condominium in a large building. A person visiting another unit trips on a loose rug in the lobby and breaks a leg. Are you liable? Yes. Common areas are owned by all the unit owners and the liability for those areas is equally shared.

Holliston's Best Value

Two Bedroom Brick Townhouses
Values from $68,900
Financing Arranged-Only 10% Down!

- Modern Kitchen & Bath
- Sun Filled Rooms
- Laundry Facilities
- Shining Hardwood Floors
- Individually Controlled Gas Heat
- Full Basement
- Parking
- Low Taxes & Condo Fee
- 10 Min. to Springford

By Appointment
177-0099
329-6288

Model Open
Sunday
12-5 PM

REGENCY PLACE
CONDOMINIUM TOWNHOUSES

Park Terrace
at Pineview

Tucked away in a secluded, woodsy neighborhood, it's only minutes from Winston, Rt. 3 and 108. Featuring hardwood parquet floors inside, a refreshing pool, tennis courts and trees outside. Garages are available at a moderate fee.

Compare the features and the price, and see how choosy you can afford to be.

ONE BEDROOM FROM $59,500
TWO BEDROOM FROM $71,500

Available now 10½% annual percentage rate.
Permanent affordable mortgage
to qualified buyers.

Park Terrace Condominiums at Pineview.
Take Rt. 3 to the Pineview Zoo Exit. (Northbound, Exit 8. Southbound, Exit 9.) Proceed past zoo.
Take left on Wyoming Ave. Park Terrace is one mile on left.

685-8978 ● 513-1700
Open Daily 12—5

The advertisements above tell about some of the advantages of condominiums.

Hidden Costs

Advertisements tell only part of the story. And, obviously, the part they tell is the most positive part. The case studies that follow show the other side of the coin.

CASE STUDY

Shirley Dorning and her mother, Marie, had lived in their two-bedroom apartment for 21 years. One day, they learned that their building had been sold to a company that was going to convert it into condominiums.

Shirley then received a notice. It said that she and her mother would have to move out when their lease was up in five months unless they chose to buy the apartment as a condominium unit. The price would be $65,000. The new owners would remodel the kitchen and bathroom and put in air-conditioning. Meanwhile, their apartment would be shown to people who might want to buy it.

Several people looked at the apartment. The Dornings began to think seriously about buying it themselves. If they bought the apartment, they wouldn't have to bother to move. The more they thought, the better it sounded. So Shirley and Marie took most of their savings out of the bank and used it as a down payment for the unit. They adjusted to the higher mortgage payments and the maintenance fee.

Three months after they bought their apartment, the Dornings were told they should come to the next meeting of the condominium association. Very important problems would be discussed.

At the meeting, another owner reported that the maintenance fees would have to be raised. Maintenance bills were higher than expected. It seemed that the old owner had sold the building because maintenance costs were eating up profits. The new owners made a quick profit by doing the minimum amount of remodeling necessary to sell the building as condominiums. Now those people no longer owned the building. The condominium owners did. And the roof and elevators needed repairs. The heating system needed to be replaced. These costs would raise the Dornings' monthly maintenance fee to $95.

Then another board member suggested that the association should build some tennis courts. This sounded like a great idea to a lot of the owners. By a majority vote, they decided to build the courts. This would raise the monthly charge another $25. The Dornings would have to pay even though they didn't play tennis.

CASE STUDY

Alonzo and Carla Robinson were looking forward to owning their first home. The suburban condominium development of Oak Hill Farms seemed perfect for an active young couple. It had a large swimming pool, tennis courts, and bike paths. All of these special features could be enjoyed for a monthly maintenance fee of $75.

The Robinsons troubles began even before they moved in. The developer who owned the land and built the buildings had promised that their condominium would be ready on May 1. They told their landlord that they would be moving from their apartment then. The landlord found new tenants. On April 15, the developer told the Robinsons that their unit wouldn't be ready until May 15. They had to spend the first two weeks of May in a motel, and it cost them a lot.

Two months after they moved in, the Robinsons had another nasty surprise. They thought that when they bought their condominium unit, they had also bought a share in the pool, tennis courts, and grounds. But it turned out that the developer still owned these facilities and planned to charge fees for their use.

Buying a condominium enables you to own a home at a lower level of investment and with less maintenance than owning a single family house.

The Smart Condominium Shopper

Real estate experts say a shopper should do at least six things before buying a condominium unit.

1. Check into the background of the developer—and take a look at other condominiums built by the same company.
2. Make sure you see a detailed statement of your monthly maintenance fee. Find out how much it is and what you get for it.
3. Find out who manages the condominium. Find out how much it costs the owners' association for this service. It's also a good idea to know when the manager's contract will need to be renewed. If the manager's fee goes up, your condominium fee will go up too.
4. Have a lawyer who is familiar with condominiums read and explain all documents presented to you by the seller.
5. Make sure the developer or owners' association has enough money to fix any construction problems that may come up after you move in.
6. Check with other owners to see that they are satisfied with the way the condominium is built and maintained.

The kit for this house comes with all the materials for a finished home. You provide the labor.

✓check your understanding ✓ ✓ ✓ ✓ ✓ ✓

1. **What benefits do condominiums offer over single-family houses?**
2. **What happens if members of an owners' association disagree about how to run the condominium?**
3. **Why is it important to learn about the developer before buying a condominium?**

HOMES BUILT IN FACTORIES

Like condominiums, factory-built housing is growing in popularity. Construction costs for this type of housing are low while quality is high. Builders can take advantage of the efficiency of factory assembly lines. They can produce housing often at half the cost of a site-built house.

Factory-built housing includes modular homes, log cabins, homes built from kits, and panelized housing. Over 12 million people in the United States currently live in this type of housing. Experts

Manufactured housing is built in factories and then shipped to the home site where it can be set up in one day.

Like cars, some manufactured housing depreciates in value as it gets older. Condominiums, like single-family houses, usually rise in value over time. If resale is a factor in your buying decision, check out the resale market for manufactured housing before you buy.

predict that in the 1990's as much as 75 percent of all housing will be factory-built.

The most popular type of factory-built housing is mobile homes, or manufactured housing as it is now called. In the 1980's, over 30 percent of all new single-family homes sold in the United States were manufactured homes. Manufactured housing accounted for over 80 percent of all new homes sold for under $50,000. About one out of every five first-time home buyers chose to live in this type of housing.

Some people think that living in manufactured housing is like living in a large truck or a camper. But many manufactured homes are surprisingly large. Small units that generally have four rooms and one or two baths sell for about $30,000. Much larger multi-section units, having as many as seven rooms and three baths, sell for about $40,000. These prices, however, do not include the land on which the unit sits.

Most manufactured houses come completely furnished. They have stoves, refrigerators, sofas and chairs, carpets, curtains, dining tables, beds, and bedroom chests. The purchase price should also cover the cost of delivery, setting the house up on the land, and connecting it to utilities.

Getting the Best Buy

As with other types of housing purchases, you should see if you can get a loan before you start looking for manufactured housing. There are two ways to finance this kind of housing. Some lenders consider manufactured houses to be the same as other types of houses. They will give you a mortgage loan to pay for the unit.

Check with savings and loan associations, finance companies, credit unions, and banks to see if they will finance manufactured housing. Some FHA and VA loans are available for this kind of housing as well. These financial institutions may require you to pay back the loan in a shorter period of time, however, such as 15 years, rather than 30. Some lenders offer loans as long as 20 years for manufactured housing.

You may not be able to finance a manufactured house in this way. In some places, lenders finance this type of housing as they would finance a car, not a house. They give you an installment loan for a much shorter period of time than a mortgage. You may not be able to get a loan for longer than seven years. Be sure to compare annual percentage rates when shopping for the best loan. You should also make sure that all loan agreements follow the rules required by the Truth in Lending Law discussed in Chapter 15.

New manufactured housing is sold by dealers in much the same way that cars are sold. Like cars, new manufactured housing comes with warranties. So it's important to find a dealer who is honest and fair and will give you good service. Check out dealers' reputations with consumer protection agencies and the Better Business Bureau. Also talk to people who already own manufactured housing to find out how reliable the dealers were who sold them their units.

Not all buyers of manufactured housing have been happy with their purchases. Recent studies show that three kinds of complaints are heard most often. First, some buyers complain that items in the unit, such as the appliances or the heating system, do not work well. Second, some buyers feel that dealers did not arrange to have the units installed properly, as promised. Third, some buyers say they do not get good service under the warranty. The following case study shows that, with manufactured housing, the best buy is not always the cheapest one.

> Modular homes are very similar to manufactured housing. They are not, however, covered by the federal regulations that manufactured housing must conform to. Makers of manufactured housing, therefore, point out that modular homes may not be as high quality as manufactured housing.

CASE STUDY

Angela and Tony Rose had been shopping for manufactured housing for a month, ever since they graduated from college. They had read a lot about manufactured houses, but they had never lived in one.

One day, the Roses found a dealer who was offering what seemed to be a great deal. The unit seemed to be what they wanted, and it had lovely wood paneling. They checked the unit carefully, inside and out. Everything looked okay. It even had a warranty. The Roses couldn't pass up the price. They bought the unit.

A month later, they went to visit Angela's mother for the weekend. While they were away, a thunderstorm hit their neighborhood, causing the streets to flood.

When they returned to their own home, they found that the roof had leaked. Rain water had completely destroyed the beautiful wood paneling in the living room that they loved so much. The ceiling was soaked in the bedroom too. The Roses immediately called the dealer. She told them that their unit would be repaired, and quickly, because it was still under warranty.

Actually, though, the Roses' home was not repaired for eight months. The Roses complained. But a neighbor showed them an article that said the Roses' problem was a common one. Many owners report that their units have leaky roofs and ceilings. They also complain about doors and windows that do not open and close properly, plumbing that doesn't work, walls that buckle, and damage done during installation. The article also said that it often took up to ten months to fix these problems. The Roses wondered if they had gotten such a good deal after all.

Setting Standards

Consumers do have some protection when they buy manufactured housing. The **Department of Housing and Urban Development** (HUD) requires manufactured housing to meet certain standards of design, construction, and safety. Here are some of the things that HUD requires.

- Doors and windows that can be removed from the inside in case of emergency
- At least two doors leading to the outside
- Good light and ventilation in each room
- Smoke detectors in sleeping areas
- Furnaces made out of fire-resistant materials
- Protection against fire for the walls and ceilings that surround the water heater and stove
- Tie-down straps for protection against wind damage
- Insulation to maintain a comfortable temperature inside

HUD gives state agencies the job of inspecting and approving manufactured housing. When a unit meets HUD standards, a state inspector puts a red and silver plate on the outside. In addition, the manufacturer puts a plate inside the house telling the buyer important facts about it. For example, the plate has a map showing what climates and weather conditions the house is designed to withstand.

Sellers also must give you a homeowner's manual explaining what to do if you have problems with your manufactured housing. The manual tells you how to maintain and safely operate the items in the unit. It also tells you how to contact state agencies that will enforce HUD standards.

Warranties on manufactured housing are not all alike. Some warranties give little coverage and for a very short time, such as 90 days. If you have a 90-day warranty, make sure everything works before the warranty expires. For example, even if you buy a unit in summer, turn on the heat. By the time winter comes, the warranty may have run out, and you'll be left out in the cold.

Before you buy, ask to see the manufacturer's warranty. Warranties vary among sellers. Make sure the one you get covers problems with the construction of the unit, plumbing, electrical and heating systems, and built-in appliances.

Before signing a purchase contract for manufactured housing, check the contract to see that it clearly describes the manufactured house and its features. Also make sure that the price in the contract is the price you agree upon with the dealer. Read all of the papers presented to you. Be sure you understand them. If something is not clear, have a lawyer read them.

✓check your understanding ✓ ✓ ✓ ✓ ✓ ✓

1. **Why do factory-built houses cost less than site-built houses?**
2. **Where can you get financing for manufactured housing? What is the difference between financing for this type of housing and for site-built houses?**
3. **How can you check out the reputation of a dealer of manufactured housing?**
4. **How do you know if a manufactured house meets HUD specifications?**

Finding Land

If you buy manufactured housing, you must find a place to put it. It does not automatically come with land, as site-built single-family houses do. You must buy or rent the land. And most communities do not let you put housing just anywhere you want. Most places have zoning laws.

Zoning laws are regulations passed by local governments describing the kinds of buildings that can be built in various parts of the community. Many communities limit the places where factories can be built, for example. They may wish to keep housing in one place and commercial buildings in another place. They may also wish to keep some land open, with nothing built on it. Zoning laws help create neighborhoods. They may guarantee, for example, that, if you buy a house in an area zoned only for single-family houses, a factory will not be built right next to you.

Factory-built housing may often be placed on land zoned for single-family houses. But you must make sure that the particular housing you plan to buy is allowed in the actual place you plan to put it. Zoning laws can be very specific. The laws may say that the house you plan to buy is too big for the amount of land you own. The laws may tell you where on the land you can put the house. You may have to apply for a **building permit**—a license granted by the local government giving you permission to build something on your land. Do not buy a factory-built house before

The British royal family still owns large amounts of the land under the city of London. People owning buildings on the royal family's land must pay rent to the landowners every year to be able to keep their buildings where they are.

Factory-built homes are built in sections. From the factory, they are shipped to the site, where they can be set up on a site-built foundation.

Sometimes, it is easier to get a mortgage if you buy a factory-built house. Since factory-built houses are built to high standards, lenders often have confidence that the houses are worth the asking price.

you have a place to put it and a permit allowing you to put it there. Zoning laws for manufactured housing can be particularly strict.

Many people who buy manufactured housing solve the problem of where to put it by renting land. There are over 24,000 communities in the United States designed just for manufactured housing. They are called **manufactured-housing communities** or, sometimes, *trailer parks*. Some of these manufactured-housing communities are lavish, with swimming pools and clubhouses. Others are poorly planned and poorly located. The rent for land and facilities can be anywhere from $50 to $500 a month. If you plan to put your manufactured house in one of these communities, rent the land before you buy the unit. Otherwise, you may end up like Al and Connie Fletcher in the case study below.

CASE STUDY

Al and Connie Fletcher were getting desperate. Their new housing unit was going to arrive in about two weeks. But they had no place to put it. They had not found a vacancy in any of the nearby manufactured-housing communities. Then they heard of one about 15 miles away that might have an opening. It was called Rolling Hills. The Fletchers decided to drive over and see what it looked like.

The owner of Rolling Hills explained that she would have a vacancy that week. But the Fletchers would have to pay an entrance fee of $500 to get it. This seemed unreasonable, but what else could they do? They paid the fee and planned to have their unit sent to the site.

After their unit was put in place and hooked up to the community's electricity, water, and sewerage, the park owner came by. She said that the Fletchers would have to buy all of their heating oil and cooking gas from her supplier. Al and Connie were shocked at the prices for the oil and gas. They were much higher than those of most other suppliers.

Al and Connie talked to other residents and heard more complaints about conditions in the community. The Fletchers decided to organize a homeowners' association to fight for better conditions.

That week, all of the residents got a notice telling them that next month the rent would go up $50. Al went to the owner and complained. Al and the owner got into an argument. She told Al to take his unit and leave. She said she didn't want troublemakers. Al and Connie couldn't afford to move. Besides, where could they go? They decided to sell their unit.

The Fletchers found a buyer right away. But the park owner said there was a rule against selling manufactured housing and leaving it in the park. They would have to pay to have it moved away. Or, she said, the rule could be dropped for a fee of $500.

1. Can manufactured housing be located anywhere in a city or town? Explain.
2. What are zoning laws and how can zoning laws help create neighborhoods?
3. What are some of the conditions zoning laws help regulate?
4. Why do you need a building permit when you plan to build on any property?
5. What were the problems that the Fletchers had in the park? How could those problems have been avoided?

SUMMARIZING
the chapter

Many people cannot afford to buy a single-family house. Condominiums and factory-built housing can be lower cost alternatives. Condominiums are multi-family dwellings owned by the people who live in them. Each family owns its own unit.

Together all of the families own the common areas. An owners' association makes decisions about maintaining and expanding common property. Each owner gets a vote in these decisions. Each owner must also share the cost of maintenance and additions to common property.

Before buying a condominium, check the reputation of the developer. Ask other owners of the condominium about the way the building is managed. Get a detailed description of the condominium fee. For your protection, have a lawyer read through all documents.

Manufactured housing is the most popular form of factory-built housing. It is often the least expensive way to buy a single-family dwelling.

Buying manufactured housing is in some ways like buying a car. You receive a warranty in the same way you would from a car dealer. And you should check on the manufactured-housing dealer in the same way you would check on the reputation of a car dealer. Manufactured housing must meet safety and quality standards set up by the Department of Housing and Urban Development.

Before buying factory-built housing, make sure you have a place to put it. Be sure you have a zoning permit if you are putting it on your own land. If you are renting land at a manufactured-housing community, find out how happy other tenants are in that community.

CHAPTER ACTIVITIES

BUILDING CONSUMER VOCABULARY

Number your paper from 1 to 6. Then write the term that best matches each numbered definition.

building permit
Department of Housing and
  Urban Development
maintenance fee

manufactured-housing
  communities
owners' association
zoning laws

1. Regulations that describe the kind and nature of buildings permitted in various parts of a community
2. The federal agency that regulates manufactured housing requiring it to meet certain standards of design, construction, and safety
3. The organization that makes decisions about the maintenance and expansion of a condominium
4. The monthly charge for using, maintaining, and repairing the common areas in a condominium
5. A license issued by a local government giving a land owner permission to build on that land
6. Places where people can rent land on which to put manufactured housing

BUILDING CONSUMER UNDERSTANDING

1. What expenses do condominium owners have in common with single-family house owners? What additional expenses do condominium owners have? What additional expenses do house owners have?
2. What problems might a condominium owner have with an owners' association?
3. In what ways is buying a condominium exactly like buying a single-family house?
4. What are the advantages of manufactured housing over a site built house?
5. In what ways is buying manufactured housing like buying a car? In what ways is it like buying a house?
6. Why is it necessary for HUD to set regulations for manufactured housing?
7. Suppose you buy a manufactured house in Florida. How do you know where in other parts of the country you can safely put it?
8. What things should you check out before locating a manufactured house in a rental community?

1. Using the ads on page 360, determine how large a down payment you would need to buy Regency Place's lowest price unit. If a 10 percent down payment is required at Park Terrace, how much would the down payment be for the lowest price unit in that development? How much of a down payment would you need for a two-bedroom unit at Park Terrace?
2. You find a two-bedroom unit at Park Terrace that you like for $80,000. But to get the best mortgage rate you need to put down 20 percent. How large a down payment would that be?
3. The lender tells you that the monthly mortgage payment, including real estate taxes, is $685. The owners' association says the monthly maintenance fee is $137. You expect to spend another $100 a month on utilities and $35 a month on homeowners' insurance. What is your total monthly housing cost?

Compare these two ads for manufactured housing.

NOW OPEN
BUY YOUR OWN LOT

ORANGE TREE II
ADULT COMMUNITY

★ **$49,999** ★
Price Includes
TOTAL PACKAGE: HOME, LOT & SET-UP!

On Lake Monarch
3 Recreational Buildings
Heated Pool and Tennis Courts
Shuffleboard, Golf and Shopping

Fully Developed Lots
45' x 70'
only **$9,000**
$500 Down
$150 Monthly

11%

ORANGE TREE II
3800 Country Road
Lake Monarch, FL 23800
(813) 623-5001

Up To 2 Years To Buy Home

A Beautiful Waterfront Community
Come live with us at **LAKE MONARCH**
Enjoy peaceful living in the rolling hills
by **LAKE MONARCH**

LAKE MONARCH FEATURES:
• Club House
• Superb Water and Sewer Facilities
• Shuffleboard and Planned Activity Program
• Excellent Fishing – Boat Ramp and Boat Launch
• Garbage Pickup

Lot Rents from
$88.00 per month
**DOUBLE WIDE
HOMES FROM
$36,990.00**

LAKE MONARCH PARK
1100 Lance Blvd.
Lake Monarch, FL 23800
(813) 623-1100

1. Why is the starting price higher at Orange Tree II?
2. What kind of financing arrangement can you expect at Orange Tree II? How might this affect your decision to buy?
3. List three important questions that you should ask at each place if you were interested in buying.
4. Using the information given in the ads, summarize the advantages and disadvantages of each place.
5. In your opinion, which deal is better? Why?

Check with your town or city hall to find out what zoning requirements there are for manufactured-housing units in your community. Where can manufactured housing be placed in your town? What other regulations does your community place on manufactured housing?

INSURING YOUR HOME

Every year, people in the United States lose over $3 billion worth of property and possessions in home fires. They lose more than $1 billion at the hands of home burglars. Fortunately, you can get insurance to protect against these and other misfortunes.

◆ Do renters need property insurance?

◆ What risks are covered by homeowners' insurance?

◆ How much insurance do you need?

◆ What sort of additional coverage is available?

You learned in Chapter 23 that mortgage lenders often require house buyers to insure their houses. It's not hard to understand why. If the house burns down, the lender loses the collateral for a very large loan—and the homeowner loses a place to live.

WHY RENTERS NEED INSURANCE

Some people think that if they don't own their own home they don't need insurance. But, if you rent, your landlord's insurance does not cover your own possessions. Think how much it would cost you to replace your clothes if they were lost in a fire. Just about everyone has possessions worth more than it costs to insure them. As the following case study shows, even small losses can be expensive to replace.

CASE STUDY

Pete DiMaggio, a high school teacher, returned home one evening to find the door to his apartment wide open. When he rushed in, he saw that his portable TV and brand new stereo were gone.

A police officer was there. He said the building manager had reported the break-in an hour earlier. The officer explained that the burglar probably came up the fire escape and through a window Pete had left open.

Pete was upset as he headed for the manager's apartment. The manager said he was sorry about the break-in. "But," he said, "I suppose you have property insurance to cover your losses."

Pete had no insurance. He thought the building's owners carried insurance. The manager said they did, but only on the parts of the building they controlled, not on tenants' possessions. He said it was Pete's job to insure his own property.

Back in his apartment, Pete sat down to figure out how much it would cost to replace the stolen TV and stereo. Then he thought he had better add in the cost of some insurance to cover future losses.

Pete is one of the estimated 20 million renters who do not have insurance. When Pete adds up his losses, he will find that they come to much more than the cost of renters' insurance. Renters' insurance averages a little over $150 a year for a typical tenant. And the less you have, the less it costs for this type of insurance.

Not only is Pete unprotected from losses caused by theft and fire, he is also unprotected from lawsuits. You may think that if you don't own a building or a car, you don't need liability insurance to protect against lawsuits. But it is possible to cause accidents in all sorts of ways.

Jill Hanson was trying out her new golf clubs in the yard behind her apartment. She tried a few easy shots to get the feel of the clubs. Unfortunately, she put a little extra swing into one of her shots. It bounced off the house and hit a delivery person in the eye.

The delivery person sued Jill for medical bills, loss of income while recovering, and legal expenses. Jill lost a lot more than a golf ball.

Tenants, like Pete and Jill, are concerned mainly about two types of losses. First, like Pete, they can lose personal property. The law defines **personal property** as all tangible possessions except land and anything fixed permanently to the land. So personal property includes clothes, stereos, furniture, books, and so on. Losses to this property can be caused not only by fire or theft but also by smoke or water damage, windstorms and hail, vandalism, and collisions of cars or planes, to mention just a few dangers.

In addition, like Jill, tenants should have liability insurance to protect against financial loss from lawsuits if they cause someone

Loss of your property can be due to more than theft. Some insurance policies will also cover damage resulting from "acts of God."

injury. Fortunately, Jill had **personal liability insurance** to help pay the expenses of injuries she causes to others. It not only paid for the actual damages to the delivery person but also paid Jill's legal expenses. Jill's personal liability insurance also protects her when she is away from home. It will protect her, for example, if she injures someone on a golf course.

✓ check your understanding ✓ ✓ ✓ ✓ ✓ ✓

1. **If you rent, what property is protected by your landlord's insurance? What property is not covered by your landlord's insurance?**
2. **Why do renters need to be protected by personal liability insurance?**
3. **What kinds of property are classified as personal property?**
4. **What sort of dangers can cause personal property losses?**

WHY HOMEOWNERS NEED INSURANCE

As you would expect, once you buy a house or condominium, your need for insurance increases. Like tenants, homeowners are concerned about loss of personal property. In addition, owners of houses, condominiums, manufactured housing, and other types of factory-built houses have another kind of property. They own **real property**, which the law defines as land and all buildings attached to the land. It is not hard to see why it is important for homeowners to insure their homes. They stand to lose tremendous amounts of money if their homes are destroyed or damaged.

Homeowners also have a greater need for liability insurance than renters do. Homeowners are responsible if someone is injured on their property. If the newscarrier trips on your front stairs, you are liable. In the previous case study, Jill's landlord is also responsible for the delivery person's injuries because the person was injured on the landlord's property.

How Homeowners Buy Insurance

Most people buy a package of insurance that includes both liability insurance and protection for personal and real property. This package is called a **homeowners' policy**.

Homeowners' policies can be purchased from an insurance agent. This person may represent one or more insurance companies. A wise consumer will check with two or three agents to compare prices and kinds of coverage. In the interview that follows, an insurance agent describes many of the different kinds of homeowners' policies a consumer can buy.

Your dog, Booboo, is a friendly, tail-wagging pooch. A neighbor's child claims she was bitten by Booboo. Are you responsible? It all depends on the situation, but probably not. Most laws say the dog gets the first bite for free. Unless owners know their dogs are dangerous, they do not have to do anything special to protect people from their pets.

In 1735, the first fire insurance company in the United States was formed in Charleston, South Carolina. Five years later, a fire burned down about half the town. The insurance company went out of business shortly afterward.

Homeowners' Insurance Pyramid

Perils

Basic (HO-1)

1. fire or lightning
2. loss of property removed from premises endangered by fire or other perils
3. windstorm or hail
4. explosion
5. riot or civil commotion
6. aircraft
7. vehicles
8. smoke
9. vandalism and malicious mischief
10. theft
11. breakage of glass constituting a part of the building

Broad (HO-2)

12. falling objects
13. weight of ice, snow, sleet
14. collapse of building(s) or any part thereof
15. sudden and accidental tearing asunder, cracking, burning, or bulging of a steam or hot water heating system or of appliances for heating water
16. accidental discharge, leakage or overflow of water or steam from within a plumbing, heating or air-conditioning system or domestic appliance
17. freezing of plumbing, heating and air-conditioning systems and domestic appliances
18. sudden and accidental injury from artificially generated currents to electrical appliances, devices, fixtures and wiring (TV and radio tubes not included)

Comprehensive (HO-5)

All perils **EXCEPT:** earthquake, landslide, flood, surface water, waves, tidal water or tidal wave, the backing up of sewers, seepage, war, and nuclear radiation.

Categories of insurance policies are determined by the number of perils they cover.

In addition to automobile, life, and fire insurance there are many types of homeowners' insurance

We carry six different types of homeowners' policies. Four are designed for people who own houses. One is for renters. The last one is for people who live in condominiums. My company sells all four kinds of house insurance.

All of our policies for house owners protect against losses from theft. Most policies also pay hotel and living expenses if you have to live away from your home for a while because it has been damaged. In addition, they all pay costs resulting from lawsuits if someone is injured on your property and you're at fault. This is important because many people do sue. This personal liability coverage is usually limited to $100,000 in personal injury claims, $1,000 in medical claims, and $500 worth of damage to someone else's property per claim.

The differences in our four policies have to do with the number of other dangers covered by the policy. The more dangers (or perils, as we in the insurance industry call them) the policy covers, the more it costs. First, we have the basic form, called HO-1 (Homeowners'-1). It covers damage to a house and its contents from eleven perils, including fire, windstorms, and theft. You can see what perils are covered in the chart I have here (page 376). Next, we have the broad form, called HO-2. This policy covers everything that the basic form covers and also seven more perils. The third form we carry is called HO-3. This policy provides the most coverage for the house itself but less coverage for personal property. The last type of house insurance we carry is the comprehensive form, called HO-5 or all-risks policy. This package provides maximum coverage to both the house and the personal property in it. All four policies protect not only your house but also other buildings on your property, such as garages and tool sheds.

Comprehensive insurance protects you against a great many perils. But no insurance company can protect you from everything. Some perils cause such widespread damage that insurance companies cannot afford to offer protection and still keep premiums at reasonable levels. So you'll find that none of our policies covers damage from floods, earthquakes, mudslides, war, nuclear accidents, chemical contamination, or any other peril specifically said to be left out.

We also sell HO-4, a renters' policy. It insures household contents and personal belongings against all of the perils included in the broad form policy. Since a renter doesn't need insurance on the building, this type of policy costs less than a regular broad form policy. The renters' policy also provides funds for living away from home in case the apartment is damaged.

The last type of insurance, HO-6, is for condominium owners. It is much like the renters' policy. It covers personal property, but not the building. This policy also covers any additions or alterations that the owner has made to the condominium.

I'd recommend any one of the homeowners' package policies. They're all about 20 percent cheaper than the same protection would be if you bought separate policies for fire, theft, liability, and additional living expenses. Also, if you can buy a homeowners' policy for three years instead of one year, you would get a better rate.

DON WILLIAMS
Insurance Agent

"

An inventory of your personal belongings will help your insurance company settle your claim.

Today's homeowners' policies provide more coverage than those of a few years ago. For example, students' personal property in dormitories is covered in their parents' homeowners' policies. Some condominium owners' policies now include coverage to pay for their losses stemming from lawsuits involving common areas if these losses are not fully covered by the joint insurance covering the condominium.

Some policies now provide **full replacement cost coverage** on your home and personal property. If your house or any personal property is destroyed, the insurance company will pay to have it replaced rather than pay you what your personal property is currently worth. In general, personal property is always worth less than it costs to replace it because, like a car, it depreciates. For example, say your five-year-old television is stolen. Because it's five years old, it has depreciated. When it was new it cost $450. At the moment it's worth only $75. But a new one of the same kind now costs $575. If you have full replacement cost coverage, the insurance company will give you enough money to buy a new set—$575. If you do not have full replacement cost coverage, the insurance company will pay you only what the set is worth now, or $75.

Flood Insurance

About 7 million people live in places that could be flooded. Because homeowners' policies do not cover flood damage, about two thirds of these people are not insured for this risk.

One third of these people, however, are insured. They are covered because they have chosen to participate in the federal government's National Flood Insurance Program (NFIP). To be able to buy this insurance, you have to live in a community that has agreed to participate in the program. Once your community agrees, it must follow several steps to help reduce the risk of flood damage. The more your dwelling is at risk from flooding, the more flood insurance will cost you—but the more you probably need it as well. You can buy this type of insurance through your local insurance agent.

If you are insured for at least 80 percent of the market value of your home, this insurance will pay to rebuild your house if it is destroyed in a flood. To get a VA or FHA loan, you must buy this type of insurance if you live in a flood hazard area. Many other lenders also require it.

How Much Insurance Do You Need?

You can insure a house for any amount up to its market value—the price you could sell your house for right now. If the house is completely destroyed, by fire for example, the insurance company will pay you the full amount of your policy. Suppose you own a house that's worth $100,000. You insure it for $100,000. A tornado wipes out the house. The insurance company will pay you $100,000. If you had insured the house for $75,000, though, the insurance company would only pay you $75,000, no matter what the house is worth. If you had full replacement cost coverage, the insurance company would pay to have the house rebuilt.

Experts advise you to insure your house for at least 80 percent of its full market value. Generally, that is enough because it is rare for a house to be completely destroyed. Usually, the foundation and the land are still left even in the worst disasters. So 80 percent of the full market value of a house is generally enough money to cover the cost of rebuilding if a house is completely destroyed.

There is another reason why you should insure a house at 80 percent of its full market value. Suppose you have a fire and only the kitchen is destroyed. If your house is insured for at least 80 percent of its full market value, the insurance company will pay the full cost of replacing your kitchen. But, if your house is only

In a fit of anger, a homeowner hits a door-to-door salesperson. The salesperson sues for injury. Will the homeowners' insurance policy cover the damages? No. Policies don't cover damages that insured people cause on purpose.

Installing safety devices, like fire extinguishers and smoke detectors, can save you money on your insurance.

If you have an insurance claim and can't agree on a settlement with your insurance company, what do you do? Call your state's insurance commissioner. He or she will explain your legal rights under the policy. If your insurance company is in error, the commissioner will step in. The help and advice the commissioner gives you are free.

partially insured, your insurance company will deduct depreciation, as it would for car insurance. So, if your kitchen were old, your insurance company would settle for much less than it would cost you to replace it at today's prices.

Most homeowners' policies have deductible clauses. As with car insurance, you must pay the deductible before the insurance company pays the rest. The larger your deductible, the lower your insurance premiums.

You can also reduce the cost of homeowners' insurance by installing smoke detectors, fire extinguishers, security systems, and deadbolt locks.

✓check your understanding ✓ ✓ ✓ ✓ ✓ ✓

1. **Why might it be wise to have replacement cost coverage?**
2. **Which kind of house insurance is the most expensive to purchase? Which is the least expensive? Why?**
3. **Why does the broad form of house insurance cost more than the insurance for renters?**
4. **How can you reduce the cost of homeowners' insurance?**

MAKING A CLAIM

If you suffer a loss, your insurance company will pay up to the total amount you are insured minus the deductible. But you may be asked to prove how much you have lost. How can you do that if your property is gone? Before anything happens, you should take an inventory of your personal property. An **inventory** is a list of all your possessions—your furniture, your clothes, and your other belongings. The list should include the age of each item, what it originally cost you, what it is worth now, and any model numbers. Some insurance agents will give you forms for taking the inventory. It is also helpful to keep any receipts you have for more expensive personal property such as steroes and video cassette recorders. If you take care to keep this inventory up to date as you purchase additional items, you will have a much easier time if you have to make a claim.

If you have a loss, your agent will tell you how to report it. If the damage to your home is so great that you need to move out while repairs are being made, your agent will also tell you how to apply for the money that may be needed to cover the additional living expenses. If you have a partial loss, you must prepare a list of all damage that was done. As you can see, it is important to shop around not only for the best insurance rates but also for a good agent who will be helpful in an emergency.

EXTRA PROTECTION

Your homeowners' policy probably will not fully cover special types of property such as jewelry, fine art, stamp and coin collections, boats, and computers. For these items, you need to make additions to your policy. These additions to cover specific items of personal property are called **floater contracts**. They are called floaters because the policies float with the property wherever it goes. If, for example, you take out a special policy to protect a diamond engagement ring, your ring is protected no matter where it is. It does not have to be in your home to be covered. Floaters generally have no deductible. As you might expect, floater contracts add to the cost of your policy.

Another kind of policy, called an **umbrella policy**, gives you additional liability coverage. This policy gives you $1 million of personal liability coverage. It costs about $150 a year. Many insurance companies require you to buy a homeowners' policy and auto insurance from them before they will sell you an umbrella policy.

A floater contract to a homeowners' policy is required to cover antiques or other special items.

1. What help is an inventory?
2. Why might a person need a floater contract added to an insurance policy?
3. From whom can you buy an umbrella policy? What is an umbrella policy for?

SUMMARIZING
the chapter

Renters and homeowners lose billions of dollars worth of property each year as a result of fire, theft, and other perils. They lose both personal property—such as stereos and clothes—and real property, like houses and garages. In addition, both renters and owners may owe thousands of dollars if they lose a liability suit.

To protect against these possible dangers, insurance companies offer different packages of insurance. One package is just for renters. Another is designed especially for condominium owners. Four packages are offered to owners of houses. These policies protect against fire, theft, vandalism, and windstorms. Three of the policies offer house owners protection against a number of other perils.

Homeowners' policies have expanded their coverage in recent years. Some companies now offer full replacement cost coverage on dwellings and personal property.

None of the homeowners' policies protects against floods, earthquakes, mudslides, chemical contamination, or nuclear war. It is sometimes possible to take out special policies to protect against these risks. The most common of these special policies is the National Flood Insurance Program funded by the federal government.

You should insure your house for at least 80 percent of its current market value. If you don't, you will not be paid the full amount of a claim if your house is only partially damaged. To make sure that you will be able to recover your losses, be sure to make an inventory of your possessions.

You can reduce the cost of your homeowners' insurance if you comparison shop, buy three-year policies, install safety equipment in your home, or accept a larger deductible.

If you feel you need additional coverage, you may take out floater contracts to protect special items of personal property such as jewelry or boats. You may buy additional liability insurance through an umbrella policy.

CHAPTER ACTIVITIES

BUILDING CONSUMER VOCABULARY

Number your paper from 1 to 12. Then write the term that best matches each numbered definition.

basic form
broad form
comprehensive form
floater contracts
full replacement cost coverage
homeowners' policy

inventory
perils
personal liability insurance
personal property
real property
umbrella policy

1. Possible dangers—such as fire, windstorms, or theft—that could cause damage to personal or real property
2. The homeowners' insurance policy that covers the least number of perils
3. An insurance policy that provides $1 million worth of protection against liability lawsuits
4. Additions to your homeowners' policy that cover special items
5. The homeowners' insurance policy that provides the most coverage for both a house and the personal property in it
6. An option of homeowners' insurance that pays the replacement cost of personal property, with no deduction for depreciation
7. A homeowners' insurance policy that covers everything covered by the least expensive kind of house insurance plus seven more perils
8. Insurance that protects against personal injury claims
9. A kind of property consisting of land and anything permanently fixed to the land
10. All possessions except land and everything permanently attached to the land
11. An itemized list of an individual's personal property
12. An insurance package that includes both liability insurance and protection for personal and real property

BUILDING CONSUMER UNDERSTANDING

1. Why do homeowners and tenants need property insurance?
2. How much personal property would a tenant need to own to make buying renters' insurance worthwhile?
3. Why should you insure your house to at least 80 percent of its full market value?

4. Which homeowners' policies would cover damage caused by a broken water pipe? theft? earthquakes?
5. Why do people who own condominiums need a kind of insurance that is different from the kind house owners buy?
6. Why don't homeowners' policies protect against nuclear war?
7. If your house is destroyed in a flood, what will flood insurance do? Who can buy flood insurance?

BUILDING CONSUMER MATH SKILLS

1. How much coverage do you need if you own a house whose market value is $90,000 and you wish to collect the entire cost of losses from partial damage to your dwelling?
2. Suppose you bought a house for $92,000 in 1985. This year, it could sell for $140,000. To be fully protected, how much homeowners' insurance did you need when you first bought the house? How much insurance do you need now?
3. Three years ago, you bought a computer for $2,100. This year, it was destroyed in an electrical fire. You are insured, but you do not have full replacement cost coverage. The insurance company tells you that the computer has depreciated 40 percent since you bought it. You have a $100 deductible. How much will the insurance company pay to cover your claim for the computer?

APPLYING CONSUMER SKILLS

Imagine that you just moved into an older one-bedroom apartment. The building is run-down and in a high-crime area. But the rent is cheap.

Your parents have let you take most of your old bedroom furniture. You estimate that it would cost you about $2,000 to replace all of your clothes. Relatives and friends have given you some used living and dining room furniture and kitchen equipment. You have used most of your savings to buy a new 19-inch color television for $525. You also have a good stereo system, but it's broken and needs $135 in repairs.

A local insurance agent offers to sell you a renters' policy with a $250 deductible for $135 per year.

You must decide whether to buy the policy for $135, keep the $135 in a savings account to use in case something happens to your things, or use the $135 to fix your stereo. Construct a decision-making grid to find out which would be the best choice for you.

GETTING INVOLVED IN YOUR COMMUNITY

Assume that you have a single-family house worth $110,000 in your neighborhood. Visit three insurance agents and find out how much a comprehensive homeowners' policy would cost to insure that house up to 80 percent of its value. If the rates differ from agent to agent, find out why.

**CRITICAL
THINKING**

**THINKING
ABOUT:**

*Real
Estate
Ads*

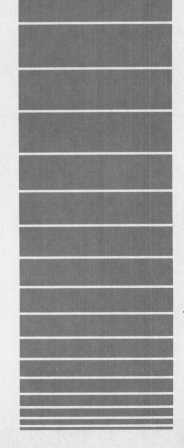

Jason and Melissa have finally saved enough for a down payment on a house. However, as they read real estate ads, they discover that the ads make the houses sound much better than they look. For example, "cozy" homes turn out to be small and cramped. Houses described as having "original charm" are disasters of poor taste. "Handyman special" or "needs TLC" means that a house is falling apart.

When reading ads, Jason and Melissa have learned to separate facts from judgments. For example, "three bedrooms" is a fact; "beautiful" is a judgment. What is beautiful to one person might be ugly to another. Read these real estate ads. Then answer the questions that follow on a separate sheet of paper. Use complete sentences.

- Exciting possibilities! This quaint home is nestled in a beautiful, secluded rustic setting. It needs a little fixing up, so it's perfect for the buyer with more vision than money. This country home features two lovely bedrooms and an airy, open kitchen. Call today!

- A sweeping staircase leads you into an interesting and unusual floor plan. This updated colonial features four bedrooms, two bathrooms, a fireplace, a living room, a formal dining room, and a kitchen that is sure to delight an antique lover. A newer roof and nice, level lot complete the picture.

1. What are the facts in each ad?

2. What are the judgments, or opinions, in each ad?

3. How might the features differ from the judgments?

Write real estate ads for the following properties. Make the negative features seem like positive features.

- This home is in the suburbs. It has three bedrooms, two baths, a living room, a dining room, and a kitchen. The fenced yard is overrun by destructive squirrels, moles, and raccoons. After heavy rains, small streams flow through the backyard and flood the basement. The kitchen cabinets are 50 years old and very scarred.

- A small, two-bedroom, one-bath condominium on a busy, heavily trafficked downtown street. There is no room for parking. A restaurant is located next door. The air usually smells of roasting garlic, fried onions, and hot olive oil.

YOUR FINANCIAL SECURITY

SAVING YOUR MONEY

People often talk about the importance of putting some money aside for the future. It's easier said than done. If you have a plan, though, saving money doesn't have to be hard. Some ways of saving are safer than others. Some ways are more profitable than others. Which savings choices are for you?

- **What are some of the reasons people put money into savings?**

- **What is compound interest?**

- **Where can you save your money?**

- **Into what types of accounts can you put your savings?**

It is very easy to spend all of your income. In fact, it may be very hard not to. But if you spend all of your money as you earn it, you may never get some of the things you really want.

SAVINGS GOALS

Perhaps you've heard people say that it's wise to save some money for a rainy day. Do you agree? Do you believe that this advice applies to you? Maybe you feel that you won't need to save until you are much older. Maybe you believe that only rich people can afford to put money into savings.

Certainly, if you don't have money, you can't save it. But saving is important for anyone who wishes to reach long-term spending goals. It may be more important for people with lower incomes than for those with money to spare. By saving a little at a time, you may be able to put aside enough to reach spending goals you could not otherwise achieve.

The case studies that follow show how some people reached their goals through saving while other people didn't.

People can save for other people's futures as well as their own. Parents often set up *school savings accounts* for their children's education. If they open an account when a child is an infant, there won't be a scramble for college tuition later.

Wise money management will enable you to save enough to buy the things you want.

CASE STUDY

Saving for spending

Curtis Lyons and Lee Miller worked after school at the Brown Bag grocery store. They each took home about $80 a week. They each had the same dream—of being set free on a KamiKaze 250 moped.

To make his dream a reality, Curtis saved some of his pay. He put about $40 of each weekly paycheck into a savings account. By the end of the year, he had over $650, enough to buy a brand new KamiKaze.

Lee was shocked the day Curtis pulled into the Brown Bag parking lot on the KamiKaze. "How'd you get that bike?" Lee asked.

"I just saved some of the money I earned here," Curtis said.

Lee didn't understand. They both worked at the Brown Bag, but Lee didn't have nearly enough money saved for a KamiKaze.

CASE STUDY

Saving for your dreams

Gordon and Connie Holman had always wanted to buy a house, but they never could save enough money for the down payment. Finally, Gordon went to see Michelle Barnes at his company's credit union. Michelle arranged for Gordon to have $250 a month deducted from his paycheck. It would be deposited directly into the Holmans' credit union savings account. In this way, Connie and Gordon would automatically save $250 each month.

In five years, the Holmans had saved $15,000, plus interest. They used their money for a down payment on a house. Gordon and Connie learned that it is not always easy to save. After all, that extra $250 a month would have made life a lot easier. They had to make many sacrifices during those five years. But their goal of buying a house made the sacrifices worthwhile.

Saving money is hard work. To make it a little easier, experts recommend that you set savings goals—that you know what you are saving for. Your savings goals, of course, will be determined by your values, lifestyle, and other life goals. Like Curtis, many young people save for motorcycles or cars. They also save to pay for further education. As you grow older, you may, like the Holmans, wish to save for the down payment on a house or a condominium. You may also want to save money for your retirement. Remember, saving today means you'll have money to spend tomorrow.

1. **How did Curtis Lyons realize his goal?**
2. **How can a person save automatically?**
3. **Name three savings goals many people have.**

SAVINGS PLACES

Once you have decided on your savings goals, you must decide where to put your money. You could put it under your mattress, in a cookie jar, or in a shoe box in your bedroom closet. Years ago, many people did just that. But you may be able to see some problems with that approach. First, your money may not be safe from fire or theft. Second, you may be tempted to spend it if it is so easy to reach. Third, your money will earn no interest in these places. For these three reasons, most people put their savings in one of a number of financial institutions. Financial institutions include commercial banks, savings and loan associations, mutual savings banks, and credit unions.

In the past, federal regulations created sharp differences in the kinds of services these different institutions were allowed to provide. Today, however, many of these federal regulations have been lifted, and the lines between the different types of financial institutions are not as clear-cut as they used to be. Still, there are some differences. Different institutions may offer better rates on some services because most of their business is still concentrated in certain areas.

In colonial times, anybody could start a bank. As in different countries today, each bank printed its own money, called *bank notes*. Hundreds of different bank notes were issued. But these notes were only as reliable as the bank that printed them. So, many of the notes were not worth much.

Commercial Banks

A commercial bank is one that provides a wide range of banking services. As a matter of fact, it is often called a *full-service* bank. Commercial banks offer savings accounts and checking accounts to both consumers and businesses. These banks lend the money that they get from these accounts to a variety of borrowers. They may lend money to businesses. They may lend money to foreign countries. They may lend money to consumers. In addition, these banks offer other services. They may manage other types of investments such as stocks and bonds, offer multipurpose credit cards, and exchange foreign money.

Savings and Loan Associations

In the past, savings and loan associations mainly offered savings accounts and home mortgage loans. They still fund about 50 percent of the mortgage loans taken out in this country. Now they may offer checking accounts and other consumer services that commercial banks provide. But you may find that some savings and loans still specialize in consumer services. So interest rates on consumer savings accounts may be slightly higher at a savings and loan than at a commercial bank.

Mutual Savings Banks

Mutual savings banks are much like savings and loan associations. Interest rates tend to be similar on savings accounts, and most of their loans are also home mortgage loans. They are called "mutual" because they are mutually, or jointly, owned by their depositors.

Credit Unions

You know that a credit union is a place where you can get a loan. But there would be no loans without savings. You may recall that credit unions often have fewer expenses than commercial banks and savings and loan associations because some of their employees are unpaid volunteers. So credit unions may not only offer low interest on their loans, they also tend to offer higher interest on their savings accounts.

KEEPING YOUR MONEY SAFE

Your money is safer in a financial institution than it is under your mattress. But your money is not completely safe even in a financial institution. The institution can make bad loans and lose your money. It can go out of business. But your money is safe in a financial institution if it is insured.

Fortunately, accounts in most financial institutions are insured. In general, if the institution goes out of business, or is robbed or burns down, your money is insured up to $100,000. If you have more than $100,000 in savings, you should keep the money in separate savings institutions. If you have two accounts in your name in the same bank that together total, say $150,000, you will not be insured for the additional $50,000.

The Federal Deposit Insurance Corporation (FDIC) insures accounts in commercial banks and mutual savings banks. The Federal Savings and Loan Insurance Corporation (FSLIC) insures accounts in savings and loans. The National Credit Union Association insures money in credit unions.

Savings and loan associations may also be called "building and loan associations," or "homestead associations," or "cooperative banks." Although they provide a variety of services today, they were started for the sole purpose of providing mortgage loans.

After the stock market crash of 1929, about 10,000 banks went bankrupt. The banks had put a lot of money into bad investments and had kept very little money in reserve. When the banks' depositors tried to withdraw their money, there wasn't much there. And the money was not insured. The FDIC was created at that time to prevent future depositors from losing their savings.

Not all financial institutions are insured. If you don't see the FDIC or FSLIC symbol displayed in a commercial bank, mutual savings bank, or savings and loan, ask for proof of membership. Before putting your money in a credit union, ask for proof of insurance. Do not put your money in a financial institution that is not insured.

✓check your understanding ✓ ✓ ✓ ✓ ✓ ✓

1. **Why are commercial banks also called full-service banks?**
2. **What do financial institutions do with the money consumers put in savings accounts?**
3. **Suppose you had $130,000 in a single savings account in a commercial bank that was insured by the FDIC. How much of your money would be insured? What could you do to make sure all of it was insured?**

MAKING YOUR MONEY WORK

This graph indicates what saving $50 a month would earn. The black line shows savings earned without interest. The blue line shows a savings account earning 7 percent interest.

When you save, your money should work as hard for you as you worked to earn it. It will work for you if it earns interest. By earning interest, your savings will grow. If you put your money in a financial institution's savings account, it will earn interest. If you leave your savings in a cookie jar or under a mattress, you earn no interest.

How much of a difference does interest make? The graph below can show you. The graph shows what happens if you put $50 a month in a financial institution that pays 7 percent interest. It also shows what happens if you put that money in a cookie jar and it earned no interest.

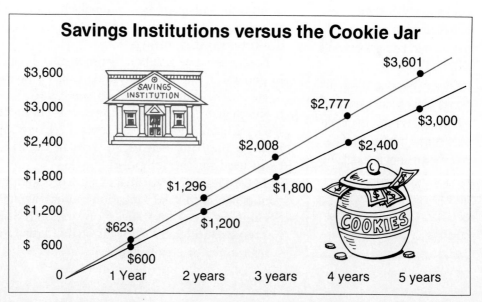

Savings Institutions versus the Cookie Jar

$3,600	
$3,000	$3,601
$2,400	$2,777
$1,800	$2,008 $3,000
$1,200	$1,296 $2,400
$ 600	$1,800
	$623 $1,200
	$600
0 1 Year 2 years 3 years 4 years 5 years	

Do You Need a Safe Deposit Box?

Where would you store the inventory for your homeowners' insurance, the deed to your house, or your birth certificate? Since these documents would cost a lot of time or money to replace, many people would lock them up in a *safe deposit box*. Safe deposit boxes are rented from banks.

Into this box you can also put jewelry, stamp collections, or small items of sentimental value, such as photographs, which could be impossible to replace if stolen or lost in a fire. It is not wise to store money in the box because your money will not earn any interest.

Safe deposit boxes are rented from banks for a small annual fee ranging from $25 to $75. The box is stored in the bank's safe, which protects your valuables from fire and theft. Access to it, however, is limited to the bank's business hours. So you have to plan ahead if you want to wear your diamonds to the party on Saturday night.

A safe deposit box is the best place to store those items that are difficult or even impossible to replace.

At the end of five years, you will have $3,000 in the cookie jar. But at the end of five years, you will have $3,601 in the financial institution. Just by putting your money in the right place, you come out $601 dollars ahead. Economists call that extra $601 earnings. **Earnings** are the amount you receive from a return on an investment. In this case, you are putting your money in a savings account and receiving interest in return. So the amount of money you receive in interest is your earnings. In the next chapter you will learn about other types of investments, such as stocks and bonds, and the ways in which those investments produce earnings.

Compounding Your Earnings

Suppose you put $1,000 in a financial institution at a 6 percent interest rate. You leave it there for ten years. You might expect to have earnings of $600 (6 percent of $1,000 = $60; $60 a year for ten years = $600). Adding the earnings to your original $1,000, you'd have $1,600 in your savings account. Right?

Wrong! You will be pleased to find that you will have more than that. The financial institution pays **compound interest**. That is, it will pay interest not just on your principal, but on the interest you've already earned.

Here's how it works. Suppose the financial institution compounds interest annually. At the end of one year, it will pay 6 percent interest on your $1,000 principal. Your $60 earnings, added to your principal, gives you a total of $1,060. The second year, the institution will pay 6 percent interest on the full $1,060, not just on your original investment of $1,000. So at the end of the second year, you will have earnings of $63.60 instead of $60. Adding the $63.60 to your first-year total of $1,060 will give you $1,123.60.

Today's high yield interest rates

	RATE	YIELD
Certificates of Deposit		
32 Days but less than 6 Months	5.500%	5.576%
6 Months but less than 12 Months	5.600%	5.678%
12 Months but less than 18 Months	5.850%	5.936%
18 Months to 30 Months	6.200%	6.296%
Money Market Accounts		
Ultimate Money Market	5.250%	5.378%
Super NOW Account	5.250%	5.378%
Super Saver Account	5.500%	5.576%
IRA 18 Month Variable Rate	5.720%	5.844%
IRA 18 Month Fixed Rate	6.400%	6.555%

Most financial institutions compound interest more than once a year. They may compound interest four times a year, once a month, or even every day. The interest on the graph on page 392 was compounded monthly. The more often a financial institution compounds the interest, the greater your earnings.

Also, the more often a financial institution compounds interest, the higher your yield. **Yield** is the percentage by which your savings grows in a single year. The yield takes into account both the interest rate and the frequency of compounding. So, for example, if a financial institution offers 8 percent interest compounded once a year, the yield is 8 percent. But if the interest is compounded monthly, the yield is about 8¼ percent.

An important thing to remember when deciding where to save your money is how the interest is compounded. On some accounts, called "day in-day out" accounts, the interest is figured from the day you put the money in until the day you withdraw it. Other, less desirable, savings accounts pay interest only if you keep your money in until the day the interest is paid. For example, your account may pay interest on the last day of each month. If you withdraw your money a day earlier, you earn no interest for that month.

In finding the right savings institution, look not only for plans that offer safety and high interest rates but also for the compounding method that gives the highest effective yield. Often, this is a plan that compounds interest daily and pays interest from the date of deposit to the date of withdrawal.

Money When You Need It

Finding the right place to put your money is not just a matter of finding the account that pays the highest yield. You must consider other factors too. For example, like checking accounts, many savings accounts have fees or pay no interest if your account falls below the minimum balance required. You may not even be able to open some accounts without a minimum balance. In general, the higher the yield, the higher the minimum balance required. To get the highest yields, you may have to have quite a lot of money, perhaps as much as $1,500.

Another factor to consider is liquidity. Your savings may have high or low **liquidity**. That is, they may be more or less quickly changed to cash. If you put your money under a mattress in your bedroom, it has very high liquidity. You can take it out and spend the cash whenever you want. Some types of savings accounts also have high liquidity. You can take your money out simply by going to the bank, writing a check, or even using an automatic teller machine (ATM).

You cannot always take your money out of a savings account anytime you want. Some accounts require you to give advance notice, sometimes a month's notice, perhaps as much as three

The Bank Secrecy Act requires banks to keep a record of customers' deposits and withdrawals. All papers concerning a person's account must be kept for five years. Banks must make these records available to federal agencies, such as the Internal Revenue Service (IRS) and the Federal Bureau of Investigation (FBI), if asked to do so.

months' notice. Other kinds of savings accounts do not allow you to take money out for a year—or even as long as ten years. If you do, you lose interest. These accounts have very low liquidity.

Which is better, high liquidity or low liquidity? As a general rule, the lower the liquidity, the higher the interest rate and yield. But high interest will do you no good if you can't get to your money when you need it. If, for example, you are saving for a down payment on a motorcycle, which you want to buy in six months, you do not want to put your money someplace that won't allow you to take it out for a year.

√check your understanding √ √ √ √ √ √

1. **Where should you put your savings in order to receive earnings?**
2. **Why should you compare yields, rather than interest rates, when deciding where to save your money?**
3. **What is the relationship between liquidity and yield?**

SAVINGS CHOICES

Even after you have decided what you are saving for and where you would like to put your savings, you still have more choices to make. Financial institutions offer consumers a variety of accounts. Here is a run-down of your savings choices.

Modern banking began in Italy over 500 years ago. Our word *bank* comes from the Italian word *banco,* meaning "bench." Why? In early times, Italian bankers set up benches along the streets to do business.

Banks offer many savings plans that provide high interest or easy access to your money

Passbook Accounts

Commercial and mutual banks, savings and loan associations, and credit unions offer **passbook accounts**. These accounts pay a low rate of interest, about 5½ percent, but they have very high liquidity. Many banks and savings and loans require a small minimum balance, generally not more than $20. If your balance falls below the minimum, the financial institution may not pay you interest. You may even be charged a fee.

Money Market Savings Accounts

Money market savings accounts are offered by banks and savings and loan associations. They are also known as *money market deposit accounts*. They pay an interest rate similar to a passbook account until your account reaches a certain balance level, usually $1,000 or $2,500. Then you get a higher rate. As with money market checking accounts, this rate varies, depending on market conditions.

A money market savings account is very liquid. When you open the account, you are given checks, as you would be with a checking account. You may withdraw money from the account whenever you wish with these checks. However, the number of checks you can write in a month is limited.

Many financial institutions charge a fee if your money market savings account slips below the minimum balance required. Some may also charge you if you write more than the minimum number of checks in a month. They may not let you deposit, or withdraw, less than a certain amount at a time. For example, some accounts may not let you write a check for less than $250 at a time.

Certificates of Deposit

Banks, savings and loans, and credit unions offer **certificates of deposit** (CDs), also called *savings certificates*. CDs offer you some of the highest interest rates available. But you give up liquidity to get those rates. With a CD, you deposit a lump sum of money for a certain length of time, commonly three months, six months, one year, two and one-half years, or five years. Many financial institutions even let you set your own length of time. The date when you may withdraw your money is the **maturity date**. The interest rate is usually set at the time you make the deposit, and this rate doesn't change. In times when market conditions cause interest rates to fall, putting your money in a CD is a good way to lock in a high rate of interest for the length of the term. If, however, interest rates go up while your money is in the CD, you cannot move your money to another account to take advantage of the better rates without paying a penalty. Be sure to find out how large the penalty is. It can amount to several months' interest.

How do we compare as savers with people in other countries? On average, people in the United States save about 6 percent of their money. People in West Germany save over 13 percent, on average. People in Japan save over 19 percent.

Where do we put our savings? Over 40 percent of us invest in certificates of deposit. Why are CDs so popular? Although CDs have low liquidity, they often pay high interest rates. People saving for long-term goals, such as retirement, may be looking for accounts with low liquidity. If their money is safely tucked away in a CD, they cannot spend it sooner than they intended.

Some financial institutions offer variable rate certificates. When interest rates rise, your CD's rate also goes up. But when interest rates fall, your CD's rate will fall.

Interest-Bearing Checking Accounts

Remember from Chapter 4 that financial institutions offer interest-bearing checking accounts. These accounts pay interest and often let you write as many checks as you wish, making them probably the most liquid of accounts. They often require a minimum balance, and you must pay a service charge or lose interest if your balance falls below that minimum. The interest rates for these accounts are usually lower than for money market savings accounts or for certificates of deposit. They may be lower than passbook accounts.

To meet minimum balance requirements, you may find it convenient to combine your checking and savings accounts. However, you may find it difficult to separate your savings from your spending money if they are both kept in the same account.

Money Market Funds

There is one kind of savings account that is not found in a savings institution. This account, called a **money market fund**, is offered by companies that sell stocks and bonds and other types of investments. The fund's managers lend the money put into these accounts to businesses and government for very short periods of time, usually less than a year, at fairly high rates of interest. Money market funds, therefore, usually have higher yields than bank, savings and loan, or credit union accounts.

The interest rate of a money market fund changes daily. The rate may be high today, but it could fall in a very short time. These accounts are riskier than money market accounts in banks not only because the rates change so often but also because the accounts are not insured by any government agency.

Money market funds offer high liquidity. With some funds, you may write checks from a money market account as you would from a checking account. There are no penalties for withdrawing your money. You may add any amount to your account at any time.

✓check your understanding ✓ ✓ ✓ ✓ ✓ ✓

1. **What kind of account offers the highest liquidity?**
2. **What happens if you withdraw money from a certificate of deposit before its maturity date?**
3. **Which type of account is not insured?**

SHOPPING FOR A SAVINGS ACCOUNT

In the case study that follows, Karen Wolff discovers the variety that consumers are offered when shopping for a savings account.

CASE STUDY

Karen Wolff received $150 in cash gifts from her relatives for her sixteenth birthday. With that much money suddenly on hand, she wanted to start a savings account. Her father said that different savings places offer different advantages. So Karen decided to shop around.

First National Bank

Karen's first stop was the First National Bank. Mr. Frazier, a savings representative, told Karen she could get 5½ percent interest, compounded daily, on a passbook account. She could also open an interest-bearing checking account that would pay 5¼ percent interest and let her write checks. However, if her balance ever fell below $100, she would have to pay a $6 service charge.

With a minimum first deposit of only $150, Karen could open only these two kinds of accounts. She would need more money if she wanted to buy a certificate of deposit. Perhaps, Mr. Frazier suggested, when Karen saved enough money she might want to buy a CD. The CD would pay about 2 percent more than a passbook or checking account. Mr. Frazier explained that Karen would have a choice of certificates. Maturity dates ranged from 90 days to eight years. The longer the term, the higher the interest rate. Mr. Frazier said the bank paid interest on the money in each certificate four times a year (March 31, June 30, September 30, and December 31). Karen thanked him and went on.

Sagamore Savings and Loan Association

Karen's next stop was Sagamore Savings and Loan Association. There, Ms. Parsegian, the savings counselor, offered Karen a passbook account that paid 5½ percent interest. But Karen wanted all of the facts. "How often do you compound interest?" she asked.

"Four times a year," Ms. Parsegian said. "And we also have interest-bearing checking accounts that pay 5¼ percent interest, but our minimum balance is $200. If you have less than $200, you will not receive interest. Like a bank, we have CDs, but you would need a lot more money."

Karen knew that the accounts at the bank and the savings and loan associations would be safe. She had seen the FDIC and FSLIC symbols on the doors.

Karen thought, however, that she could find higher interest rates. She decided to look into a money market fund. Her father told her that brokerage houses, companies that sell stocks and bonds, often offer money market funds. She decided to visit the Loyalty Brokerage House.

Loyalty Brokerage
At Loyalty, Mrs. Gonzales, the account representative, told Karen she could put her $150 into their money market fund. The fund was currently paying 7½ percent interest. But the interest rate changed every day. "Has it been going up or down?" asked Karen.

"Over the last six months, it has been going down slightly," Mrs. Gonzales replied, "but just this week, it started going up again."

"I know the money is not insured," said Karen. "How safe do you think it is?"

"Well," replied Mrs. Gonzales, "no one has ever lost money in one of our funds. We put the money in short-term investments. A lot of it is lent to the federal government. I think that our funds are about as reliable as the government. But you have to understand, that's just my opinion."

✓ check your understanding ✓ ✓ ✓ ✓ ✓ ✓

1. **Why would Karen's money be safe at the bank or savings and loan association?**
2. **Where would Karen be sure to earn the most interest now?**
3. **What other things besides interest should Karen think about in deciding where to put her money?**

*S*UMMARIZING
the chapter

Saving money now means being able to spend money in the future. Experts say that it is both easier and wiser to set specific spending goals before you save money. People save money for many reasons, for example, to buy cars, to pay for their education, to buy homes, and to save for their retirement.

Savers should put their money where it will earn interest. They can earn interest in commercial and mutual banks, in savings and loan associations, in credit unions, and in investment houses.

Interest is the percentage rate paid on your savings; the dollar amount paid is called the earnings. Most savings places pay compound interest. The yield is the percentage your savings will grow over a year. It depends on both the interest rate and the frequency of compounding.

Passbook savings accounts pay a low rate of interest and have high liquidity. Certificates of deposit pay higher interest rates, but have low liquidity because savers must leave their money in for a certain period of time. Many financial institutions offer interest-bearing checking accounts and money market savings accounts. Brokerage houses offer money market funds, which are completely liquid and usually have the highest rates. However, they are not insured.

C·H·A·P·T·E·R C·T·I·V·I·T·I·E·S

BUILDING CONSUMER VOCABULARY

Number your paper from 1 to 9. Then write the term that best matches each numbered definition.

certificate of deposit   money market fund
compound interest   money market savings account
earnings   passbook account
liquidity   yield
maturity date

1. The percentage by which your savings grows in a single year
2. The amount received from a return on an investment
3. Payment of interest not only on the principal but also on the interest already earned
4. The ease with which savings can be changed into cash
5. A kind of savings account in which a fixed amount of money is held for a certain period of time by a savings institution
6. A kind of savings account offered by businesses other than savings institutions
7. A savings account with high liquidity but low interest rates
8. A kind of savings account that offers a low interest rate when the balance in the account is small and a higher, variable rate after the balance reaches a certain level
9. The date on which you may withdraw your money from a CD without penalty

BUILDING CONSUMER UNDERSTANDING

1. How does compound interest help your money grow faster?
2. Why can the same rate of interest yield different earnings?
3. Why should you find out how liquid an account is?
4. What trade-offs might you have to make to get the highest yield on your savings?

5. What is the advantage of having a long-term savings account such as a certificate of deposit? What are the disadvantages?
6. What are the advantages of keeping your savings in an interest-bearing checking account? What are the disadvantages?
7. How do money market funds operate?

BUILDING CONSUMER MATH SKILLS

1. If you put $500 in a savings account at the beginning of the year, how much more in earnings would you have at the end of a year if the interest rate were 7 percent rather than 6 percent, compounded annually?
2. You put $200 into an account that pays 5½ percent interest, compounded annually. How much money will you have in the account after ten years? after 20 years?
3. If your bank compounds interest semiannually, how much will you earn in one year on $400 deposited in an account that pays 6 percent interest?

APPLYING CONSUMER SKILLS

How do you think your savings goals will change as you grow older? What are some things you're saving for now? What might you be saving for when you're 25? when you're 40? As your savings goals change, why might you choose different types of savings accounts? Give examples of a good account for you now, at age 25, and at age 40. Explain why you chose those accounts.

GETTING INVOLVED IN YOUR COMMUNITY

Where can you get the highest yield on your savings? Compare rates of interest on passbook accounts and certificates of deposit at three savings places in your community. For each account, answer the following questions:

1. What is the rate of interest?
2. How often is interest compounded?
3. When is interest paid?
4. Is interest figured from day of deposit to day of withdrawal? If not, how is it figured?
5. Are the savings insured? If so, who insures them? Where is the best place to save? What is the best savings plan?

INVESTING YOUR MONEY

When you have money left after paying your expenses, you may think about investing it. People invest their money in the hope that it will grow. How can you decide which investments are wise? How do you begin investing? How do you go about protecting an investment?

◆ How do businesses raise capital?

◆ What are the differences between stocks and bonds?

◆ What are capital gains?

◆ What do stockbrokers do?

◆ What are the advantages and disadvantages of investing in mutual funds?

NEW YORK STOCK EXCHANGE

In this chapter, we'll explore the exciting but unpredictable world of investing in stocks and bonds. We'll learn why more than 30 million people in the United States own stocks and bonds. We will learn ways to evaluate and choose among different investments. Finally, we'll see how the consumer with very little money to invest can enter this exciting, risk-filled arena.

WHY BUSINESSES SELL STOCKS AND BONDS

In Chapter 5, you learned that land, labor, capital, and entrepreneurship are the four resources that are required to produce goods and services. Capital refers to the machines, tools, and factories that businesses need to make products or provide services. Businesses also need another kind of capital. Businesses need money. In order to raise the large amounts of money necessary, corporations may sell **securities**—another name for stocks and bonds. By selling securities, a corporation can raise money to buy equipment and build factories. Selling securities helps a corporation grow.

Buying a Piece of the Business

In Chapter 6, you learned that the owners of a corporation are called stockholders. They become owners by buying stock in a corporation. People buy stock in units called *shares*. That's why stockholders are also called *shareholders*. A share of **stock**, then, is a share in the ownership of a corporation. Some stockholders may own only one share of stock. Others may own thousands of shares.

People who buy shares of stock risk only the money that they pay for that stock. If the corporation goes bankrupt, they may lose some or all of their investment. They will not have to use personal funds, however, to pay the debts of the corporation.

The word *bond* comes from the early English word *band*, which meant a "fastening." As a fastening holds a garment together, those who issue bonds are held to pay back the money that they've borrowed.

When buying or selling stocks you should have a professional, called a stockbroker, make the transaction for you.

Corporations can sell, or issue, two kinds of stock: common and preferred. All corporations must issue **common stock** in order to get started. Holders of common stock generally have the right to vote for the board of directors, which is the group of people who set corporation policies and hire the top management. Common stockholders may also have the right to vote on changes in corporate policy proposed by the board of directors.

As owners of the corporation, stockholders receive reports telling them how the corporation is doing. They may also receive part of the profits of the corporation in payments called **dividends**. If a stock is paying an annual dividend of $1 per share, for example, a stockholder who owns ten shares will get $10 that year. A stockholder who owns 100 shares will get $100. As a rule, corporations pay dividends only if they are making a profit.

The board of directors decides whether dividends will be paid each year. Dividends may vary from year to year depending on how much profit the corporation makes and whether the board of directors decides to distribute that profit to the stockholders. The board may decide, for instance, to put all of the profits back into the company. They may use the profits to raise employees' salaries or to buy capital equipment.

If dividends are paid by the corporation, preferred stockholders must receive theirs first, before the common stockholders. **Preferred stock** pays fixed dividends, such as $5 a year per share. No matter how much the dividend may be for the holders of common stock, if the company is paying dividends, the preferred stockholders will receive their $5 a share.

Lending a Business Money

Another way a corporation can raise money is by issuing bonds. While a share of stock represents ownership in a corporation, a bond represents a debt. A **bond** is a promise to repay, at some future date, money lent to the corporation by buyers of the bond. For example, you may buy a bond from the Granite Corporation for $10,000. You will be lending $10,000 to Granite Corporation. At a future date, also called the **maturity date**, Granite will pay you back your $10,000—plus interest. For most bonds, interest is paid periodically from the time the bond is bought until it matures.

Because a bond is a debt, bond interest is an expense for a corporation. Unlike dividends, interest must be paid—and it must be paid before any dividends are distributed. In addition, if a corporation goes bankrupt, the bondholders receive their money first. Stockholders receive what, if anything, is left after all debts are paid. Investing in bonds is usually safer than investing in stocks. Exceptions may be periods when interest rates are increasing, which can cause bond prices to fall.

The federal government, states, cities and towns, and government agencies issue bonds to raise money too. Your school system

Some executives in a corporation have "inside" knowledge about the corporation's plans. For example, they may know that a merger is planned, which usually causes stock prices to increase. If the executives who have this special information buy stock, knowing they will make a big profit, that's *insider trading*, and it's illegal.

In the investment world, what's hot and what's not changes. The best investments in the late 1980's were (in order) bonds, stocks, and Old Master paintings. But over a 15-year period, the best investments were (in order) oil, rare United States coins, and gold.

Construction costs for things such as this arena are often financed by the sale of bonds.

may issue bonds. It may have sold bonds to raise money to make repairs or to buy land, new buildings, or expensive equipment.

You may be familiar with one kind of bond that the federal government sells, **United States savings bonds**. With as little as $25, anyone can lend money to the federal government by buying one of these bonds. When the bond matures, the bondholder gets twice as much money as it cost to buy the bond. So, if you buy a United States savings bond for $25, you will receive $50 when it matures. These bonds do not pay a fixed rate of interest. If interest rates rise while you hold the bond, your bond will mature faster. If interest rates fall, your bond will take longer to mature. A rate of 6 percent with a 12-year maturity period is guaranteed at the time of purchase, however. The Federal Reserve Bank suggests that bondholders check with their banks, from time to time, to find out the interest rate and the estimated maturity date of the bond.

The Payoff

One reason people buy stocks and bonds is the same reason they might put their money in an interest-bearing savings account—to receive earnings in the form of dividends or interest. Economists call this savings goal *investing for income.*

The yield on a share of stock or on a bond is figured by dividing the dividend or interest by the amount invested. For example, if you bought a share of stock for $20, and after a year you received a $1 dividend, your yield would be 5 percent ($1 dividend ÷ $20 stock investment = .05, or 5 percent). You can now compare this rate of return against other savings and investment options.

Another important reason why investors buy securities is the hope that the price will go up. In other words, investors are hoping

Suppose a person invests $1000 a year at 7.5 percent interest for 42 years. Only $42,000 would be paid in, but at retirement time, there would be $295,000 to retire on. In fact, you could withdraw $1930 a month (interest) and never touch the principal.

to sell their stocks or bonds at a price higher than they paid for them. Economists call this savings goal *investing for growth*. For example, suppose you bought 100 shares of the Dolphin Publishing Corporation at $15 per share. A year later, you sold them for $20 per share. You gained $5 per share—what the tax people call a **capital gain**. In this case, the capital gain was $500 ($5 per share × 100 shares). Your yield from the capital gain was 33 percent ($500 capital gain ÷ $1,500 investment = .333, or 33 percent).

It is difficult to predict whether stock prices will go up or down. To some degree, the more profitable a corporation is, the higher its stock price will be. But that is not always true. No one can tell for sure whether the price of any particular stock will go up or down on any given day.

The prices of bonds change mostly as interest rates in general change. If you buy a $10,000 bond that pays 9 percent interest, for example, the value of your bond will fall if interest rates go up. That's because people will want to buy the bonds with higher interest rates. They won't want to buy your bond that has a lower interest rate. If you plan to keep your bond until its maturity date, you don't need to worry about the fall in the price of your bond. You will get the full $10,000 back then. But if you should need to sell your bond before that time, you could find that you have to sell it for less than you paid for it.

Investors who have purchased securities at low prices hope for a **bull market**, a market of rising prices. Unfortunately, a **bear market**, or a market of falling prices, can also occur. Sometimes, as the case study that follows shows, the payoff can be deceiving.

Why is a rising stock market called a *bull market?* Because bulls fling their horns up when they fight. So, the prices are going up as if on the horns of a bull. When stock market prices fall, it's called a *bear market* because bears strike downward with their paws when they fight.

CASE STUDY

As usual, Wally was standing on his patio bragging to his neighbor Paula about something he did. This time it was about the $450 interest payment he received on the $5,000 worth of bonds he purchased from the Electric Data Corporation. Wally explained that he knew a lot about securities. Paula was feeling envious. The $450 was a lot more interest than she could have ever gotten if she had put that $5,000 in a savings account. Terrific, thought Paula, but who has $5,000 to put into any investment? All she could afford to buy was 10 shares of Connors Corporation for $10 each, and that took a lot of courage for Paula. On top of that, she was embarrassed to mention, she got only 95 cents per share in dividends all last year.

1. **Calculate the yields for both investments. Which investment did better?**
2. **If Paula had paid $5 per share for her stock, what would her yield have been?**

1. Why do corporations sell stocks and bonds?
2. What are the differences between common and preferred stock?
3. How does a share of stock differ from a bond?
4. What is the difference between dividends and interest?

HOW TO GET STARTED

Investing in stocks and bonds is not a good idea for everyone. The first rule of investing in securities is never to use money you need for emergencies. Your job should be secure, and you should have money to provide for essential living expenses with some left over. Your savings should be large enough to meet emergencies and short- and long-term needs. In addition, money management experts point out that you should have a sound insurance program before investing in securities. You need adequate insurance protection for your life, health, home, and car.

Financial experts also believe that the right psychological attitude is important for investing in securities. Studies have shown that sensible investors make more money than gamblers. As an investor, you should expect moderate gains, and you must be willing to work hard to get them. You should carefully study the stocks and bonds you're interested in before you buy.

Going to a Stockbroker

After you've done your homework about the market, you are ready to go to a stockbroker. A **stockbroker** is a professional who buys and sells stocks for other people. For a fee called a *commission*, the stockbroker will arrange for you to buy and sell stocks. The stockbroker's commission is not based on how much money you make. The broker makes a commission each time you buy or sell stock.

Some stockbrokers work for traditional stock brokerage firms. These brokers will often give you advice about which securities they believe to be good investments. The company may send out reports about market conditions to help you as well. If you feel you don't need this help, you might want to do business with a discount stock brokerage firm. You will pay lower commissions using a discount firm. But you won't get any advice, and you may not get your own stockbroker. At some firms, whoever answers the telephone will take care of your trade.

Shares of stock are traded on a stock exchange. The New York Stock Exchange and the American Stock Exchange are the two

One financial consultant suggests a way to measure how good securities are as an investment. Compare the yield you make on securities with the yield you make on money in the bank. If the rates are about even, it's best to have your money in the bank. Your money is safer there.

What is a good return on an investment in the stock market? Financial experts say that the average long-term return on common stocks, historically the best performing investment around, is about 9½ percent per year.

best known stock exchanges in the United States. There are also regional stock exchanges in Chicago, Denver, Cincinnati, and elsewhere in the country.

Not all stocks are traded through stock exchanges. Some corporations, especially new ones and small ones, may have difficulty meeting the strict requirements of the exchanges. Other corporations just prefer not to have their stock traded on a stock exchange. Stock not traded through an exchange is called **over-the-counter stock**. Such stocks are bought through stockbrokers

The first stock exchange in the United States was founded in 1792. Before that time, people who wished to buy and sell stocks first had to find the stockbrokers. The brokers were often found gathering under a buttonwood tree on a particular street in New York City. Which street? Wall Street.

Ownership of millions of shares of stock changes hands daily on the floors of stock exchanges throughout the world.

who are able to give you the current price of an over-the-counter stock. Over-the-counter stock prices are also listed in the financial section of most daily newspapers.

Finding Information About Stocks

Every day, the results of trades on the New York and American stock exchanges are listed in many newspapers across the country. These listings hold a wealth of information that investors may use to make investment choices. But first, like the Bensons in the case study below, you have to find out how to read the stock listings.

CASE STUDY

Al and Rita Benson were more than a little concerned about how the stock market worked. They had received some common stock as a wedding present from Rita's uncle five years ago. They wanted to own more stock, but didn't know how to go about it. One day at work, Al's friend Nick mentioned that his sister-in-law, Ellen Stavros, was a stockbroker. Al called Ellen and made an appointment with her to talk about investing. At the meeting, Ellen explained the stockbroker's role.

"One way to invest is to use a brokerage firm like mine," said Ellen. "The people here are trained to help you plan your investments. Today we'll discuss your goals in investing, and I'll try to suggest a few stocks that you may want to look into.

"If you decide to buy, I'll telephone the order to our brokerage firm member on the floor of the stock exchange. He'll try to buy at the best price he can get at that particular time. Then we'll make sure you get your stock certificate, which we can send to you or hold here in the office. For these services, you pay us the price of the shares that you buy, plus our commission. If you want to sell your stock, we handle it about the same way. We're members of most stock exchanges, so we can get you just about any company's available stocks and bonds."

Al was very pleased with Ellen's advice and the materials she gave him. He took the material home, and he and Rita studied it. They read about a number of different companies. But they were stumped when they tried to read the stock listings in the newspaper to see how these companies' stocks had been doing recently.

The next day Rita called Ellen, who was happy to explain. When Al came home that evening, Rita turned to the financial section of the newspaper to share with him the new knowledge she had acquired.

"Here's the New York Stock Exchange general listings," she said, pointing to a page filled with small print. "And here's the company we're most interested in, General Leedown.

52 Weeks		Stock	Div.	Yld %	P-E Ratio	Sales 100s	High	low	Close	Net Chg.
High	Low									
55½	28¾	Gen Led	3.40	6.3	9	225	35	33¼	34¾	+ 1

Highest and lowest prices this year

Number of shares traded today

Dividend paid

Difference between last sale yesterday and today

Highest and lowest prices paid today

Net Chg.

Abbreviated stock name

Price-Earnings ratio

Price paid for last sale today

"You'll notice the abbreviation for General Leedown under the word *stock*. To the left of the stock name is the price range for the past 12 months, which has been as high as $55.50 and as low as $28.75 per share. To the right of the name is the annual dividend—$3.40 per share. The yield percentage based on the dividend is 9.8 percent. I got that by dividing the dividend, $3.40, by the price of a share.

"The next column is the **price-earnings ratio**, which Ellen explained as well. That's a figure arrived at by dividing the price of the stock now by the earnings per share over the past 12 months. This figure is used to judge how well a stock is doing—the lower, the better.

"In the *Sales 100s* column, you can find the number of shares traded, or changing ownership, today. To see how many shares of General Leedown were traded today, you multiply the number in the column by 100. Let's see. The number there is 225, so 22,500 shares of General Leedown were traded today. Further to the right, you can find the high and low prices for the day. Al, what were they?"

"A high of $35.00 per share and a low of $33.25," Al replied.

"Good. Now comes the hardest one. If the last sale, or closing price, of General Leedown stock was $34.75, what do you think the *Net Chg* means?"

"I think I read in one of Ellen's pamphlets that it means the difference between today's closing price and yesterday's. Since the net change is one, that means that yesterday's closing price was 33¾ or $33.75."

"Right! Now we both understand how to read the financial page. Let's find the listing for that stock my Uncle Jay gave us as a wedding present and see how it's doing."

✓ check your understanding ✓ ✓ ✓ ✓ ✓ ✓

1. **What services do stockbrokers provide? How do they earn their commissions?**
2. **What role does a stock exchange play in trading stocks?**
3. **What is the yield percentage on a stock? the price-earnings ratio?**

THE SMALL-TIME INVESTOR

Suppose you'd like to invest in stocks or bonds but don't have a lot of money to work with. Many such investors put their money in mutual funds. A **mutual fund** is a pool of money that is used by an investment company to buy a variety of stocks or bonds. The big advantage to investing in a mutual fund comes from *diversification*, which allows you to spread your money over several different investments. The value of some stocks or bonds may drop, but others will probably rise, so the risk of losing money is lower than if you put your money in a single stock or bond.

Another advantage of a mutual fund is that you save money on commissions. As an individual investor, you can end up paying a lot when you buy and sell stocks and bonds through a broker. But big mutual fund companies usually pay a lower percentage in commissions because of the large size of their purchases and sales. That savings is passed on to you.

Choosing a Stock Fund

There are many different kinds of stock mutual funds. Before you choose one, you must decide on your investment goals. One kind of mutual fund has growth as its goal. Its investments are designed to create capital gains. Its managers try to choose stocks of growing companies. The prices of those stocks are expected to rise quickly. If the mutual fund managers can buy those stocks at a low price and then sell them when they reach a higher price, the fund and its investors will earn capital gains.

Other funds have income as their goal. Managers of these funds choose stocks that they believe will pay high dividends. Still other types of funds combine both growth and income goals, so some of the stocks are selected because they are expected to rise in price while other stocks are chosen because they are expected to pay good dividends.

Stock mutual funds can be broken down in other ways. Some funds specialize in buying stocks of companies within one specific industry, such as entertainment or health care. Some specialize in foreign stocks and even in stocks of a single foreign country such as Japan. Some buy mainly over-the-counter stocks. Others buy stocks of large, very stable companies.

What about investing in gold and diamonds? Their prices go up and down. Over a long period of time, gold and diamonds grow in value, but if the market is down and you need to sell, you'll lose money.

Choosing a Bond Fund

There are several types of bond funds. Some are composed entirely of bonds issued by federal or state governments. These funds are often advertised as "tax-free" funds because the interest on some types of government bonds is not counted as taxable income. However, the interest rates on these government bonds are lower than on other bonds. You must decide, based on your income, whether a tax-free fund is a good deal for you. Generally, the higher your income, the better the deal.

Investing in IRAs

Even if you are covered by a company pension plan and social security, a personal retirement fund can help maintain a pre-retirement standard of living. You can establish an individual retirement account (IRA) if you do not have a company pension plan where you work or to supplement an already existing pension plan.

To encourage saving for retirement, the United States government does not tax, as part of your annual income, the dividends you earn in an IRA account until you withdraw from the account. If you wait until retirement to withdraw the funds, you are usually in a lower income bracket. The money, therefore, is not taxed at as high a rate as when you were a full-time wage earner making deposits into the fund.

There is an individual retirement account, called KEOUGH, for self-employed people. An individual can even establish an IRA account for a non-working spouse. A two-income couple can have two separate accounts.

Financial institutions such as banks, insurance companies, and investment firms sponsor IRA accounts. You can have your money invested in CDs, Treasury bonds, mutual funds, or other similar investments. You are allowed to transfer your funds from one kind of IRA account to another. If you leave your job, you are permitted to withdraw your funds from a company retirement plan for deposit in an IRA. The money you withdraw is not subject to a tax penalty as long as you reinvest it within 60 days from the time of withdrawal.

Money you withdraw from an IRA or Keough account before you reach age 59½ is subject to a tax penalty, and you must start withdrawals by age 70½. As with other investments, rates of return can vary widely. Shop around to find the account that best suits your savings objectives and future needs.

How much risk is there in junk bonds? One study showed that the default rate on junk bonds is 20 times higher than on high-quality corporate bonds. You may make a lot of money fast. But you may lose it all just as quickly.

Some funds specialize in high-quality, low-risk bonds. These are usually issued by large, established companies that grow at a slow but steady pace. Some funds specialize in very risky bonds, often called low-quality, or *junk bonds*. These bonds are issued most often by new, fast-growing companies that may produce high profits quickly but may also fail. The higher the quality of a bond, the lower the risk but the lower the interest rate too. You must decide how much risk you want to take to get a higher rate of interest.

Choose your mutual funds wisely. They're not all alike. They differ in terms of goals, fees, and performance. Get information about the funds you're interested in, and check how they've been performing in the past five or ten years. A fund that has done well over the last six months may have simply benefited from a bull market. One that has done well over ten years would appear to have smart managers.

✓ check your understanding ✓ ✓ ✓ ✓ ✓ ✓

1. How does a mutual fund operate?
2. What are the advantages of buying shares in a mutual fund instead of stocks or bonds of one company?
3. Describe two different goals stock mutual funds may be designed to reach.

SUMMARIZING
the chapter

Corporations sell both stocks and bonds to raise financial capital. Stocks are shares of ownership in a corporation. Shareholders receive dividends based upon the number of shares they own and the profits of the corporation. Common stock must be issued when a corporation gets started. This type of stock does not guarantee a dividend. Preferred stock guarantees dividends if the corporation makes enough to pay them. Bonds are the debts of the corporation.

People invest in stocks and bonds for many reasons. Some investors buy stocks and bonds to get high dividends or interest. They are said to be investing for income. Other investors buy stocks and bonds in hopes that their prices will go up and they can sell at a higher price than they paid. These investors are investing for growth. Many securities are traded by representatives of brokerage firms at the New York or American stock exchanges. Stocks not traded on a stock exchange are traded as over-the-counter issues.

Be careful if you invest in stocks and bonds. Use only money you can afford to lose. Even though your broker may recommend stocks to buy, you should check them out carefully yourself, and you should follow their progress in the daily newspaper stock listings. Your money will be safer if you try to earn steady yields than if you to try earn money quickly by investing in high-risk securities. For those interested in having a variety of securities, a mutual fund may be the answer. Mutual funds are run by professionals. Their aim is to gather small amounts of money from thousands of people and invest it in many different stocks or in corporate and government bonds.

C·H·A·P·T·E·R A·C·T·I·V·I·T·I·E·S

BUILDING CONSUMER VOCABULARY

Number your paper from 1 to 15. Then write the term that best matches each numbered definition.

bear market	over-the-counter stock
bond	preferred stock
bull market	price-earnings ratio
capital gain	securities
common stock	stock
dividends	stockbroker
maturity date	United States savings bonds
mutual fund	

1. The figure obtained by dividing the current price of a stock by the earnings per share over the past 12 months
2. Shares of ownership in a corporation
3. Stock that is not purchased through an exchange
4. A market of falling prices
5. A professional dealer in stocks and bonds
6. Stock that pays fixed dividends when a company pays dividends
7. Corporate profits paid to shareholders
8. A pool of money that is used by an investment company to buy securities from several different companies or sources
9. A market of rising prices
10. The amount realized by selling stocks or bonds at a price higher than that at which they were purchased
11. A loan to a corporation that must be paid back on a specific date
12. The kind of stock a corporation issues in order to get started
13. Another name for stocks and bonds
14. A debt of the federal government
15. The date on which a bond debt must be repaid

BUILDING CONSUMER UNDERSTANDING

1. Who decides what to do with a corporation's profits? In what ways can these profits be used?
2. Why and for what purpose can a school system issue bonds?
3. Which of the following people meets the requirements for a successful investor? Why?

a. Vic Polonna wants to buy common stocks. He has saved $5,500 in his first two years as an accountant. Vic is single, has auto insurance, and makes $26,000 a year. He is hard working, keeps up with fashions, and plans to buy stock based on careful research. He hopes for future capital gains.

b. Alice Slocum wants to buy securities because she thinks it could her double her money in a year. Alice plans to use part of her $18,000 savings to buy securities. Alice is divorced, has a seven-year-old child, and earns $17,500 in her fifth year with the bus company. She has a large life insurance policy plus renter's, health, and auto insurance.

4. Why is it unwise to use money you need for paying expenses to invest in stocks and bonds?

5. Name some of the requirements the experts feel you should have before starting an investment program.

6. What is meant by diversification? Is diversification a good thing or a bad thing? Explain.

7. Name some sources you could read to find information about stocks and bonds.

8. If you had a small amount of money to spare and wanted to invest it in securities that would give you money to use this year, where might you put it? Why?

BUILDING CONSUMER MATH SKILLS

1. Below is a stock price quotation from a daily newspaper. Examine the quotation, and answer the questions that follow.

Wednesday, May 3, 19— Sales										
52 Weeks				Yld	P-E	Sales				Net
High	Low	Stock	Div.	%	Ratio	100s	High	low	Close	Chg.
7¼	4¼	BAC Ind	5	1.10	8	10	5 ⅛	5	5	– ¼

a. What is the annual dividend of Bacon Industries?
b. What was the highest price it sold for in the last 12 months? What was the lowest price of the last 12 months? What are the highest and lowest prices it reached today?
c. What was yesterday's closing price for Bacon Industries?
d. What is the net change in the stock today?

2. Figure the annual yields of the following investments.
a. You buy a share of stock for $25 and receive an annual dividend of $1.50.
b. You buy bonds for $5,000 and get total annual interest of $600.

Ronnette Johnson is a 45-year-old widow with two children. She has $60,000 in savings from her late husband's life insurance. She is now working as a registered nurse. Her house is paid for, but Ronnette still has one child left to put through college. She is considering buying securities with all or some of her savings. What do you think she should do? Explain your reasoning.

Suppose you, together with one or two of your classmates, have $100,000 to invest. Go to the school or public library and research some securities you would like to buy. If possible, talk to stockbrokers and people you know about what to buy. Get many opinions. Select three stocks. Imagine that you bought those stocks. Graph the stocks' prices every day. Two weeks from the day you buy, "sell" your securities. How did you do?

INSURING YOUR LIFE

For many people, planning for the future involves buying life insurance. Life insurance policies provide protection for families if a wage earner dies. Life insurance policies are also used as a way to save for retirement. How do you know whether you need life insurance protection? How do you know whether saving through a life insurance policy is a good idea for you?

● Why do some people need life insurance while others don't?

● How should you determine how much life insurance you need?

● What is the difference between term insurance and cash-value insurance?

● How can you shop for the best buy in life insurance?

Life insurance can become complicated, but the main idea behind it is simple. If you have life insurance, you can provide financial security for someone who depends on your income.

Life insurance is similar to other kinds of insurance in that the policyholder, the person who is insured, pays premiums to the insurance company regularly—perhaps yearly, quarterly, or monthly. When the policyholder dies, the insurance company pays money to one or more people called **beneficiaries**. The beneficiaries, who are usually family members, are so named because they receive the benefits of the insurance.

The amount of money the beneficiaries receive is the **face value** of the policy. A $10,000 policy will pay the face value of $10,000 to the beneficiaries upon the death of the insured.

Life insurance differs from other kinds of insurance in that it may be used for a purpose other than providing protection against loss of income if a wage earner dies. Life insurance policies are also used as ways to invest money in long-term savings plans.

IS LIFE INSURANCE FOR YOU?

Some people, like most high school students, need no life insurance protection. Why? Because no one else depends on the money they earn. Other people, particularly people with children, need a lot of protection. Children would have no way of earning a living themselves if the person or people who support them suddenly died.

Unless this teen-ager's family depends on her income, life insurance for her life is not a necessity.

Since the main purpose of life insurance is to provide income for dependents, most of the insurance protection should be on the wage earner or wage earners. Insuring a wife or husband who is not employed also can make sense. In a family where there are small children who need child care, the death of a non-working husband or wife could also cause financial hardship.

In addition to insuring the family wage earner, it may also be important to insure the parent who stays home to care for young children.

How much life insurance is enough? One guideline used by an insurance association is to multiply your current salary by six. So, if you make $20,000 per year, that's $120,000. From that figure, subtract any group insurance, pension plan, or death benefits survivors would get from other sources. The remaining amount is how much life insurance you need.

In deciding how much life insurance protection you need, other things need to be considered too. Does the family have debts? A family with large debts needs more protection than one with small or no debts. The surviving family members would have to pay the debts if the wage earner died.

Another factor to think about is whether the dependents can count on money from other sources, such as social security or a company pension plan. A family that expects no other income needs more life insurance than a family that will receive money from other sources.

The family's goals are important too. Would the dependents be willing to change their lifestyle after the wage earner's death? Would they be willing to move if they could no longer afford their home? Is a lot of money needed for the children's further education?

Finally, a family must consider rising prices. A family should think ahead and try to have enough insurance to provide for needs and wants in future years.

✓check your understanding ✓ ✓ ✓ ✓ ✓ ✓

1. **What is the difference between a policyholder and a beneficiary?**
2. **Why do few high school students need to buy life insurance?**
3. **Who in a family should be covered by life insurance? Why?**

TYPES OF LIFE INSURANCE

All life insurance provides benefits to dependents if the policy-holder dies. Life insurance can also have other goals, such as providing a savings plan. Life insurance policies can be divided into two basic categories: those that do not accumulate cash value and those that do. A variety of policies is available within each category.

Policies Without Cash Value

Insurance that does not accumulate a cash value is called **term insurance**. A term policy is effective for a certain period of time called a term. Coverage stops at the end of the term, say five years, unless you renew the policy. Each time you renew, you are older and the risk of dying is greater, so the cost of your premiums goes up. Term policies pay only if the policyholder dies during the term of the policy. If the policyholder outlives the term and does not renew the policy, the beneficiaries get no money.

Level-term insurance There are two types of term insurance. With **level-term insurance**, the amount of protection stays the same while the premium increases each time the policy is renewed. Most level-term policies need to be renewed every year or every five years. If you buy a level-term policy, you should make sure the policy has the feature of **guaranteed insurability**. That is, make sure you can buy additional insurance in the future no matter what the state of your health. This feature can be purchased as a **rider**—an addition to your life insurance policy.

Decreasing-term insurance With the other kind of term policy, **decreasing-term insurance**, your premiums stay the same, but the amount of protection goes down. For example, a policy may give $10,000 protection the first year but only $2,000 in the last year. Decreasing-term insurance makes good sense if you have a home mortgage. As your mortgage grows smaller, your insurance needs also decrease. Since the value of most houses grows, though, the decrease in coverage may be too great. Instead, you may prefer to buy level-term insurance, and then drop the policy when you no longer need it.

The most common way to buy term insurance is through a **group life insurance** policy. Some people work where employers pay for this insurance, or they are members of an association that is able to get this type of policy. Since an entire group is insured, the premiums are usually lower than they would be if you bought the same insurance on your own.

Group life is a special bargain for older people who would have to pay high rates if they bought their own term policy. A disadvantage of group life, however, is that policyholders lose insurance protection if they leave the company or group.

Suppose you have a five-year term life insurance policy. If you get seriously ill after three years, can the insurance company cancel the policy? No. An insurer can't cancel the policy as long as you're paying the premiums.

After age 70, a person cannot buy a term life insurance policy in New York State. Would that worry most older people? Probably not. The income of most 70-year-old people is in the form of social security, pensions, or investments. Their dependents would still be able to live on that income even if they were gone.

Policies with Cash Value

Some life insurance policies use part of the premium to pay the cost of the insurance and the remainder to provide for savings. Such insurance is called **cash-value insurance** because it accumulates savings. The amount of savings increases each year and earns interest.

This kind of insurance gives you the opportunity to invest in a savings plan while providing financial protection for your dependents. Cash-value insurance provides less protection for your insurance dollar than term insurance, but anytime you wish to cancel your insurance, you receive the cash you've been saving. The money you receive when you cancel your insurance is called the **cash surrender value** of the policy.

Unlike some other savings plans, however, your money is not very liquid. In order for you to have access to your savings, you must either cancel the policy, thus giving up your insurance protection, or borrow against it.

This ability to borrow against the cash surrender value is a big advantage of cash-value insurance over term insurance. Although you must pay interest on your loan, the interest is usually much lower than rates for commercial loans. If you die before paying back the money to the company, the unpaid amount is deducted from the money paid to your beneficiaries.

Whole life insurance Insurance companies have many kinds of cash-value policies. One kind is called **whole life insurance**. You pay premiums on this type of policy as long as you live. The face value of the policy and the premiums stay the same. The cash surrender value of a whole life policy grows slowly. It would become as large as the face value if you lived to be 100 years old.

You can turn the policy in for its current cash surrender value at any time. Since once you retire you no longer need to be insured as a wage earner, many people cash in whole life policies to get additional retirement income.

A whole life policy does not give as much insurance protection for your dollar as term insurance. However, it does give more protection, although less savings, than other cash-value policies.

Whole life used to be the most common type of cash-value life insurance. But today, life insurance companies offer a wide range of new policies, and competition spurs companies to keep bringing out new ones. All of them offer some variation of insurance combined with a savings account. If you buy whole life insurance, you get a guaranteed cash surrender value. Because it is guaranteed, the yield may be low. Many of the new types offer the chance to get higher yields on the savings portion of the insurance. These yields are not guaranteed, however, and you may need to take more risk than you would with a whole life policy.

Universal life insurance One of these newer types of policies is called universal life. With **universal life insurance**, the cash surrender value of the policy depends on current interest rates. For example, if you decided to cash in your policy after a few years and interest rates had decreased, you would receive less money than you had expected. If interest rates had increased, you would receive more money than expected. A minimum yield, usually 4 percent, is guaranteed. In effect, you are buying term insurance, and the company invests, as the savings portion of the plan, the difference between the total premium and the dollars to be used for the insurance protection. You may increase or decrease the amount of your premium as long as you pay enough for the life insurance coverage.

Universal life is popular because the interest earned on the savings portion is not taxed. But you must be careful since some companies offer high interest rates the first year and then lower them. Some companies also use a lot of your money for expenses and commissions for the agent.

Variable life insurance A type of universal life policy that lets you invest your money in several mutual funds is called **variable life insurance**. These funds are managed by the insurance company. You may tell the company to invest in bonds, stocks, or a savings account. If you choose correctly, you can earn high yields on the savings part of your insurance payments. If you choose incorrectly, your yield could be low, or you could even lose money. Because of the added risk, *Consumer Reports* calls variable life "insurance roulette."

Single-premium life insurance The newest type of cash-value life insurance is called **single-premium life**. This type of life insurance provides the least amount of insurance protection for the money and the most amount of savings for your insurance dollar. You pay one premium of at least $5,000. After deducting expenses and sales commissions, the insurance company invests most of it for you. The money you earn is tax free as long as you don't cancel the policy and withdraw the cash. You may still use the cash without paying taxes, however, by borrowing it at a very low interest rate.

Life Insurance Trade-offs

Both term and cash-value insurance provide income protection for dependents if a wage earner dies. But how do you decide which is best for you? To help answer this question, an investment adviser and an insurance company vice president give some advice.

I recommend term insurance, and I'll use examples to show why it's better. First, let's say you want as much insurance protection as you can get. We'll take two 30-year-olds with $300 a year to spend on life insurance. The person buying whole life can buy a $15,000 policy, and the person buying term can buy a $100,000 policy for the same amount of money. If both of them die that year, the beneficiary of the person who bought whole life will get only $15,000. The beneficiary of the one who bought term will get $100,000. You simply get more protection for your dollar when you buy term insurance.

But we know you shouldn't buy life insurance that way. The first thing you should do is decide how much protection you need. So take another example. Let's say both people buy $100,000 policies, but one buys term and the other buys whole life. In 20 years, the person who bought whole life might have several thousand dollars in cash value. That looks good, but the person who bought term took the difference in the premium costs and saved it. That money earned interest. Now what happens if both policyholders die? The beneficiary of the cash-value policy gets $100,000. The beneficiary of the term policy gets $100,000, plus all of the money saved and all of the interest that money earned.

Now, an insurance agent can show you figures that seem to say that in 20 years a whole life policy will cost you nothing. The cash value of the policy will be greater than all of the premiums you paid in. What's wrong with this argument? It ignores interest. Money that earns 10 percent interest doubles in seven years. So buy term and invest the difference. You'll be money ahead, and you won't have to cancel your life insurance in order to collect that money.

THOMAS LOFGREN
Investment Adviser

*B*uying whole-life insurance is a good deal, especially when you're young. If you buy a whole-life policy while you're young, you'll pay the same low premium as long as you keep the policy. If you buy level-term insurance, the price keeps going up; if you buy decreasing-term, the amount of protection goes down. Sure, term insurance is cheap when you're young, but it gets expensive as you get older.

If you turn in your whole-life policy, the cash is all yours. Or you can keep the policy and borrow the cash value at a low rate of interest. That's a good way to send the kids through college.

Buy term and you have to die before anyone can collect. Buy whole life and you'll get cash if you live—cash for retirement or cash for the things you really want in life. A whole life policy isn't really free, as a few agents claim, but it is a good deal.

Of course, you could buy a combination of whole life and term. Buy a basic package of whole life and add term when you have young children or a lot of debts, such as a home mortgage. Also, after you buy basic protection, you might try universal life. I think whole-life should be bought first, though, because the guaranteed yield on a universal life policy is small.

JILL GLENNON
Liberty Pole Insurance Company

Insurance companies sometimes offer lower premiums to non-smokers and people who stay in good physical condition.

1. **What is the major advantage of cash-value insurance over term insurance?**
2. **What is the difference between level-term and decreasing-term insurance?**
3. **Explain the differences among whole life, universal life, variable life, and single-premium life insurance.**

BUYING LIFE INSURANCE

A popular myth about life insurance is that all companies charge the same rates. In fact, the cost of insurance varies widely. And some companies are safer than others. You should shop with care. Because you are counting on the company to pay benefits years from when you buy the policy, consider only the safest companies.

Quality and Cost

How do you know which companies are safe? You can find out by studying *Best's Life Insurance Reports*. This publication ranks insurance companies according to their financial strength, the soundness of their investments, and their ability to meet emergencies. The companies are rated as follows:

A+ and A	Excellent
B+	Very Good
B	Good
C+	Fairly Good
C	Fair

A high *Best's* rating doesn't mean the company offers low prices. It means that the company will probably be in business when your beneficiaries make claims on the policy. But since you can't assume that the high-rated companies sell the lowest cost policies, you need to compare prices in addition to ratings.

Term policies are the easiest to compare. Basically, the lower the premium cost, the better the deal. Make sure the policy is guaranteed renewable, and consider the price of the premiums for 10 or 20 years. Some companies have low initial premiums and then raise them sharply.

Comparing cash-value policies is more difficult because the lowest premium is often not the best deal. To tell which deal is best, you have to make a comparison of the cost of the cash-value premiums with the cash surrender value of the policy. There are studies that rank the cost of cash-value policies by determining the interest-adjusted cost. A policy's **interest-adjusted** cost is calculated by comparing the cash surrender value of the policy with

---

Can you take out a life insurance policy on anyone, such as a neighbor or a friend? No. If you take out a life insurance policy on someone else, you must have an *insurable interest*. In other words, you would have to suffer a financial loss if the person died.

What happens if a person forgets to pay a premium? Most companies will keep the policy in force for 30 days after the premium is due. After the 30 days, the policy coverage ends. The insured must reapply to put the policy back into effect.

the amount the premiums would earn if the money had been deposited in a savings account at a fixed rate of interest.

Fortunately, you do not have to figure out this cost yourself. *Consumer Reports, Changing Times* magazine, and some state insurance offices have already done this by ranking policies according to their interest-adjusted cost. The lower the interest-adjusted cost, the better the policy.

Selecting an Agent

Most of the time, consumers buy insurance through an agent rather than directly from an insurance company. A good agent judges your needs and sells you a tailor-made policy. A good agent also keeps in touch after the sale to answer your questions and update or change your policies. A good insurance agent is worth a lot, therefore, while a poor agent is useless or even harmful.

An insurance agent who does the job well will sell you a policy that meets both your present and future needs.

How much life insurance can a person get? One Canadian land developer took out a policy for $44 million from a California agent.

But make no mistake about it. An agent's main job is to sell you a life insurance policy. Some agents may try to sell you much more than you need because they get up to 55 percent commission on your first-year premium. Since they get only 5 percent after the first year, you may not see them again. In fact, one study found that only 13 percent of the policyholders surveyed had found an agent useful after the sale was made. Few agents stay in the life insurance business more than five years.

Watch that Rider

In addition to the basic life insurance policy, an agent may try to persuade you to buy a **rider**, an addition to the policy. The cost of these riders varies greatly among companies. If you want a rider, compare its cost as well as the cost of the basic policy. These are the four most common riders.

- **Accidental Death Benefit**. If you buy this rider, your beneficiary will get double the face value of the policy if you die in an accident. Although the extra cost is small, it's difficult to justify the expense since most people do not die in accidents. Life insurance is supposed to protect your dependents. In fact, their financial needs may be greater if you die a natural death after a long illness than if you die in an accident.
- **Waiver of Premium**. With this rider, the insurance company will pay the premiums for you if you are totally disabled and can't work for six months or more. Suppose you become disabled. Without a waiver of premium, you might have to drop your policy because you could no longer afford the premiums. The cost of this rider is small. It probably is a good idea to buy it, particularly for a policy with large premiums.
- **Guaranteed Insurability**. This rider allows you to buy additional term insurance regardless of your health. Of course, the price of a new term policy goes up as you grow older, but, under this rider, you can't be turned down because of poor health. The rider is usually not offered to people over 40. It is valuable if you feel you will need more insurance in the future and you don't want to risk being turned down.
- **Convertibility**. This rider to term policies allows you to switch the policy to a cash-value policy regardless of your health.

What does a beneficiary have to do after an insured person dies? The beneficiary has to give the life insurance company a copy of the death certificate. The insurance company will do the rest.

When an agent comes to sell you life insurance, be ready to ask questions like these.

- "Why do I need insurance?" (An agent who does not plan a program for your specific needs is not giving you the service you should be getting.)
- "What is the company's *Best's* rating?" (Ask to see it in writing.)
- "What is the interest-adjusted cost of this insurance policy?" (Ask for that figure in writing too. Then check it in *Consumer Reports* or *Changing Times*. The lower the cost the better.)

Since a good agent is so valuable, you should not wait for an agent to phone you or show up at your door. Search for one yourself when you feel you need life insurance. If you don't, you may get one like the agent who showed up at Ryan Daily's home and tried to sell Ryan insurance. For easy reference in the case study that follows, the sales arguments are numbered, together with Ryan's replies.

CASE STUDY

1. "Hi, Ryan. I'm Terry Wetzel. I represent the James Polk Insurance Company, and I'd like to talk to you about your financial security.

2. "You may be young now, but soon you'll be married and have a family. How will they get by if you're not around to take care of them? Even now there would be high funeral costs if you died. Do you want your parents to bear this burden?

   "Now, let me tell you about life insurance. It's best to buy it when you're young. Later on, the cost will be higher, and you may not be in good enough health to get it.

3. "We have just the package for you—our 'Young Person's Protector Plan.'

4. "Now, let me show you some figures. This plan not only gives you $10,000 worth of insurance protection but also builds up cash for your future. In 40 years, you'll have more cash than you paid into the policy. In other words, you get $10,000 protection for 40 years, and it costs you nothing."

5. "Sounds good," Ryan agreed. "But I can't afford it right now."

   "No problem." said Terry. "You can get the protection now and pay nothing for two years. How about that? We know a young person's needs."

6. "Sounds better," Ryan said. "Could I get a copy of the policy to show my dad?"

   Terry frowned. "Come on now, you'll be a college graduate soon. Are you always going to rely on your dad? After all, this program is designed for you. This is why the decision should be one that you make."

How should Ryan handle this situation? Let's go back and see what he could do at each point in the discussion.

1. Right away, Ryan should ask what the James Polk Insurance Company is, and what its *Best's* rating is. He should ask for the rating in writing.

2. The agent's scare tactic should make Ryan suspicious. If all Ryan has to worry about are funeral expenses, he might risk going without life insurance. Ryan probably has high college expenses and can't afford life insurance. The price of life insurance will not be very much higher a few years later, when Ryan graduates, and he could save the cost of the premiums in the meantime. Ryan's health might get bad when he is older, but the odds are strongly against it.

3. The "Young Person's Protector Plan" has a fancy name, but what type of insurance is it? It soon becomes clear that it's some kind of cash-value insurance. But is it whole life, universal life, or what? Ryan should find out, and he should also ask why the agent didn't mention term insurance, which has a much lower premium.

4. Ryan should realize that the agent did not figure the interest the premiums could earn for those 40 years. He should ask for the interest-adjusted cost of the policy. After he gets the cost in writing, signed by the agent, he should compare it with the interest-adjusted costs in *Consumer Reports* or *Changing Times*.

5. "Pay nothing for two years" is a deal often offered to young people short on cash. Ryan would be borrowing money from the insurance company to pay for the first two years' premiums. If you buy life insurance, you can cancel it at any time and you are off the hook. But if Ryan takes this deal, his loan cannot be canceled. The interest rates on these loans can be very high. He can be sued if he doesn't pay.

6. Ryan should tell the agent that he would never buy insurance without seeing a sample policy. While Ryan is capable of making his own decision, he should not limit his sources of information. He probably should discuss an important decision like this with several people. Although Ryan has put up with this sales pitch until now, it's time to say good-bye, and fast.

✓ check your understanding ✓ ✓ ✓ ✓ ✓ ✓

1. **Why is it important to check the reputation of an insurance company before buying life insurance?**
2. **Name three facts you need to know about an insurance company in order to judge its reliability.**
3. **How does an insurance agent make money? What does this mean in terms of dealing with an agent?**

People buy life insurance as financial protection for their families in case of death. They also buy life insurance for use as a long-term savings plan. The person insured is the policyholder, and the beneficiary is the person who receives the benefits of the insurance.

There are two major kinds of life insurance, term and cash value. Term insurance provides coverage for a certain period of time. Cash-value life insurance policies provide a combination of protection and savings. Each individual and family must decide whether insurance is needed, how much protection is enough, and what kind to buy depending on their circumstances.

To evaluate life insurance companies, use *Best's Life Insurance Reports*. When buying term insurance, look for the lowest premiums. Using the interest-adjusted costs of policies that appear in magazines like *Consumer Reports* helps you find the best deals in cash-value life insurance. Consumers need to choose their insurance agent as carefully as they choose their insurance company. The agent should plan an insurance program especially tailored for each consumer.

CHAPTER ACTIVITIES

BUILDING CONSUMER VOCABULARY

Number your paper from 1 to 15. Then write the term that best matches each numbered definition.

beneficiaries	level-term insurance
cash surrender value	rider
cash-value insurance	single-premium life insurance
decreasing-term insurance	term insurance
face value	universal life insurance
group life insurance	variable life insurance
guaranteed insurability	whole life insurance
interest-adjusted cost	

1. A life insurance policy for which the face value and the premiums stay the same for as long as the policyholder lives

2. A life insurance policy that allows you to tell the insurance company where they should invest the money that you pay in premiums
3. A life insurance policy for which the amount of protection remains the same, but the premium increases each time the policy is renewed
4. The people who receive the money from a claim on a life insurance policy
5. Cash savings received when an insurance policy is canceled
6. A measure of the cost of whole life insurance by which its cash value is compared with the amount that the money paid in premiums would earn if put in a savings account at a fixed rate of interest
7. A category of life insurance that combines a savings program with protection against loss of income
8. The amount of money beneficiaries receive from a policy
9. Life insurance bought by people through a business or an association
10. A provision that allows you to buy additional insurance at an older age, regardless of any change in the state of your health at that time
11. A life insurance policy in which the amount of protection goes down, but the premiums stay the same
12. A life insurance policy in which the cash surrender value is determined by current interest rates
13. A life insurance policy has the least amount of income protection and that is almost all savings
14. A category of life insurance that has no cash surrender value
15. An addition to a life insurance policy

BUILDING CONSUMER UNDERSTANDING

1. How is life insurance similar to car and homeowners' insurance? How is life insurance different from these other kinds of insurance?
2. Why might a young married couple need more life insurance protection than a college student who lives with parents?
3. List some factors that would reduce the amount of life insurance someone might need.
4. For what reasons would someone want to buy decreasing-term insurance?
5. Suppose you had bought a universal life insurance policy. Why might you wish to increase the amount you pay in premiums?
6. How do you know if a life insurance company is financially strong?
7. What should you look for to get the best buy in term insurance? in cash-value insurance?

Assume that you are 25 years old and have decided to buy a $50,000 whole life policy. You know agents from the William McKinley Insurance Company and the Grover Cleveland Insurance Company. You looked up cost information in *Consumer Reports* and read the following information:

Company	First-Year Premium	Twenty-Year Interest-Adjusted Cost Index
William McKinley	$290	0.69
Grover Cleveland	388	0.15

1. How much lower is the first-year premium for William McKinley Insurance compared with Grover Cleveland Insurance?
2. How much lower is the interest-adjusted cost of Grover Cleveland Insurance compared with William McKinley Insurance?
3. Which policy is the better buy? Why?

1. Rank the following people in order of their need for life insurance. The person you rank number 1 needs the most protection. Then explain why you ranked each of these people the way you did.
   a. Marcia Cassidy, 24, is married and is a high school teacher expecting her first child. She and her husband agree that she will continue working only until their baby is born.
   b. Dave Lorch, 22, works as a welder. He is getting married in a few months. Both he and his future wife plan to keep working at their current jobs.
   c. Tyrone Bearden, 30, is married and has two children, ages 2 and 5. His wife worked as a secretary before their marriage but has no plans to work outside the home until the children are much older. They have a home with a $70,000 mortgage.
   d. Walter Linn, 45, has two children, 19 and 17. His wife, Arlene, works part-time as a travel agent. They have a home with a $60,000 mortgage.
2. Assume you must advise a young family on the type of life insurance they should have. The husband is 28, and the wife is 25. Both are nurses, and each earns about $24,000 a year. They have one child, 2 years old.
   a. Should both the wife and husband buy life insurance? Why or why not?
   b. Should they buy term or cash-value insurance? Discuss the advantages and disadvantages of each kind.

c. What additional information would you want to know before telling them how much life insurance they should have?

3. You have just graduated from high school and plan to attend college next fall. A life insurance agent comes to your home and wants to sell you a policy. How would you reply to the agent?

GETTING INVOLVED IN YOUR COMMUNITY

Get together with other students in your class in small groups to interview three life insurance agents in your community. Find out what specific policy each agent recommends for the following family. The husband is 30 and earns $25,000 a year as an accountant. The wife, 25, is a substitute teacher. They own a $75,000 house with a $55,000 mortgage. They have two children, both under five years old.

Report to the class on which agent offered the best policy. Explain why it is best. Some questions that should be discussed are:

1. Did each agent design the insurance for the family's needs?
2. Did any agent advise either too much or too little insurance?
3. How financially strong is each agent's company?
4. How does each policy's interest-adjusted cost compare with others in the life insurance industry? Check these figures in *Consumer Reports* or *Changing Times*.

INSURING YOUR INCOME AND HEALTH

Many people would say that the two things that most need to be protected by insurance are their incomes and their health. They are so important, in fact, that the federal government provides some protection in the form of social security. Consumers may also buy health insurance and additional protection against loss of income stemming from illness or accidents.

■ What kind of income protection do workers and their families have?

■ Who pays the bills if you become disabled or unemployed?

■ Why do you need health insurance?

■ What group health plans are offered by employers?

■ How do you shop for individual health insurance?

Life insurance is a form of income protection. This type of insurance supports dependents if a wage earner dies. But what if a wage earner becomes too sick to work? What if a wage earner is laid off a job and cannot find another? Both of these cases would cause at least as much financial hardship as the death of a wage earner. Neither is covered by life insurance. Fortunately, there are a number of insurance programs that do provide income in the case of such misfortunes.

THE CASE FOR INCOME PROTECTION

Loss of income from illness or unemployment may be worse for a family than loss of income caused by the death of one of its members. If a spouse dies, life insurance money may be available. Also, the surviving spouse may remarry. But if a working spouse becomes disabled or unemployed, there may be no income for the family. And a disabled worker may need full-time care. For these reasons, financial experts say that disability insurance is one of the most important insurance plans a consumer can buy.

Disability Insurance

Disability insurance replaces some of the income lost if you cannot work because you are sick or injured. It can be purchased privately, but it is often paid, in whole or in part, by employers. There are two types of disability insurance: *long-term disability* and *short-term disability*.

Long-term disability insurance usually pays 60 percent of your salary, tax-free, for life in case you are permanently unable to work because of an accident. It will pay that money until you turn 65 if you cannot work because of an illness.

These policies have an **elimination period** or a time period before coverage starts. These periods can be from one month up to three years, depending on the policy. If an accident or illness occurs during this elimination period, you will not receive benefits.

Short-term disability insurance pays part, or sometimes all, of your income if you cannot work during the elimination period. If you break your leg, for example, and you can't go back to work for six weeks, short-term disability insurance will cover you. If you are permanently unable to work, short-term disability payments will cover you at first, and long-term disability payments will cover you after the elimination period is over.

Workers' Compensation

Disability insurance will protect you no matter how you become disabled. But if a person is injured while at work, income protection called **workers' compensation** insurance then takes over.

Every year, one out of every five people in the United States needs to see a doctor.

What does the term "total disability" mean to you? It has different definitions in different policies. In some policies, "total disability" means that you can't do any job at all. In other policies, it means that you can't do work for which you have experience or education. So, under one policy you might be totally disabled while under another policy, you may not be.

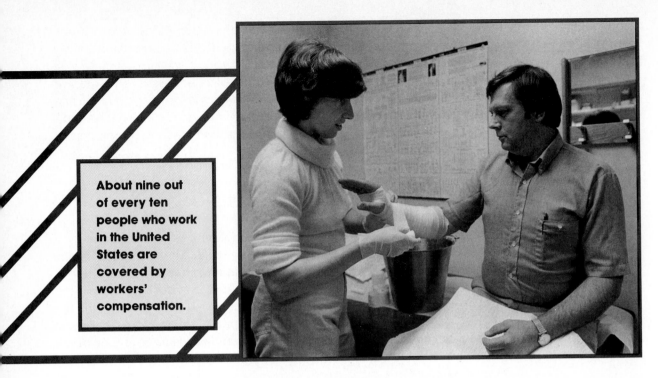

Employers pay for this insurance as required by their state laws. Each state-run program sets the weekly compensation an insured employee will receive. This amount is often 60 to 80 percent of the wages lost. A worker usually needs to be out of work a certain number of days before payments begin.

In addition, workers' compensation often pays most of the medical bills that result because of the job injury. If a worker dies as a result of an on-the-job accident, compensation is also paid to the family.

Unemployment Insurance

Another form of income protection administered by state government is called **unemployment insurance**. This type of insurance covers workers who are laid off from their jobs. Employers pay for much of this insurance. The benefits are paid weekly to people who are qualified. Workers who quit their jobs or are fired for misconduct usually do not qualify. In addition, your job must be covered by this insurance plan.

The amount of benefits and requirements for qualification are determined by each state. Benefits are generally based on the average wage in the state. These benefits usually last 26 weeks, but in some cases can be extended to as long as 52 weeks.

For eligible unemployed people to receive benefits, they must report to their state employment office and register for work. While receiving unemployment benefits, they must look for a suitable job and be willing to take one if offered. Otherwise, they may lose their benefits.

Social Security

Run by the federal government, **social security** is an insurance program that provides disability payments, survivors' benefits, and retirement income. The program insures almost 90 percent of the workers in this country. Workers pay a specific percentage of each paycheck for this insurance. Their employers are required to match this payment. All money is deposited in a special trust fund. Self-employed people pay a rate between the individual rate and the combined amount paid by employer and employee together.

Your earnings are identified throughout your working life by your social security number. Everyone over the age of 5 is required to have a social security number.

If you work in a job covered by social security, you begin to pay for it from your first paycheck. However, you can't receive any benefits until you have worked for a certain amount of time. That amount changes as Congress changes the laws associated with social security. Social security work credit is measured in quarters of coverage, four to a year. Currently, you must work for 40 quarters (or ten years) before you are eligible to receive benefits. The amount you receive in benefits is based on the average amount you have earned in the five years before your benefits begin.

Although the payments provide a very important source of financial help, few people can live on this money alone. Most people think it is wise to supplement social security with private disability and life insurance, as well as with additional retirement income.

The major benefits provided by social security are listed below.

Disability benefits People who have an illness or injury that prevents them from working for at least 12 months may receive social security payments. They receive payments as long as they are unable to work. People who are severely disabled can receive checks even though they may be able to work a little and earn some money.

Survivors' benefits Like life insurance, social security will pay benefits to dependents if a worker dies. However, to be eligible the surviving husband or wife must be at least 60 years old. Children must be under 18 years of age. Parents who depend on a grown child's income may also receive survivors' benefits.

Retirement income Most people receive their first benefits from social security when they retire. About one out of every seven people in the country receives a monthly social security check.

Most people elect to get retirement checks at age 65 to 67, but some people start collecting retirement income as early as age 62. The younger you are when you start collecting, the lower your monthly payments. These payments increase automatically as the cost of living goes up.

After hospitalization, many people prefer to recover at home instead of in a hospital. Hospital equipment is set up at the sick person's home. A nurse is hired to make visits. Many group health insurance plans cover home care. Why? Home health care is cheaper than hospital care—sometimes as much as 90 percent cheaper.

If you decide to keep working after you turn 65, you may not get full retirement benefits. The amount that you can earn after retirement and still be eligible to receive social security benefits usually varies each year.

√ check your understanding √ √ √ √ √ √

1. **What is disability insurance? Why do some experts believe this is one of the most important kinds of insurance?**
2. **When would an employee receive workers' compensation insurance payments? What benefits does this insurance provide?**
3. **What requirements must a person meet to receive unemployment insurance payments?**
4. **In what situations do people qualify for social security payments?**

THE CASE FOR HEALTH INSURANCE

As an indication of how high medical costs are, in one New England hospital there is an official rule that heart-attack patients should never be shown the bill for their hospital stay. It is feared that the shock could give them another attack.

People in the United States spend an average of $2,000 per person on health care each year. Some people spend a great deal more. For example, the total hospital expense for open-heart surgery can cost over $30,000. A few days' stay in a hospital to treat a broken leg can cost more than $2,500. Many of us have some form of health insurance, so we don't have to pay the full cost of these expenses. But health insurance covers less than half of all health care costs. And 40 million people in the United States have no health insurance at all.

You may feel that, since you are young, you don't need to worry about medical insurance. But, as the following case study shows, there's no knowing when something might happen that would leave you with big medical bills.

CASE STUDY

Mike Kucala had always been healthy. Why shouldn't he be? He was only 22 and played sports regularly. He was really in shape. So when his employer gave him a chance to buy health insurance, Mike turned it down. He felt the $40 monthly charge was too much for something he thought he wasn't going to use. Three months later, though, Mike was hurt in an auto accident. His two-week hospital stay cost $8,000. The doctor's bills were another $2,000. Mike had no idea how he could ever raise enough money to pay his medical bills.

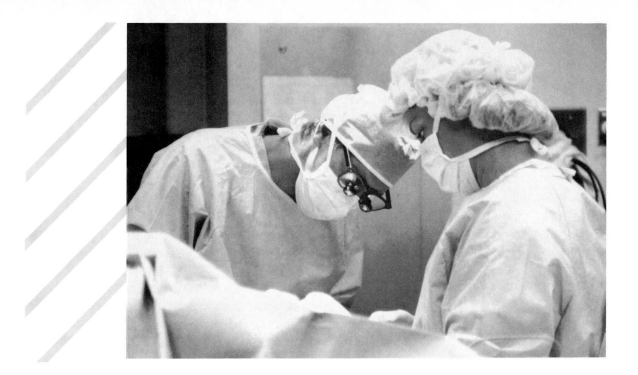

Often surgical expense insurance pays a limited amount for an operation. If the surgeon charges more, you have to pay the rest yourself.

If you doubt that you need hospital insurance, consider that in one hospital it costs $70 a day merely to lie in a bed. This cost does not include the cost of staying in the room, the cost of meals, or the cost of any medical care.

Kinds of Health Insurance

Health insurance coverage is important protection for you and your family. What type of basic insurance policy should you have? Do you need additional coverage? Here is a run-down of the main kinds of health insurance coverage.

Hospital expense insurance Insurance that pays for all or part of your hospital bill is called **hospital expense insurance**. It might cover such things as the room, meals, laboratory tests, x-rays, nurses' care, and medicine. Such insurance usually has a deductible and may have limits as well. It may cover you only for a certain amount of time or up to a certain amount of money.

Surgical expense insurance If you have an operation, **surgical expense insurance** pays part or all of the surgeon's fee. Most policies list the kinds of operations the company covers and the amount they pay for each operation.

Medical expense insurance Fees charged by doctors for services other than surgery are covered by **medical expense insurance**. It covers doctors' fees stemming from hospital stays, visits to a doctor's office, or visits by a doctor to you at home. It also covers the cost of tests the doctor performs. It usually is available only in combination with hospital and surgical coverage. Such a combination of hospital expense, surgical expense, and medical expense insurance is sometimes called *basic health coverage*.

Major medical insurance A serious illness can use up all of your basic health coverage in a hurry. **Major medical insurance** picks up where other health insurance ends to cover big expenses. Usually, you pay a deductible amount, such as the first $100 or $500. The major medical policy then covers most of the rest. The most common policy pays 80 percent of your expenses beyond $500. There is usually a limit to what the policy will pay you, either in a year or in your lifetime. This limit, however, is much higher than limits for basic health coverage.

Buying Group Health Insurance

Health insurance can be bought in two forms: by an individual policy or through a group. Most health insurance in the United States is **group health insurance**. Most businesses offer group plans for their employees. A group can also be made up of members of a labor union, social or professional organization, religious organization, or credit union. All members of the group can be insured, whatever their age or health. In most group plans offered by businesses, new employees can become members of a group health plan simply by filling in an application form.

> The idea of health insurance goes back to ancient China. People paid doctors to keep them well. If a person got sick, the payments were stopped.

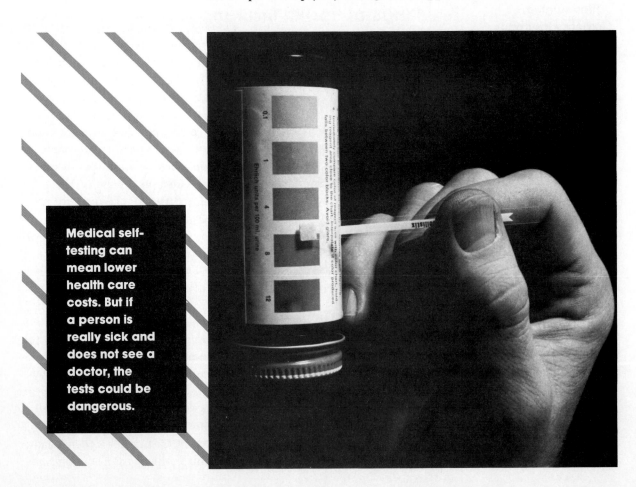

> **Medical self-testing can mean lower health care costs. But if a person is really sick and does not see a doctor, the tests could be dangerous.**

Health Insurance Buying Guide

If you must buy an individual health policy, make sure you know what you're getting. You should always read a sample policy before you buy. Here are a few good questions to ask.

- What percentage of the premiums is actually paid out in benefits?
- If you make a claim, can the policy be canceled or the rates raised to unreasonably high levels? To protect you from this problem, be sure to buy a policy that cannot be canceled. In addition, you want one that is *guaranteed renewable*.
- What conditions or illnesses are not covered by the policy?
- How much time must go by after the policy starts before it pays benefits?
- What exact benefits does the policy pay? Will it cover the same illness more than once?
- How does the policy compare with a good group plan?

Many employers pay all or part of the cost of the insurance for their employees. But even if workers themselves pay, a group policy usually costs much less than an individual policy. When dealing with large groups, insurance companies have less paperwork and other expenses. So, over 90 percent of the payments for an average group are returned in benefits.

You learned in Chapter 14 that you may receive medical care from doctors in private practice in a fee-for-service arrangement. You may also receive medical care from doctors who work in group practice—in health maintenance organizations (HMOs), independent practitioner associations (IPAs), and preferred provider organizations (PPOs). Group medical insurance is available for both fee-for-service and group arrangements. Usually, group insurance that covers HMOs, IPAs, or PPOs pays for more medical fees than does insurance covering private practice.

In communities having group practices, most employers must give their workers the option of subscribing to either fee-for-service arrangements or group arrangements.

Group insurance plans have some disadvantages. If you leave the group, you have no health protection. However, federal law requires that employers offer workers who leave voluntarily or are laid off the option of paying for the group plan for at least 18 months after they leave the company.

According to one estimate, if the whole nation joined HMOs, the national health care budget would drop by about $25 billion dollars. Does that sound like a lot of money? It's only five percent less than we are paying already.

Shopping for an HMO

By 1995, half of us will be subscribers to some type of HMO. We need to shop as carefully for group health arrangements as we do for any major purchase. Here are a few good questions to ask about an HMO before signing up.

- How many patients are there for each doctor?
- How many specialists are in the group? Are they board-certified?
- What hospital is the group affiliated with? Is the hospital associated with a major medical school?
- Can you visit any specialist within the group without a primary-care physician's okay?
- Will the group pay for use of a specialist outside the plan?
- If you are ill or injured away from home, will the HMO cover all necessary treatment at an outside hospital or emergency clinic?

Before buying insurance, make sure it's the plan you really want. In an effort to cut costs, insurance companies have increased deductibles and required more out-of-pocket payments by the insured. HMOs and other group practices have tried to cut down the time their subscribers stay in the hospital to reduce costs. As a result, studies show that patients are becoming more unhappy with the quality of their medical care. Some patients are being sent home from the hospital too soon and end up having to go back. The studies find many more complaints coming from users of HMO plans than other types of group health insurance.

Buying Individual Policies

How much more expensive is individual health coverage than group health insurance? If you have group insurance, the premiums will be 15 percent to 40 percent cheaper than if you buy coverage as an individual.

If you are in a group plan, you will be insured for everything the plan covers, and at a reasonable cost. However, millions of people in the United States can't get into a group plan because their employer doesn't have one. Others are self-employed or unemployed. These people must buy individual health insurance policies.

Individual health insurance coverage is expensive. So in buying an individual policy, you need to think about the coverage that you need most. Individual policies also are more difficult to get than group policies. Most insurance companies require you to pass a medical examination before you can be covered. And even if you pass the examination, the policy may not cover a serious illness if you had it before buying the policy. Furthermore, insurance companies can cancel your policy whenever they wish. As you can see in the following case studies, some people find it hard to get good health insurance of any kind.

CASE STUDY

When Lester Hingham worked as an engineer he had company medical insurance, but when he quit his job to become a fishing guide, Lester tried to get individual health insurance. His application was turned down because he had high blood pressure. Later he had to face the expenses of a heart attack without insurance.

CASE STUDY

Joyce Fulton went into a hospital with a pain in her right foot. She told the insurance company she had never had any trouble with that foot or leg before. But 12 years earlier, her left foot had needed medical attention. The insurance company refused to pay the hospital bill because, they said, the problem must have existed before Joyce was insured by them.

CASE STUDY

Cesar Budo bought a policy for himself and his family when he started his own business. He had a child who often had colds. The doctor had diagnosed the problem as asthma, but did not tell the parents. For that reason, the parents did not mention the problem on their application for individual health insurance. Later, when the insurance company found out about the child's asthma, they canceled the policy for the entire family. The Budo family had to sell their home in order to pay medical bills.

✓check your understanding ✓ ✓ ✓ ✓ ✓ ✓

1. **What are the advantages of group health insurance?**
2. **What does basic health coverage consist of?**
3. **In what ways is individual health coverage more difficult to get than group health coverage?**

Buying Government Insurance

People over 65 may be entitled to coverage by government health insurance without paying any premiums. This health insurance program, called **Medicare**, is run by the Social Security Administration of the federal government.

Medicare is made up of two parts: Part A and Part B. Part A of Medicare is like hospital expense insurance. It partially pays for hospital care. It also covers part of the expense for approved nursing home care and home care visits by medical professionals. In addition, it pays for some medicines and equipment used in providing this care. The patient must first pay a set amount each day, and Medicare pays some of the rest.

Part B, like medical expense insurance, partially pays for non-surgical doctors' services, supplies, tests, and x-rays. After subtracting a deductible and determining a set fee for these services, the government pays 80 percent of that fee for these services. Medicare does not pay all costs, so many people buy additional coverage through major medical insurance.

Medicaid is another federal health care plan. It pays for health care for the poor, including the blind, disabled, elderly, and dependent children. Medicaid is usually run by state or local human services agencies.

Buying Dental Insurance

One of the fastest growing medical insurance plans is dental insurance. Currently over 80 million people have part of their dental bills paid by these plans. Health insurance is usually a way of guarding against the large unexpected medical bill that could mean financial disaster. Dental insurance, instead, is aimed at preventing small problems from becoming big ones. Therefore, it partially pays for regular exams, x-rays, treatment, and dental surgery.

One of the benefits of Medicare is partial payment for care in an approved nursing home.

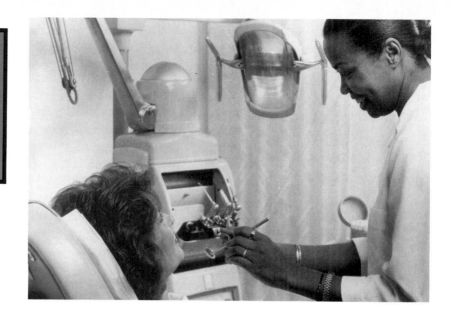

The insurance company usually pays a specified percentage of the bill after the patient pays a deductible. Because almost all people sooner or later need dental care, insurers would rather sell group policies to help reduce their level of claims. Since it is usually the case that only people who expect to spend a lot on dental care buy individual dental policies, these dental policies have very high premiums.

✓check your understanding ✓ ✓ ✓ ✓ ✓ ✓

1. Should you buy individual health insurance with the idea that it will pay for all your medical expenses?
2. How much of your medical expenses will major medical insurance cover?
3. For whom is Medicare intended? For whom is Medicaid intended?
4. Why are few individual dental policies sold?

*S*UMMARIZING
the chapter

Disability insurance protects against loss of income if a wage earner cannot work because of injury or illness. Many employers offer both short-term and long-term disability insurance. State government provides workers with workers' compensation. This type of insurance, which is paid for by employers, provides a weekly compensation for employees injured on the job. Another state program is unemployment insurance, which pays weekly benefits to workers who are laid off. Social security provides some disability income, survivors' benefits, and retirement income.

Health care costs are high. Health insurance helps reduce these expenses. Group health insurance obtained through a company or an organization is the most common type of coverage. With group health insurance, employees often have a choice of using fee-for-service doctors or those who practice in group arrangements. Group insurance is often paid in full or in part by employers. Even if you pay the premiums yourself, though, it is generally less expensive than individual medical coverage.

Not all employers provide group insurance, however, and not all people are employed. Those people must buy individual medical coverage.

Medicare and Medicaid insurance, run by federal and state governments, provide health care and protection for the elderly and the poor.

One of the fastest growing medical insurance plans is group dental insurance. Most dental insurance is sold as group plans, since insurance companies find the costs of providing individual dental coverage very high.

C·H·A·P·T·E·R A·C·T·I·V·I·T·I·E·S

BUILDING CONSUMER VOCABULARY

Number your paper from 1 to 12. Then write the term that best matches each numbered definition.

disability insurance	medical expense insurance
elimination period	Medicare
group health insurance	social security
hospital expense insurance	surgical expense insurance
major medical insurance	unemployment insurance
Medicaid	workers' compensation

1. Insurance that pays part of your salary if you are out of work for a long time due to injury or illness
2. Insurance that pays the surgeon's fee for an operation
3. Health insurance provided through a company or other organization
4. Insurance that pays for all or part of the expenses associated with staying in a hospital
5. Federal insurance program that provides retirement benefits, disability insurance, and survivors' benefits

6. Insurance that pays for fees charged by doctors for services other than surgery
7. A federal program of health insurance for the poor
8. Income protection for workers laid off from their jobs
9. Insurance protection against long-term or very costly health expenses
10. A state-run program paid for by employers to provide income protection for workers injured on the job
11. Health insurance for the elderly
12. The amount of time that must go by before long-term disability insurance goes into effect

BUILDING CONSUMER UNDERSTANDING

1. What is the difference between disability insurance and workers' compensation insurance?
2. Describe three mishaps that could disable a worker. At what age does a worker need disability insurance? Do workers who support only themselves need disability insurance? Why or why not?
3. You read the following advertisement in the paper:

    Money while you are sick
    $200 a day in cash
    Pays double for cancer

    Contact Guardian Health Insurance Company now! What would you want to know about this insurance policy before buying it?
4. June Grazianno injured her back while bowling. She was in a hospital for two weeks and spent much of that time in traction. What kind of health insurance coverage would pay her bills?
5. Eddy O'Brien was ill for 15 weeks and missed work. His employers paid his salary for only three of those weeks. What kind of insurance policy would give him additional income?
6. Gary Shock owns the Action Software Company. He feels he earns enough to pay for regular hospital and doctors' expenses himself, but he is worried about the cost of a major illness or accident. What type of health coverage should he buy?

BUILDING CONSUMER MATH SKILLS

1. Assume that you have hospital expense and major medical coverage through an individual health insurance policy. After minor surgery and a four-day hospital stay, you have the following bills: $1,700 for surgery, $1,400 for room and meals, $2,400 for lab tests and x-rays, and $200 for medication. Your hospital expense insurance will cover $4,300 of the bill. How much of your total bill is not covered by your hospital expense insurance?

If your major medical pays 80 percent after you pay a $100 deductible, how much of the remaining bill is paid by this coverage? How much must you pay?

2. Two HMOs are offered at your place of work. In addition, a fee-for-service group plan is offered. Your company will pay your entire premium for individual coverage under the fee-for-service plan and half the premium for family coverage. If you choose an HMO, your employer will pay the same dollar amount that would have gone for the fee-for-service plan and you will pay the rest. The monthly costs of all the programs are:

	Fee-for-Service Plan	HMO Supercare	United Cities HMO
Employee	$100	$ 88.87	$ 81.24
Family	160	130.85	146.26
TOTAL	$260	$219.72	$227.50

   a. How much will your employer contribute toward an HMO program if you choose to subscribe to one for yourself alone?

   b. Assume that you wish to buy family coverage. Which plan is least expensive? By how much?

   c. How much will your company save if you choose individual coverage under the Supercare plan rather than the fee-for-service plan? What percentage savings is this amount?

APPLYING CONSUMER SKILLS

Assume that, after you graduate, you are offered two identical jobs. Job A pays $1.50 an hour more than Job B for a 40-hour week. Both have the same working conditions. Job A offers no health insurance. Job B offers a group health insurance plan that includes full basic health insurance coverage, major medical coverage, and long-term disability insurance. Both jobs are covered by social security, workers' compensation, and unemployment insurances.

Construct a decision-making grid with your values and goals along the top and the alternatives (Job A or Job B) down the left side. Complete the grid.

Which job alternative appears to be best for you? Why?

GETTING INVOLVED IN YOUR COMMUNITY

Go to the personnel office of a large company in your area and find out what group health benefits are available. Make a chart showing their coverages and costs. If HMO plans are available, compare their features with the fee-for-service group plan. Now evaluate each using the shopping guides on pages 443 and 444.

Jason and Melissa want to invest $20,000 that they have inherited. They plan to use the return on their investment for retirement and for their children's college education. They are considering the following investment options.

COMMON STOCK IN ACME CORPORATION
The broker charges a 5 percent commission. Stock costs $89 per share. Five years ago the stock cost $75 per share. Yearly dividends per share for previous years to last year were $5.00, $2.30, $6.56, $7.80, and $9.10.

PREFERRED STOCK IN LEVINE ELECTRONICS CORPORATION
The broker charges a 3 percent commission. Stock costs $20 per share. Two years ago, when the company was formed, stock cost $12 per share. Dividends have not yet been paid. The company is putting profits back into the company to encourage growth.

BAYVIEW STOCK MUTUAL FUND
There is no broker's commission. Stock costs $95 per share. Five years ago, stock cost $79 per share. Yearly dividends per share for previous years to last year were $7.11, $6.40, $12.35, $12.61, and $13.30.

BANK CERTIFICATE OF DEPOSIT
There are no fees. A ten-year certificate earns 9.5 percent interest per year, guaranteed.

Answer the following questions on a separate sheet of paper. Use complete sentences.

1. If Jason and Melissa had invested their money a year ago, how much in interest or dividends would they have made last year in each of the investment options? For stocks, figure whole shares. Remember to deduct broker's fees.

2. In which investment option would their money probably be the safest? Why?

3. Which investment option seems to offer the greatest chance for high return? Why?

4. Which investment option seems to be the most risky? Why?

5. Rank the investment options from 1 (best) to 4 (worst). Explain your rankings.

6. How do you think the couple should invest their $20,000? Explain.

CRITICAL THINKING

THINKING ABOUT:
Investment Choices

THE CONSUMER AND THE UNITED STATES ECONOMY

MEASURING ECONOMIC ACTIVITY

The United States economy is enormous. It's hard to keep track of so much economic activity. Some parts of the economy may be very healthy while other parts are not. How do we know how strong the economy is as a whole? We can measure the total value of all the goods and services produced in a given year. We can count the number of people out of work. We can keep track of prices. How do we measure the ups and downs of the economy?

- What is GNP, and how does it measure the state of the economy?

- Why is unemployment a measure of how well our economy is doing?

- What is the consumer price index, and what are the advantages and disadvantages of using it to measure inflation?

- What are the stages of a business cycle?

How do we know if the economy of our country is healthy or not? For many years, the definition of a healthy economy has been full employment without inflation. Economists describe **inflation** as a general rise in the price of goods and services. Although the United States has never been able to reach this goal, we came close during the mid-1960's. During that time, prices rose less than 3 percent a year, and the unemployment rate averaged around 4 percent.

The condition of the economy affects each one of us. It is hard to find a job when unemployment is high, and many people with jobs worry that they will lose them. Rising prices make it difficult to plan for the future. Inflation can bring poverty to people living on fixed or slowly rising incomes.

You can affect the economy through your voting power and through your buying decisions. In order to vote for candidates with sensible economic programs, you must have some understanding of economic matters. For instance, do you understand these headlines describing our country's economy?

As you read this chapter, you will learn what these headlines mean. You will see how economists measure and determine the health of our economy.

MEASURING GROSS NATIONAL PRODUCT

Economists often use the **gross national product** (GNP) to measure the size of our economy. GNP is the total dollar value of all the final goods and services produced in the United States in a year. Notice that only final goods and services—those not used to make something else—are counted in order to give an accurate picture. If the value of all steel and all automobiles were counted, we would be counting the same steel twice, since some of it is used to make cars. Therefore, only the cars are counted in GNP. They are the final goods.

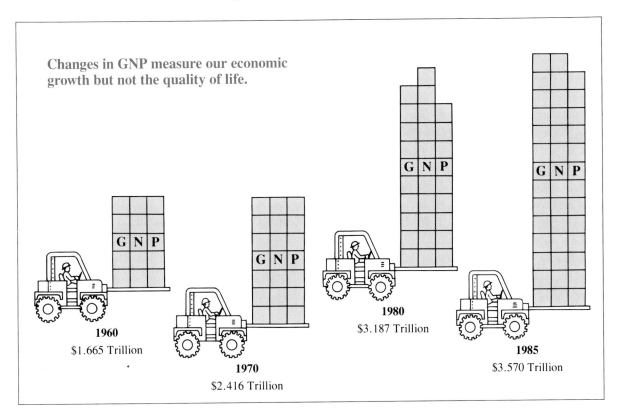

Changes in GNP measure our economic growth but not the quality of life.

1960
$1.665 Trillion

1970
$2.416 Trillion

1980
$3.187 Trillion

1985
$3.570 Trillion

The Components of GNP

GNP is divided into three basic parts: consumption, investment, and government expenditures. *Consumption* refers to all of the goods and services consumers buy. About two thirds of GNP is made up of consumption expenditures.

Investment consists of those expenditures that businesses make on new factories and machinery, often called capital investment. It also includes the purchase of new homes by consumers. Although they make up the smallest part of GNP, about 17 percent, investment expenditures are important for our economic health. If businesses do not expand, the economy will not grow in the long run.

More and larger businesses mean more job opportunities. When you read in the newspaper that investment expenditures are down, you can expect higher unemployment to follow. If these expenditures are up, you probably can look forward to better times and more employment.

Government expenditures are the third part of GNP. Federal, state, and local governments spend money for such things as the construction and maintenance of highways and public transportation systems, education, parks, national defense, and police and fire protection. About 20 percent of GNP consists of direct government expenditures to purchase such goods and services. This percentage may seem lower than you would expect. In part, this is because transfer payments are not counted as part of GNP. **Transfer payments** are money taken from some people and given to other groups. This money is usually collected as taxes and is distributed through programs like social security, unemployment compensation, and welfare. Transfer payments are excluded from GNP because the government is only moving money around. This money will be counted when the people who finally receive it buy goods and services.

Using the Right Measurements

The real GNP of the United States is around $4 trillion. Does this figure represent health for our economy? By itself, the figure does not say much about our economy. Economists are more interested in whether GNP is rising or falling. So they look at the growth rate of GNP to measure economic health. The *growth rate* of GNP is often given as a percentage increase or decrease as compared with the preceding time period. So an annual growth rate of 5 percent would mean that the GNP is 5 percent higher this year than it was last year. If the rate is very low or even declining, obviously the economy is not doing well. In recent years, the economy has grown at an annual rate of about 3.5 percent.

Because GNP consists of the dollar value of all final goods and services, GNP can go up if prices go up. This can happen even if the country is not producing more goods and services. For example, if prices rise by 10 percent and we produce no more goods and services, the GNP will go up by 10 percent.

One way to make sure the GNP measures increases in production, and not just increases in prices, is to use what economists call a **real dollar** as a unit of measurement for the value of goods and services. A real dollar is the value of a dollar in a given year. This year then becomes the **base year** for comparing different years and for determining the real growth in GNP, or *real GNP*.

The year the government currently uses as the base year is 1982, and the real increase in the production of goods and services is figured in terms of what the dollar was worth in 1982. Inflation has caused prices to rise since 1982. So you cannot buy as many goods and services with a dollar today as you could in 1982. Say the price of an apple was 10 cents in 1982, so you could buy ten apples with a dollar that year. Suppose apples now cost 12 ½ cents, so you can buy only eight apples with a dollar today. That means that this year's dollar is worth the same as 80 cents was worth in 1982. By using real dollars, economists can compare GNP in different years using the same measuring stick.

Another way we use GNP measurements is to compare growth rates among countries. To compare GNP among countries, we use per capita GNP. **Per capita GNP** is the total GNP of a country divided by its population. A country with a large population, like the Soviet Union, has a much higher GNP than a small country like Switzerland only because far more people live in the Soviet Union than live in Switzerland. Individuals in Switzerland are actually each producing more goods and services than those in the Soviet Union. This situation is indicated by the fact that the per capita GNP of Switzerland is more than twice as high as the per capita GNP of the Soviet Union. Therefore, per capita GNP is a better indicator of the production of the two nations than the total GNP figures alone.

> Inflation is often anticipated in such things as union contracts. Cost-of-living clauses in those contracts are used to keep up with inflation. Thus, when the inflation rate rises, workers' wages often do too.

The Value of Measurement

Some people say that GNP is not the best measure of our country's economic welfare. They point out that GNP measures only the prices of goods and services. It does not measure the quality of those goods and services. Automobiles that break down and need repairs increase GNP while cars that last a long time lower it. If you drive your car in a crowded city, get stuck in a traffic jam, and use a lot of gas, GNP goes up. You could have taken a clean, air-conditioned train and spent less money. You would have been more comfortable, but GNP would have been lower.

In addition, GNP does not judge the usefulness of the goods and services produced. An expensive program to build housing for poor people will increase GNP, but so will a war.

GNP leaves out many things that money can't buy. Many people value clean air, a beautiful view, and peace and quiet. A new factory may increase GNP, but it may also pollute the air, spoil the view, and increase the noise and activity level.

Most economists would agree that not all economic growth improves our welfare. But they say that, in general, people are better off when GNP is rising. An increase in GNP means more jobs. And many of the goods and services measured in GNP do improve the quality of our lives. For example, building public transportation systems and installing anti-pollution equipment increase GNP. Most of the time, people in countries with a high per capita GNP are better off than those who live in countries with a low per capita GNP. When the rate of growth of GNP slows or drops, it usually means hard times ahead.

Economic Graphs

Study these graphs on GNP, the unemployment rate, and the CPI. Then answer the following questions based on the graphs.

1. A recession is usually defined as a period when real GNP drops for six months or more. During which years did we have recessions?
2. What happened to the unemployment rate during these recessions?
3. What happened to the consumer price index during and after these recessions?
4. Real GNP increases during a period of economic expansion. During which years did the economy expand?
5. Which was the longest period of economic expansion? Which was the shortest period of economic expansion?
6. What happens to the unemployment rate during periods of economic expansion?
7. When did the highest rate of inflation occur? When did the lowest rate of inflation occur?

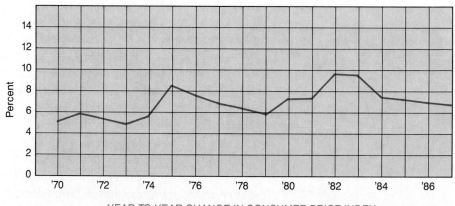

UNEMPLOYMENT RATE, ALL CIVILIAN WORKERS

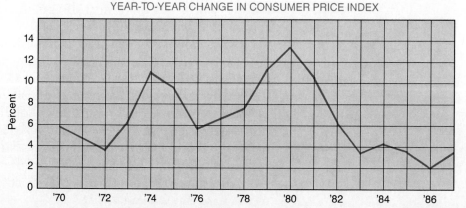

YEAR-TO-YEAR CHANGE IN CONSUMER PRICE INDEX

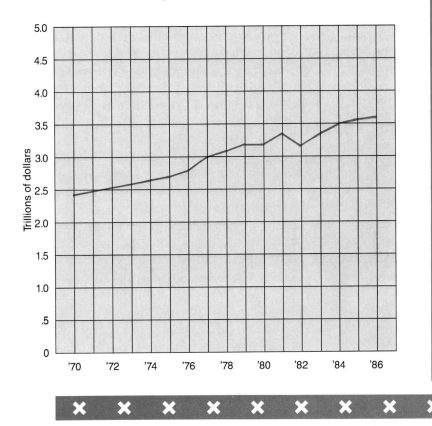

Gross National Product (GNP): 1970 to 1985
(in 1982–1984 dollars)

Trillions of dollars

✓check your understanding ✓ ✓ ✓ ✓ ✓ ✓

1. **What is GNP?**
2. **What are the three major parts of GNP? Which part is biggest?**
3. **Why is investment in factories and equipment important for the health of the economy?**
4. **Why are real dollars used to measure GNP?**

MEASURING UNEMPLOYMENT

You will recall from Chapter 2 that the unemployment rate is the percentage of people who are looking for work but can't find a job. It may not surprise you that the unemployment rate is an economic measurement that many people watch very closely. In times of high unemployment, even people who are working may worry that their jobs could be the next to go. People who are unemployed may feel frustrated and useless because they want to work, but no jobs are available.

Unemployment is higher for teen-agers than for any other group.

Unemployment does not affect all people equally. The unemployment rate for married men is usually lower than for any other group. The unemployment rate for women is now about the same as for men, although it traditionally has been higher. The unemployment rate for blacks often is about twice as high as the rate for whites. Teen-age unemployment is usually highest of all, often double or triple the national average.

How is unemployment measured? During the third week of each month, some 1,000 interviewers working for the Bureau of the Census talk to people in 65,000 households across the country. This sample of the country's population has been chosen according to scientific principles to make sure that it is an accurate reflection of the entire work force of the United States (not counting people working in the armed services).

Anyone over 16 who does any work for pay during that week is considered employed. If you work just one hour for pay, you will be considered employed. If you work 15 hours or more for a family business for no pay at all, you will also be classified as employed.

Anyone over 16 who is not working but is actively looking for work is considered unemployed. The interviewers find out if people are actually seeking work by checking to see if they registered at an employment agency, met with possible employers, asked friends about job possibilities, answered want ads, or used other methods to find a job during the previous four weeks. People who were laid off from a job but are waiting to be recalled to that job are counted as unemployed even if they are not looking for another job.

Increased automobile manufacturing usually reflects a healthy economy.

A person who is not actively looking for work is not counted as part of the labor force. Some people quit looking for work because they never have any luck finding a job. These people are called *discouraged workers*. Some people say the number of discouraged workers is much higher than the Bureau of the Census admits.

✓ check your understanding ✓ ✓ ✓ ✓ ✓ ✓

1. Which groups have the highest unemployment rates? Which groups have the lowest unemployment rates?
2. How would you be classified if an interviewer from the Bureau of the Census interviewed you?
3. What is the difference between an unemployed person and a discouraged worker?

MEASURING PRICES

The prices of all goods and services in the country do not go up and down together. Some go up while others go down. Economists are interested in knowing whether prices in general are rising, which is the general rate of inflation. To find out, they have developed price indexes, which compare the prices of a number of goods and services over time.

The Consumer Price Index

The **consumer price index** (CPI) is the nation's most important price index. The CPI is a measure of the rise or fall in the prices of a certain set of goods and services between one time period and others. The prices of this collection of goods and services, called a *market basket*, are recorded for the first time period, called the *base period*. The prices for the base period are set equal to 100. At another time, say one year later, the prices of the same set of goods and services are recorded again. The prices are then compared on an index scale. Suppose that prices a year later turn out to be 50 percent higher than they were in the base period. The CPI for that year would be 150 (150 − 100 = 50; 50 ÷ 100 = 50%). If the price index was 75 ten years ago and now is 150, prices have risen 100 percent in those ten years (150 − 75 = 75; 75 ÷ 75 = 100%).

In order to make the consumer price index, the Bureau of Labor Statistics checks the prices of about 400 goods and services in 85 cities. The individual businesses selling the goods and services are selected by computer. A consumer price index is made for each city, in addition to the national index, which combines all of them together. The individual indexes are more accurate indications of inflation for those cities than is the national index.

Actually, there are two consumer price indexes. The one reported most often in the news is based on the spending habits of urban wage earners and clerical workers of moderate income. This index covers about 35 to 40 percent of the population. The other, the *all-urban index* illustrated below, covers the buying habits of urban consumers only.

> CPI measures just price change. Price change is only one of many things that affect your cost of living. Other factors include the area you live in, your values, and your lifestyle.

Change in Consumer Price Index
All Urban Index

Base Year = Average of 1982–1984

The index for urban wage earners and clerical workers is often used to determine salary increases in labor contracts. It is based on the buying habits of urban wage earners and clerical workers between 1982 and 1984. Products are ranked according to their importance in the family budget. The index assumes that consumers spend their money according to the following budget:

Good or Service	Percentage of Budget
Housing	43
Transportation	19
Food	18
Clothing and upkeep	6
Medical care	5
Entertainment	4
Other items	5

How much the changes in the CPI affect you depends on how similar your buying habits are to this budget.

Problems with Price Indexes

Price indexes are our most important source of information about inflation, but they can be misread and misinterpreted. They tell where we have been, not necessarily where we are headed. It is misleading to use one month's rate of change in a price index as a prediction of the annual rate of change. Things can happen in a month that will not happen throughout the year.

In addition, there are problems in measuring the real level of prices. For instance:

The CPI assumes a "fixed" market basket. In other words, it assumes that people keep buying the same things, even when prices increase. However, most people don't do that. If the price of beef goes way up, for example, most people will buy more chicken and fish.

- With what year should price changes be compared?
- How heavily should each product or service be weighted? Should everything be counted equally? Should the goods and services people buy most be counted more?
- Whose buying habits should be used: urban workers, the rich, the poor, farmers?
- What should be done when the quality of goods or services improves? Consumers may be paying more, but they are also getting more. For example, if a car with improvements, such as safety devices, has a higher price tag than last year's model, should this be considered a rise in price?

✓check your understanding ✓ ✓ ✓ ✓ ✓ ✓

1. **What does the consumer price index measure?**
2. **List and explain three problems involved in using a price index.**
3. **Why is housing such an important area in the CPI?**

Economic changes from good times to bad times, and then back again, are like a roller coaster.

GNP

∿ Actual growth rate
— Average growth rate

Recovery

Peak
(Prosperity)

Valley
(Recession)

Recession

Valley
(Depression)

Recovery

Peak
(Prosperity)

Years

MEASURING ECONOMIC CYCLES

Over time, real GNP tends to rise and fall according to a pattern. Rather than climbing steadily upwards, it tends to move up and down in an almost geographical pattern of peaks and valleys. The peaks represent good times, and the valleys represent bad economic conditions. Economists call the progression of real GNP from peaks to valleys and back to peaks again the **business cycle**.

A business cycle may go through four stages: prosperity, recession, depression, and recovery. During times of economic health, or **prosperity**, most people are employed and wages are increasing. Businesses are expanding and new homes are being built.

Since World War II, the average length of a period of recovery and prosperity has been slightly less than four years.

Prosperity is sometimes accompanied by inflation. Increasing wages give people more money to spend. If they spend money faster than new goods and services can be produced, prices rise.

In a typical business cycle, recession follows prosperity. Officially, **recession** occurs when the level of real GNP declines for two quarters or half a year. In a recession, businesses reduce spending for new factories and equipment and unemployment rises. Fewer people have jobs, and so, as a group, consumers' income decreases. Lower income decreases demand for goods and services and, therefore, prices fall. Much of what has been made cannot be sold, and inventories of unsold products fill stores and warehouses. At the bottom of the recession, the economy is in bad shape.

If real GNP falls far enough and if unemployment becomes extremely high, a more serious condition than recession occurs. It is called **depression**

During the Great Depression, one out of every four people who wanted to work couldn't find a job.

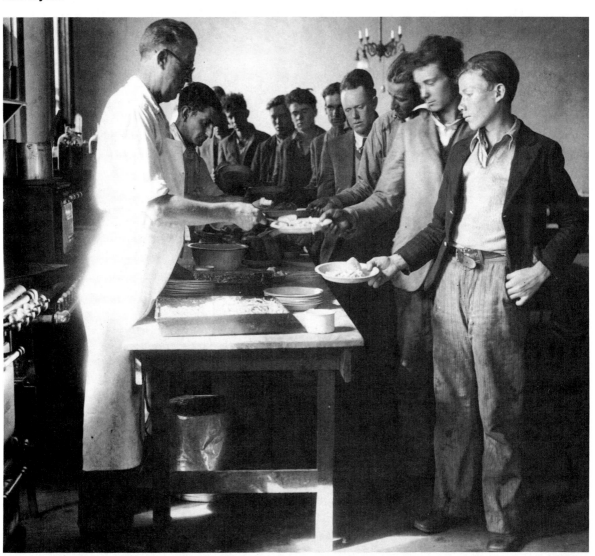

Eventually business picks up, and more people are employed and earning wages. Consumer demand increases and prices rise again. The economy enters the next cycle, a period of **recovery**, leading to another period of prosperity.

However, things do not always work this way. The United States has had prosperity without inflation (in the 1960's), and recessions with inflation (in the 1970's). In 1980 the rate of inflation topped 12 percent with 8 percent unemployment. An economic situation that combines high unemployment and inflation is called **stagflation**. This term comes from the words "stagnation" and "inflation," and it means double trouble.

√ check your understanding √ √ √ √ √ √

1. **What are the stages of a typical business cycle?**
2. **Why is a recession bad for businesses?**
3. **What is the situation called when we have inflation in times of recession?**

S UMMARIZING
the chapter

The goal for our market economic system is full employment without inflation. One way to determine how well the economy is doing is to add up the dollar value of all final goods and services produced in the country in a year. This figure is the gross national product (GNP). Using a real dollar base to eliminate the effects of inflation, we can determine a more accurate figure for GNP, called real GNP. A real GNP rate that is rising means our economy is in good shape.

The unemployment rate tells us what percentage of the people who want to work actually have jobs. Anyone working one hour a week for pay is counted as being employed. People not looking for work are not counted as part of the work force.

Inflation, a general rise in the price level, is measured by price indexes. The Consumer Price Index (CPI) measures the prices of goods and services most commonly bought by urban consumers or wage earners and clerical workers.

Business cycles are a kind of map of economic activity. The stages in the cycle include prosperity, recession, and recovery. Not every cycle follows this pattern. Sometimes, recessions become so severe that they turn into depressions. Also, in the 1970's and 1980's, we have had several periods of stagflation, high inflation with high unemployment.

CHAPTER ◆ A ◆ CTIVITIES

Number your paper from 1 to 13. Then write the term that best matches each numbered definition.

base year
business cycle
consumer price index
depression
gross national product
inflation
per capita GNP

prosperity
real dollar
recession
recovery
stagflation
transfer payments

1. A measure of the rise and fall in price of a certain set of goods and services over time
2. The value of a dollar in a given year, used to compare prices in different time periods
3. A decline in real GNP for at least six months
4. The total dollar value of all the final goods and services produced in the United States
5. A period of high unemployment and high inflation
6. Money collected from one group of people by government and distributed to other groups
7. The ups and downs of our economic system's activities
8. The total GNP of a country divided by its population
9. The period of time upon which the value of a real dollar is set
10. A serious condition of very high unemployment and a severe drop in real GNP
11. Generally rising prices for goods and services
12. A period of economic health, when businesses are expanding production and new homes are being built
13. A period of improving economic activity following a recession

1. Why do economists feel that people are generally better off when GNP is rising? What could cause GNP to rise that would not contribute to people's welfare?
2. What are some of the disadvantages of using GNP to measure our economic welfare?
3. How is unemployment measured?

4. How would the following people be counted in the unemployment statistics? Why?
   a. Frank Basile, a 17-year-old student who works five hours a week at a local gas station
   b. Rebecca Moy, a 22-year-old secretary who decided to be a homemaker after she lost her job
   c. Eileen Bandy, a recent high school graduate who has been looking everywhere for a job but has had no luck
   d. Mark Aleman, a 45-year-old wire cutter who lost his job two years ago and gave up looking for work about six months ago
5. A friend of yours just told you the consumer price index increased 8 percent last year. "Everyone's money is buying 8 percent less than last year," your friend explains. Is your friend right? Why or why not?
6. Identify each of the following stages of the business cycle:
   a. High employment, increasing wages, expanding businesses
   b. Rising unemployment, unsold goods, falling prices
   c. Steep fall in GNP, very high unemployment
   d. High unemployment, high inflation

BUILDING CONSUMER MATH SKILLS

You look at the consumer price index and find the following numbers:

Year	CPI
1984	311.1
1985	322.2
1986	323.4
1987	335.0

1. What was the rate of inflation from 1984 to 1985?
2. What was the rate of inflation from 1985 to 1986?
3. What was the rate of inflation from 1986 to 1987?
4. From 1984 to 1987, was the rate of inflation increasing or declining?

APPLYING CONSUMER SKILLS

1. Senator Marie Shelley is quoted as saying, "If the United States were to double its GNP, I think it would be a much less livable society than it is today." Do you agree or disagree? Why?
2. "America is no longer number one," Congressman Ward Melville claims. "Several other nations have higher per capita GNPs than the United States. We must regain the top spot at any cost." Do you agree with Congressman Melville? Why or why not?

3. Do you believe the unemployment rate shows how well-off people are in this country?

4. In the past, the unemployment rate for women has usually been higher than that for men. In recent years, the gap between the two rates has narrowed so that they are about the same. Why do you think this has happened?

Find out the unemployment rate for your city or area. How does it compare with the national average? Why do you think the average for your area is higher or lower than the national average? Is there a CPI for your city or area? If so, how does it compare with the national CPI? Why do you think your area's CPI is higher or lower than the national CPI?

CONTROLLING PROBLEMS IN THE ECONOMY

Citizens and political leaders frequently argue over how well the economy is performing. They become concerned when either the inflation rate or the unemployment rate is high. Government can do a number of things to bring these rates down. What tools can government use to keep the economy healthy?

■ What causes inflation and unemployment?

■ Does anybody benefit from inflation? Does anyone benefit from high unemployment?

■ How does government attempt to control inflation and unemployment?

■ What role does money play in controlling inflation and unemployment?

In the last chapter, you learned various ways to measure our economic performance. You also became acquainted with the stages of a business cycle. Now you'll examine in detail the problems of inflation and unemployment. These two economic problems occur frequently and have widespread effects.

INFLATION AFFECTS EVERYONE

From the end of World War II in 1945 until the mid-1960's, the economy of the United States enjoyed low unemployment while avoiding high inflation. But in the last part of the 1960's and throughout the 1970's, prices rose rapidly. Most public opinion surveys showed that citizens in the United States ranked inflation as the number one or number two economic problem in the country. Why were people so concerned about it? Why should we be on the alert for it?

Who Is Hurt by Inflation?

Sooner or later, just about everybody loses if inflation is high. Working people who don't receive pay increases equal to the price increases are hurt by inflation. But some people are hurt more than others, especially retired people, those with low incomes, savers, and creditors.

Most retired people live on fixed incomes—incomes that stay the same year after year. They may receive a set amount from a pension, insurance, or a savings plan. When prices rise there are few ways, if any, for them to get more income. So they are forced to buy less.

Low-income people use a large part of their budgets for food, housing, and clothing. When prices rise, they must make difficult choices. They may have nothing at all left over for savings. If inflation continues a long time, they may have to cut necessary expenses, such as food, as they find their small incomes buy fewer and fewer goods and services.

People who have money in savings accounts or who own government bonds are also hurt by inflation. With inflation the purchasing power of your savings goes down. If high rates of inflation continue, many consumers will decide to spend their money rather than save it. But spending their savings will not solve their problems. Consumers without savings will not be ready for emergencies. Also, as you learned in Chapter 5, higher consumer spending can lead to higher prices—that is, to still more inflation.

In times of inflation, creditors lend out money that is paid back months or years later in dollars that are worth less. If the inflation rate is 10 percent a year, a lender must charge 10 percent interest just to break even. That is one reason interest rates are high and loans hard to get during periods of inflation.

If the inflation rate becomes very high, economists call it *hyperinflation.* In Germany in the 1920's, the inflation rate was so high that prices doubled every other day. Workers were paid twice a day so that they could go shopping during lunchtime and avoid the higher prices they would have to pay if they waited to shop after work.

Who Benefits from Inflation?

As bad as inflation is for many people in the United States, it is not bad for everyone. Some people actually benefit from inflation.

As you might expect, if inflation is bad for creditors, it can help out borrowers. Suppose, for example, that you borrowed $100 a year ago at an interest rate of 11 percent. Now you owe the lender $111. But suppose the inflation rate during that year was 13 percent. If you pay back the loan this year, you will be paying with money that is worth less than it was last year, when you borrowed and used the money. This year, the $111 could buy only about as much as $98 could buy last year ($111 − $13). You've come out ahead. The lender, of course, has not.

The borrowers most likely to benefit from inflation are people who borrow to buy a home. As you know, mortgages are long-term loans, sometimes as long as 30 years. Over that time, the interest rate paid on many mortgage loans can turn out to be lower than the inflation rate for the same period.

Stockholders also suffer during inflation. From 1970 to 1980, the cost of living just about doubled. However, the average price of stocks hardly changed at all. The buying power of those stocks was cut in half. They were worth less than when they were bought.

✓check your understanding ✓ ✓ ✓ ✓ ✓ ✓

1. **Why are people with fixed or low incomes hurt by inflation?**
2. **How are creditors and savers hurt by inflation?**
3. **How do borrowers gain from inflation? Which borrowers gain the most?**

Why do most people consider inflation the number one problem in this country? Because while prices are rising, the purchasing power of their income is going down.

Inflation Takes a Bite Out of Your Tax Dollar

Annual Rate of Inflation	Value of Today's $100,000 in		
	5 Years	15 Years	25 Years
6%	$74,726	$41,727	$23,300
8%	$68,058	$31,524	$14,602
10%	$62,092	$23,939	$ 9,230
12%	$56,743	$18,270	$ 5,882
14%	$51,937	$14,010	$ 3,779

Federal and state governments fund programs to teach new job skills to the unemployed.

THE MANY FACES OF UNEMPLOYMENT

People can find themselves out of a job for a number of reasons. The case studies that follow show some of the many faces of unemployment.

CASE STUDY

Marcus Thomas got a job in drafting after graduating from vocational school. It was a good job, but after two years he became tired of northern winters. He read that there were a lot of jobs in the Southwest. At the library, he read the want ads in some newspapers from southwestern cities. Marcus quit his job in January and went south. He was looking for a job with a good salary and benefits. He wouldn't jump at the first opportunity.

CASE STUDY

At 19, Laurie Phillips has not seen the inside of a school for three years. She has seen the inside of car washes, restaurant kitchens, and service stations—but only for short periods of time. Mostly she has been unemployed. Laurie has heard that the unemployment rate is falling, but there seem to be no jobs for her. Although there are thousands of want ads in the paper, Laurie never turns out to be qualified for the jobs offered. Most of them require a high school diploma, and many require much more training.

CASE STUDY

Ric Lopez is a highway construction worker who often works 14 hours a day during the warm months. The fantastic paychecks plus unemployment compensation help tide him over during the winter when there is no work. Of course, he must look for work to get unemployment compensation, but there is no highway work during the winter. Next year, Ric plans to spend two months of that time in Florida. He has started his savings plan already.

CASE STUDY

Joan Pitrowski had put in a good four years at the local car assembly plant. Until this year, in fact, business was so good that Joan got extra pay to work long hours. This year, however, the economy slowed down. Any auto worker knows that when times are tough new cars are among the first things people stop buying. The lots outside the plant were full of new cars, and dealers said they already had enough. The company decided to close the plant until more cars were sold. Joan was unemployed.

Each person described in the case studies above is unemployed, but each is unemployed for a different reason. Economists divide the different kinds of unemployment into four main categories: frictional, structural, seasonal, and cyclical unemployment.

Frictional Unemployment

Some unemployment occurs simply because people are changing jobs. A certain number of people are always looking for jobs with higher pay, better benefits, or a nicer location. This kind of unemployment is called **frictional unemployment** because it is caused by "friction" in the system. People can't find new jobs immediately, so time, or friction, is involved in the search for a new job. Frictional unemployment can actually rise during times of prosperity because increased confidence allows people to quit their old jobs to look for better ones. Many economists believe that frictional unemployment accounts for about 3 percent of the work force. This is one reason unemployment cannot be eliminated.

Structural Unemployment

Another type of unemployment is caused by changes in the organization, or structure, of the economy. This kind of unemployment is called **structural unemployment**. Factories become more

The unemployment rate is highest for teen-agers and lowest for married men.

and more automated. Some areas of the country grow while others decline. New products and services replace old ones.

As a result of these changes in the economy, people trained for some jobs may find there are now few openings in their field. Learning new skills to get a job is hard. In addition, many people, particularly high school dropouts, never learn the skills necessary to find jobs in today's economy.

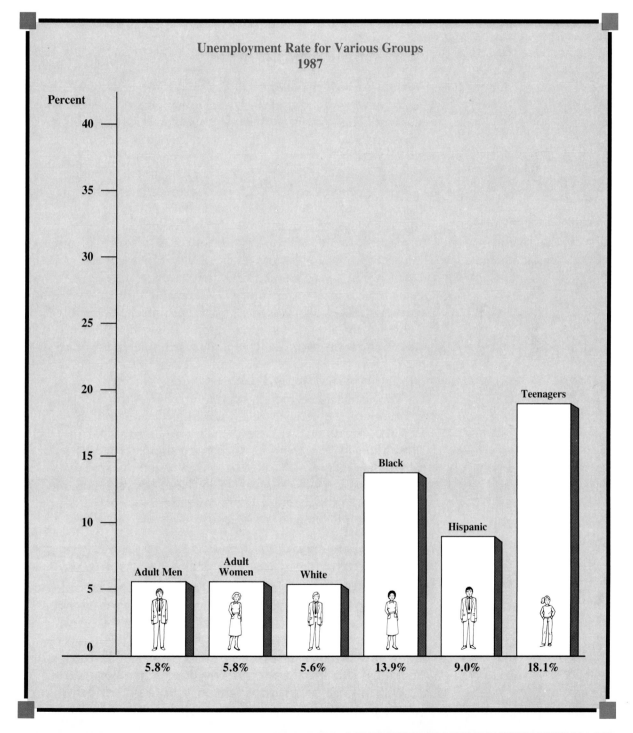

Unemployment Rate for Various Groups
1987

Adult Men	Adult Women	White	Black	Hispanic	Teenagers
5.8%	5.8%	5.6%	13.9%	9.0%	18.1%

Seasonal Unemployment

Some industries hire workers at certain times of the year and regularly lay them off during the rest of the year. This situation is called **seasonal unemployment**. Farm workers, construction workers, camp counselors, and vacation resort employees are among those who work only during certain months. Some industries, such as the automobile industry, close for a while when the companies change production line equipment for the next year's models.

Cyclical Unemployment

As you learned in the last chapter, when the economy enters a period of recession, businesses may cut back operations and lay off workers. This **cyclical unemployment** is caused, therefore, by a downturn in the general economy as part of the business cycle. Such downturns can be caused by lower consumer spending, lower levels of investment, or decreases in government spending.

When spending levels decrease, businesses find that they are keeping on hand more of the goods they should be selling. This build-up of goods is called **inventory**. Too much inventory forces businesses to cut back on production of new goods in order to reduce their inventories. As a result, they lay off production workers.

When employees are laid off, they have less money to spend, so demand shrinks even more. As demand shrinks, even more workers are laid off. This cycle may repeat itself several times.

Investment also slows down during this time. Why invest in new factories or machines when the present ones aren't being fully used? More of the people who build factories or machines are laid off. These people also now have less money to spend.

How ironic! The nation has enough resources to produce goods and services people want and need. Skilled workers are available to work, but no one will hire them and millions are unemployed. The nation is in a recession. If the recession is bad, it is referred to as a depression.

Throughout history we have had periods of cyclical unemployment. One of the main goals of economic policy is to keep these periods from becoming too severe.

One economist believes that if the unemployment rate for teen-agers were the same as it is for older workers, the total unemployment rate would drop by 1 percent.

Some economists say that minimum wage laws cause high teen-age unemployment. Why? Because many employers would hire teen-agers if they could pay them less. However, since employers must pay a minimum rate, employers hire older people who have more experience and don't have to be trained.

✓ check your understanding ✓ ✓ ✓ ✓ ✓ ✓

1. At the beginning of this section you read about four unemployed people and their reasons for being jobless. What kind of unemployment does each person represent?
2. Which kinds of unemployment are most serious, and which are least serious? Why?
3. Which kind of unemployment occurs most often in a recession? in a period of prosperity?

If budget cuts caused this worker to be out of work, his unemployment would be cyclical. If his job could not be done in winter, his unemployment would be seasonal.

Wage and price controls are often used in time of war. Consumer goods are in very short supply during wartime. But income is high, as most people have jobs in the military or helping the war effort. Without controls, the high demand combined with short supply would lead to prices so high that only the rich would get necessities, such as food.

A POLICY OF TAXING AND SPENDING

The federal government's taxing and spending can have an enormous effect on the nation's economy. Because this is so, some economists believe that government can help control the ups and downs of our economic system with a deliberate policy to change taxing and spending. This policy of controlling the amount of money taken in from taxes and the amount spent through government services is called **fiscal policy**.

Fiscal policy and inflation One of the factors that causes inflation is increased consumer and business demand. Government can use fiscal policy to control inflation by reducing consumers' disposable income (or take-home pay), thus reducing consumer demand. Government reduces the income of consumers and businesses by raising taxes. The more they have to pay in taxes, the less they can spend. So raising taxes lowers demand.

In order for this fiscal policy to work, however, government must also cut back its own spending. Increased taxes will not help fight inflation if government puts the money back into the economy by spending the taxes on government programs. So, in times of inflation, government should have a surplus in its budget. It should save the additional money it takes in from the higher taxes to lower total demand.

Hans DEPARTMENT STORE
AUTOMATIC PRICING PLAN
Prices are EXTREMELY LOW to
sell on sight before reductions of
25% after 12 selling days
50% after 18 selling days
75% after 24 selling days

During periods of inflation, consumers look for all sorts of ways to increase the buying power of their incomes.

Fiscal policy and unemployment When unemployment is high, the government needs to put more spending power into the consumers' hands. If Congress and the President cut income taxes, people and businesses will have more money to spend and demand will increase. The increased demand will cause businesses to expand, thus increasing the number of jobs and lowering unemployment.

This process takes a certain amount of time, however. Some economists argue that the amount of time it takes to cut the unemployment rate by cutting taxes is too long. They believe government should help unemployed people more quickly and more directly by hiring them itself. They can be hired to build highways, housing, mass transit, and public buildings, for example. Government can also help unemployed people by giving them money directly through unemployment compensation and through higher social security and welfare benefits. This money doesn't help just unemployed people. When they spend the money, demand increases. More workers are then needed to produce the goods and services the unemployed people can now buy. Thus, many of these unemployed people may be able to find jobs and no longer need government help.

But remember that in times of high unemployment, government cuts taxes. How can a policy work that requires the government to cut taxes and at the same time increase spending? Generally, it must go into debt. When government spends more than it has, it is said to be operating with a **budget deficit**. Many economists believe that budget deficits are healthy for the economy in times of high unemployment.

However, once people get used to a certain level of government spending, they often find it difficult to vote to reduce that level. And budget deficits are not healthy for the economy in times of low unemployment. If the government spends more money than it receives in taxes during a period of low unemployment, the result can be inflation. If government pumps money into the economy when no more goods and services can be produced because labor is in short supply, the only outcome can be higher prices. Economists often describe this situation as "too much money chasing too few goods."

> In the United States, people think of money as coins and paper bills. Another kind of money, however, makes up the largest part of our money supply. Bankers call them *demand deposits*. We call them the balances in our checking accounts.

√check your understanding √ √ √ √ √ √

1. At what two areas is fiscal policy directed?
2. What fiscal policy should the government follow during a period of inflation?
3. What fiscal policy should the government follow during a period of high unemployment?

CONTROLLING THE MONEY SUPPLY

The second major tool that is used to help control the economy of the United States is monetary policy. **Monetary policy** is a plan to increase or decrease the amount of money in circulation. The main idea is to increase the money supply during a recession or depression, and to decrease the money supply during an inflationary period.

Who controls the money supply? Fiscal policy in the United States is set by Congress and the President. Monetary policy, however, is determined by an independent banking system regulated by the federal government. This system, the Federal Reserve System, was established by Congress in 1913.

The system consists of 12 Federal Reserve Banks in various parts of the country and a board of seven governors appointed by the President for a term of 14 years each. Because the President appoints only one new governor every two years, even a President who serves two four-year terms can only appoint four of the seven governors during the time in office. For this reason, the members of the Board of Governors are somewhat free from political influence.

How does monetary policy work? Because the money supply affects the economy, the Federal Reserve System must regulate it. If the Federal Reserve thinks the economy is in a recession, it probably will increase the amount of money in circulation. This situation is often called an *easy money policy*. An easy money policy usually means lower interest rates for consumers and businesses. Interest rates are determined by the supply of money and the demand for money. If the amount of money people want to borrow increases while the amount available to lend stays the same, interest rates will go up.

If the Federal Reserve increases the amount of money in circulation, interest rates should go down. Consumers feel this is a good time to buy something on credit because they can borrow money at lower interest rates. An easy money policy may also encourage people to buy houses since mortgage interest rates are lower. Businesses may borrow money to invest in new equipment and factories. All of this economic activity should help the economy recover from a recession.

To help ease a recession, the Federal Reserve Board will issue an order to increase the amount of money in circulation.

What Is Money?

Before people traded with money, they traded one good for another under the *barter system*. A person traded ten chickens for one pig, for example. But bartering is inconvenient. What the two traders need is a **medium of exchange**—something that helps them trade goods and services more easily. Suppose that the traders agree then that gold will be the medium of exchange. The pig trader can give gold to the chicken trader, and the chicken trader can use the gold to buy a cow.

Money is also a **measure of value**—a way to compare how much two different goods are worth. Today you can use money as a way to compare the value of your income with the value of the goods and services available in the market. You can decide what you can afford to buy because your income is measured in the same units as the prices of what you want to buy.

If you don't want to spend your money today, you can save it for use at a later time. This ability of money to be saved is called a **store of value**. When you put these functions of money together, you see that money is really much more than just coins and bills.

In times of inflation, the Federal Reserve will probably pursue a *tight money policy*. Decreasing the amount of money in circulation should help cure inflation, as less money chases available goods and services. In addition, interest rates will rise. Higher interest rates should discourage borrowing and investment and take excess demand out of the system. Of course, if money is too tight, the Federal Reserve could bring about more unemployment.

OTHER ECONOMIC APPROACHES

Fiscal policy is supposed to work because it regulates demand. When demand is low and unemployment is high, lower taxes and more government spending boost the economy. When high demand causes inflation, higher taxes and less government spending help take the steam out of the economy.

To many economists of the 1980's, too much or too little demand could not be the cause of our problems. After all, too much demand should cause inflation, and too little demand should cause unemployment. How can we have a lot of both at the same time? These

Does the Money Supply Matter?

Most economists believe the money supply is one of several important influences on economic activity. But some economists, called *monetarists*, believe that the size of the money supply is by far the most important cause of economic activity.

In this century, monetarists point out, there has been a close relationship between the amount of money in circulation and economic activity. For example, during the Great Depression of the 1930's, the money supply fell drastically. To end the depression, the money supply should have been gradually increased, the monetarists say. These economists say the reduction in the money supply was the reason the depression lasted so long. In the 1970's, the money supply increased rapidly. This, say the monetarists, is the main reason for inflation.

Another group of economists, called Keynesians (after economist John Maynard Keynes—pronounced "canes"), believe that although the money supply does affect the economy, other factors are important too. They point out that in many countries, notably Japan after World War II, large increases in the money supply have not led to inflation. The economy is also affected by government spending and by interest rates, the Keynesians say.

The debate between the monetarists and the Keynesians has been going on for much of this century. It is one of the reasons different economists offer different solutions to the country's economic problems.

economists, often called **supply-siders**, believe that both unemployment and inflation are caused by supply problems. They believe that we just aren't getting as many goods and services from our resources as we used to.

Controlling Productivity

Supply-siders believe that lower taxes will make people and businesses work harder and take more chances on new ideas. They will be able to keep more of what they earn from this extra work or risk taking. They also suggest removing government regulations and giving tax breaks for business investment made to compete in the world economy. More efficient businesses can produce more from the same number of resources. Even if tax cuts increase demand, supply will also be higher, so there will be less inflation and less unemployment.

Wage and Price Controls

Some people think the simplest way to end inflation is to control wages and prices. Most economists do not believe wage and price controls work. Because controls keep prices from rising, people want to buy more. But businesses have no reason to produce more because they can't raise prices, and workers have no incentive to produce more because their wages won't go up. The lack of goods and services causes shortages. Because people can't get goods and services by paying more, they turn to illegal or "black" markets. The whole economy operates less efficiently.

Another problem with wage and price controls is that it is hard to check up on millions of prices and the wages of more than 130 million workers. Free markets usually work more efficiently than government bureaucracies.

✓check your understanding ✓ ✓ ✓ ✓ ✓ ✓

1. What is monetary policy?
2. What does the Federal Reserve System do?
3. How do supply-siders believe productivity can be increased?

SUMMARIZING
the chapter

The major economic goals of the United States are full employment with little or no inflation. Inflation hurts retired people, low-income people, savers, and creditors. Inflation is of some benefit to borrowers, especially those who take out long-term loans.

Unemployment is a problem with many causes. Frictional unemployment results when people changing jobs do not find new ones right away. Structural unemployment is caused by changes in the organization of the economy. Seasonal unemployment occurs because some work can be done only at certain times of the year. Cyclical unemployment results from a downturn in the business cycle.

The federal government tries to control the economy using fiscal policy to change the amount it takes in from taxes and the amount it spends through government programs. During periods of inflation, the government should increase taxes, reduce spending, and have a surplus in its budget. During periods of high unemployment, the government should cut taxes, increase spending, and have a deficit in its budget.

The Federal Reserve System tries to control the economy by regulating the supply of money. During periods of high unemployment, the Federal Reserve should expand the money supply. During periods of high inflation, it should reduce the money supply.

Supply-siders believe that we just aren't getting as many goods and services from our scarce resources as we used to. They suggest giving businesses tax breaks and removing government regulations to encourage investment. In the process, they believe, the supply of goods and services will become greater so there will be less inflation and less unemployment. Although wage and price controls are favored by many citizens as a control over inflation, these measures have rarely worked well.

◆ C·H·A·P·T·E·R 𝒜 C·T·I·V·I·T·I·E·S ◆

BUILDING CONSUMER VOCABULARY

Number your paper from 1 to 12. Then write the term that best matches each numbered definition.

budget deficit
cyclical unemployment
fiscal policy
frictional unemployment
inventory
measure of value

medium of exchange
monetary policy
seasonal unemployment
store of value
structural unemployment
supply-siders

1. A situation that results when the government spends more money than it takes in from taxes
2. A way in which the federal government can affect the economy through taxation and spending
3. The function of money that makes it possible to keep it and use it later
4. Unemployment caused by a downturn in the economy
5. The function of money that makes it acceptable to use for purchasing goods and services
6. Unemployment caused by changes in the organization of the economy
7. The function of money that makes it possible to compare the worth of one thing to the worth of another
8. A way in which the Federal Reserve affects the economy by increasing or decreasing the amount of money in circulation
9. Unemployment caused by work that is done only at certain times

10. Unemployment caused by people looking for new or better jobs
11. Economists who believe that economic problems can be solved by encouraging business to use resources more efficiently
12. Goods that a business has not sold.

x

BUILDING CONSUMER UNDERSTANDING

1. What can you and your family do to protect yourselves from the effects of inflation?
2. If you were a government official, what kind of information would you want to have before designing policies to reduce unemployment?
3. Which type of unemployment is decribed in each case below?
   a. It's February, and Sam Johnson, a gardener, is out of work until spring.
   b. Maria Santos used to work as a typesetter for a newspaper, but the paper installed computer typesetting systems, which she did not learn how to use.
   c. Harry Andrews has been looking for a job ever since he graduated from college. Everywhere he goes, employers say they are not hiring because business is slow.
   d. Amy Wong has decided to move from Florida to Maine so that she can take up skiing. She will be looking for work as a teacher.
4. Congressman Paul Mays believes a tax cut and higher government spending are needed to lower the unemployment rate, which is at 8 percent. Inflation is also going up at an 8 percent annual rate. Argue against Congressman Mays' ideas.
5. Why would the Federal Reserve System follow an easy money policy?
6. In a television interview, Senator Leona Lopez declared: "We know exactly how to control inflation—with permanent wage and price controls." Do you agree with Senator Lopez's view? Why or why not?

BUILDING CONSUMER MATH SKILLS

1. Assume that the rate of inflation last year was 8 percent. If you had $700 in a passbook savings account paying 5½ percent interest did you gain or lose money? How much did you gain or lose?
2. Using the chart on page 475, assume that the work force is 120 million.
   a. How many total workers were unemployed?
   b. How many times greater is the unemployment rate of black workers than white? Teen-age workers than adult men?

The following data are for an economy like that of the United States.

	Year B	Year C
Unemployment rate	6%	9%
Consumer Price Index (Year A − base = 100)	104	105
Major interest rates	8–10%	6–8%
Real GNP (Year A = 4,000 bil.)	4,200 bil.	4,100 bil.

1. How does the unemployment rate in Year C compare with that in Year B? How does the inflation rate compare? interest rates? real GNP?
2. What phase of the business cycle is Year C?
3. What fiscal policy do you recommend for Year C? What monetary policy would you recommend? Why?
4. What economic policy do you think the government should pursue for Year D? Why?

Find out what the current rate of unemployment is in your community or area. Is it higher than the average for the country? Which kinds of unemployment can be found in your community? Write a letter to your congressional representative recommending an economic policy to deal with this unemployment.

GOVERNMENT TAXING AND SPENDING

Where do governments get the money needed to pay for the goods and services that they buy? Taxes! Local, state, and federal governments all tax and spend. What makes a good tax? How do we want our governments to use this tax money? To us, both as consumers and citizens, these are important questions.

- Why do governments have taxes?

- How is income taxed?

- How are property, goods, and services taxed?

- What are the differences among progressive, proportional, and regressive taxes?

- How large is the national debt?

It is said that nothing is as certain as death and taxes. It is also certain that people dislike paying taxes. Remember the American Revolution. It was fought with the battle cry: "No taxation without representation!"

Taxes are the money we pay to governments to support the services they provide. As Supreme Court Justice Oliver Wendell Holmes said, "Taxes are what we pay for civilized society." The amount we pay for taxes depends on what we want our governments to do for us and how efficiently they do these things. If citizens want government to provide police and fire protection, schools, national defense, and social security benefits, the citizens must pay taxes to provide the money for these services. If people vote for more services, such as newer libraries or more mass transportation, taxes will probably rise. However, more efficiency could lower taxes without decreasing the level of services.

Local, state, and federal taxes take about one third of the income people earn. An average person works about four months of the year just to pay taxes. The total tax bill for a typical family is larger than what it spends for any other single item—such as food or housing. Since we spend more money paying for government services than for anything else, it is important for us to study the taxes we pay—and what services we get for them.

WHERE THE MONEY COMES FROM

The money government has to spend comes from its citizens in one way or another. The amount people pay in taxes depends on where they live, what they earn, what they buy, and what they own.

How a Tax Works

All taxes have some things in common. They are all figured on a base and a rate. The base might be the income you earn in a year. The rate is the percentage of that income that you pay in taxes.

Some taxes have both a nominal and an effective tax rate. The **nominal tax rate** is the "official" one, but the **effective tax rate** is what people actually pay. For example, the nominal federal income tax rate for incomes between $17,850 and $43,150 is 28 percent. But for reasons you'll learn about later in this chapter, the effective tax rate is actually less than that.

Federal, state, and local governments use three bases of taxation: income, wealth, and consumption. Income refers to the amount of money a person earns, usually as a wage or salary, during a certain time period. Wealth is the dollar value of all the things a person owns, minus that person's debts. Wealth includes such things as real estate, cars, jewelry, stocks, and bonds, while income usually refers only to money. Consumption includes all the goods and services purchased by individuals, businesses, and governments.

Tax rates in the ancient world were high. In India and China, kings were paid one fourth of each crop. In Egypt, the king received a fifth of each crop. If a peasant had nothing to give the tax collector, he could be forced to sell his wife or daughter into slavery to get the money.

Taxing Income—At Least Twice

Most people in the United States pay taxes on their income to both federal and state governments. In addition, some cities and counties tax income if they are permitted to do so by the state. So an individual could pay taxes on income as much as three or even four times!

Corporations, which are regarded as individuals for legal and tax purposes, also pay an income tax to both the state and federal governments. Corporations are taxed on their profits—what's left after costs have been deducted from earnings. The corporation's shareholders also pay taxes on any dividends they are paid by the corporation. The corporation's profits are thus taxed at least twice.

Federal income tax The United States Congress determines tax rates through the legislation it passes into law. Currently, the nominal rates of the federal income tax are 15 percent and 28 percent. Married couples pay 15 percent on combined incomes up to $29,750, and single taxpayers pay 15 percent on incomes up to $17,850. People earning incomes above those amounts pay 28 percent on the amount that exceeds $29,750 for married people and $17,850 for single people. This two-tier system of taxation was created by the 1986 Tax Reform Act.

The effective federal tax rates are not as high as 15 percent and 28 percent because a lot of personal income in the United States is not taxed. Why is this?

When the 1986 Tax Reform Act was passed, about 6,000,000 low-income people were dropped from the tax rolls. As of 1988, a family of four making less than $14,480 does not have to pay any federal income tax.

> Income tax on corporations was started in 1909. It was only a 1 percent tax at that time. By the 1980's, the tax rate was 48 percent of income, before deductions.

> **If you don't pay your taxes, the government can take what you have in savings accounts and auction what you own to raise the money you owe.**

Why does the IRS give families with children a tax break? In 1960 it cost $37,274 to raise a child to age 18. It cost $132,414 in 1982, and it keeps going up.

In addition, many welfare payments, most social security payments, and most veterans' benefits are not taxed. The interest received from most bonds issued by state and local governments is also considered to be tax free. For example, if you owned a bond issued by your school district that paid $60 in interest a year, that interest would not be taxed.

Exemptions and deductions

Another reason the effective tax rate is lower than the nominal rate is that taxpayers can exempt, or exclude, a certain amount of money for each person they support from the income on which they are required to pay taxes. This **exemption** amounted to $2,000 in 1989. A family of four, for example, could exempt $8,000 in 1989.

There are other amounts that may be excluded from income. These amounts are called **deductions**. Medical expenses may be deducted if they are over 7.5 percent of a wage earner's taxable income. Expenses such as donations to charities and union dues also may be deducted if they are over 2 percent of taxable income. State and local income taxes and property taxes are fully deductible, as is interest on home mortgage loans.

If taxpayers don't have many of these possible deductions or don't keep track of them, they can deduct, instead, a certain overall percentage of their income. This percentage is called a **standard deduction**. In 1988 the standard deduction was $3,000 for a single taxpayer and $5,000 for a married couple. Starting in 1989, exemptions and the standard deduction will be adjusted for inflation. After the exemptions and deductions are subtracted, the taxpayer figures the tax owed on the balance.

The Internal Revenue Service (IRS) employs 100,000 people and processes 100 million tax returns a year.

Payroll tax Nine out of ten workers have a payroll tax deducted from their incomes. As you learned in Chapter 29, this payroll tax is for social security and is used to supplement the incomes of retired people, to provide survivors' benefits, and to provide disability income.

Workers are not the only ones who pay social security taxes. Their employers are required by law to match the contributions of their employees dollar for dollar.

Taxing Wealth

The income tax raises money based on an individual's annual income. In contrast, a tax on wealth raises money by taxing the possessions that an individual has accumulated. The wealth tax that raises the most revenue is the real estate tax. Basically, the **real estate tax** is a tax on land and what is built on it. As you recall from Chapter 21, real estate taxes are also called property taxes.

The real estate tax is the most important source of revenue for local governments. Counties, cities, towns, and school districts obtain about 75 percent of their money from it. The real estate tax is the third largest source of tax money in the United States. Only the personal income and the social security taxes raise more revenue than the property tax.

Another wealth tax is the **personal property tax**. Items such as cars, jewelry, stocks, and bonds are considered wealth and are taxed by some state and local governments. Other wealth taxes are paid by people who receive inheritances or make large gifts to relatives. Both the federal and state governments collect these taxes, although the federal tax is mostly on large estates and gifts. Inheritance and estate taxes account for less than 1 percent of all revenues.

To raise money, the government taxes what you own, as well as what you earn.

Taxing Purchases

A tax collected on the goods and services that we buy is called a consumption tax. You probably know this type of tax as a sales tax. The **general sales tax** is collected by individual states as a straight percentage of the purchase price of many products. Sales tax rates vary from state to state, but range from 2 to 8 percent.

Consumers are most directly affected by the general sales tax because most items they buy are taxed. In states with high tax rates, the sales tax can add considerably to shopping expenses. In some states, certain items are excluded from sales taxes. These items may include food, medicine, clothing, repairs, and legal and medical fees. Low-income people, who spend a greater proportion of their limited incomes on food and clothing, are helped when sales of these necessities are not taxed.

An **excise tax** is a consumption tax that unlike the general sales tax is levied on specific items. Often it is "hidden" because it is collected from the manufacturer or producer and passed on to the consumer indirectly through higher prices on certain products. The highest excise taxes are levied on gasoline, utilities, alcoholic beverages, and cigarettes. Although gasoline and utilities are necessities, alcoholic beverages and cigarettes certainly are not. Because people will buy these items even if the price goes up, they are a good source of revenue for the government.

√ check your understanding √ √ √ √ √ √

1. **Why does every government—federal, state, and local—have taxes?**
2. **What is the difference between the nominal and the effective tax rate?**
3. **Why isn't all income subject to the federal income tax?**
4. **What is an excise tax? Name four excise taxes. Why are they effective for raising revenue?**

IS THERE A GOOD TAX?

Everyone favors improving the tax system—and usually by reducing taxes! "Reduce my taxes, but don't take away education, highways, parks, or national defense." For economists, tax reform is not so simple. They know there are several characteristics of a good tax, and not every tax is likely to have them all. Designing a tax system involves trade-offs. If citizens and politicians weighed the costs—as well as the benefits—of each type of tax before adopting it, they could improve the quality of the tax system. Here are some questions they could consider when judging a tax.

Different countries use income taxes for different purposes. In Germany, taxes are used to make the economy grow. In Sweden, taxes are used to make the economy stable. In this country, taxes are used to make the economy grow and to make the country stable.

The most famous tax protester probably was Lady Godiva. According to the legend, her husband was a cruel person who taxed the village people to the point where they were near starvation. Lady Godiva asked her husband to show mercy and lift the taxes. He said he'd lift taxes when she rode naked through the streets. She did, and he lifted the taxes.

Is It Fair?

What happens when you and the IRS don't agree on how much you owe in taxes? Many people go to Tax Court. If you ask, the IRS office handling your case can give you information on the procedure. Or, you can write to Clerk of the Court, U.S. Tax Court, 400 Second Street N.W., Washington DC 20217. Ask for the Small Tax Case Kit.

Some people define a fair tax as one that taxes people based on the benefits they receive. Those who use the most services should pay the most, and those who use less should pay less. This theory is called the **benefits-received principle** of taxation. It is the reason that property owners are charged for street, sidewalk, and sewer improvements that directly benefit them. Another example of the principle is the gasoline tax. All the money raised by the gasoline tax is used to build and maintain roads and highways.

Other people feel that richer people can afford to pay more taxes than poorer people and, therefore, should pay higher taxes. This theory is called the **ability-to-pay principle**. It is the reason that the employed are taxed to help the unemployed. In general, the rich pay more taxes to support all the services of government, whether those services benefit them or not. Let's look at examples of various tax structures to see if the ability-to-pay principle can be used as a yardstick of a fair tax.

Progressive Tax One way of putting the ability-to-pay principle into practice is by increasing the rate of taxation as a person's income increases. This kind of tax is called a **progressive tax**. Let's look at how it works.

CASE STUDY

John Bankson, an editor, has a gross income of $22,850. Exemptions and deductions reduced his taxable income to $17,850. He paid 15 percent of this income for his income tax. This amounts to $2,677.50 ($17,850 × .15 = $2,677.50).

Gina Norman is an administrative assistant with a gross income of $30,000. Exemptions and deductions reduced her taxable income to $25,000. She paid 15 percent on the first $17,850 and 28 percent on income above $17,850. Her income tax is $4,679 ([$17,850 × .15] + [$7150 × .28] = $4,679.50).

The person with the higher income not only pays more taxes but at a higher rate. Some people believe that progressive tax rates can get so high that people may become unwilling to make more money. If people are less willing to work and invest, the economy would be hurt.

Proportional tax If the effective tax rate remains the same regardless of an increase in income, the tax is a **proportional tax**, and it works like this. Jill Carter makes $15,000 a year and has an effective tax rate of 10 percent. She pays $1,500 in income tax

($15,000 × .10 = $1,500). Gerald Lee, making $25,000 a year, also has a 10 percent tax rate. As a result, he pays $2,500 in taxes ($25,000 × .10 = $2,500). Both people pay the same percentage of their income in taxes, but, because he earns more money, Gerald pays a larger amount.

Regressive tax If the effective tax rate goes down as income increases, it is a **regressive tax**. Here are examples. Jill Carter pays 10 percent on an income of $15,000, or $1,500. But Gerald Lee now pays 7 percent on an annual income of $25,000, or $1,750 ($25,000 × .07 = $1,750) Notice that Gerald Lee still pays more dollars in taxes. With a regressive tax, though, the person with the higher income pays a lower percentage of income in taxes than a lower-income person.

Almost all of our consumption taxes turn out to be regressive. For example, suppose you and a friend each pay $100 a year in gasoline tax. If you earn $15,000 and your friend earns $20,000, you will pay a greater portion of your income for the gasoline tax.

Is It Efficient?

A good tax should be efficient. It's foolish to spend a lot of tax money just to collect taxes, yet in some small cities over 10 percent of the income tax received is spent collecting it. Since it is hard to track down some personal property, the personal property tax is an inefficient one. For instance, people don't wear their best jewelry or display stock certificates on the coffee table when the personal property tax assessor comes around.

For income tax, on the other hand, it costs the federal government less than one-half penny for every dollar of income tax it collects. Excise taxes are collected at one time from manufacturers.

The state government doesn't have to go to every single consumer to collect the general sales tax. The money is collected mostly from stores, and the government gives the cost of figuring and collecting back to the stores.

Does It Hurt the Economy?

A good tax should not discourage people from working or cause them to change their lives in ways that may hurt the economy. As we said earlier, some people believe that high tax rates on persons with large incomes discourage them from working, saving, and investing.

The property tax has been blamed for causing the deterioration of buildings and neighborhoods. When people improve their property, the assessed value of the property increases. As a result, taxes on the property will rise if the tax rates remain the same. Rather than paying higher taxes, some property owners may choose to let their buildings fall apart. Many local areas exempt the cost of improvements from taxation for a certain period of time to encourage people to fix up their property.

> **If property taxes are too high, people might let their property get run down to lower the value and therefore be required to pay less.**

Does It Bring in Enough Revenue?

If too many property improvements are excluded from the real estate tax, the tax might not bring in enough revenue to pay for government services. A good tax, therefore, should bring in the money it is intended to raise.

When a tax has a base that keeps on rising, additional revenue can be brought in without increasing rates. This kind of tax is called an **elastic tax**. The federal income tax is a good example of an elastic tax. Because this tax is progressive, the government gets a higher percentage of incomes as they rise. Politicians favor such a tax because they don't have to raise taxes continually or create new ones to bring in additional funds.

In order to keep the federal income tax from getting too large and unfair, Congress can pass a new tax laws to set tax rates. The Tax Reform Act of 1986 lowered tax rates on personal income and required indexing. **Indexing** is adjusting income levels for the calculation of income tax to allow for inflation. Personal exemptions and the standard deduction will also be indexed, or adjusted, beginning in 1989.

Is It Politically Acceptable?

Politicians are especially concerned about whether a tax is acceptable to the people. In 1665, the Minister of Finance commented to the King of France that "The art of taxation consists of so plucking the goose as to obtain the largest possible amount of feathers with the smallest possible amount of hissing." Voters often complain to lawmakers that taxes are too high and services too poor. One way to get around this problem is to design taxes that are so politically acceptable that voters don't realize they are paying them. For the politician, a good tax is not seen or felt—only paid.

A large number of regressive consumption taxes owe their existence and survival to the fact that they are politically acceptable. Most people probably could not tell you how much they pay in taxes on utilities, gasoline, alcohol, or cigarettes. They may not even realize they pay them at all.

> A Colorado woman owed $1,725 in taxes. The IRS sold the woman's home, valued at $50,000, for $1,725 to collect what was owed.

> Some people say there should be a *flat-rate* income tax with no deductions allowed. They say that if everyone, including corporations, paid the government 10 percent of their income, the government would have enough income from taxes. Unfortunately, the flat-rate tax doesn't consider a person's ability to pay.

✓ check your understanding ✓ ✓ ✓ ✓ ✓ ✓

1. **Describe the benefits-received principle of taxation. Give one example of a tax that follows this principle.**
2. **Describe the ability-to-pay principle of taxation. Give one example of a tax that follows this principle.**
3. **Give a description and examples of the five tests used to determine a good tax. Does any one tax meet all five tests?**

WHERE THE MONEY GOES

As you learned in Chapter 7, the federal government uses your tax dollars to provide those services that we as citizens expect. Each level of government—federal, state, and local—spends its tax dollars to provide different services.

Federal Government Expenditures

The federal government spends over 40 percent of its revenue for social welfare programs. Such programs are designed to assist various groups of needy people in our society. Through its social welfare agencies, the federal government provides payments for the poor, the disabled, and the elderly. Some government programs provide funds for retraining those who have been laid off their jobs. Unemployment benefits are also available for such people.

From the graph below, you can see that the federal government spends more (dark blue) than it takes in (light blue).

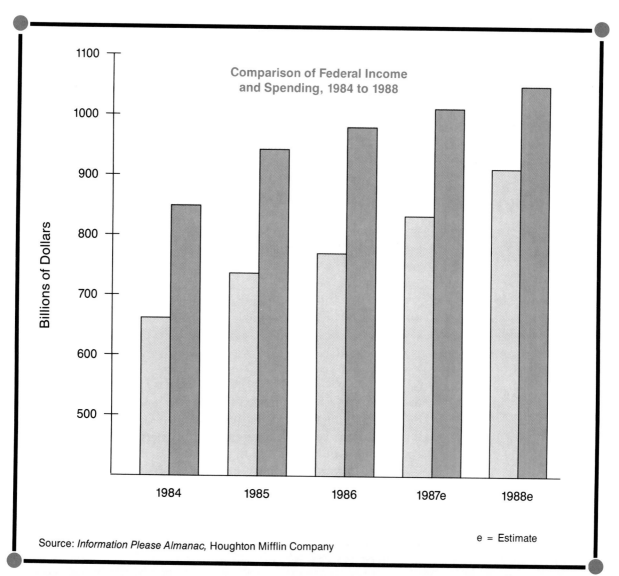

Source: *Information Please Almanac,* Houghton Mifflin Company

e = Estimate

The second largest expenditure of the federal government is for national defense. In recent years, an increase in spending for national defense, as well as for other government services, has caused the national debt to rise rapidly. Interest paid on the national debt is the third biggest expenditure of the federal government. When the federal government spends more than it collects in taxes, the government goes into debt. This practice is called *deficit spending*. How can the government spend more than it takes in? By borrowing.

The size of the national debt is a matter of great concern to many people. They fear that the government has gone beyond its ability to decrease the debt to a manageable size in the near future. The United States has changed from a position as the largest creditor nation in the world to the largest debtor nation in the world.

The federal government has two ways to finance its debt. It can sell government securities, which adds to the debt because interest must be paid on those securities. Or, the government can borrow from the Federal Reserve, in effect creating more money. Both forms of borrowing can create problems in the economy.

If government borrows in the marketplace by selling securities, then money may not be available for consumer and business needs. Government securities are one of the safest forms of investment, so people are more likely to buy those rather than leaving their money in savings accounts where it can be borrowed by consumers or businesses. As a result, consumers and businesses have a harder time borrowing money. Interest rates usually go up. Businesses can't expand, and productivity may be lower. Growth in GNP may decrease.

If government borrows from the Federal Reserve by creating more money, the additional money in circulation can cause inflation. And inflation causes problems for everyone since our dollars are worth less.

In an effort to reduce the size of the national debt, Congress passed the Gramm-Rudman-Hollings law in 1985. This law requires the federal government to decrease the size of the debt each year.

State and Local Expenditures

State and local governments also spend a good share of your tax dollars. The biggest expenditures for most state governments are for education, social programs, health programs, hospitals, and construction and upkeep of highways.

Although much of the money for social welfare programs is provided by the federal government, these programs are administered by the states. These programs include Aid to Families with Dependent Children (AFDC), unemployment compensation, Medicaid, and other programs for the poor. While the federal government provides a considerable amount of the money, the

A simple filing system can help a lot at tax time. Using large envelopes, save your receipts. Have one envelope for medical expenses, one for taxes paid, one for interest income, and so on. At the end of the year, organizing your tax return will be a lot easier.

states also administer funds for the maintenance and construction of highways and for mass transportation.

Local governments provide the services that most directly affect us as citizens and consumers. If you attend a public school, a lot of your costs are paid for by local tax dollars. Local governments provide police and fire protection, supply water, take care of streets, and maintain parks and playgrounds. In addition, many local governments collect trash, provide for sewage removal, operate and staff public libraries, and even offer emergency ambulance service.

√check your understanding √ √ √ √ √ √

1. What is the national debt?
2. Name some of the social welfare services provided by the federal government.
3. Name some services that are provided for people by local government.

SUMMARIZING
the chapter

In the United States, workers pay about one third of their income in taxes. These taxes finance the activities and services of local, state, and federal governments. The three bases on which the government raises revenue are income, wealth, and consumption. The largest taxes that most of us pay are federal and state income taxes.

Economists consider some taxes to be better than others. A "good" tax should be fair, efficient, not harmful to the economy, able to bring in enough revenue, and politically acceptable.

Over 40 cents of each dollar spent by the federal government goes into social welfare programs such as social security, disability insurance, and Medicare. National defense is the second greatest expense. Interest on the national debt is the third largest expense.

When the federal government does not take in enough tax money to pay its expenses, it goes into debt. The size of the national debt is a concern to many people. In an attempt to decrease the national debt, in 1985 Congress passed the Gramm-Rudman-Hollings law.

At the state level, the biggest expenditure is for education. While the federal government helps considerably, a second big expense is social welfare programs. For local governments, too, education accounts for a large share of the tax dollars spent. Other major local government expenditures are for services such as police, fire, and park departments.

C·H·A·P·T·E·R A·C·T·I·V·I·T·I·E·S

BUILDING CONSUMER VOCABULARY

Number your paper from 1 through 16. Then write the term that best matches each numbered definition.

ability-to-pay principle
benefits-received principle
deductions
effective tax rate
elastic tax
excise tax
exemption
general sales tax

indexing
nominal tax rate
personal property tax
progressive tax
proportional tax
real estate tax
regressive tax
standard deduction

1. A tax on land and what is built on it
2. The official tax rate
3. A tax for which the effective rate goes down as income increases
4. Adjusting income tax bases to account for inflation
5. The idea that those who get the most government services should pay the most taxes
6. A tax that is levied on goods or services and collected from the manufacturer or producer
7. A tax for which the effective rate rises as income rises
8. An exclusion from income tax for persons supported by the taxpayer
9. A tax for which the base keeps rising
10. The tax rate that people actually pay
11. The exclusion of a certain percentage of income from tax payments
12. A tax for which the effective rate remains the same regardless of an increase in income
13. A flat-rate tax on the consumption of most goods
14. The idea that the more income you have the more taxes you should pay
15. A tax on wealth such as cars and jewelry
16. Amounts that may be excluded from taxable income

BUILDING CONSUMER UNDERSTANDING

1. For each of the following situations, decide whether the tax is progressive, regressive, or proportional. Explain why you think so.
   a. A tax of 3 percent of the income of taxpayers regardless of how much they make

  b. A tax of 1 percent on the first $1,000 in income, 2 percent on the next $1,000, and 3 percent on the next $1,000

  c. A tax of 15 percent on the first $1,000 of income, 12 percent on the next $1,000, and 10 percent on the next $1,000

  d. A sales tax that does not tax services, but does tax food

  e. A tax of 20 cents on a gallon of milk

2. Give one example of a tax that meets each of the tests for a good tax: fair, efficient, not harmful to the economy, able to bring in enough revenue, and politically acceptable.

3. Give an example of a tax that illustrates the benefits-received principle. What is a tax that illustrates the ability-to-pay principle?

4. How can a general sales tax be made less regressive?

BUILDING CONSUMER MATH SKILLS

1. The following chart shows the federal budget receipts and outlays for 1965 to 1985. Study the graph and then answer the questions that follow.

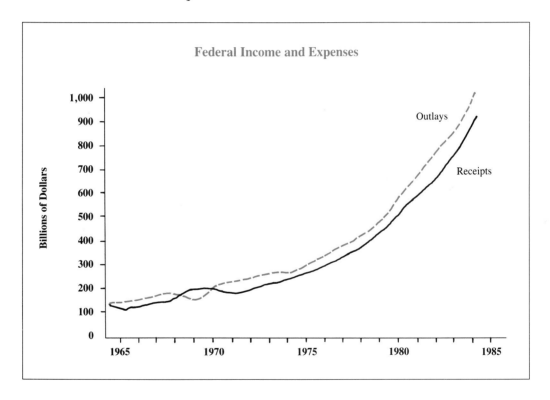

Federal Income and Expenses

a. In which years were federal receipts and outlays about the same?

b. Approximately how much did outlays rise between 1980 and 1985?

c. Which five-year period saw the smallest increase in both receipts and outlays?

d. Approximately how much did income rise between 1980 and 1985?

2. Assume your state has a sales tax rate of 5 percent. Figure the amount of tax and the total price you must pay for the following items.

Items	Price
Color television set	$489.00
Two record albums	7.98 each
Jeans	34.95
Sweater	25.00
Shoes	39.95

APPLYING CONSUMER SKILLS

1. Which areas of federal spending do you think should be cut? Which areas do you think should be increased? Why?
2. Prepare a grid with the five criteria for a good tax listed on the horizontal axis and various taxes listed on the vertical axis. Limit the number of taxes to be analyzed by listing the three most important taxes: income, sales, and real estate. Evaluate each tax according to each criterion either with a plus if the tax meets the criterion, or with a minus if it does not.
3. Which tax is based more on the ability-to-pay theory: the personal income tax or social security tax? Why do you think so?
4. Do you think taxes can get so high that people would be unwilling to make more money? Why do you think so?

GETTING INVOLVED IN YOUR COMMUNITY

Obtain a copy of the annual budget of your city or town. Determine the following:

1. The source of the largest amount of revenue
2. The largest expenditure of tax dollars
3. What percentage of the budget is spent for education and for police and fire protection

Jason was recently elected to the Mayor's Finance Committee. Because the city is short of money, some city services must be cut back or eliminated. Here is a list of possible cutbacks that Jason prepared.

1. Cut police and fire protection. Cutbacks would result in a 20 percent reduction in police and fire department personnel. Some emergency calls might have to "wait their turn" to be answered.

2. Eliminate aid to the homeless. Currently, a city shelter provides cots, showers, and two meals a day for 200 homeless people. Without city funding, the shelter would have to close. The homeless would be forced to find other shelter or sources of aid.

3. Cut parks and recreation services. Cutbacks would mean eliminating summer youth camps and outdoor programs. Maintenance and landscaping staffs would be reduced. Many city swimming pools and playgrounds would be closed.

4. Cut roadworks spending. Road repairs would be minimal. New construction would be halted on a much-needed expressway through the city. The expressway would relieve traffic jams that paralyze city streets every morning and evening.

Answer the following questions on a separate sheet of paper. Use complete sentences.

1. Which cutback will probably affect the most people in the community? Which cutback will affect the least number of people? Which cutback will have the most severe impact on a group?

2. If the issue were voted on, which cutback do you think most voters would be in favor of? Why?

3. Should the mayor consider how his decision will affect his re-election campaign? Explain.

4. What are some of the possible outcomes if the mayor decides not to make any budget cuts at all?

5. What do you think the mayor should do? Can you suggest other ways that the city's budget problems could be solved?

Glossary

A

ability-to-pay principle
The idea that the more income you have, the more taxes you should pay.

abrasion
Wear caused by rubbing.

acceleration clause
A statement in a loan contract requiring you to pay back the full balance if you miss a payment.

additives
Extra ingredients put into food to improve flavor, color, or nutritional value.

adjustable rate mortgage
A mortgage loan in which the interest rate changes according to financial market conditions.

adjusted balance method
A way to determine finance charges by basing them on the balance owed after payments have been made each month.

annual percentage rate (APR)
The interest rate paid in a single year on any money that is borrowed.

antibiotic
A drug that is effective in fighting illnesses caused by bacteria.

antihistamine
A drug that relieves the symptoms of allergies, such as sneezing.

antitrust laws
Laws that prevent the formation of monopolies by setting up rules for fair competition.

arbitration panel
A group that hears and helps settle disputes between consumers and car manufacturers.

attorney general
The top law enforcement official in a state.

automation
The use of machines to produce goods.

average-daily-balance method
A way to figure credit card finance charges based on the average amount owed for each day of the billing period.

B

baby boomers
The large group of people born after World War II, between 1945 and 1960.

bait-and-switch advertising
Advertising a product of poor quality, then encouraging a consumer to buy a higher priced product.

balance
The amount of money that is in an account, such as checking or savings.

balloon-note mortgage
A mortgage that is paid off at a fixed monthly rate for three to five years, after which the remaining balance is due in full.

balloon payment	A final payment on an installment loan that is more than twice as large as the other payments.
bankruptcy	A legal judgment of a person's inability to pay his or her debts.
bar association	A professional organization of lawyers.
base year	The period of time upon which the value of a real dollar is set.
basic form	An insurance policy that covers damage from eleven perils to a house and its contents.
bear market	A market in which the price of stocks is falling.
beneficiary	The person who receives the benefits from a life insurance policy.
benefits-received principle	The idea that those who get the most government services should pay the most taxes.
Better Business Bureau	A group of local businesses that police themselves and help with consumer complaints.
bond	A loan to a corporation that must be paid back on a specific date.
book value	The price recognized by banks and insurance companies for a car of a particular model and year.
brand	The name a manufacturer gives a product or a line of products.
broad form	A kind of insurance that covers seven more perils than the basic form does.
budget	A plan for spending and saving money.
budget deficit	A situation that results when the government spends more money than it takes in from taxes.
building permit	A license issued by a local government giving a land owner permission to build on that land.
bull market	A market in which the price of stocks is rising.
business cycle	A period of the ups and downs of our economic system's activities.

canceled checks	Checks that have been paid from a checking account and that are returned with the statement.
capital gain	The amount of money earned by selling stocks or bonds at a price higher than the price at which they were purchased.
cash surrender value	The cash savings received when an insurance policy is canceled.
cash value insurance	A kind of life insurance that combines a savings program with protection against loss of income.
cashier's check	A check that can be purchased and is written by a bank from its own funds.
category killer	A specialty store that carries a single type of product and practically every product that exists of that particular type.

certificate of deposit	A savings account in which a fixed amount of money is held for a specified length of time.
certified check	A personal check that is guaranteed by the bank in which the account is held.
check	A written order telling a financial institution to take money out of an account and to give it to someone else.
check register	The section of a checkbook where checks and deposits are recorded.
circular flow of income and expenditure	The interrelationship in the economy of consumers, producers, and government.
citizen	A person who lives in a community, state, or country.
Civil Rights Acts/laws	Laws that protect people from unfair treatment because of race, sex, religion, or age.
claim	The money paid out by insurance companies to their customers to cover insured losses.
clearance sale	A sale to encourage customers to buy items in low demand.
clearing	The process of taking money out of a checking account and giving it to the payee named on the check.
closing	The meeting at which the ownership of a house is transferred from the sellers to the buyers.
closing costs	Fees paid to the lender to obtain a mortgage.
collateral	Something of equal value to a loan that serves as protection for the money borrowed.
collection agency	A business specializing in debt collection.
collection agents	Professional debt collectors.
collision insurance	Pays for the damage to your car if it is hit by another car.
command economic system	An economic system in which the government makes the production decisions.
common stock	The kind of stock a corporation issues in order to get started; holders of common stock can vote for the board of directors and for policy changes.
comparison shopping	Gathering information about prices and quality.
competition	Two or more businesses selling the same or a similar product or service.
compound interest	Interest that is earned not only on the principal but also on the interest already earned.
comprehensive form insurance	Insurance that provides maximum protection for a house and the personal property in it.
comprehensive insurance	Protects your car against damage caused by something other than a collision.
condominiums	Multi-family housing owned by all of the people who live in the units.

consumer	A person who buys goods and services.
consumer price index	A measure of the rise and fall in the price of a certain set of goods and services over a specific time period.
contingency clause	A protective clause put in a purchase-and-sale agreement.
contingency fee	A lawyer's fee based upon the percentage of money won in a lawsuit.
contract	A written legal agreement between two or more people.
convenience foods	Food that is partially or completely prepared by the manufacturer.
corporation	A business organization in which the owners are stockholders who do not operate the business.
co-signer	Someone who agrees to make the payments on a loan if the original debtor does not.
credit	The opportunity to borrow money or to receive goods or services in return for a promise to pay later.
credit bureau	A company that gathers and sells credit information about consumers.
credit rating	How good or bad a credit risk a person is thought to be.
creditor	One who lends money.
cyclical unemployment	Unemployment that is caused by a downturn in the economy.

D

dealer's cost	The amount a car dealer pays to the manufacturer for a new car.
debt consolidation loan	A long-term loan used to pay off other loans.
debtor	One who borrows.
decreasing-term life insurance	A policy in which the premiums stay the same, but the amount of protection goes down.
deductible clause	Requires the insured to pay a certain amount of a repair bill before the insurance company will pay the rest.
deductions	Money taken out of a paycheck for such things as federal income tax, union dues, and health insurance; the amounts of money that may be excluded from taxable income.
default	To fail to meet payments on a mortgage loan.
deferred payment price	The total cost of a purchase using installment credit that includes down payment, principal, and finance charges.
deficiency judgment	A legal notice stating that more money is owed on an installment debt even though the item has been repossessed.
demand	The amount of goods and services consumers are willing and able to buy at a certain time.
demonstrator	A car used by a car dealer to show features to potential customers.

department of consumer affairs	A local government agency that can take legal action against businesses that break consumer protection laws.
Department of Housing and Urban Development	The federal agency that requires manufactured housing to meet certain standards of design, construction, and safety.
deposit	The amount of money put into a checking or savings account.
depreciation	The amount an item loses in value as it ages.
depression	A serious condition of very high unemployment and a severe drop in real GNP.
derived demand	The change in consumer demand for goods and services and the effect it has on available jobs.
developer	A person or company that builds new housing.
diagnostic center	A shop equipped with electronic equipment to test cars.
disability insurance	Insurance that pays part of a person's salary if that person is out of work due to injury or illness.
discretionary income	The money a person has left over after paying for necessities.
discrimination	Singling out a group of people for unfair treatment.
disposable income	Take-home pay or the amount left after deductions.
distributor	A business that moves goods and services from one company to another.
dividends	Corporate profits paid to shareholders.
down payment	A certain percentage of the purchase price of an item bought on credit that the borrower pays first in cash.
drawee	The financial institution that pays out the money specified on a check.
drawer	The person who orders a financial institution to take money out of an account and to pay it to someone else.

earnest money	A deposit made on a house.
earnings	The amount of money received from a return on an investment.
effective tax rate	The tax rate people actually pay.
elastic tax	A tax in which the base keeps rising.
Electronic Funds Transfer	A computer-run system used to transfer funds from one bank account to another without using checks or cash.
elimination period	The amount of time that must pass before long-term disability insurance goes into effect.
emergency care	Immediate medical attention for an accident or illness.
endorse	Signing the back of a check in order to cash it or give it to someone else.
Equal Credit Opportunity Act	A law preventing creditors from denying credit for any reason other than a person's ability to pay.

evict	To force a tenant to leave a house or apartment.
excise tax	A tax levied on goods or services and collected from the manufacturer or producer.
exemption	The amount of money allowed for persons supported by the taxpayer that is excluded from taxable income.
express warranty	A written warranty.

F

face value	The amount of money the beneficiaries will receive from an insurance policy.
factors of production	Resources that a country has.
factory-built homes	A house built in a factory and moved to the home site.
fad	Something that is very popular for a short period of time.
Fair Credit Billing Act	A law that provides a process by which consumers can correct credit card or charge account mistakes.
Fair Credit Reporting Act	A law granting borrowers the right to know about and to challenge information that credit bureaus have about them.
Fair Debt Collection Practices Act	A federal law regulating the methods used by collection agents.
fear sell	Pressuring a consumer into buying a product by warning about dangerous consequences if it is not purchased immediately.
fee-for-service	A way of paying for medical care in which you are able to select the doctor you wish and to pay for the doctor's bills out of your own funds or to turn them over to a health insurance company.
FHA loan	A mortgage loan guaranteed by the Federal Housing Administration.
FICA (Federal Insurance Contributions Act)	A law that requires employers to withhold money from employees' salaries to pay for social security benefits.
finance charge	The interest paid on a loan.
fiscal policy	The policy that controls the amount of money taken in from taxes and the amount of money spent by the government.
fixed costs	Expenses that remain the same no matter how much a business sells.
fixed expenses	Bills that are the same each time you pay them, such as rent, loans, and insurance.
fixed-rate mortgage	A mortgage loan in which the interest rate remains the same for the entire life of the loan.
floater contract	An addition to an insurance policy that covers special items of personal property.
foreclosure	Repossession of a house by a mortgage lender.
four basic food groups	Categories of food that are good sources of necessary nutrients.

franchise	The right of one company to use the name, business methods, and advertising of another company.
fraud	Getting money or other gains through deception.
free gimmick	Offering what appears to be something for nothing.
frictional unemployment	Unemployment caused by people looking for new or better jobs.
full replacement cost coverage	An option for homeowners' insurance that pays the replacement cost, with no deduction for depreciation.

G

garnishment	The taking by a creditor of wages or salary for payment of a debt.
general sales tax	A flat-rate tax on the consumption of most goods.
generic foods	Foods that have no brand name.
goals	The things a person tries to reach or obtain in life.
goods	Things we can touch that satisfy our wants.
grace period	The length of time you have in which to pay a bill so that you can avoid paying a finance charge.
gross income	The total amount of money, before deductions, that a person earns.
gross national product (GNP)	The total dollar value of all the final goods and services produced in the United States in one year.
group health insurance	Health insurance provided through a company or other organization.
group life insurance	Life insurance bought by people who are employees of a business or members of an association.
guaranteed insurability	A provision that allows a person to buy additional insurance at an older age, regardless of health.

H

high ball	Offering a customer a high price for a car that is to be traded in and also a high price for the car that the customer wants to buy.
holder in due course	The new creditor when an installment loan contract is sold.
homeowners' policy	An insurance package that includes both liability insurance and protection for personal and real property.
hospital expense insurance	Insurance that pays for all or part of the expenses associated with a hospital stay.
house brands	A store's own brand, which is usually cheaper than a nationally advertised brand.

I

implied warranty	An unwritten warranty.
impulse buying	Buying something without thinking first.
income	The money a person or a business makes.
indexing	Adjusting income tax bases to account for inflation.
inflation	A general rise in prices for goods and services that is caused by a change in the amount of money in circulation.
information costs	Time and money spent gathering information about prices and quality.
innovation	Improving or inventing new products or services.
installment cash loan	A money loan that is paid back in equal monthly payments.
intangible	Something that cannot be touched.
interest	Money a financial institution pays for the use of the money in an account.
interest-adjusted cost	A measure of the cost of whole life insurance by which its cash value is compared with the amount that the money paid in premiums would earn if placed in a savings account.
inventory	An itemized list of personal property; the items owned by a business.

L

landlord	The owner of a rental house or apartment.
law of demand	A rule stating that people will buy less when prices rise and more when prices fall.
law of supply	A rule stating that producers are willing to provide more of a product if the price rises and less if the price falls.
lease	A rental agreement that states the rights and duties of the landlord and tenant.
legal clinic	A group of lawyers who specialize in simple legal services and charge a fixed fee for performing them.
legal referral service	A service that recommends lawyers.
lemon laws	State laws designed to help consumers with new cars that have many problems.
level-term insurance	A policy in which the amount of protection stays the same while the cost of the premium increases each time the policy is renewed.
liability insurance	Pays the cost of bodily injury and property damage you cause to others.
line of credit	The limit that can be charged on a revolving charge account.

liquidity	The ease with which savings or an investment can be changed into cash.
loss leader	A product priced close to the wholesale cost to encourage people to come to a store.
low ball	Offering a low price on a car and then changing to a higher price, hoping the customer is still willing to buy.

M

maintenance fee	The monthly charge for using, maintaining, and repairing the common areas in a condominium.
major medical insurance	Insurance protection against long-term or very costly health expenses.
malpractice	Carelessness or unusual mistakes made by a doctor.
manufactured-housing communities	Places where people can rent land on which to put manufactured housing.
manufacturer	A business that makes goods from raw materials.
market economic system	An economic system in which production decisions are determined by the consumers.
market price	The point at which the quantity demanded by the consumers is equal to the quantity supplied by the producers.
marketplace	An opportunity for producers to sell, and consumers to buy, goods and services.
markup	The percentage that retailers increase the price of an item over its wholesale cost.
maturity	The date on which you may withdraw money from a savings plan without penalty.
maturity date	The date on which you may withdraw money from a CD; the date on which a bond debt must be repaid.
measure of value	The function of money that makes it possible to compare the worth of one thing to that of another.
Medicaid	A federal program of health insurance for the poor.
medical coverage	Auto insurance that pays doctor and hospital expenses for injuries to you no matter who is at fault.
medical expense insurance	Insurance that pays for doctor fees for services other than surgery.
Medicare	A federal program of health insurance for the elderly and the disabled.
medium of exchange	The function of money that makes it acceptable to use for purchasing goods and services.
mixed economic system	An economic system in which the government, producers, and consumers together make the decisions.
monetary policy	A plan to increase or decrease the amount of money in circulation.

money-market fund	A savings account that is offered by companies that sell stocks and bonds.
money-market savings account	A savings account in which the interest rate varies depending on stock market conditions.
money order	Like a purchased check, it is an order to pay a specific amount of money.
monopoly	A business that sells goods or services that no other business has.
mortgage	An installment loan for housing.
multi-family dwelling	A building that contains the homes of more than one family.
multipurpose card	A revolving credit card that may be used in different businesses.
mutual fund	A pool of money used by an investment company to buy a variety of stocks and bonds.

N

natural fibers	Fibers made from materials found in nature, such as plants or animals.
no-fault insurance	Protects the insured person no matter who is at fault in an accident.
nominal tax rate	The official tax rate.
non-exclusion	The principle that people cannot be excluded from using certain public goods or services even if they are not paying for them.
nutrients	The ingredients in food that provide you with nutrition.
nutrition	The process by which the body uses nutrients from food to maintain health and promote growth.
nutritional labeling	Labels on food items giving information about the nutritional content.

O

odometer	The instrument on a car that measures how many miles the car has been driven.
open dating	Labeling a food product to tell the consumer the last date on which it can safely be sold.
opportunity cost	What you give up to be able to buy something else.
options	Extra items, such as air conditioning, that add to the base price of a new car.
over-the-counter (OTC) drugs	Drugs that can be bought without a doctor's prescription.
over-the-counter stock	Stock that is not purchased through an exchange.
owners' association	The organization that makes decisions about the maintenance and expansion of a condominium complex.

P

partnership	A business owned and operated by two or more people.
passbook account	A savings account with high liquidity but usually a low rate of interest.
patent and copyright laws	Laws that prevent people from making or selling a product that belongs to another person or company.
payee	The person, business, or group to whom a check is written, and who will receive the money.
per capita GNP	The total GNP of a country divided by its population.
perils	An insurance term for the possible dangers that could cause damage to personal or real property.
permanent care labels	Labels sewn into clothing to tell you how to clean it.
personal liability insurance	A policy that provides protection against injury or damage caused to another person.
personal property	All possessions except land and things permanently attached to land.
personal property tax	A tax on possessions such as cars and jewelry.
personal resources	Things such as money, time, or skills that we use to satisfy our wants.
point	A charge made by a mortgage lender equal to 1 percent of the cost of a mortgage loan.
pollution	Something harmful added to land, water, or air.
predelivery inspection form	A list of things to be checked on a new car by a dealer's mechanic.
preferred stock	Stock that pays fixed dividends when a company pays dividends.
premium	The amount a person pays for insurance.
prepaid legal services	Legal services available through professional organizations, labor unions, or credit unions.
prescription drugs	Drugs that cannot be bought without a doctor's prescription.
preservatives	Extra ingredients put into food to keep it from spoiling.
previous balance method	A way of determining credit card finance charges based on the entire amount owed from the past month and allowing no deductions for payments made.
price-earnings ratio	The figure obtained by dividing the current price of a stock by the earnings per share over the past year.
primary-care physician	The doctor who is seen first for routine care.
principal	The amount of money borrowed, excluding the interest.
producer	A person who makes goods or provides services.
profit	The money a business has left after selling its goods and services and paying expenses.

progressive tax	A tax in which the rate increases as a person's income increases.
promissory note	A written agreement stating the terms of an installment cash loan.
promotional sale	A sale on new items or items just coming into season to compete with other stores on the basis of price.
proof-of-purchase label	The part of a box or label sometimes required by a manufacturer to qualify for a rebate.
property tax	A tax on land and what is built on it. Also known as real estate tax.
proportional tax	A tax in which the effective tax rate remains the same regardless of an increase in income.
prosperity	A period of economic health, when businesses are expanding production and employment is high.
pro-tenant leases	Leases that spell out the duties of the landlord as well as those of the tenants.
public goods	Goods and services that only government can provide.
purchase-and-sale agreement	A contract signed by the buyer and the seller of a house setting up the terms of the sale.

R

rain check	A written promise for the consumer to be able to buy an item at the sale price if a store is sold out of the item.
raw-goods producers and processors	Businesses that provide and process natural resources.
real dollar	A unit of measurement for the value of goods and services, based on the value of the dollar in a given year.
real estate brokers	People who sell housing as a profession.
real estate taxes	Taxes collected by local government, based on the value of land and what is built on it.
real property	Land and all buildings attached to land.
rebate	A refund on part of the price of a product.
recall	The manufacturer's notice to return cars of a certain model and year to the dealer to repair defects at no charge to the owner.
recession	A decline in the level of the GNP for six months.
recommended daily allowance (RDA)	The amount of nutrients a person needs daily to stay healthy.
recovery	A period of improving economic activity following a recession.
referral selling	Offering customers free merchandise or an amount of money if they buy a product or service.
registered identification number	A code substituted for the manufacturer's name on a clothing tag.

regressive tax	A tax for which the effective rate goes down as income increases.
regulatory agency	Any government body that has the power to make and enforce rules and regulations.
rent control laws	Laws telling landlords how much they can raise rents.
repossession	Taking back a purchased item if a loan is not repaid.
retail installment credit	Credit given by a seller of goods and services that is paid for in equal amounts for a set time period.
retailer	A business that sells directly to the consumer.
return on equity	A measure of the success of a business by comparing the profits with the amount the owner has invested in a business.
return on sales	A measure of how well a business is doing by comparing the profits of the business with its sales.
revolving charge account	A loan that does not have to be paid back in a specified period of time.
rider	An addition to a life insurance policy.
Rule of 78	A way of determining how much borrowers owe when they want to pay off loans early. It states that the initial payments were interest and the later ones, principal.

S

seasonal unemployment	Unemployment caused by work that is done only at certain times during the year.
second opinion	Another doctor's views about a medical problem.
securities	Another name for stocks and bonds.
security deposit	Money held by the landlord to pay for any damage caused by a tenant.
service firm	A business that sells services rather than goods.
services	Things we can't touch that satisfy our needs and wants.
shared consumption	A characteristic of a good or service that it can be used by more than one person at the same time.
shoplifting	Stealing merchandise from a store.
shortage	The situation when there is not enough of a product for everyone who wants to buy it.
side effects	The ways a drug affects the body in addition to the way it is meant to work.
single-family house	A type of housing, not attached to any other buildings, in which a single person or family lives.
single-premium life insurance	A policy that offers the least insurance protection and is almost all savings.
single-purpose card	A credit card that be used only in one company's stores.

small-claims court	A court that deals with minor legal matters involving limited amounts of money.
social security	Federal insurance that provides retirement benefits, disability insurance, and life insurance.
sole proprietorship	A business owned and operated by one person.
specialist	A doctor who practices in a single branch of medicine.
stagflation	An economic situation that combines high unemployment and high inflation.
standard deduction	The exclusion of a set percentage of income from tax payments.
standard features	The items that are included in the base price of a car.
standards of identity	Standard recipes established by the Food and Drug Administration for certain products.
sticker price	The base price of a new car, as suggested by the manufacturer, and the cost of the options that have been added.
stock	Shares of ownership in a corporation.
stockbroker	A professional dealer in stocks and bonds.
store of value	The function of money that makes it possible to keep it and use it later.
structural unemployment	Unemployment caused by changes in the organization of the economy.
sublease	To rent an apartment from a tenant.
suburb	An area of homes just outside a city.
sun protection factor (SPF)	A rating system that indicates how well a product protects against the rays of the sun.
supply	The amount of goods and services producers are willing to sell at a particular time.
supply-siders	Economists who believe that economic problems are caused by supply problems and that they can be solved by encouraging business to use resources more effectively.
surgical expense insurance	Insurance that pays the surgeon's fee for an operation.
surplus	The amount of a product that producers want to sell that is more than consumers want to buy.
symptoms	The signs that a person may be suffering from an illness.
synthetic fibers	Fibers that are made from chemicals.

T

tangible	Items that can be touched.
technology	The application of scientific knowledge in business or industry.
tenancy at will	Renting a house or apartment without a lease.

tenants	People who live in a house or apartment owned by someone else and who pay rent to the owner.
term insurance	A life insurance policy that does not accumulate cash value.
Textile Fiber Products Identification Act	A law requiring labels be sewn into clothing to identify fiber content.
thirty-day charge account	Credit that costs nothing in finance charges if the bill is paid in full each month or within the billing period.
title insurance	Insurance that protects a house buyer in case something turns out to be wrong with the title.
title search	Examination of ownership records of a property to establish the legal owners.
trade-in	A car taken by a car dealer to cover all or part of the down payment on another car.
trade-off	Getting more of one thing by choosing less of something else.
traditional economic system	An economic system in which decisions are made based on past customs, laws, or practices.
transfer payments	Money collected by the government from one group and given to others.
travel-and-entertainment card	A multipurpose credit card that does not usually charge interest but requires that the entire balance be paid off upon receiving the bill.
traveler's check	A check that is purchased for use while traveling.
trust	A plan by which one person holds and manages property for someone else.
Truth in Lending Law	A law requiring all creditors to state finance charges and interest rates in the same way.

U

umbrella policy	An insurance policy that provides $1 million worth of protection against liability lawsuits.
underinsured motorist insurance	Makes up the difference if the person at fault in an accident does not have enough insurance to cover your losses.
unemployment insurance	Income protection for workers who are laid off from their jobs.
unemployment rate	The percentage of people who are looking for work but cannot find a job.
uninsured motorist insurance	Provides protection against a driver who does not have liability insurance.
unit pricing	A way for consumers to compare the cost of different sizes of the same item.
United States savings bond	A loan of money to the federal government.

universal life insurance	A policy in which the cash surrender value is determined by the current interest rates.
utilities	Expenses such as phone, gas, electric, and water that should be included in the cost of housing.

V

VA loan	A mortgage guaranteed by the Veterans Administration.
values	Inner feelings about what is good or desirable.
variable costs	Expenses that change with the amount of goods and services a business sells.
variable expenses	Bills that are different each time, such as for food, clothing, and recreation.
variable life insurance	A policy that allows a person to tell the insurance company where to invest the premium money.
voluntary compliance	A settlement of a consumer complaint by a business without an admission of guilt.

W

walk-in clinic	A medical office set up to treat people without an appointment.
wants	Goods or services that consumers need or would like to have.
warranty	The retailer's promise that a product is of a certain quality or will perform in a certain manner.
warranty of habitability doctrine	Laws that make landlords responsible for services whether or not they are mentioned in the lease.
whole life insurance	A policy in which the insured pays the premiums as long as he or she lives, but for which the cash surrender value remains the same.
will	Instructions on how money and property will be distributed after a person's death.
Wool Products Labeling Act	A law requiring the three kinds of wool used in clothing to be identified.
workers' compensation	A state-run program paid for by employers to provide income protection for workers injured on the job.

Y

yield	The percentage by which savings or investment grows in a single year.

Z

zoning laws	Regulations that describe the kind and nature of buildings permitted in various parts of a community.

Index

HUD, 366
hyperinflation, 471

I

implied warranty, 123
impulse buying, 166
income
    and granting of credit, 224
    defined, 86
    discretionary, 259
    disposable, 35
    education and, 7
    estimation of, 34–36
    gross, 35
    retirement, 439
    variable, 36, 38
income protection
    disability insurance, 437
    unemployment insurance, 438
    workers' compensation, 437–438
income taxes, 36
independent practitioner association (IPA), 207, 443
indexing, 496
individual retirement account, 414
inflation
    credit and, 471–472
    defined, 454
    effects of, 471–472
    fiscal policy and, 477
    hyperinflation, 471
    monetary policy and, 481
    stagflation, 466
    stockholders and, 472
    wage and price controls and, 48
information cost, 116
innovation, defined, 93
installment credit
    cash loan, 224, 250
    co-signer for, 250
    FTC and, 250
    holders in due course, 250
    life insurance on, 249–250
    mortgage, 319
    reading contracts for, 249–250
    retail, 223, 249

    Truth in Lending Law and, 247
insurance
    car. *See* automobile insurance.
    claim, 299, 380
    dental, 446–447
    disability, 437
    flood, 379
    health. *See* health insurance.
    homeowners'. *See* homeowners' insurance.
    liability, 375
    life. *See* life insurance.
    premium, 299
    renter's, 373–375
    social security, 439
    unemployment, 438
intangible products, 22
interest
    compound, 394–395
    defined, 74
    from checking account, 398
    on savings, 392–395
interest rate, 231
    credit card, 242
    inflation and, 471–472
    monetary policy and, 480
inventory, 380, 476
investment, defined, 455
IPA, 443
IRA, 414

J

Jefferson, Thomas, 168
Johnson's Charts, 412
joint checking account, 52
junk bond, 414

K

Keynesian economists, 482

L

label
    cosmetic, 197–198
    food, 163, 165
    medicine, 193
    merchandise, 121–122

labor, 68
  laws affecting, 106
land, as resource, 68
landlord-tenant matters, lawyers' role
  in, 210
law
  antitrust, 105
  civil rights, 106
  consumer protection, 106–109
  copyright, 104
  fair labor, 106
  "lemon," 295
  patent, 104
  zoning, 367
law of demand, 75
law of supply, 76
lawsuits, 210
lawyer
  choosing, 212
  fees, 213
  finding, 210
  function of, 209–210
  types of practice, 211
lease, 331–335
  defined, 331
  pro-tenant, 334–335
  sublease, 335
legal clinic, 211
legal referral service, 210
legal services, prepaid, 211
lemon law, 295
letter writing, 144–145
liability
  limited, 90
  unlimited, 89
liability insurance, 302, 375
life insurance
  agent, 428–431
  beneficiary of, 420
  Best's reports, 427
  cash-value, 423
  choosing, 427–431
  decreasing-term, 422
  face value of, 420
  group, 422
  interest-adjusted cost, 427–428
  level-term, 422

  need for, 420–421
  rider to, 422, 429
  single-premium, 424
  social security as, 439
  term, 422
  types of, 422–426
  universal, 424
  variable, 424
  whole, 423–424
limited liability, 90
liquidity, 395–396
loan
  debt consolidation, 258, 261
  FHA, 345
  home equity, 346
  VA, 346
loss leader, 119
losses, minimizing, 88

M

Magnuson-Moss Warranty Act, 123
mail fraud, 135
mail order, 126–127
  problems with, 126
  regulation of, 127
malpractice, medical, 207–208
manufactured-housing community, 368
manufacturer, defined, 84
market
  "black," 483
  bull vs. bear, 407
  economic system, 71–73
  price, 77
marketplace, defined, 72
markup, 119
MasterCard, 241
maturity date
  of bond, 405
  of CD, 397
Medicaid, 446
medical care. *See* doctor; health care; health
  insurance; medicine.
Medicare, 445–446
medicine
  acne, 191

P

paper money, 221
parent company, 91
partnership, 89–90
passbook account, 397
patent law, 104
payee, defined, 53
payment, transfer, 456
payroll tax, 36, 491
peer pressure, 12
permanent care label, 182, 184
personal identification number, 60
personal liability insurance, 375
personal property, 374
   taxes on, 491
personal resources, defined, 3
physician. *See* doctor.
PIN number, 60
point-of-sale terminal, 60
points, mortgage, 352
Poison Prevention Packaging Act, 106
pollution, defined, 105
POS terminal, 60
postal money order, 58
PPO, 443
predelivery inspection form, auto, 292
preferred provider organization (PPO), 207, 443
preservatives, food, 162
previous-balance method of figuring interest, 243
price fixing, 94
price-earnings ratio, 411
prices
   market, 77
   measuring, 461–463
   supply and demand affecting, 74–77
primary-care physician, 202–203
principal, of loan, 222
producer, defined, 2
production problem, 69
productivity, control of, 482
products, 22
profit
   defined, 72
   figuring, 86–87
   maximizing, 87–88
progressive tax, 492

promissory note, 250
promotional sale, 119
proof-of-purchase label, 119
property
   personal, 374
   real, 375
   taxes on, 320, 491, 495
proportional tax, 492–493
proprietorship, 89
prosperity, defined, 464
public goods, 99
purchase-and-sale agreement, 351

R

rain check, 167
raw-goods producers and processors, 84
real dollar, defined, 456
real estate
   broker, 322
   lawyer's role in, 209
   taxing, 491, 495
real property, 375
rebate, 119
recall, auto, 295
recession, defined, 465
recovery, economic, 466
Red Book, auto prices, 278, 291
referral selling, 131–132, 135
registered identification number (RN), 180
regressive tax, 493
regulatory agencies
   federal, 148–150
   state and local, 146–147, 336
rent, 320, 323–324
   apartment, 331–332
   defined, 74
rent control, 337–338
renter's insurance, 373–375
repossession, 247
resources
   costs of, 4
   natural, 68
   personal, 3
restrictive endorsement, 54

Credits

Text

27, Excerpts from *High Schools and the Changing Workplace,* © 1984 by the National Academy of Sciences.

139, "The Hotel Guest as Thief" by Michael Lasky, from *The New York Times,* January 27, 1974. © 1974 by the New York Times Company. Reprinted by permission.

192, Sentence about dandruff, from *The Medicine Show,* Fifth Edition, by the Editors of *Consumer Reports,* published by Consumers Union, Mount Vernon, New York, 1980.

Art

Book design: Marjorie Millhon
Cover design: Ellen Taurins, Taurins Design Associates
Cover photography: Michael Groen
Illustration: Graphics etcetera, Terry Presnall, and Meg Kelleher Aubrey

Charts, tables, and graphs on the pages listed are based on information from the following sources:

21, Bureau of the Census
22, *Monthly Labor Review,* Vol. 106, No. 11, November 1983, Table 2, p. 45
57, The First National Bank of Boston
121, *Money Management, Your Shopping Dollars,* Household Finance Corporation
166, *Supply Guide: Average Monthly Availability of Fresh Fruits and Vegetables,* 11th ed., 1981, United Fresh Fruit and Vegetable Association
208, *Statistical Abstracts*
285, Hertz Corporation, 1980
290, *Consumer Reports Magazine,* April 1987, pp. 204–205
300, National Safety Council
376, Insurance Information Institute
455, *Statistical Abstracts* and *Facts on File*
462, *Statistical Abstracts*
475, Bureau of Labor Statistics
497, *Statistical Abstracts*
501, *Statistical Abstracts*

Photography

x Steve Krongard/Image Bank **2** Joe Toto **4** Martin Rogers/Stock Boston **5** Stock Boston **13** Image Bank **16** Masterfile **19** Bill Gallery/Stock Boston **20** (top) Alan Bergman (bottom) John Coletti/Picture Cube **23** Jon Goell/Picture Cube **28** After-Image **32** Comstock **39** Peter Chapman **52** John Zoiner/Uniphoto **61** Bill Barley/Shostal **66** Bobbie Kingsley/Photo Researchers **69** (top right) Bettmann Newsphotos (top left) Peter Chapman **70** Paul Perry/Uniphoto **71** Sygma **76** Dick Currance/Woodfin Camp **83** Keith Jenkins/Boston Globe **84** Doug Menuez/People Weekly © 1987 Time Inc. All Rights Reserved **87** Alan Carey/Image Works **91** G. Desteinheil/Shostal **92** Peter Chapman **93** Photo Source **94** Shostal **98** James Archambeault **100** George Hunter/Shostal **101** Shostal **103** Uniphoto **105** Spencer Grant/Taurus **107** Bettmann Newsphotos **110** Brian Seed/Click/Chicago **115** Chuck Keeler/Click/Chicago **117** Peter Chapman **118** Peter Chapman **120** Gabe Palmer/After-Image **125** Eli Reichman **130** Bettmann Archive **135** Tim Davis/Photo Researchers **136** Peter Chapman/Stockphotos, Inc. **137** Image Bank **138** Mark Antman/Image Works **142** Uniphoto **144** Jon Bailey/Picture Cube **147** Peter Chapman **148** Carroll Seghers/Uniphoto **149** Leonard/Click/Chicago **151** Comstock **157** Jeffry Myers/Stock Boston Peter Chapman **166** Daniel Grogan/Uniphoto **167** Robert Llewellyn/Picture Cube **169** (top) Andrew Brilliant/Picture Cube (bottom) Bob Daemmrich/Uniphoto **174** Stephanie Pfriender/Stock Market **176** (bottom left) Walter Bibikow/Image Bank (bottom right) Wendy Ledis/Uniphoto **178** (top) Frank Siteman/Stock Boston (bottom) Michael Grecco/Stock Boston **179** Peter Chapman **180** Arthur Sirdofsky **183** Peter Chapman **184** Peter Chapman **188** Les Morsillo **190** Paul Fry/Uniphoto **192** Bob Daemmrich/Uniphoto **196** Tim Ribar/Uniphoto **197** Photophile **201** Kay Chernush/Image Bank **202** Tom Tracey/Photophile **204** Matt Bradley/Uniphoto **209** Russ Kinne/Comstock **213** Mug Shots/After-Image **218** Peter Chapman **220** Richard Wood/Picture Cube **221** Robert De Gast/Lensman **223** Don Smetzer/Click/Chicago **231** Everett C. Johnson/After-Image **237** John Lei/Stock Boston **241** Tom Tracey/Photophile **242** Roy Morsch/Stock Market **244** Jonathan Taylor/Uniphoto **247** Shostal **255** Jon Riley/After-Image **263** J. P. Laffont/Sygma **264** Gabe Palmer/After-Image **270** Herb Snitzer/Stock Boston **274** Dan McCoy/Rainbow **276** Richard Steedman/Stock Market **278** Don Smetzer/Click/Chicago **281** Bob Daemmrich/Uniphoto **284** Peter Chapman **287** Dario Perla/After-Image **288–289** Mark Segal/Click/Chicago **292** Gabe Palmer/After-Image **298** William L. Hamilton/Shostal **299** David Strickler/Click/Chicago **302** Augustus Upitis/Shostal **305** Brad Claire/After-Image **308** Shostal **314** Shostal **316** Ellis Herwig/Stock Boston **319** Lisa Ebright/Nawrocki **320** Tom Ives/Comstock **322** Al Henderson/Click/Chicago **328** Krasner/Uniphoto **332** Joel Gordon **333** Bob Daemmrich **334** FPG **337** Click/Chicago **342** James Ballard **348** Claire Fabvier/Black Star **350** Daniel MacDonald/Stock Shop **353** Vautier Denanxe/Click/Chicago **354** Bart Bartholomew/Black Star **358** Steve Rosenthal/Graham Gund **362** FPG **363** Comstock **364** Dan McCoy/Rainbow **367** Dan McCoy/Rainbow **372** Michael Patrick/Picture Group **374** Arthur Ross/FPG **377** David Bentley/Nawrocki **378** Dave Schaffer/Picture Cube **380** Stock Boston **381** S. McCarrol/FPG **386** Bettmann Archive **388** Michael Hayman/Photo Researchers **393** Arnold Zann/Black Star **394** T. J. Florian/Nawrocki **396** David Bentley/Nawrocki **403** Kunio Owaki/Stock Market **404** Joe McNally/Wheeler Pictures **406** Shostal **409** Stock Boston **413** Jon Riley/Click/Chicago **419** William Hubbell/Woodfin Camp **420** Stock Market **421** Robert Wagoner/Stock Market **426** Index Stock **428** Jim Pickerell/Click/Chicago **436** Elliot Varner Smith **438** Donald Dietz/Stock Boston **441** Comstock **442** Mottbe Weissman/Photo Researchers **446** Gabe Palmer/Stock Market **447** Comstock **452** A. Pierce Bounds **460** Nawrocki Taurus **464** Craig Aurness/Click/Chicago **465** Wide World **470** MacNelly/Tribune Media Services **473** Liane Enkelis/Stock Boston **477** Peter Menzel/Stock Boston **478** Richard Pasley/Stock Boston **480** William S. Nawrocki/Nawrocki **487** Barbara Rios/Photo Researchers **489** Brent Petersen/Stock Market **490** Michael Weisbrat/Stock Boston **491** Ted Horowitz/Stock Market **494** Phylane Norman/Nawrocki **495** Philip Jon Bailey/Stock Boston